Praise for *Phantom Lady*

"*Phantom Lady* sheds welcome light on a woman producer of both motion pictures and television and a key member of Hitchcock's inner circle. The entertaining narrative spans Hollywood's Golden Age and the rise of television, with insightful takes on many of the greats."

—**Robert Matzen,** author of *Dutch Girl:*
Audrey Hepburn and World War II

"Christina Lane skillfully evokes Harrison's intelligence and charisma, offering an analysis of how she navigated the power relations of the classical Hollywood studio system and later the new industry of television, and how she determinedly carved out a space where she could successfully exercise her own agency. *Phantom Lady* traces the story of a remarkable woman but has wider resonances for our understanding of gender, creativity, and collaboration in media and creative industries."

—**Helen Hanson,** associate professor of film history,
University of Exeter, and author of *Hollywood Heroines:*
Women in Film Noir and the Female Gothic Film

"A fascinating chronicle of one of the key writer-producers of classic film and television, a woman who charted the path for today's generation of female showrunners and movie producers."

—**Shelley Stamp,** author of *Lois Weber in*
Early Hollywood and *Movie-Struck Girls*

"Hitchcock's name is on the cover, and Christina Lane's book does provide useful new angles on the great man's work. But its value goes far beyond this, as the carefully researched account of the career of a pioneering woman writer and then producer, in Britain and then America, in cinema and then TV. An instructive and inspiring story."

—**Charles Barr,** author of *English Hitchcock*

"*Phantom Lady* provides a rich and compelling portrait of a dynamic, indefatigable woman whose multidecade Hollywood career will be a revelation to readers."

—**Diane Negra,** professor of film studies and
screen culture, University College Dublin

PHANTOM
LADY

HOLLYWOOD PRODUCER
JOAN HARRISON,
THE **FORGOTTEN WOMAN** BEHIND
HITCHCOCK

CHRISTINA LANE

CHICAGO
REVIEW
PRESS
An A Cappella Book

Library of Congress Cataloging-in-Publication Data
Names: Lane, Christina, author.
Title: Phantom lady : Hollywood producer Joan Harrison, the forgotten woman
   behind Hitchcock / Christina Lane.
Description: Chicago : Chicago Review Press, 2020. | Includes
   bibliographical references and index. | Summary: "The untold story of
   Hollywood's most powerful female writer-producer of the 1940s, Joan
   Harrison, who grew from being the worst secretary Alfred Hitchcock ever
   had to one of his closest collaborators, critically shaping his brand as
   the "Master of Suspense.""— Provided by publisher.
Identifiers: LCCN 2019041981 (print) | LCCN 2019041982 (ebook) | ISBN
   9781613733844 (cloth) | ISBN 9781613733851 (adobe pdf) | ISBN
   9781613733875 (epub) | ISBN 9781613733868 (kindle edition)
Subjects: LCSH: Harrison, Joan, 1907–1994. | Women motion picture producers
   and directors—Great Britain—Biography. | Women screenwriters—Great
   Britain—Biography.
Classification: LCC PN1998.3.H3688 L36 2020 (print) | LCC PN1998.3.H3688
   (ebook) | DDC 791.4302/33092 [B]—dc23
LC record available at https://lccn.loc.gov/2019041981
LC ebook record available at https://lccn.loc.gov/2019041982

All images are from the author's collection unless otherwise indicated

Typesetting: Nord Compo

Printed in the United States of America
5 4 3 2 1

For Gaspar

"You can just see a little *peep* of the passage in
Looking-glass House, if you leave the door
of our drawing room wide open:
and it's very like our passage as far as you can see,
only you know it may be quite different on beyond."

—Alice, *Through the Looking Glass,
and What Alice Found There* by Lewis Carroll

CONTENTS

PROLOGUE
WANTED: YOUNG LADY, BY PRODUCER

November 1933

TWENTY-SIX-YEAR-OLD JOAN HARRISON didn't like waking up without a sense of purpose, which is why she was likely happily surprised when something unusual caught her eye: a blue note tucked into the morning newspaper that the family housemaid carried into her room with the usual breakfast platter of tea and crumpets.

Having only recently moved back to the Grove, her parents' estate in the town of Guildford, Surrey, Joan was still in the habit of sleeping late. She had little intention of abandoning the bachelorette ways she had cultivated while living thirty miles east in Kensington, a district of London. She could still hop aboard the train to enjoy late-night parties at friends' flats in the city.

Joan had returned home after a few years of working as a typist and a salesgirl in the British capital. Despite an active social scene there, boredom had set in. Just what was she going to do with her life? The question vexed her. She had confessed her malaise to a girlfriend only a short while ago. Her friend evidently took the conversation to heart, for it was she who had risen early, read the *Daily Telegraph*, and sent it along to Joan at the Grove. With it was a hastily jotted note that read, "For your consideration."

The announcement began with the title "Wanted: Young Lady." It specified, "Highest educational qualifications, must be able to speak, read, and write French and German fluently, by producer of films." The ad had been placed by the Gaumont-British Picture Corporation, the leading movie studio in Britain.

1

There was only one catch: the interview was in two hours. Setting aside her breakfast tray, Joan promptly began preparing.

Joan's dissatisfaction with her direction in life had been building for some time. Years earlier, her parents had expected her to marry the boy next door, the son of a barrister, whom they adored. At the time, Joan feared she would be entering a trap. Did she really expect nothing more from life than "a town-and-country marriage, a commuting husband, babies and four o'clock tea with the ladies' auxiliary of the local sons of Eton"? As she reflected later, many of her early actions were driven by anxiety over the emotional suffocation such a life would bring her. "I think that I was subconsciously seeking an escape," she said.

She had first sought that escape at the Sorbonne in Paris, and then Oxford. Upon graduation, she declared to her father, Walter, that she wanted to be a newspaperwoman.

It was not a random aspiration. As publishers of the weekly *Surrey Advertiser*, the family ran what amounted to a newspaper dynasty. Joan's maternal grandfather, Alexander Forsythe Asher, had been the *Advertiser*'s sole proprietor (as well as Guildford's mayor). Walter, who had married into the business, was the *Advertiser*'s managing director. "I expect you to give me a job," his daughter announced.

"Why don't you marry that nice young boy?" Walter countered. When he realized that his daughter would not be dissuaded, he acquiesced. But not fully. She had better put aside any ideas of becoming a reporter, he instructed. "You can go to work if you like, but not in journalism. You'll harden. You'll turn ugly. You'll become rough and tough and masculine," he asserted, adding, "Besides, you will never be a success in a tough field like the newspaper business."

Joan found his male bias illuminating. He was right to deter her, but not for the reasons he presumed. If she were to enter the family business, she would like to run it her way. She had her own ideas about things. So she went to London instead.

Now back home and still adrift, she was not going to miss out on this job interview at Gaumont-British.

On her way out the door to catch the commuter train, Joan told her mother, Amelia, that she was en route to Gaumont-British Pictures to see about a job. "Be sure to wear a hat," Amelia advised. Though Joan never liked to be told what to do, she knew her mum was right. One must always dress like a lady.

Joan, in fact, never had trouble affecting that role. On this day, like every day, she was impeccably attired in a designer suit, with her golden blonde hair stylishly coiffed. At five foot four, she had a trim, petite build. Her slightly turned-up nose and powder-blue eyes added a twinkle to her naturally gregarious personality. She was often told that she should think about a career in the movies; she was luminous enough to be a star.

She didn't mind hearing this. The truth was that Joan was movie struck. She had often frequented the Electra Cinema and the Oxford Theatre (later the Super Cinema) when she attended Oxford, and had even written film reviews for the *Surrey Advertiser* as a way to acquire free passes to the London movie houses. This trip to Gaumont-British would make for stimulating sightseeing, regardless of the outcome.

She arrived at the Gaumont's Lime Grove studio complex in Shepherd's Bush just after noon. It was only then that she realized that the person who had posted the ad was Alfred Hitchcock. The then thirty-five-year-old had made more than a dozen feature films and was the best-known director in Britain. He was not yet the internationally renowned "Master of Suspense," but he was already making a name for himself.

As Joan made her way down the hallway, she saw a long line of applicants, perhaps as many as forty women—or even one hundred, if certain later (likely inflated) reports are to be believed. Panic set in. Hitchcock would surely hire someone before she even got her foot in the door.

Joan went into action. According to a later *New York Times* account, "She stalked up to the gentleman in charge, requested his ear, whispered that her sister was having a baby and could she be the next one in to see Mr. Hitchcock, so she could run back to the hospital and be there when the baby came?" She did have sisters, but neither one was anywhere near married, much less expecting a baby. The "commissionaire" took her at her word. He moved her to third in the queue.

It was 12:50 PM when Joan was ushered into Hitchcock's office. The director was already hungry in anticipation of his usual one o'clock lunch hour. He was also dissatisfied with the parade of potential secretaries he had seen thus far. At first, he simply stared at Joan. Then he asked her to remove her hat. She took this as a good sign.

Hitchcock's first words were "Do you speak German?" He needed someone to communicate with the actor Peter Lorre and art director Alfred Junge, who would both be working on his next picture, *The Man Who Knew Too Much*.

Joan hesitated. In all her studies of the classics, first at the Sorbonne and then at Oxford, she had attained only a passing acquaintance with German. "No, but I speak French," she replied, with a slight hint of the coquette. Resigned to defeat, she started toward the door.

But Hitchcock apparently had already been sold. A quick appraisal of Joan's comely appearance and fair features told him this was his new hire. Hitchcock (like most men, in his view) was vulnerable to sophisticated blondes. "Well, you're hired anyway," Hitchcock concluded, "provided you'll have lunch with me. I'm starving to death!"

The lunch conversation between the new secretary and the seasoned director only confirmed for him that he had made the right decision. She had seen a great number of his films and evinced a keen eye. Moreover, she disclosed that as a child she had had "an absolute passion on the subject of crime—how criminal acts were committed and who did them." She had voraciously "read every type of book written on the subject." She had also spent many a day sitting in on actual court cases. Her uncle, Harold Harrison, was the keeper (the person in charge of assigning cases to judges) of the Old Bailey court in London. Knowing of her obsession with crime stories, he kept her abreast of current trials and made it easy for her to sit in.

Hitchcock looked on with delight as Joan recounted "every grisly detail" of several cases while consuming her meal. He had found a kindred spirit; at a young age, he too had savored visits to the Old Bailey (and would later impress people with recollections of the court's exact floor plans) and had amassed a library of criminal cases and true crime fiction.

In only a few hours, Joan had gone from contemplating an idle life over morning tea to winning the favor of a critically acclaimed director. Her decision to take the job would perplex her parents; the movie industry, as viewed from the upper reaches of Guildford society, was a foreign land. And they did not especially like that it would draw her back to the city. As they saw it, this was yet one more in a string of misadventures. But to Joan, it was as if the puzzle pieces that had been just beyond her grasp were suddenly falling into place. A picture of where she wanted go was finally taking shape.

It was only a few weeks before it became apparent that Joan was ill equipped for the job of secretary. She had meager patience with answering phones, taking dictation, or typing up story conference notes. What she did possess, however, was an uncanny sense of what made for a good story. Hitchcock could always hire another secretary. Joan instead would become the director's closest professional collaborator and personal confidante after his writer-editor wife, Alma Reville. Joan would be entrusted with their secret creative codes. She would become the most loyal and enduring screenwriter and producer Hitchcock ever employed.

Harrison would contribute to all of Hitchcock's late British achievements, including *Young and Innocent* and *The Lady Vanishes*, and his early Hollywood successes, notably *Rebecca*, *Foreign Correspondent*, and *Suspicion*. Together, these films established Hitchcock as a master of the seriocomic thriller and gothic suspense. Joan was at his side at the most pivotal point in his career, and in his life—as he bid England adieu, embarked on worldwide fame, and set about creating his signature style. Plainly put, Alfred Hitchcock would not have become "Hitchcock" without her.

Within five years of joining Hitchcock, Harrison was functioning as a creative producer, mastering every aspect of technical continuity and carving out her own bold artistic sensibility. After collaborating on nine feature films with Hitchcock, she struck out on her own, producing female-centric investigative thrillers, including the noir gem *Phantom Lady*.

Deemed a "superb masterpiece" by *Film Daily* upon its release in 1944, the film follows a young, attractive secretary turned amateur sleuth as she gambles everything to save her boss, wrongly accused of murder, from the electric chair. Now considered by many to be the high point of film noir, this landmark picture launched the American career of director Robert Siodmak and made Joan the most powerful female producer in Hollywood—and the first woman to become a full-fledged producer at a major studio.

If her story is singular, it is also representative of a wave of female power that was overtaking the industry, one that has been obscured by history. The classical studio era was a golden age for women, who enjoyed key positions as board members, agents, publicists, editors, designers, researchers, story editors, and, of course, screenwriters, as J. E. Smyth illuminates in *Nobody's Girl Friday: The Women Who Ran Hollywood*. Screen stars who have become household names, such as Bette Davis and Barbara Stanwyck, were exerting influence and making change by leading participation in guilds, unions, protests, political organizations, war bond work, and more. Meanwhile, Harriet Parsons and Virginia Van Upp soon joined Harrison in the producer ranks. The only three female producers in 1940s Hollywood, they would find it a constant struggle to maintain their foothold. But they prevailed.

Though never acknowledged as such, Harrison was unquestionably a producer-auteur. Taken individually, her films are often seen as having been authored primarily by her male collaborators. When her oeuvre is considered as a whole, however, the pieces fit together to form a singular, distinctive vision: gritty, risky, wry portraits of love, marriage, and family awash in psychological and often-physical violence. She traded in moral ambiguity and shadowy struggles for self-empowerment with indelible imagery: the footsteps of a woman alone on a dark, rain-slicked city street (*Phantom Lady*) or a fiery surprise when a thieving secretary wearing a dime-store wedding ring meets her death in a burning car (*They Won't Believe Me*). The *London Times* eulogized upon her death that "she placed a recognizable mark on all her work, involving primarily an impish, dark and off-beat sense of humor and a clear understanding of the close relationship between the giggle and the scream."

As a powerful female role model, Joan paved the way for generations of women that followed. Part of her standing in the classical Hollywood studio system was founded on the star image she fashioned for herself. Taking a cue from her mentor, Joan placed herself center stage as a ravishing and success-ful career woman.

Harrison sported casual-chic suits by Adrian and Coco Chanel, accented with carefully chosen jewels, handbags, and shoes. In the vanguard of design trends, she set the pace in refined women's workday styles. "From my New York point of view, Joan was so far above the other ladies I knew," remarked Eleanor Kilgallen, former talent agent at MCA/Universal. "She was impeccably groomed, very chic. Other women were so eager to become her, at least the ones I knew." Joan's glamour portraits graced the pages of *Life*, *Vogue*, *Collier's*, and a host of Hollywood fan magazines, often accompanied by advice for working women: "Be ambitious," and "Work seven Mondays a week."

"But for Joan, I don't think we would have had Gale Anne Hurd, Kathleen Kennedy, or Amy Pascal," observed actress Carol Lynley, who knew her in the 1950s. "Looking back, I realize what a precedent she set for me and particularly other girls, who only saw women as homemakers, or teachers, or nurses, or wallflowers."

At the height of her film career, Harrison lived at the center of Hollywood society, enjoying acceptance in the most elite circles. She counted among her friends Charlie Chaplin, Claude Rains, David Niven, Sam Spiegel, Marlene Dietrich, Billy Wilder, John Huston, Evelyn Keyes, Paul Henreid and his wife, Lisl, and Lewis Milestone and his wife, Kendall. Her paramours included Irwin Shaw, Kirk Douglas, and Gilbert Roland. One of her most public liaisons was her on-again, off-again affaire de coeur with Clark Gable, following Carole Lombard's tragic death in 1942. Many even predicted she would be the next Mrs. Gable. But it was the romances she kept out of the spotlight that ran the deepest, including an infatuation with a woman that she kept most secret. When Joan finally did marry, in 1958, she chose not a celebrity but a literary star: the inventor of the modern-day spy thriller, Eric Ambler.

Her unconventional streak extended to her relations with her Hollywood bosses. More than twice, she stunned studio chiefs by resigning from a project rather than compromise her creative principles. When Universal Pictures vetoed her preferred ending for the film *The Strange Affair of Uncle Harry*, she broke her contract and walked off the lot for good. And when Howard Hughes issued a blanket directive declaring that from then on all RKO pictures would be about one of two things—"fighting and fornication"—she knew he'd written it for her and made her exit from that studio as well.

Following her success in movies, Harrison established herself as a television pioneer, launching the enterprising series *Janet Dean, Registered Nurse* (featuring *Phantom Lady* star Ella Raines) in 1954. Soon thereafter, legendary talent agent Lew Wasserman conscripted her to reteam with Hitchcock to produce the *Alfred Hitchcock Presents* series, which (in its original half-hour incarnation and later as the retitled *The Alfred Hitchcock Hour*) ran on television from 1955 to 1965.

Arguably, the weekly show did more to raise Hitchcock's public profile than all the movies he made during the same period. In building up the Hitchcock brand, Joan reinvented herself. With full creative control, she oversaw story selection, scripts, casting, and crew, working closely with both established talent (Joseph Cotten, Claire Trevor, Cloris Leachman) and promising newcomers (Steve McQueen, Robert Redford, Angie Dickinson). She found herself not only at the forefront of thoughtful, original programming but also on the front lines of the media mergers and the turbo-driven production schedule that would come to characterize MCA-Universal-Revue Studios in the 1960s.

As a prototype of the modern-day showrunner, Joan certified that Hitchcock's elevated sensibilities, literary values, and style were sustained week in and week out. Film historian Eddie Muller says, "There's no mistaking that the Hitchcock brand sold the *Alfred Hitchcock Presents* series. But it was Joan Harrison who ensured the continuity of the Hitchcock brand. She 'made' that show."

As Hollywood's conservative climate was pushing progressives out—by underwriting the House Un-American Activities Committee and implementing the blacklist against so-called subversives—Joan was angling for ways to bring exiled writers, directors, and actors back. She used her position on the *Alfred Hitchcock Presents* series as a way to strike back, doggedly campaigning to employ blacklisted talent.

So why has so little attention been paid to Harrison? Even as countless volumes have been devoted to Hitchcock, from his films and fans to his fancies, she continues to live in his shadow. Donald Spoto's influential *The Dark Side of Genius: The Life of Alfred Hitchcock* (first published in 1983) treats her as a sick infatuation of the director, who "nursed his unarticulated longings in a kind of silent, gray, romantic gloom that hung over [his] family." John Russell Taylor's *Hitch: The Life and Times of Alfred Hitchcock* (1978) glosses over her in a single paragraph. In the more recent *Alfred Hitchcock: A Brief Life* (2015) by Peter Ackroyd, she makes only a cameo appearance as "Hitchcock's secretary"—and this is *after* she earned a writing credit for *Jamaica Inn* (1939). More often, as in the Fox Searchlight film *Hitchcock* (2012) and HBO's *The Girl* (2012), Harrison receives no mention at all.

Phantom Lady seeks to return Joan Harrison to her rightful place in the Hitchcock universe and restore her reputation as an important, trailblazing film and television producer in her own right. Tracing her complicated, creative relationship with Hitchcock and her deep influence on his work, her dramatic struggle to become a no-holds-barred producer, and her many personal challenges and triumphs, this book will chronicle one of the last great untold stories of the classical Hollywood era—the kind of story Joan herself might have brought to the screen, if she hadn't been so busy starring in it.

1 | AT HOME

ON JUNE 20, 1907, Joan Harrison's life began in the quintessentially British borough of Guildford, Surrey. The village had hosted kings, castles, chapels, and Lewis Carroll, who (according to locals) wrote *Through the Looking-Glass*, the sequel to *Alice's Adventures in Wonderland*, in his provisional second home, surrounded by ancient archways and rabbit burrows. Joan was born into an Edwardian time—a "golden afternoon" of prosperity—replete with green pastures, gas streetlamps, and the romance of yore. A dazzling mist would rise at dawn from its many rivers, and a special hillside stream was ascribed healing powers.

Named for the golden sands ("gold ford") along its riverside, Guildford is sandwiched into a gap along the Harrow Way trail on the banks of the River Wey. Founded during the Saxon period, it is dotted with medieval architecture, anchored by the ruins of a twelfth-century stone Norman castle. Located about thirty miles southwest of London, Guildford began to boom when the railway arrived in the mid-nineteenth century, after which dormitories for London commuters sprang up, and eventually dairies, breweries, and an engineering industry. By the 1860s the town was starting to course with the energy of new artistic and literary interests and, if Carroll's frequent presence was any indication, a great force of imagination. It attracted people with foresight, ingenuity, and pluck.

Among them was Joan's maternal grandfather. Alexander Forsythe Asher had been born in 1839 in the commercial district of Keith in Banffshire. He was the sixth son of James Parker Asher, a writer and bookbinder who hailed from the small Scottish town of Huntly. The enterprising, industrious Alexander

11

discovered his talents for newspaper reporting in his teenage years and began moving up the ranks of local papers. Feeling a bit unmoored at the age of twenty (his mother died when he was young), he sought career advice from a trusted minister. The local vicar counseled him, "My friend, do as Abraham did: go south." And so he did. He trekked southeast to Wellington and then to Sevenoaks in Kent, earning accolades at each job along the way. Alexander could sniff out a story.

The cold, wet climate of a South Wales post took a toll on his health. On doctor's orders, he accepted an assignment with the *Surrey Standard*, and soon confronted an unusual proposition: the chance, at the age of twenty-eight, to become chief proprietor of a successful weekly newspaper. Along with fellow reporter Angus Fraser Walbrook, Alexander signed on as a financial partner to the *Surrey Advertiser* in November 1867.

The *Surrey Advertiser* was barely four years old, but it had grown rapidly in influence since launching as an eight-pager with a circulation of three thousand. An old-form "pennysaver"—the paper cost "one penny (where not sent free)," according to its cover—its purpose, as its name suggested, was to advertise local businesses. Still, the original owners had decided almost right away that it served them well to integrate legitimate news with ads. The paper was so successful that it transitioned from a monthly to a weekly periodical within its first quarter.

With the paper's growing clout in Guildford and the surrounding county of Surrey, Alexander became quickly beholden to the paper's conservative backers, the businessmen and community leaders who had ushered him into power. Despite Alexander's espoused claims of impartiality and a "guiding mission" that stated the *Advertiser* would "on all occasions be gentlemanly in tone and temperate in language, advocating the right, denouncing the wrong," his paper was hardly neutral. The *Advertiser* positioned itself in direct contrast to the *Surrey Times*, a competitor that appealed to the labor party and more liberal readers. Alexander was in fact proud to be cast as a pro-business conservative. It aligned with his values and was a formula that worked.

The most widely circulated paper in West Surrey, the *Advertiser* projected a youthful, industrious image. The article announcing Asher and Walbrook's ascendancy referenced the English essayist Lord Thomas Macaulay, who reputedly proposed, "Advertising is to business what steam is to machinery. The grand propelling power." This was a vision of a forward-thinking team assuring rapid progress, fueled by ad sales. "Advertising keeps the steam up," the article declared.

The *Advertiser* was emerging at precisely the moment the British newspaper industry was adopting more commercial and sensationalistic practices. Though Asher and Walbrook stayed away from tabloid and entertainment journalism, and maintained a conservative tone ("by gentlemen, for gentlemen"), they were forging the paper in the context of an increasingly competitive marketplace. If in the early days the paper had made an effort to balance news and ballyhoo (and to camouflage the latter), it shifted briskly. Advertising—specifically, purely ad-driven content—became more and more crucial to the operation, "keeping the steam up."

On June 11, 1867, in the same year that Alexander took control of the *Surrey Advertiser*, he married a determined Scottish woman named Eliza Mure. Her father, James Mure, had entertained ambitions as a writer before taking up law, presumably for financial stability. Known for her love of education and children, Eliza, like her father, fostered literary instincts. At the time of her meeting Alexander, Eliza had been working as a governess for families across southern England. The marriage represented a major step up for her.

The Ashers embarked upon starting a family, eventually bearing four children; daughter Amelia McWhir Mure (born August 1871) would be Joan's mother. By now, the Ashers were living at the Grove, an orange brick Georgian Revival house that would be Joan's family home. Located on Farnham Road, an ancient route that led up a steep hill out of the town's center, the house was in the neighborhood of the Mount, which scaled west Guildford. The Mount offered an aerial view of both downtown and the surrounding countryside. The Grove property, which included an expanse of land and buildings that stretched well beyond the estate grounds, was perched strategically along the railway bridge, giving the Ashers a front row to the flow of industry and commerce.

The Ashers were part of the rising middle class, stitching their way into the social fabric of a place that was becoming increasingly appealing to affluent families. Villas and well-sized homes sprung up from farmlands and fields, as did working-class communities, drawn to new service and manufacturing jobs, and especially the giant Dennis Brothers automobile plant, which opened in 1895. Guildford's pulse was also quickening with the arrival of electricity and water pipes, conveying modern comforts, even if horse-drawn buggies were still common on the village's gray granite streets.

After some deliberation, Alexander chose to locate the *Advertiser*'s office in the middle of town on Market Street, anchored by its hotels, pubs, and markets, just a stone's throw away from advertising row, where the walls and windows of local businesses featured poster-sized signs.

Remain in the hub, attuned to the action, but stay out of the headlines—this was the careful positioning that spelled success for Alexander and his family. They grew accustomed to adhering faithfully to Guildford's social rules and customs, taking center stage when it was called for, but mostly abiding quietly in the margins. To mention themselves in the *Advertiser* would have been objectionable, even garish; to see their lives reported on in the *Surrey Times* would mean that something had gone truly awry.

The year 1900 began with sorrow: Eliza died of heart failure at the Grove on January 9. She was sixty-one. She was laid to rest in the cemetery on the Mount. Several weeks later, devastating floods wiped out the old Town Bridge—the lifeline in and out of Guildford—spelling disaster for local businesses. With commerce at a standstill, the newspaper stumbled, but only temporarily.

Meanwhile, inside the *Surrey Advertiser* office, a romance had been blooming. Alexander's daughter Millie (as Amelia was called), considered a spinster at twenty-eight, had developed a fondness for a young man who had joined the business department a few years prior. Walter Harrison, the Irish-born son of a clerk, had been raised in West Sussex and trained in banking. With angular features and a serious, businesslike demeanor, he appealed to Millie. Walter had led a peripatetic existence growing up (it's likely that his father, Charles, had some affiliation with the British army, as Walter was born in Longford, an army town) and was drawn to the firm ground that the Ashers had established in Surrey. And he was keen on Millie, who was lovely looking with bright cobalt blue eyes.

On July 11, 1900, six months almost to the day after her mother's death, Millie married Walter in Guildford's Holy Trinity Church. This twisted pattern, in which tragedy and joy occurred close together, would become familiar for the Harrisons.

Living at the Grove, they had cemented into one family now, with Walter having fully integrated himself. A shared triumph came when Alexander was elected mayor of Guildford in November 1901. Millie, in her mother's absence, served as unofficial mayoress, shining in a role of public leader and social hostess typically reserved for women with decades more life experience.

As the still-grieving bride took on new official duties, she continued the familiar pattern of meeting life's challenges in intense privacy. If it was the Asher way, so it would be with the Harrisons.

Mayor Asher's greatest deed, one memorialized in stone, was the completion of the new Town Bridge in February 1902, just shy of the flood's two-year anniversary. The opening of the new bridge signaled the village's financial and psychological rebirth at the dawn of the new century.

Millie and Walter welcomed their first child, Muriel Mary, on August 6, 1902. Jack Forsythe followed on October 18, 1904. With their brood expanding, the Harrisons moved to the Craigmore residence a short distance away at 3 Mareschal Road. The Victorian two-tone house (redbrick bottom, light stucco on top), with its spacious ten rooms, was rich in architectural detail and flanked by a stately brick wall and an arched entrance, but it did not come close to the grand scale of the Grove. It ran more along the lines of young Charlie's Santa Clara home in Hitchcock's *Shadow of a Doubt*.

It was in Craigmore that Joan was born on June 20, 1907. (Though some official documents list June 26, her original birth certificate reports that she was born on June 20, which is when she celebrated her birthday.) Her early life was marked by music, songs, and plays—pursuits nurtured by her father, who supervised the music programs at the family's church. Thus, it became customary for young Joan or one of her siblings to appear at a prominent home to perform a short dramatic scene or at a local recital to play a pianoforte. By the time Joan was seven, with soft curls in her fair hair, dimples, and her mother's blue eyes, she received accolades in the *Surrey Advertiser* for her part in a local musical concert. (The *Advertiser*'s editorial policies notwithstanding, the Ashers were not immune from occasional displays of pride, particularly when it came to their children.)

Walter's devotion to youth education was manifest in an unflagging commitment to local school boards and church activities. He was commended for knowing "no parochial bounds to his churchmanship," during his lengthy time as rector's warden for St. Nicolas' Church and for committing years of faithful service to the Guildford Diocesan Conference. Joan did not inherit her father's reverence for religious institutions; many who knew her later in life commented on her strong disavowal of organized religion. And though she rarely disclosed recollections of her early years to anyone, when she did, she painted her childhood with a dry brush. It was unduly formal and often exacting.

While other children spent their days romping among the Guildford castle ruins or rock climbing up a favored hill near St. Catherine's Chapel, leisure time for Joan and her siblings tended to be more rigid. They might be found rehearsing for an upcoming Saturday afternoon matinee or cheering for their father's cricket team (often playing against a rival newspaper). Some days must have glided by as little bits of fun in "fairyland" (Jack, in fact, played the part of a forest chestnut in a play titled "Fun in Fairyland"), while on others, the children may have felt like props trotted out for show.

Joan might have been just old enough for one of Guildford's most historic occasions to have made an impression: the royal festivities surrounding the coronation of King George V on June 22, 1911. Nearly every one of the town's twenty thousand residents gathered in the heavily decorated downtown streets to witness a grand procession of over thirty-five floats. She would be a royalist all her life, never so far from her roots that kings and queens did not impress her.

Still, it's unlikely that, for Joan, the crowning of a new monarch came anywhere close in importance to the arrival of Faith Mary, her younger sister (and final sibling). Born May 26, 1912, Faith arrived almost like an early birthday present for the soon-to-be five-year-old Joan, who doted on the little girl. The two became inseparable. The elder sister later recalled that they were always pursuing their next venture. One of their signature projects was a newspaper, which they designed all by themselves and printed on the family printing press when Joan was in her early teens and Faith around eight or nine. The publication consisted of "poems, stories, nature items, and columns." Joan and Faith called door to door on their neighbors, selling the paper for "a tuppence" (two pennies). The mechanics of putting it out fascinated them. "I think she and Faith were more interested in the process of printing than anything else," says Joan's niece (and Faith's daughter), Dr. Kate Adamson. "They liked the idea of seeing an issue through from start to finish."

This kind of entrepreneurial spirit was encouraged by the girls' schooling. It's difficult to underestimate the impact of Guildford High School for Girls (GHS) in shaping the kind of woman Joan would become. She began attending GHS at the age of six. (In the British educational system, the term *high school* was applied more generally at that time.) College degrees had become a more attainable goal for women by the turn of the century as secular universities began to allow them to sit for exams and, then gradually, admit them to degrees. As a progressive school, GHS's stated mission was to prepare female students to go on to university, unlike the conventional finishing schools available to most girls and women at that time. Guildford High School emphasized intellectual ability, leadership, and moral character, as well as the arts and physical fitness, educating students to resist Victorian norms of feminine passivity.

The standard curriculum included German and French, drawing, singing, and gymnastics. Physical activity was deemed so important that students were required to choose at least one sport in which they would specialize (such as hockey, lacrosse, or swimming). Joan chose tennis and soon eclipsed most of her peers.

Guildford High School was deeply embedded in the life of the community. Even though it was a day school, it afforded an exclusive private education, catering to the daughters of merchants, doctors, stockbrokers, and architects. Muriel and Faith attended, as did Jack, through age eight. (The school enrolled boys through the third grade.)

As the children grew, the Harrisons moved back to the Grove. Millie and Walter assumed an increasingly public role in both the business and the borough, which had grown in sophistication. It was a happy marriage, though as with all families, there were episodes that were not to be discussed in public. Joan's aunt Anna Hairstens Robison Asher, Eliza's younger sister, had married a celebrated war correspondent's son, a local reporter named William Puxley Pearse, in August 1897. By January 1908 the thirty-one-year-old Anna had abandoned her husband and was living in a Bayswater, London, apartment with an unmarried man. She was, according to her husband's divorce filings, cohabitating and "habitually committing adultery" with Lancelot Miller.

One can only guess as to what would have prompted a woman of Anna's standing to stray so far from societal norms. Two months after the divorce decree became final, she was dead. The burial registry listed her cause of death as "apoplexy," implying stroke or sudden shock. The death certificate, signed by her brother, an Anglican priest who was by her side when she passed away, lends more insight. The cause of death was indicated as "alcoholism, enteritis, and exhaustion," following a seven-day binge. She had been on a bender, the culmination of a long downward spiral.

Anna's tribulations were kept out of the papers, perhaps in deference to the family. It could be that they were kept so secret, even within inner circles, that Joan may not have known much at all about her aunt Anna, ever. (She was, after all, only a baby when Anna died.)

It's difficult to say how much of Anna's story ever saw the light of day, although it no doubt hovered in the background. As Joan grew into adulthood and honed her powers of observation, she began to see for herself the tensions between the depths and surfaces of domestic life. She would notice that certain burdens were borne without mention. She recognized that high drama, near horror, and buried tragedy were not only the features of fiction; they were part of everyday life. Later, she explained why she enjoyed making thrillers and horrors with "ordinary persons for characters—secretaries, housewives, a man in an ordinary job" who, in the end, revealed themselves to be villains. She remarked, "The most interesting murderers are the most mild-seeming men. Inside, the most extraordinary things are happening to them." The "most extraordinary things" were happening inside the most ordinary-looking people; of this she was certain. This must have been true of someone like Anna, who played the role of victim and victimizer in her own life.

Joan, in time, would further her notions about female self-destruction and why women writers had a special skill for capturing a raging violence hiding in the everydayness of life: "Women have written lots of mysteries, perhaps some of the best," she concluded. "We like to deal in terms of the normal family in which something horrible happens." The decompensating sister, husband driven to despair, or secretly psychotic neighbor—these were the stuff of nightmares.

2 | WARTIME

ANY FAIRYLAND AURA TO JOAN'S CHILDHOOD was dramatically altered by the outbreak of World War I. On Sunday, June 28, 1914, a telegram from the Press Association was deposited in the mailbox of the *Surrey Advertiser*. It conveyed that Archduke Franz Ferdinand of Austria and his wife had been assassinated in Sarajevo. Normally, if a recorder saw anything of significance in a message such as this, he posted it in the office window; however, on this day, the recorder saw nothing that stood out. He was on his way to visit the Grove anyway, so he delivered the note to Alexander Forsythe Asher (then seventy-five years old), who read it, set it aside, and published the news item the next day, giving it no particular weight. How was the *Advertiser* staff to know that within weeks this seemingly remote event would lead to an international war that would change the world forever?

In early August, with the European crisis looming, crowds would gather in the town center to glean the latest news. Outside the *Surrey Advertiser* office on High Street, they were anxiously awaiting Germany's response to Britain's demand that the country abide by its neutrality agreement with Belgium. Reports of mounting tensions were cascading in: Austria had declared war on Serbia; Russia was rallying forces against Austria; Germany had declared a state of war, which forced Russia and France into a climactic confrontation. As each report arrived off the wire at the *Advertiser*, the staff would post it on one of the large windows that lined the first-floor offices, while throngs of Guildfordians peered in from the sidewalk.

By 11:00 PM on Tuesday, August 4, the deadline by which Britain's ulti-matum to Germany expired, the crowd had swelled. Just after 11:30 PM, the *Advertiser* announced, "England has declared war on Germany." Loud cheers erupted, followed by the singing of the national anthem. By midnight, the streets had cleared except for small groups here and there; everyone else had rushed home to deliver the message to their families.

Seven-year-old Joan may have lain awake that night at the Grove, waiting to receive news of the growing confrontation. What is certain is that Joan would have noticed changes in her usual way of life almost immediately. Guildford High School, which was just about to welcome students into a new building for the fall season, was converted for military use. It served as a short-term camp for thousands of London Territorial soldiers who came through in mid-August, and soon thereafter as a makeshift Red Cross hospital. Joan and her fellow pupils grew accustomed to attending classes hosted in the larger homes around the neighborhood, which were made available to the students by private citizens.

No one in the immediate Harrison family would be called to serve. Joan's father was past the age of conscription, and her brother too young. (Men ages nineteen to forty were eligible for enlistment.) However, chances are that ten-year-old Jack was given basic military training by local rifle clubs or cadets. (Even before the war, churches and schools were mobilizing young boys' clubs for weekend shooting sessions.) And the Ashers and Harrisons were at the cen-ter of activity when it came to galvanizing community efforts. British officials put heavy pressure on businesses, newspapers in particular, to aggressively encourage young men to enlist and all citizens to contribute resources.

When blackout rules were imposed, the nation's war footing was felt even more deeply. In January 1915, Guildford's blackout went into effect, with a 5:00 PM daily cutoff. No lights could emanate from homes, automobiles, storefronts, or streetlamps, to prevent enemy aircraft from making out targets from above. This "plunged the town into inky black darkness" each night.

These precautions did not spare Guildford from the terror of Wednesday, October 13, 1915, the night a German zeppelin reached the village. It was a perfectly clear sky that evening. The first sign that anything was amiss came at 10:00 PM, with the loud whirring of engines overhead. This drew a number of people into the street, where they saw a large aircraft circling overhead shoot out an electric-blue flare. Just as it seemed to be moving on, the airship turned back and dropped a second flare. And then as quick as a flash, at 10:25 PM, the zeppelin released ten explosives in a direct line that ended less than half a mile from the Grove. Eyewitnesses couldn't believe how low the airship had flown before rising to the approximately ten-thousand-foot elevation where it deployed the bombs. One person recalled with awe and dismay seeing its "unmistakable shape . . . silhouetted in the moonlight like a cigar suspended in space."

If Joan wasn't awakened by the droning engines, there is little doubt that she heard the bombs hit. Her contemporaries describe the ground shaking from terrific booms, "causing the windows to rattle and the house . . . to shake to its foundation." Those who were there that night heard constables shouting, people running in all directions, and "lots of loud, excited voices." Such zeppelin attacks were designed, more than anything else, to "scare the hell out of people." While Joan rarely if ever commented on her childhood experiences of war, her mother, Millie, summed them up in one word: "terrifying." Incredibly, and to everyone's great relief, no lives were lost that night, but it would take months for the collective shock to wear off.

According to one chronicler of the era, "The home front in Guildford had to get used to: a military presence like it had not witnessed before; fears of German spies in their midst; food shortages that eventually led to rationing; the continued call for men to enlist until it became compulsory in 1916; [and] women taking jobs left vacant by men who had gone to war."

By war's end, an estimated five hundred of the town's men would die in battle, and thousands returned wounded. Frightening stories made their way back from the trenches, as did letters hinting at horrors better left untold. The idyllic world Joan had known was gone forever.

Wartime in Guildford brought another loss. On Christmas Day 1916, Alexander Forsythe Asher died. The beacon of the *Surrey Advertiser*, and the family patriarch, was gone. He had, however, prepared the way for Millie and Walter to run the lion's share of the business. Though he had married a second wife, Alice Maud, in 1904 and assigned her some company shares, she did not take on an official role with the *Advertiser*. Alexander's brother, James Parker, who also owned shares, had sold them back to the Ashers when he left Guildford for New Zealand in search of a new lease on life. This left Walter in charge as commercial and advertising manager, as well as joint managing director (working alongside editor W. H. Oakley). Millie had been secretary for over a decade when her father passed away. Between the shortage of paper and materials, problems hiring staff, and reduced profits, it was not easy ushering the *Advertiser* through the war. Millie and Walter survived by their wits and sheer perseverance.

The Harrisons continued to show this kind of ingenuity as the Great War ended. Walter, in particular, seized upon the implicit business opportunities of the postwar period, enlarging the paper's format, investing in new technology, and broadening the *Advertiser*'s vision in an effort to satisfy the growing consumer demands of a booming mass culture.

As Guildford welcomed troops home, Joan moved away to Tudor Hall, an esteemed boarding school in Chislehurst, Kent, just outside London. Tudor Hall offered an elite education: visiting lecturers; requisite French, German, Latin, and Italian; a commercial Art Press School; and an interschool tennis cup. Yet the curricular focus was not so different from GHS—public service, the arts, languages, fresh air, and physical activity. For reasons uncertain, Joan stayed only a year.

By 1920 she was back at home and thriving at Guildford High School. At thirteen, Joan's canvas was expanding. She was winning tennis tournaments, taking part in the dance club and the literary society, and acting in supporting roles in school plays. She was active in the social service committee, which was in tune with broader political changes in the country. Britain had granted women voting rights in 1918; in the postwar years, women were invigorated by open debate, seeking to increase their access to the public sphere.

Many GHS girls wanted to exercise their political voices. As the student body began to experiment with new principles of governance, Joan played an important part. She served for multiple years on school council, which at the time had its eye on abolishing hierarchies—in athletics, for example. As the council secretary, she reported that "after a term's trial, it was discovered, that the machinery of government did not run so smoothly without a School Captain," however. In senior year, she contributed to the formation of a junior branch of the League of Nations Union, which gave students an avenue to become more involved with international politics.

It was during this time that she discovered her greatest passion: writing. As a regular contributor to the *Guildford High School Magazine*, she enjoyed many occasions for practice. In one entry, Joan and her coauthor, M. Allen, recounted a "Book Dance" given by their class, in which everyone was required to come dressed to represent the title of a book (e.g., *Two Little Vagabonds* or *Oliver Twist*). They explained, "Before tea, we danced as hard as we could while a friend kindly played for us and after tea, which lasted a good while, we invited our friends to do some competitions." One game involved unjumbling the names of great men, written down on scraps of paper. Another guessing game had obliged participants to figure out that a *C* drawn in red ink was meant to signify the Red Sea and a drawing of "old candle grease" referred to Ancient Greece. Winners enjoyed boxes of Turkish delights. "After this," they concluded, "we danced waltzes, polkas, one-steps, and many others until we were tired out. After the Sir Roger de Coverly [an English country dance], we had cheers for everyone, and then went home."

Around the age of fifteen, Joan began writing movie reviews for the *Surrey Advertiser*. With the rising popularity of movie palaces, the one-thousand-seat Picture Playhouse went up just off High Street in 1922. Housed within a larger complex called Winter Gardens, the cinema was really a glorious entertainment mecca, boasting an arcade, restaurant, and dance hall. Many of Guildford's "bright young people" (as the tabloids had deemed the generation) saw the space as an escape, a place to see and be seen. It was the pictures, however, that mattered most to Joan. Even penning the reviews was a means to an end, she later confessed, "so I could get the passes" for free. Also by this time, Joan was indulging her passion for horror and mystery books, keeping her fascination hidden from her parents. She was also obsessed with "how criminal acts were committed and who did them," reading every true crime book she could lay her hands on.

In spring 1925, as Joan rounded out her final year of high school (her sixth form, in the English schooling system), she was flourishing in every way. She was vice head girl of the school, the equivalent of vice president of her class. Each year she had excelled, earning special certificates or honors in history, French, English, Latin, scripture, and mathematics. The fact was that all the Harrison girls shone academically. Muriel, having graduated from North Middlesex School for Girls in Enfield in 1919, was attending the Bedford College for Women (part of the University of London). Faith demonstrated proficiency in multiple subjects while also contributing to the high school magazine. Millie had done a fine job encouraging their curiosity and independence.

No one, however, was quite prepared for just how high Joan's aspirations had risen. She had gradually begun to envision a path that departed from that of her older sister, for it was assumed that Muriel was en route toward embarking on a teaching career. Joan saw that as too conventional. One of the University of Oxford's women's colleges, St. Hugh's, might set her up for greater opportunity. When Joan announced her intention, Millie and Walter were taken aback. It's not that they doubted her abilities, only that they assumed she would be happier spending the next few years going out on the town and plotting her move into an office job. Yes, she was prone to burying her nose in a book, but that didn't necessarily translate into "university" material. Muriel had always been the scholastic one, Joan the social butterfly. The family could barely hide its surprise: *Joan, college, really?*

She stood her ground. She performed well on the London General School Examination, which granted her the Higher School Certificate she needed to qualify for an "ancient" such as Oxford. She passed the test in six subjects—including English, history, Latin, and mathematics—and earned a special certificate in spoken French. Adding to her parents' amazement (and pride), she earned a distinction in French, which led to a new development. Based on the test, she was offered a one-year scholarship at the Sorbonne in Paris. This was ideal; she could improve her fluency before proceeding to Oxford, where she hoped to concentrate in spoken French. But her parents couldn't help but worry: Would she spend more time shopping than studying?

In the end, Walter and in particular Millie gave Joan their blessing and encouraged her to take the leap. If she had set her sights on Paris, then so be it. From here on, her life would be what she made of it.

3 | BEYOND THE VILLAGE

JOAN ENTERED THE UNIVERSITY of Paris at the Sorbonne in early November 1925, the start of the fall term. There she took French honors at the Faculty of Letters, making her home in the heart of campus at 6 Rue de la Sorbonne. With the school's *bibliothèque* a stone's throw away, this was a dream for a young woman enamored of books and romance languages. Living in the Latin Quarter, in the heart of the Left Bank's intellectual center, she was steps away from the Notre Dame Cathedral and the Louvre. She embraced the rigors of academic life but made time to enjoy the pleasures and freedoms afforded by the French capital. Though too young and as yet too unaware to know of the literary cohort Gertrude Stein dubbed the Lost Generation, Joan's Paris was nevertheless the Paris of Fitzgerald and Hemingway, the city the latter would later remember as a "moveable feast." Joan, no less than Hemingway, feasted on the wonders spread out before her.

Joan was part of a female vanguard. When she arrived, the Sorbonne was feeling the effects of a protracted feminist battle against the centuries-old "separate spheres" model of education. Though the school had been admitting women for fifty years, they had been treated as second-class citizens, prevented from full entrée to subjects such as medicine, law, and engineering. If the purpose was to groom women to be teachers, homemakers, or good citizens, what possible good could come from "masculine" scientific training? What use was women's mastery of the modern languages? The view was overturned in 1924, when France's presiding minister of instruction determined that the option should at least exist in girls' high schools for them to take an identical educational course of preparation of that afforded to men, leading to the same university entrance exam, the *baccalauréat*.

Upper-class and upper-middle-class female students, Joan among them, seized the opportunity presented by the governmental policy change, which was in part a by-product of World War I. (With so many Frenchmen lost to the war, it became clear many women would go unmarried or otherwise unsupported and would need the type of education that would allow them to fend for themselves.) On the one hand, Joan was riding a French Republic feminist wave, taking advantage of open doors that had been long closed except to a select few. On the other hand, she faced an "adverse political and cultural climate" in her classrooms; the male-dominated Sorbonne would not become a congenial place for women overnight.

Her year at the Sorbonne had always been meant to be a mere stepping stone—a language immersion—that would lead toward a college career at St. Hugh's College, University of Oxford. A "personal project" of its founder, Elizabeth Wordsworth (a great-niece of the poet William Wordsworth), St. Hugh's had been founded in 1886. By 1923 it was Oxford's largest women's college, with 151 undergraduates. As at the Sorbonne, this was a watershed period for St. Hugh's, as the university's expectations shifted, requiring all women to "read" for degrees beginning in 1920. Before this, they could sit through lectures and even had the option of taking equivalent examinations as their male counterparts, but most women had not followed the requisite high school curriculum (which included Greek and Latin) to obtain degrees.

When female students ventured beyond the St. Hugh's campus to take coursework at Oxford's men's colleges, as was often necessary to meet their requirements, they faced resistance. One professor required them to sit "in the back of the hall, where he hoped he could not see them." Still, the tide had turned, and most female students felt they had "arrived," a sentiment fondly expressed by one of Joan's contemporaries as she recalled walking into her first law class, happily surprised to receive cheers from the male students (though she admitted she was bewildered by the attention "a little bit").

In the fall of 1926 St. Hugh's offered Joan a return to the familiar, mirroring the more intimate (and punctilious) female-centered setting of her Guildford High adolescence. Daily rituals were modeled after those of British middle-class family life. The young women followed a set schedule, as though they were "at boarding school or in an especially strict family home," according to

St. Hugh's historian Laura Schwartz. A typical day consisted of rising early for homework and, after breakfast, heading out with friends for tea or coffee at a popular spot, such as the Cadena on Cornmarket Street, the Super Cinema's café (the luxury movie theater catered to a breakfast clientele), or the restaurant inside the Elliston & Cavell department store (which, according to St. Hugh's women, was "the place to be seen and to see gorgeous men"). Next, it was time for lunch, then class, and after that, afternoon tea and sports or recreation. Students were expected to dress for dinner, as if for a social event. Chapel service was a regular requirement in the evenings, yet many found ways around this by maintaining busy cultural calendars.

Although the rule-bound, rigid structure was designed to preserve a Christian educational foundation—and thus had the effect of monitoring the young women's potential contact with men—the students rarely let the surveillance hinder them from enjoying their new lives away from home. They went about as they liked during the day, and if a special occasion arose in the evening, they would take a chaperone (an elder girl) along. As one alumna commented, the mid-1920s at St. Hugh's "was a period of great fun and great hope." They felt privileged to be there—especially having endured the adversity of war—and they were going to savor the experience.

It was in this very spirit that Joan approached Oxford. She spent long hours in the campus drama department, a lively world fueled by surrounding professional theaters. Having just opened, the Oxford Playhouse featured up-and-coming actors John and Val Gielgud and Flora Robson. At the Savoy, the D'Oyly Carte Opera Company frequently staged the operettas of Gilbert and Sullivan, a favorite of St. Hugh's students, who often broke curfew to stay until the very end of a performance or made a hectic dash back to avoid penalty. (Upon returning to their rooms, the young women often played "Tea for Two," "What'll I Do," and "I Want to Be Happy" quietly on their gramophones.)

St. Hugh's students were most mesmerized by the Oxford University Dramatic Society (OUDS), an independent forum for plays put on by Oxford students. Dominated by productions of Shakespeare, OUDS groomed actors and actresses who would soon become Britain's greats, such as Gyles Isham ("We lost our hearts to him!" remembers one student) and Peggy Ashcroft, who took the OUDS stage in 1931 (and would, within four years, appear in a Hitchcock film).

For the time being, Joan devoted most of her extracurricular time to St. Hugh's productions and writing for several school publications. One of her classmates, Rita Landale, recalled, "My strongest memory of her is that she was always reading a play! I suppose she read other things but I could not help noticing that I always saw her reading a play." While there are few available records to credit Joan's involvement with specific shows, it is most likely that her role consisted of writing or working behind the scenes. (Although, given how warmly Rita Landale remembered her "delightful little singing voice," Joan may have also sung in musicals or one of the school choirs.) She certainly would have participated in the spring 1928 premiere of Edmond Rostand's late nineteenth-century *Les Romanesques*. Put on by the second-year class, it was one of the most ambitious and best-received plays of her college tenure. (The "second-year" play was a highlight of the academic experience at St. Hugh's.)

Joan chose courses that fed her passion for drama and literature—courses on Molière, Jean Racine, Greek tragedy, and nineteenth-century literature (concentrating on such Romantics as Honoré de Balzac, Victor Hugo, and Gustave Flaubert). At the same time, she polished her writing skills as a contributor to the *Fritillary*, a joint publication of all of Oxford's women's colleges, and the *Imp*, the literary magazine of St. Hugh's. (The *Fritillary* and the *Imp* would prove to be significant springboards for women who made writing their career. Renée Hayes, Margaret Lane, and E. M. Challens, who later took the pen name Mary Renault, were contemporary contributors.) Joan wrote movie reviews for the *Fritillary*, under a regular column titled Super Cinema (which referenced the nearby movie palace of the same name), though which ones exactly she penned are hard to say, owing to a lack of attribution. Joan contributed what she called "airy, refined character sketches" and other items to the *Imp*, which carried original stories, poems, gossip, and wide coverage of social and sports activities. Most articles here too were unattributed to an author; anonymity was meant to empower the writers and ensure freedom of speech. It is likely, though, that if the budding writer contributed an ounce—and she did—then she gave tons. This was a small-scale editorial staff, constantly reiterating to readers not to lose sight of the importance of keeping the publication going.

One *Imp* sports review, authored by "J.H." and likely written by Harrison, displays a flair for humor. Covering a lacrosse game between third-year students and the fellows of the SCR (senior common room), she opens, "By untiring efforts and unflagging zeal, the Third Year have won back the laurels snatched from them last year by the S.C.R." She continues, "We must render well-deserved homage to Miss Rowe's indefatigable play; to Miss Perham and Miss Downie, whose cooperation on the field was as harmonious as it is in the library; and to Miss Goulding, whose intrepidity in attempting to wrest the ball from Miss Glover compelled our admiration. Miss Fowle, too, was very eloquent on the subject of rolls-in." A distinctive voice shines through in this recap, in its playful attempt to elevate the form, while capturing action, spectacle, and particular personalities.

Beyond strengthening her writing skills, the *Imp* and the *Fritillary* supplied Joan with the opportunity to indulge in the exchange of ideas. This was the greater gift of St. Hugh's—a milieu in which conversation constantly flowed, over morning coffee or Sunday tea, on a bicycle ride, or in a friend's room. Most of Joan's contemporaries report these exchanges as playing the most crucial role in their passage from girlhood into adulthood. As one woman put it, "We certainly set the world to rights over hot cocoa in each other's rooms."

Another classmate captured the ambience in those idealistic interwar years, surrounded by women with newly won rights and a growing awareness of the world around them. With a hint of irony, she reflected, "Six years had gone by since the end of the Kaiser's War and plainly, we believed in a utopian future, guided by a League of Nations, and of course the League of Nations Union, which would forever establish international order, justice, and peace." Some at St. Hugh's were finding their political and philosophical belief systems exposed and challenged. Others, like Joan, were expanding on horizons that had formed earlier. The League of Nations Union had been critical in sensitizing her to international relations and, specifically, the role women might play in making the world just and equal. Meanwhile, they were considering their career prospects against the backdrop of a depressed British economy.

Even with such uncertainty, the general mood remained lively and spirited. House parties or private dances took place frequently on weekends. Joan was right in the middle of it all; as Rita Landale recalled, "Joan led a gay life at Oxford. She was always smartly dressed and very noticeable." Joan's fashion sense and stylishness came naturally. She used it to draw attention to herself, never afraid of wearing a color that was too bright or a hat that was "too much." She once told a story of how, for her coming-out party, when all the debutantes wore pastel colors on their big day, she had chosen to wear a red dress.

While Joan's rebellious streak had its appeal, it could work against her when she tried to test the college's rules. One night Joan went with her friends to a pub that was off-limits according to the college's code of conduct. Just as she was about to take her leave, she noticed a student monitor (called a "runner") coming through the front door. In a mad dash to camouflage her identity, she raced back to take refuge in the ladies' room. She piled on lipstick, rouge, mascara, and powder. Then she attempted the performance of her young life, sashaying her hips from left to right, until she reached the bar and requested a double brandy in the huskiest voice she could muster. "Feel[ing] like one of the world's greatest actresses," she watched as her friends were herded out the door, heads hung low in shame. Joan was about to claim victory when the runner turned back, peered his head in the door and asked, "Aren't you coming too, Miss Harrison?" She fell in line, resigned to pay the same penalty as her friends. If this episode taught her anything, it was an early cue that she shouldn't make any grand plans for the stage; but it didn't stop her from future antics.

Joan struggled in her first two years of coursework. According to her tutorial reports, she did well in Latin ("very satisfactory") but poorly in French language ("low, too many big mistakes"). Her *Tartuffe* tutor commented that her work should be stronger considering that she was in "French honors." Her medieval literature report observed, "This is a competent student, but I don't know if she is likely to develop much." Another faculty member expressed concern that Joan lacked the necessary depth and substance: "She has shown intent and appreciation, but is rather inclined to produce catalogs of facts. Her style is dangerously colloquial, even 'chatty.'" Another one expressed similar criticism about her apparent superficiality: "Her work is often spoilt by lack of personal thought. I think she has more intelligence and could get over this secondhandedness." These were not the kinds of reports that newly admitted Oxford students dreamed of taking home.

But by her second year, some of her tutors were seeing a spark. Her Rousseau teacher wrote on her report that while Joan's paper was not perhaps the best of the class, "it was the most interesting." In nineteenth-century literature, she was showing "more original[ity] and relying on her own judgment." By her final semester, her tutor (for an unidentified course) surmised that she still lacked healthy habits of revision but displayed "a good style, and a fairly extensive vocabulary." Another concluded that she "asked good questions and had a mature writing style."

While it's likely that Joan made a bit of a show out of her own careless-ness—after all, she had many diversions—it may also be the case that the St. Hugh's academic structure was not the most conducive for her. Some of her classmates voiced regrets that they did not have more personal direction. One alumna reflected, "I could have done with more guidance, I was a bit immature, [and] should have taken an extra year before Oxford." Another woman explained, "I suppose I was conscientious enough. For me and others like me, it was a disappointment that the principal and my remote personal tutor never showed any interest or concern in what I intended to do when I came down." Given Joan's natural determination and willfulness, her impulse would have been to resist the school's hierarchies and resent being steered away from her growing loves—of stage, writing, and, of course, the movies. Why confine herself to a classroom when wide worlds were opening up on screens at the nearby Electra Cinema and the Super Cinema, which granted easy entrée to Hollywood first-runs, and the Scala (later the Phoenix Picturehouse), which offered international and art-house fare?

In finals week of spring 1929, Joan, like every other Oxford student, would be judged not by her grades up to that point but by her performance on her exams. The highest possible ranking, first-class honors, was awarded to a very small percentage of students (usually those bound for graduate school). Then came second-class honors, third-class, and the occasional (and dreaded) fourth-class.

Joan, perhaps more relieved than proud, walked away with third-class honors. Compared to some in her cohort, this was an undistinguished and underwhelming way to cap a college career. On the other hand, in the grander scheme, given how few women in Britain could say they had gone to Oxford, let alone any university, it was really the degree that mattered. Joan could capi-talize on her "honors Oxford education" regardless, dropping casual reference to it here or there, as needed. And she would.

That June, having just graduated, she went toe-to-toe with her father in the family library. At twenty-two, she was stunningly beautiful and, if she is to believed, yearning to return to London to launch her career as a reporter. That's the point at which she invited her father into the library and made her announcement: "I want to be a newspaperwoman. I expect you to give me a job."

Walter cautioned her, "You will never be a success in a tough field like the newspaper business." Joan later recounted that she held a copy of the *Surrey Advertiser* in her hand, prepared to make her defense. But at that moment, she surrendered, folding up his own newspaper and returning it to his grasp. (There is reason to question just how devastated Joan actually might have been when Walter put his foot down. "The family view has always been that Joan was never that interested in the newspaper business," says her niece, Kate Adamson. "Joan liked to be the boss, and, at that time, she would not have been able to have had the level of input that she would have liked.")

For a time, Joan remained at the Grove. She and Faith, now graduated from high school, spent time attending parties and shopping; downtown Guildford was electric with activity by the early 1930s. Brother Jack, having gone into the family business at the age of twenty-three, was guiding the *Advertiser* into the future. He was his father's son, and he wore the mantle of company secretary well, impressing Walter with his ideas for more modern technology and new financial practices. Meanwhile, older sister Muriel was covering a lot of territory. After graduating from Bedford College with an honors degree in history, she was teaching at the Maynard School for Girls in Exeter, 150 miles west of Guildford. This was her second appointment, following a brief stint at Queen Ethelburga's School, which took her two hundred miles north from home.

Following four months of dress-rehearsing her parents' vision of an English lady's life, Joan grew restless. Though her career aspirations remained undefined, London was calling. She later recalled, "When I came out of college, I was vague about a career. The thought of living in London, the big city, appealed to me." With the help of Oxford friends, she landed a position writing advertising copy for the London Press Exchange. Acclaimed writer Lesley Blanch, who befriended Joan later in life and had an ad job in the early 1930s, reflected, "It was a great moment for advertising firms, it was the beginning." But Joan didn't experience the same momentum. She hit a ceiling as a copywriter after eighteen months. "I felt I had gone as far as I could go in the advertising business," she later explained. She returned to the Grove.

After a few months of soul searching, it was time to seek some other type of employment. At this point, her father did offer to make some introductions, but on his conditions. He used his contacts to procure her a job as a sales clerk in a midtown London dress shop. Working with clothes appealed to Joan. She loved fashion. But she didn't like working under someone else's thumb, and she found kowtowing to the condescending matrons unbearable. What sense did it make to stand next to their reflections in the mirror and tell them they looked "darling" as their girdles stretched the seams of the store's latest tweed suit? "At the end of the day, I found myself loathing women," she later confessed. One story has it that her career as a shopgirl ended dramatically when she lost her patience with a customer, wadded a dress into a ball, and hurled it directly into the woman's face. She had been there six months.

Then came a moment when she arrived at the kernel of an answer. Story chasing had been in her family's blood for generations. Joan wanted to write; she wanted to tell stories. Nothing was stopping her. She began to write her own short stories and send them in to magazines. A few sold, though none were published. "I had a little talent for writing, but not enough," she said. Her wages were meager, but her passion had been irrevocably sparked. "All I'm after for twenty-four hours a day," she was fond of saying, "is a good story."

She may not have known it at the time, but Joan was gathering the tools and experiences that would inform her career for decades to come. In her spare time, she began attending court sessions at the Old Bailey "to learn about life," as she later put it. For this, she enlisted her favorite accomplice, her father's younger brother, Harold, who happened to work as the keeper at the Old Bailey. As the official who assigned all the court's cases, Uncle Harry had been sneaking Joan into some of London's most riveting trials ever since she was a child. (His stint as the keeper was so long that the *Hull Daily Mail* speculated that "he had probably heard more murder trials than any other person living." "He was one of those Uncles young girls adore," she once said of Harold (who died in 1941 in a World War II air raid). "He not only took you to lunch, but he knew all the grisly details of all the most shocking crimes." Joan spent other days visiting Scotland Yard or viewing police lineups, forever in search of narrative inspiration.

Still, by spring 1931 Joan was in need of gainful employment. If she had paused to compare her trajectory to those in her Guildford High graduating class, she would have found that a third of her peers had gone into the professions. About half the class had assumed roles as wives and mothers. A few had found success as musical or stage performers. The remaining women were teachers or secretaries. Joan elected to take shorthand and typing courses.

"A secretary can learn any business," a girlfriend had advised her. And so to secretarial school she went.

Joan managed to acquire a spot as a typist in a London publishing house. She spent her days tapping other writers' words on the keys. Single characters, one after another. But with so many interesting characters running around in her own mind, she wondered what the point of it all was. At the very least, she'd much rather be reading a book than typing one up.

Eighteen months passed. She was twenty-six years old, with no room for advancement at the publishing house and no other prospects. It was time to pack up her London life and go home. But oh, how it must have pained her! In London, Joan first lived in a Victorian gingerbread at 8 Springvale Terrace, coincidentally very close to Lime Grove Studios in Shepherd's Bush. (Or perhaps not so coincidentally—might she have entertained notions of working at a film studio as young as twenty-three?) A little later, she moved to 41 Leonard Court, in the Edwardes Square, where revitalization meant that winding garden paths mingled with bustling shops and the recently constructed neo-Greek Kensington Cinema, which was hailed at its opening as "the largest cinema in England." In London, she had been surrounded by her passions. What life could Guildford possibly offer to compete with London? She would find a way back, of that she must have been sure.

4 | BIRTH OF A MASTER

IN NOVEMBER 1933, having said good-bye to the secretarial pool and returned to the Grove, Joan had barely put her feet up when Alfred Hitchcock's "Wanted: Young Lady" advertisement landed in her lap. "You're hired. . . . I'm starving," concluded the interview, and suddenly she had a position at the Gaumont-British Picture Corporation assisting Britain's most celebrated director.

Harrison's introduction to Hitchcock has been recounted dozens of times over the years in Hollywood press releases and magazine stories, often by Joan herself, though the particulars vary. Like a good story, it has taken on a life of its own. The basic grain remains the same, but the truth is, the now epochal anecdote has never done justice to either Harrison or Hitchcock. She had much more going for her than blonde beauty. Her ambition and clever mind would have been immediately noticeable to the director, and her Oxford degree set her apart. (He probably wouldn't have held the "third-class" against her if he'd bothered to ask her honors level; he didn't think formal education defined a person.)

By the same token, Hitchcock deserves more credit than the account grants him, portraying him as "either unprofessional or lecherous or both," as film historian Eddie Muller points out. Not only was Hitchcock's personal assistant Renee Pargenter vacating her position with her eye on the altar, but the director was also leaving behind a number of key crew members as he joined a new studio. At Gaumont-British, he was looking to amass a strong team with no room for lightweights. Joan fit the bill.

Hitchcock promptly noted Joan's extensive knowledge of film and her impressive command of actors' names. "The motion picture industry fascinated me," she later remarked, surmising that what really cinched the job was when she told Hitchcock that she'd seen every one of his movies. When he offered her one pound a week, down from the three pounds she had earned in the typists' pool, she barely batted an eyelash. Any amount would do, to work in the cinema. It was an added bonus to work for Hitchcock, one of the few British directors whose name stood out on a marquee.

Born on August 13, 1899, in Leytonstone, Hitchcock was the son of a greengrocer. His family eventually moved to the Limehouse district of London's East End, on the northern bank of the Thames River, as the senior Hitchcock expanded his business into a market and fishmonger's shop. Biographer Patrick McGilligan describes a childhood filled with hard work and strict discipline (typical of parents who were devout Catholics), though not lacking in joy. The Hitchcock family took pleasures in theater, music, and sports, instilling in their son a love of entertainment. As a young man, he worked in the sales section of W. T. Henley's Telegraph Works before moving into an advertising position that held more allure. In spring 1921 he landed a job as a title illustrator at the formidable Famous Players–Lasky British Producers, located at Islington Studios.

Before long, Hitchcock had advanced through the ranks, aided by the foresight of producer Michael Balcon, who continued to mentor him when Famous Players–Lasky ceased production in the UK and conducted sweeping layoffs. Balcon was developing a new company, Gainsborough Pictures, which would produce lower-budget fare. He placed Hitchcock in various positions (including assistant director, writer, art director, and editor) during this period of British retrenchment. Betting on his protégé's future, Balcon viewed him as a boy wonder. By 1926 Hitchcock was on the verge of releasing his first feature film at Gainsborough.

The director may have been special, but it would be erroneous to account for his rise by way of a "great genius" narrative. His brisk ascent occurred because he was well supported and guided by a handful of skilled professionals. In addition to Balcon, he had the good fortune to be coached by producer-director Donald Crisp, writer Eliot Stannard, and the directors George Fitzmaurice and Graham Cutts (the latter of whom Hitchcock would quickly replace as Gainsborough's top director).

One of the earliest and most vital influences on his career was the woman who would become his wife, Alma Reville. Hitchcock had spotted her on the day of his arrival at Famous Players–Lasky in 1921, though months would stretch out into years before he conjured the nerve to speak to her. She had four years' seniority over him when he landed at Lasky, having begun at the London Film Company at Twickenham Studios as a "movie mad" sixteen-year-old. Alma worked early on as a cutter in the editing room. By the time Hitchcock joined Famous Players–Lasky, she had held positions as editor, continuity writer, second assistant director, assistant producer, and the critical role of floor director. She was the only person—man or woman—in the British industry to hold jobs as both cutter and continuity supervisor.

And she was only twenty-two. At four feet, eleven inches tall, Alma was tiny with reddish-brown hair and glasses that hid her pretty hazel eyes. She felt comfortable in men's trousers, as was customary of many working women of the day. To the average observer, her appearance marked her as bold and racy. "I regarded myself as a very attractive girl, prettier perhaps than I really was," she later recalled. "I was outgoing and social. . . . I loved movies and loved what I was doing."

When, in 1923, Hitchcock found himself in a position to hire an editor, he gave Alma a phone call. Hitchcock was the newly anointed assistant director for the Balcon-produced feature *Woman to Woman*, and he wanted her to join his team. This marked his first-ever communication with her, and it came after their respective jobs at Famous Players–Lasky had concluded. Alma surmised that he had bided his time until he held a higher position of authority, "since it is unthinkable for a British male to admit that a woman has a job more important than his." Indeed, his master plan included a marriage proposal. But he deferred such a gesture until he had forged some professional collateral. Alma negotiated a higher salary and signed on. Reville and Hitchcock would collaborate on dozens of films across Europe over the next few years. And, at a certain point, their two "imaginations met," as Alma put it. Their working relationship blossomed into a romance. They married on December 2, 1926.

Alma brought Hitchcock along, technically and artistically. He himself noted that "she'd been working in films when I met her. She knew more about it than I did. She taught me." Respected in the trade, Reville wrote an article in the publication *Motion Picture Studio* in early 1923 advising filmmakers to "try and see the films as your audience would." Her sensibilities would help lay the foundation for Hitchcock's overall cinematic approach. During his first directorial venture, *The Pleasure Garden*, he would turn to Alma after every shot and ask, "Was that all right?" (Shot in Munich in 1925, the film had so many problems it went unreleased until 1927.) When it came time to direct *The Lodger: A Story of the London Fog* in 1926, Hitchcock had grown confident in his own abilities. With Alma at his side as a trusted partner, backed by a trained, reliable crew, he was certain that *The Lodger* would enable Balcon to realize his bet on the fledgling director.

The British cinema industry had been struggling. Unlike studios in Germany, France, and the Soviet Union, which were thriving at the time, British studios had to contend with their American counterparts for the same market share: English-language films. And because Hollywood studios had the industry clout to demand block booking (stipulating that theaters buy their films in bundles) and blind bidding (requiring theaters to bid for and book their films without first previewing them), it was difficult for British studios to compete with them. The weaker UK industry faced a long-term losing battle on the world stage, unable to escape its association with poor production values and low quality. Even the British preferred Hollywood fare. By the post–World War I era, American interests had captured 80 to 90 percent of British screens. Only 5 percent of films exhibited in Britain were produced there.

What was needed, industry leaders decided, were prestige pictures made by British filmmakers elevated to master status to catapult British cinema to another level. In a sense, Balcon dreamed up this formula, and Hitchcock brought it to life. *The Lodger*, made in 1926 and released (after a protracted internal struggle) in 1927, combined European art-cinema touches with classical suspense. Upon its release, *Bioscope* deemed it possibly "the finest British production ever made."

Hitchcock rapidly ascended at Gainsborough Pictures, bolstered by supportive producers and a good deal of American technology that Famous Players–Lasky had left in its wake. But the studio's small size and house style—its orientation toward adaptations and melodramas—was stifling to Hitchcock. By the middle of 1927, with several of his films (including *Easy Virtue* and *Downhill*) still awaiting release, he signed a contract with the much larger British International Pictures (BIP).

BIP enabled Hitchcock to make a greater variety of films, with bigger budgets and higher production values, at a time when the industry was on the brink of unprecedented growth. After two years of parliamentary debate over the disastrous state of the domestic market, the UK government had just passed the Cinematograph Films Act of 1927. Block booking and other harmful practices by foreign companies were prohibited, and a quota was put in place mandating that 20 percent of all films screened in the UK had to be produced domestically. These measures would go far. In 1927, British companies released 40 motion pictures on British screens. By 1930, that number had climbed to 132. Four years later, the number of British releases hit 194. Yet the quota policy ultimately yielded mixed results, especially where "quota quickies" were concerned. With high incentives to churn out as many films as possible, British studios paid little regard to quality.

It only took a few years for Hitchcock to discover he'd arrived at another professional dead end at BIP. The studio was more interested in making quota quickies than the kinds of prestige pictures that were his strong suit, and executives fretted over the very artistic flourishes that might distinguish him from the pack. Continually dogged by management, he couldn't seem to set himself apart. And despite the fact that many of his BIP films (e.g., *The Ring*, *The Manxman*, *Blackmail*, and *Juno and the Paycock*) earned him praise or at least notice from reviewers, their reception at the box office tended to be mixed. He realized he was in a precarious position. And where was the creative freedom he yearned for? It was at this juncture in 1933 that Hitchcock made the dramatic decision to reunite with Michael Balcon and his new venture, Gaumont-British Pictures.

Balcon had poised his company for success, aggressively shifting his focus toward more lavish productions. His eye was on international markets, most directly on American audiences. He would feature only Hollywood names or those English stars who were well known overseas. Balcon was a strategist—he would treat Hitchcock's filmmaking team as if it was a separate unit all to itself. He even employed the term "Hitchcock films" as a production category, a genre that ran in tandem with "romance" and "comedy."

Joan came on board just as the Hitchcock unit settled into its new office at Lime Grove Studios in Shepherd's Bush. Having been recently remodeled, Lime Grove was a bustling place, configured as two large blocks with a lower-lying connecting building in between. The complex included half a dozen sound-stages; exterior shooting spaces; three theaters; dressing rooms; wardrobe, set, and prop shops; and a row of offices. Hitchcock's office held prime position.

And he was armed with two collaborators brought in specifically for him from his Gainsborough days, producer Ivor Montagu (who had spared *The Lodger* from the cutting-room floor) and Angus MacPhail (whom Balcon hired to head up Gaumont's story department).

The first film on the docket would be *The Man Who Knew Too Much*, based on a scenario about gentleman adventurer Bulldog Drummond, a character created by writer H. C. McNeile (whose pseudonym was Sapper). Hitchcock had developed the story at BIP with the talented writer Charles Bennett, also recruited to Gaumont. Dropping the Bulldog Drummond character, a necessary move in order to acquire the property from BIP, Hitchcock and Bennett revised it into the tale of a married couple who get caught up in an espionage plot and must rescue their kidnapped daughter.

Hitchcock once said, "I think you'll find the real start of my career was *The Man Who Knew Too Much*," deeming it "the picture that re-established my creative prestige." It contained many ingredients that would come to define the Hitchcock oeuvre: suspense, a "chaos world," a couple-driven story, an active heroine, an ambivalent villain, a "MacGuffin" ("the thing the spies are after, but the audience doesn't care about"), and a remarkable set piece. *The Man Who Knew Too Much* would launch Hitchcock's "classic thriller sextet," an accomplished series of films that not only put the director and the studio on the worldwide map but also ushered in one of the most distinguished periods in British cinema.

Joan's arrival coincided with this momentous turning point in Hitchcock's career. Though a casual observer might have summed up her role as passive— she was a mere assistant, watching, listening, and learning—she was bearing witness to the birth of a creative energy that encompassed collaborators, methods, modes, structures, decisions: the production elements that would essentially map out Hitchcock's future.

When Joan met him, Hitchcock was in his midthirties, with a receding hairline and a double chin. He was at least a hundred pounds overweight, stretching the boundaries of his dark navy suits. His boyish face could look cherubic at times, sly at others. He was a needler, an impish provocateur. Wielding startling puns and over-the-top practical jokes, he delighted in inciting reactions from friends and colleagues. "Call me Hitch, without a cock," he liked to say when introduced to new people. Yet he was capable of warmth and charm, and great depth. Actor-producer John Houseman (who would encounter him not that many years later) reflected, "I had heard of him as a fat man given to scabrous jokes. . . . What I was unprepared for was a man of exaggeratedly delicate sensibilities, marked by a harsh Catholic education and the scars from a social system against which he was in perpetual revolt and which had left him suspicious and vulnerable, alternatively docile and defiant."

Within a month or so of Joan's hiring, she was asked into the office during a story meeting between Hitchcock and Charles Bennett. The director picked up a copy of James Joyce's *Ulysses*, which he kept handy on his desk for just this occasion, and turned to an earmarked section—the vulgar "toilet scene." As he recited the passage matter-of-factly, Joan couldn't help but lose her composure, even though she must have known she was playing into his hands. Why was he doing this? According to Bennett, what seemed to bother her most was how total and complete her unmasking was; she couldn't disguise her desire to figure out what was behind Hitchcock's ritualistic need to put her through the wringer. Hitchcock's reading left her speechless, and stumped.

Joan would realize soon enough that this was Hitchcock's chief operating mode with most women he encountered both professionally and personally, a way for the somewhat socially awkward, physically self-conscious man to gain an upper hand. He employed it most especially with the actresses he had cast or was considering casting; from his perspective, part of a director's role was to encourage an actress to let down her guard; it was entirely appropriate to use humor, manipulation, and even (and sometimes especially) shock. Some women could look past the tactic. Others could not. Ingrid Bergman fell into the former category, remarking, "I knew Hitchcock liked working with me. I could feel it, and I felt that way about him. . . . He always listened. Hitch was someone I could tell just about anything. He had a delicious sense of humor, and he could be a little shocking. It wasn't so much what he said, but when he said it, always at some inappropriate moment when no one was expecting it."

But in Joan's case, Hitchcock's professional justification for such behavior held no water. His orchestration served no apparent purpose but to provoke a one-sided emotional striptease, intended for his erotic gratification. And perhaps Bennett's as well; his behavior sank lower because he included another man as a bystander. Joan was, no doubt, an ideal target; the picture of elegance and reserve, she had internalized all the necessary social mores of middle-class respectability. In a new job, she would have been on her best behavior. It seemed that to the director, the more guarded the woman, the more gratifying the takedown.

In a 1935 *Film Weekly* interview, Hitchcock elucidated what bothered him most about women raised to be respectable. While some sections of the article were tongue-in-cheek, others were more caustic, such as his discussion of the "lady pose." This stance, Hitchcock said, was the dislikable quality seen notably in upper-middle-class English women, who lacked a "real, human" dimension. He opined, "It was always their desire to appear a lady and, in doing so, they became cold and lifeless." He wished he could "knock the ladylikeness out of chorus girls," namely "English film actresses . . . from some school of acting or from the stage"—whose polish, by this logic, kept them from realizing they were chorus girls at heart. Given the degree to which he had thought this through, Hitchcock seemed unaware of the inhumane nature of his own impulses. His allusions to violence are also chilling.

The *Ulysses* passage represented Hitchcock's efforts to gauge how quickly Joan's "lady pose" could be knocked off, if at all. How thick was her mask? Who lived behind the postures and pretense? Joan had "failed" her first trial.

She soon got another chance, by way of a screen test. Upon meeting Joan, cinematographer Curt Courant convinced Hitchcock that they should audition her. Could Gaumont have an unexpected star in its midst? She happily consented. She must have wondered if her time onstage was finally paying off. Hitchcock had a routine for these moments as well. "Have you slept with anyone?" he would call out from behind the camera. On existing archival footage related to his earlier film *Blackmail*, the lead Anny Ondra and Hitchcock can be seen performing an audio test, playfully bantering in a way that reveals their warm rapport. Ondra says, "Oh my gosh, I'm terribly frightened." He asks, "Why? Have you been a bad woman or something?" She laughs and replies, "Well, not so bad, but—" "But you slept with men?" he queries. She turns away laughing and says, "Oh no!" He goads her, "You have not? Now come over here and stand still in your place, or it will not come out right, as the girl said to the soldier." She giggles uncontrollably.

With Courant behind the lens, Hitchcock put Joan through her paces. Though there is no extant footage of this audition, his script wavered very little in these situations. "Have you slept with anyone, Miss Harrison?" he likely asked. By all accounts, she held her own in the indecorous setting. She impressed him with steely repartee but proved deficient as a thespian. As the director put it, "Well, I'll not spoil a good assistant by turning her into a second-rate actress." A window had closed, but she had her foot in the door.

5 | TRUE CRIME PAYS

JOAN'S INITIAL DAYS AS A PERSONAL ASSISTANT consisted of answering telephones, opening mail, keeping Hitchcock's calendar, and taking notes during meetings. She managed the constant revolving door of actors, crew, and staff. "Everything was so large and confusing and people whose names I didn't even know kept coming in and out of the office using strange technical terms, which at the time I could never get sorted out," Joan remembered. Knowing that she was supposed to translate German to English for esteemed art director Alfred Junge and cast member Peter Lorre, she tried her best. It was not only German but also French—her métier—that failed her. According to Charles Bennett, Joan would approach Lorre on set to explain what was in store for the next scene. She spoke in French, which Lorre was fluent in, but instead of grasping what she was saying, he "listened bewilderedly for a while, then said in his halting if hopeful grasp of the English tongue, 'Please—please, speak English.'"

Joan could relate. All of Shepherd's Bush felt foreign. "I was too curious about everything," she recalled. Everything except for typing, answering phones, or opening mail, that is. To his credit, her boss recognized that she—and he—were better off playing to her strengths. He gave her a reader's responsibilities, inviting her to sit in all script meetings and empowering her to read short stories, novels, and magazine articles, which she summarized for his consideration. Hitchcock was not inclined to pore over written synopses; he preferred the bravura of verbal recital. "Mr. Hitchcock likes to have plots told to him rather than read to him," Joan explained. "I found myself trying to improve on the stories as I went along." Each day, Joan would spin a little web, performing for the master. He took pleasure in watching his protégée weave her stories.

As Hitchcock watched and listened, so did Joan. "He allowed me to see all sides of the business. . . . I suppose he appreciated my fascination for the work," she contemplated. This is where his absolute love of cinema, and high regard for those who shared it, held great benefits. If she had questions, he had answers. No point was too trivial when it came to making movies. "No detail of the work [was] too small for him to explain," Joan recalled. "With him, there's always time." Hitchcock's naturally careful and fastidious manner paid dividends she couldn't have calculated when she settled for two pounds less per week than she had earned in her previous job.

Hitchcock was a bona fide teacher, and he had a zeal for mentoring women. Jay Presson Allen, who found him "generous and diplomatic" when she worked on the *Marnie* screenplay in the 1960s, enjoyed what she called his "tutorial style." Hitchcock preferred working with women, she deduced, because he was more comfortable around them. "If he'd had his way, he wouldn't have worked with men at all. It's not that he liked to dominate women screenwriters; he gave us freedom," remarked Allen (whose credits include *The Prime of Miss Jean Brodie, Cabaret, Funny Lady*, and *Deathtrap*). This was especially true, she felt, for strong-willed women who stood their ground against his tests. "I don't have a reputation for being a docile person," she said, "but I don't have any trouble giving myself over to someone who's really gifted."

With Joan, Hitchcock was patient, walking her through what she needed to know. Hitchcock had the foresight to appreciate that this sharp-minded, Oxford-educated woman could prove to be a powerful ally. Just as Balcon had banked on him, he intuited that she was worth the investment.

At the same time, Joan benefited from a studio system that was open. In contrast to the Hollywood mode, London studios were not compartmentalized. Those who ventured through the doors of a place like Lime Grove gained exposure to most stages of production. Such an artisanal setting was in part responsible for Hitchcock's swift rise through the ranks. Now his protégée was experiencing every facet. Joan mused, "I was able to invade every department. I saw how pictures were cut. I worked with the scriptwriters. I read stories for possible production material, and of course I learned everything I know about directing from Hitch." She shadowed him through the process of dailies, editing, sound dubbing, and even marketing.

Script preparation for *The Man Who Knew Too Much* took place from fall 1933 through spring 1934. The chief story architect was Bennett, Hitchcock's most valued "constructionist," though D. B. Wyndham Lewis has a credit, likely from earlier participation at BIP. Even in the case of Bennett, who was a most reliable source of both structure and dialogue, writing for Hitchcock was a far cry from the clichéd isolated author, hunched in deep revelation over a typewriter.

On a typical writing day, Bennett would drive his car over to the director's flat at 153 Cromwell Road, where Hitchcock stood waiting at the curb. As Bennett chauffeured him to the studio, they exchanged small talk. Upon arriving, they would chat, "but only touching on the screenplay," according to Bennett, until lunchtime. Around twelve thirty, they would take lunch at the Mayfair Hotel, making little mention of the project at hand. Back at the studio, Hitchcock might repair for a nap, at which time Bennett would spend a few hours producing scenes from what the day had yielded. Otherwise, they might have a story conference. At five o'clock, it would be time to take Hitchcock home. "We'd leave the studio together," Bennett recalled, "and go back to his flat. And that's where the real work was done. Over cocktails, beautiful cocktails made by Alma. And we'd just kick around ideas. A lot of them were very useful. A lot of them were very useless. But that's the way it was done, yes."

From this description, a lot of the actual writing occurred somewhere in between the office and home, during downtime. "We practically lived together," Bennett remarked, capturing the intensity that occasionally characterized Hitchcock's writing relationships. Moreover, even Bennett (who spent his later years taking more than his fair share of the credit, often at the expense of female writers) readily admits, "the real work was done" in Alma's presence, a point made time and again by Hitchcock's British collaborators. Those may have been gorgeous cocktails she was serving up, but they were nothing compared to her bons mots on story, plot, and character.

The triangular pattern that structured Hitchcock's creativity dated back to the beginning of his British career. As film scholar Charles Barr has observed, the director's female characters were often portrayed as sympathetic when not overtly active and independent, and this was perhaps a by-product of the "dialectic between the dominant male screenwriters and the constant presence and influence of Alma." Alma—and later Joan—offered a voice that sometimes worked "with" and sometimes "against" the male writers.

The somewhat fractured nature of this relationship can be detected in Bennett's later declarations to interviewer Patrick McGilligan that Alma "never did a damned thing. . . . I don't remember seeing Alma at all during the writing. Except at the end of the day perhaps, when we would go home for drinks at Hitchcock's apartment."

It is revealing that Bennett can't describe exactly when, or how, the mechanics took place. When it came to writing with Hitchcock, who was heavily involved and took an occasional writer's credit on the British films, the process was elusive. John Houseman (who worked on several of his American titles) once pointed out, "Working with Hitchcock really meant listening to him talk—anecdotes, situations, characters, revelations, and reversals—which he would think up at night and try out on us during the day." Ivor Montagu, who took an associate producer credit on the original *The Man Who Knew Too Much*, explained that the film "was really an original idea of Hitchcock's. You see Charles Bennett had the credit for story-making in that but you see what happened with Hitch's stories was that he would want an amanuensis. He originally used Alma Reville on a lot of things. . . . He wanted a screenwriter to talk to and the screenwriter would get the credit. Hitch would go around London and he'd see something from a bus. He would go, for example, to the Albert Hall. We would work these into the stories. And that's how he would get the atmosphere of local scenes and sets, and the sets would develop collaboratively like that."

The director would visualize episodes, ask clarifying questions, or arrive at a thrilling epiphany. Some have proposed this working method came from his background in art direction; others attribute it to his editing instincts. (He thought of film first and foremost as montage, as little bits and pieces.) Whatever the explanation, he needed writers who could imbue his kernel thoughts with narrative coherence, logic, and psychological motivation. (He didn't like to let on that he needed anyone. To maintain the upper hand, he would "set the tone with idle talk, lowering the writers' defenses," according to McGilligan.) This developmental stage of filmmaking—a time for conversation and collaboration—was his favorite part. It was the moment of creation, after which the boring task of making the movie began.

It would take a little time for Joan to be included in those studio meet-ings and Mayfair Hotel lunches, but only a few months passed before she was spending evenings on Cromwell Road, gaining glimpses into how "the real work" was done. Not only was she learning from the Master, she was taking cues from the Madame. She was fast becoming the "third collaborator." Alma was likely relieved to have a new trainee, because it allowed her to apportion time to her own outside projects, when she wasn't devoting her attention to those domestic activities that gave her pleasure, including hostessing, garden-ing, cooking, and parenting.

Born July 7, 1928, the Hitchcocks' daughter, Patricia, was energetic and precocious, encouraged by her parents to have a mind of her own. Alma enjoyed motherhood, but she did not see it as her only occupation, nor was she content to merely coach Hitchcock from the sidelines. Professional oppor-tunities were mounting and, with Patricia of school age (and soon bound for boarding school), Alma embraced them. She had cowritten four screenplays between 1931 and 1934 for some of the best-known directors and performers in Britain. In fact, as *The Man Who Knew Too Much* was coming to fruition, Alma was collaborating on what would become one of Britain's most suc-cessful sound-era titles, Berthold Viertel's *The Passing of the Third Floor Back* (released in late 1935).

Alma's bustling work life was one reason Joan was welcomed so quickly into the family fold. She functioned as personal assistant to both husband and wife. She joined in the evening entertainments at Cromwell Road, which included an "informal film society of friends and associates" such as Bennett, Montagu, and MacPhail. The Cambridge-educated Montagu characterized these nights as part work, part play: "A feast of fancy and dialectic, a mixture of composing crosswords and solving them. The unfolding story was elaborated with suggestions from all of us; everything was welcomed if not always agreed."

Actors also attended, including favorite guests Peter Lorre (affectionately dubbed "the walking overcoat" by Hitchcock because of his overattachment to the garment) and Celia Lovsky, who performed the role of Lorre's nurse in *The Man Who Knew Too Much* and whom the actor married during produc-tion. In addition, Joan often found herself in the company of London's most influential intellectuals and film critics. Iris Barry, C. A. Lejeune, and critic turned producer Walter Mycroft frequented Cromwell Road.

Her world was opening up, as she met writers, artists, and actors from all over Europe and from a wide array of cultural and political backgrounds. Gaumont-British was the studio with the most European crew members both above the line (e.g., creative heads) and below the line (e.g., technicians and craftspeople), including a large contingent of German Jewish émigrés. Some of her colleagues were political or religious exiles, while many more had become deeply concerned about rising fascism and the growing possibility of war on the continent. Montagu, a self-declared Communist who had recently returned from a Russian filmmaking venture with Sergei Eisenstein, was emblematic of many in the British industry (and Gaumont in particular). They were raconteurs, whose discourse came from personal experience.

Along with Montagu, there was director Adrian Brunel and the powerful distributor and theater owner Sidney Bernstein, both of whom had been instrumental in founding the London Film Society in 1925. (An ardent anti-Nazi, Bernstein was funneling many actors and filmmakers out of Germany as early as 1933.) The goal of the Film Society was to bring a variety of noncommercial, hard-to-find prints to a broad British audience composed of craftspeople, the press, and avid cinemagoers. Helmed by a council of nearly thirty people that included not only Montagu, Brunel, and Bernstein but also Barry, Lejeune, Mycroft, the actor Hugh Miller, H. G. Wells, and George Bernard Shaw, the Film Society created a vital cultural center.

By the late 1920s, crowds of fourteen hundred were drawn to screenings of films from Germany, France, and the Soviet Union, playing each Sunday afternoon at the New Gallery Cinema on Regent Street. Afterward, these patrons would pour into local pubs and cafés or the welcoming homes of Gaumont staff to discuss not only the film but also the grand-scale musical accompaniment and the lecture that ensured each program was not to be missed. Montagu revealed that they strove to expand cinema's appeal for Britons: "In this way, we could draw into film artists, sculptors, writers, who up to then disdained films." It was a strategic effort to attract younger people with artistic inclinations and new talent into the field. In her Oxford and Chelsea days, Joan would have been a prime target for the Film Society.

Still, she was young and inexperienced when it came to the film business. She was catching on to the fact that her position would demand long hours. And if she was going to take it seriously, she would have to set everything else aside. This was a career, not a job. One day she was in Hitchcock's office taking dictation when the clock struck five o'clock. Her eyes began darting at the clock.

Hitchcock asked, "Do you have to go now?"

"I told you about this dinner party, Mr. Hitchcock," she replied.

"All right, dear, we won't be very long," he said. Seven thirty arrived, and they were still going. Meanwhile, Joan was practically throwing out her shoulder turning to look at the time. Hitchcock suddenly halted in the middle of the scene he was transmitting and announced, "You may go."

The next day, when Joan arrived at work, a new "telegram" appeared everywhere she went. "The Upper Thames Ladies Bowling Society Requests Your Presence Given at Party Tonight" was written on a slip of paper that appeared in the powder room. Another note reading "The Chelsea Cooking School Would Like You to Attend a Party" showed up on her desk. In sum, twelve "wires" materialized. The final one rolled in as she was departing for home. It simply said, "Party Party Party Party Party." The perennial practical jokester had made his point. Her social life would take a backseat.

The Man Who Knew Too Much was in production from late May through early August 1934. Bob Lawrence was played by Leslie Banks (turning in an affable, breezy performance) and wife Jill was played by Edna Best (then celebrated more for her stage roles and off-screen marriage to Herbert Marshall). Fourteen-year-old Nova Pilbeam was cast as their daughter, Betty. Pierre Fresnay played the murdered friend of the couple, and Lorre, who had first been hired for the assassin (a smaller role) was cast as Abbott, the spy-ring leader, after an initial meeting with Hitchcock proved he was well suited to play the unbalanced eccentric. Lorre's presence would also help Gaumont sell to the US market, because he was better known to American audiences than the film's top stars. With the 1931 German film *M*, he'd made quite a mark. Though Gaumont failed to realize Lorre's American market value at first, the studio quickly gave him major billing and adjusted its marketing strategies.

Over the course of the development process, *The Man Who Knew Too Much* had transformed into a tale of Londoners Bob and Jill Lawrence, who while vacationing in St. Moritz witness a murder and learn of a plot to assassinate a foreign leader. The political operatives abduct their daughter, Betty, in an attempt to deter them from going to authorities.

The character of Jill evolved significantly from early script drafts, in which she had figured only nominally. By the final draft, it is Jill who drives much of the drama—as in the rousing musical sequence at the Albert Hall, in which she is forced to choose between hindering the assassination or saving her family's lives. After she unwittingly does both, by screaming from her seat when she spots the killer taking aim across the hall, the action barely pauses before Bob (who has been taken hostage) is used as human collateral by the spies in a final shoot-out against police.

Another major change revolved around this last confrontation at Abbott's hideout. Originally, the sequence too closely mirrored the Siege of Sidney Street of 1911, in which bobbies called in the military during a standoff with armed revolutionaries. The shoot-out was a political embarrassment for the British government. In response to the British Board of Film Censors' request for changes, Hitchcock's team (and playwright Emlyn Williams, in particular) proposed a revised finale in which the harried police commandeer arms from a local gunsmith.

The new conclusion gave the wife and mother a central and extended role. In the end it is Jill—a trained sharpshooter—who winds up killing the assassin and setting free her child and husband. The last chilling minutes of the film are meant to suspend the audience on an emotional high wire, as young Betty steps out onto the roof in an effort to save herself, with the assassin close behind. In a surprise twist, it is not a policeman who takes down the villain but a perfect shot fired by Jill, who has swiped the police marksman's gun at the last minute.

This was one of Harrison's favorite scenes in all of Hitchcock's films, the one she would invoke years later as having been "seared in her mind": "Remember in *The Man Who Knew Too Much* where Edna Best saw the villain trying to push her child off the roof, and she took the rifle and took long and steady aim. To shoot the villain without hitting her [daughter]—Hitch made you feel as though you . . . were telling your own heart to be still . . . not to shake her aim." These were, at their core, the raw materials of "cinematic identification," a signature technique that would come to define the director's psychological style. This scene was one of the first times Joan saw firsthand how cinematic suspense was devised. The moment may well have stayed with Joan for its portrayal of female power, and the unlikely twist created when the woman wields the gun by surprise.

Joan experienced another "first" during *The Man Who Knew Too Much*: she made her screen debut. She is listed in the official credits as "Secretary," a description that has led some to misidentify her as the woman who sits next to Lorre in the opening dining room sequence at the Swiss hotel (though the exotic brunette in the scene bears little resemblance to Joan). The truth of Joan's participation is much more prosaic. "The actress in the movie [Edna Best] was supposed to drive a car in one scene," Joan disclosed in a 1949 interview, "and she couldn't drive. For one glorious scene, I became a double for the heroine, for the first and last time on screen."

If Joan did serve as a substitute driver for Best, her fleeting moment likely ended up on the cutting-room floor. Jill's scenes when she travels by automobile involve only taxis and police cars. In no scene is she, or her stand-in, seen driving. So why is Joan described as playing a secretary in so many credible references? One possible explanation: Joan was listed as company "secretary" in some of the film's official documents, including call sheets and credit lists, which led to ensuing confusion about her role on the production. Even at this early stage, Joan was already playing the role of phantom lady.

In December 1934 the press screening for *The Man Who Knew Too Much* was held at the Academy Cinema in the West End. This was the first time Joan attended the premiere of a film with which she was involved, and it was a smashing event. *Kine Weekly* deemed the movie a "glorious melodrama, an exciting excursion in the realm of artless fiction, staged on a spectacular scale." A *Daily Express* reviewer wrote, "Hitchcock leaps once again into the front ranks of British directors." The film would go on to break attendance records at nearly every theater where it opened, and it became Hitchcock's greatest British success up to that point. For Joan, these were personal rewards, not to be shared with her parents. They considered working in the movies to be gauche. If they chose to watch it at all, the Harrisons likely only saw *The Man Who Knew Too Much* once it traveled to their local Hippodrome Cinema in nearby Reigate in mid-February 1935.

By then, Joan had fully adopted the Hitchcocks as her second family. For Christmas 1934, she had accompanied them to St. Moritz, where they went every December to celebrate their anniversary. *The 39 Steps'* screenplay was due soon; Hitchcock and Alma wanted to have Joan in tow for the writing sessions with Charles Bennett. The trip to the Palace Hotel, which included little Patricia, allowed for plenty of relaxation, whether skiing on the slopes, sleigh riding, drinking cocoa at the lodge, or reading on the balcony. ("I like to ski," Hitchcock once said, "in my mind.") It was a symbolic postscript to her first project with Hitchcock, seeing in person the snowy resort location that launches the story of *The Man Who Knew Too Much* (even though it had been conjured only through artificial backdrops and second-unit footage).

As she greeted 1935, there wasn't any doubt that Joan had assumed a unique role within the Hitchcock entourage, and at Shepherd's Bush as well. By now, her nickname was "Joanie." And as for her boss, well, to her he was now simply "Hitchy."

6 | BIGGER STEPS

IF *THE MAN WHO KNEW TOO MUCH* showed Hitchcock's brand of suspense in nascent form, *The 39 Steps* found it well on its way to maturity. The film was grander in scale, with a bigger budget, more lush production values, better-known stars, and a modern, sexy story line. The director had read the source material, John Buchan's novel, upon its 1915 release in serial form, and he had wanted to adapt it for years. But once he acquired the rights and reread the book, he was frustrated to discover it was not as cinematic as he remembered.

The original story, set in early World War I, follows Richard Hannay, a Scottish expatriate who has moved to London after making his fortune in South Africa only to find himself drawn into an espionage plot. He offers his apartment as shelter to a frightened American stranger, and when the man turns up stabbed to death at his place, he takes up his cause and suddenly is forced on the run.

Through the months of November and December 1934, Joan closely observed while Charles Bennett and Alma Reville transformed the novel for the screen. The process went as it always did. They boiled down the story to its core in the form of a one-page synopsis, and then built a rough scene-by-scene treatment. At the final stage, a dialogue specialist (in this case, Ian Hay) came in to add the lines. *The 39 Steps*' greatest asset was its "double chase" structure (the police hunt Hannay while he goes after the villains), a staple of many Hitchcock thrillers to follow. But the writers had their work cut out for them; they needed robust characterization and richer plotting.

Toward this end, they added three female characters not present in the novel. In the new version of the story, Canadian tourist Richard Hannay (Robert Donat) visits a London music hall, where he witnesses an impressive demonstration by performing savant Mr. Memory and meets the mysterious spy Annabella Smith. He brings her home, where she makes a cryptic reference to "the thirty-nine steps" before she is murdered and he is presumed to be her killer. To prove his innocence, he goes on the lam, chasing a group of political spies halfway across Scotland while being pursued by police. During his escape, he convinces a crofter's wife to assist in a swift getaway. Further along, he kidnaps a beautiful blonde stranger and handcuffs himself to her. The woman, Pamela, gradually comes to believe in his innocence, at the same time falling in love with him.

When filming began on January 11, 1935, certain portions of the screenplay were not finished. Pamela's character, in particular, posed a dilemma that pre-occupied the writers. Originally, a less lustrous actress, Jane Baxter, had been set to play Pamela. But when, at the last minute, Baxter was forced to decline the part owing to another commitment, Hitchcock's team enlisted Madeleine Carroll (who signed her contract on January 9). Given Carroll's star power and her very different screen presence, the writers immediately set about expanding the role of Pamela. Bennett and Harrison frenetically churned out pages on the set, while Carroll strengthened her role further in rehearsals and, eventually, through her performance The increased spotlight on the character, and on the star who played her, would turn out to be pivotal in creating another trope common to Hitchcock films: the Hitchcock blonde.

"I suppose the first blonde who was a real Hitchcock type was Madeleine Carroll," Hitchcock once said, and film critics nearly universally agree. In *The 39 Steps*, Carroll was luminous, playing up her blonde beauty and exquisite facial features in her typically regal way, assisted by Bernard Knowles's camera and Hitchcock's direction. Consequently, and for the first time on-screen, she broke through her *iceberg maiden* image, revealing a sense of adventure and true moxie. She entreated the audience to laugh with her, shed tears with her, and share her doubts about the hero. The female character stood on her own two feet (even while being dragged along in handcuffs across the craggy terrain). Film scholar Leonard Leff observes, "She was 'smart and sexy' as the press book called her, as well as independent. She was also unafraid of men, or her own sexuality, which she nonetheless held in reserve."

To understand Carroll as a Hitchcock blonde is to more fully grasp the director's vision of his ideal sexual and feminine type—and, by extension, his cinematic fantasy life. It was with Carroll that Hitchcock discovered the merits of playing with (and playing on) the "lady pose" and the filmic pleasure of discovering all that was hidden and intriguing about the woman underneath. It was the seemingly unending process of withholding and revealing—the same game of hide-and-seek layered within his movies—that was the turn-on. For decades after *The 39 Steps*, Hitchcock gave interviews in which he contemplated his own notions about femininity and why Carroll represented an original template. He said he'd been delighted to add her to the cast. He had loved meeting her in person, because she was full of zest and joie de vivre. Yet when it came time to act, she "suddenly became another person. She played in a kind of mesmeric trance. I asked what had become of the gay person I'd met at our first interview. She said, 'but I thought I had to act.' I told her for God's sake be yourself."

Be yourself, be natural. On the surface, there is very little to this tale that seems erotic. But it lies at the heart of Hitchcock's fantasy life. What happens when a seemingly "cold, unfeeling, humorless" lady such as Carroll acts unexpectedly? In a telling reveal, Hitchcock explained to the BBC:

> At the heart of the English woman or the north German or the Swedish [woman] can look like a schoolmarm, but boy, when they get going these women are quite astonishing. . . . It's more interesting to discover the sex in a woman than it is to have it thrown at you, like a Marilyn Monroe or those types. To me they are rather vulgar and obvious. I think it's much more interesting in the course of the storytelling to discover the sex. . . . Anything could happen to you with a woman like that in the back of a taxi.

His film concept of a woman was a fantasy of repressed sexuality being unleashed. *Anything could happen.* "You know why I favor sophisticated blondes in my films?" he asked François Truffaut. "We're after the drawing-room type, the real ladies, who become whores once they're in the bedroom."

No one understood the director's psychological and sexual tastes better than his wife. There was a quiet perversity in this. "Madeleine Carroll was my choice for *The 39 Steps*," Alma proudly conveyed years later. "I saw her first, and told Hitch about her."The small, spectacled brunette intuited, perhaps better than the man himself, his dreams and desires—and the larger-than-life character who dominated his innermost fantasies.

The timing of the arrival of the Hitchcock blonde is impossible to ignore. She appeared on the screen, in Carroll's iconic form, at the precise moment that Joan had become a fixture in Hitchcock's daily life. The two women shared an obvious physical resemblance in their facial features, in addition to their natural ash-blonde waves and blue eyes. Only an inch separated them in height. They were born a year apart. Though their biographies are not identical, some overlaps are notable. Namely, before acting deterred her, Carroll had gone to college and from there enrolled at the Sorbonne, intending to begin her graduate studies in French. Their personalities were also similar. Both were jovial and social, but they had been socially bred to remain composed at all times. Their defensive default mode was that of the cultivated English girl: cool and removed. Harrison and Carroll, in a way, merged through an effect that resembled the director's beloved optical processing, in which the original could not be distinguished from its near-perfect duplicate.

Whether it was conscious or not, Joan was becoming more important to Hitchcock. A turning point occurred during preproduction for *The 39 Steps*. When Charles Bennett arrived one morning for work, Hitchcock had arranged for a 250-seat riverboat with full orchestra and a fully stocked bar to take them on an afternoon cruise on the Thames River. Bennett was elated, until he realized that the excursion included a third person—Joan. The pretense was to vitalize the writing process, "but not a bit of it, not a bloody word was spoken about the story," recalled Bennett. Was this informal gesture on Hitchcock's part the closest he could come to extending an exclusive social invitation to his new assistant? The cruise had all the trappings of a first date, and Bennett was right to feel a little like a third wheel. If nothing else, the writers' day out signaled a promotion for Harrison. But this also irked Bennett. Joan was now "one of the guys."

Joan's constant presence brought a certain electricity to Hitchcock's life— at the office, at Cromwell Road in the evenings, and on family trips. Not only did she turn herself out in the most fashionable styles, wearing the most ravishing scents, but she was also wickedly funny and uncommonly well read. She had an inquiring mind, and frequently (and unexpectedly) reverted to a quiet strength. "Joan had iron in her, but she masked it with a wonderful femininity. You could tell, the wheels were always turning," observes Norman Lloyd. The attraction, for Hitchcock, was creative as well as physical. But for a man whose life was ruled by his own creative mindscape and fantasy life, in the end, what was the difference?

"There are only two women I could ever have married," Hitchcock once disclosed to Charles Bennett, "Alma, whom I did, and Joan, whom I didn't." In Hitchcock's personal orbit, Joan was swiftly taking on an ever-larger role. It was during the making of *The 39 Steps*, as the Hitchcock blonde was coming alive on-screen, that a fantasized vision of Joan—a phantom lady—was being born.

The director had a bad habit of possessive thinking. Writers were "his," until he didn't want them anymore. And actresses too. He saw his cast members less as cattle (a metaphor that is often associated with the director) than as "chess figures," pawns in the mise-en-scène of his personal chess board. Eventually, the notion of the Hitchcock blonde, as a symbolic ideal, came to belong to the director—as another one of his filmic stamps.

Joan, however, refused to be possessed. She might play along, but not as someone's pawn. She wasn't the type. At the same time, there can be little doubt that she was influenced by the cinematic iconography elaborated on by Madeleine Carroll and *The 39 Steps'* Pamela. The star and the character were lighting a path for how Harrison might reenvision herself for the next stage of her career. Symbolically, she was turning the page onto a new chapter, imagining herself as a full-fledged screenwriter—*Hitchcock's* screenwriter. Refracted through a series of projections—of herself, the women around her, the object of Hitchcock's attention, and the movies she had loved since childhood—Joan began to see herself as she wanted others to see her. She was shrewd enough to know that it was part real, part performance.

Not surprisingly, Joan found that she was contending with wagging tongues and whispers, insinuating that she was rising in Hitchcock's ranks by trading sexual favors. But there was little chance of that. Joan definitely would not have entertained a physical relationship with Hitchcock; she preferred tall, suave, or rugged men. Even biographer Donald Spoto, who has made the most of Hitchcock's romantic feelings for Joan, does not believe she encouraged them.

As for Hitchcock, Spoto portrays him as a man caught in the grips of "silent, gray romantic gloom," painting a melodramatic picture that grants neither him nor Joan much agency. But it does seem likely that the director, despite his crude sexual jokes at Joan's expense, stopped short of actually propositioning her. As biographer Patrick McGilligan illuminates, he differed from his contemporaries in this regard; he was a "family man" who eschewed the clichéd temptations of the casting couch, if for no other reason than his corporeal unease. More than once, Hitchcock joked that his one and only climactic sexual experience had occurred when he and Alma conceived their daughter, and he told playwright Rodney Ackland that he thought he "would have been a 'poof' if he hadn't met Alma at the right time." Hitchcock's sexuality was complicated, masking intense desire behind his claims of impotence and celibacy and sowing confusion with offhanded remarks. Charles Bennett (whose professional relationship with the director would soon deteriorate) later reflected that Hitchcock "suffered personal discomfort, jealousy, even hate because his huge bulk rendered him unattractive to women. And I think he hated one and all, but he occasionally found that he had need of them."

McGilligan does indicate that "there are interesting gaps and ambiguities in his record. He was sometimes capable of questionable behavior." Occasionally, if he had imbibed too much at a gathering, he might grope a woman's behind. "One of his tricks was to kiss a woman hello or goodbye, then surprise her by thrusting his tongue inside her mouth," notes McGilligan. "Now and then he would escort a crush around the studio in fatherly fashion, waiting and watching—eternally waiting and watching."

So it's more than possible that early on, at some party or another, Hitchcock attempted to cross the line. If so, Joan—with her iron will—would have halted it. Meanwhile, she was becoming increasingly immune to any off-color jokes he lobbed her way. She used the same strategy that she deployed when playing tennis, rarely racing to the net when under pressure. Instead, she let men do all the work. She hung back at the baseline and kept the ball in play. She, like Hitchcock, had a lot invested in the idealized image of the cool blonde.

It is enough to suggest that Joan's presence alone turned the workspace into a place of sustained suspense for a man whose inner desires and impressions toward women were complex. If "a woman of elegance . . . will never cease to surprise you," according to Hitchcock, then each day held the element of surprise.

And from this environment *The 39 Steps* emerged as Hitchcock's most sophisticated story to date. In the film's conclusion, the character of Pamela stands equal with Hannay, playing a crucial role in his exoneration. Mr. Memory, the performer from the beginning of the film, has held the clue to the identity of the "thirty-nine steps" all along. The couple returns to the music hall and Hannay prompts him to reveal it in the public venue. The film thus conveys the idea that even if the hero did not commit this particular crime, he was due for a redemptive journey, and it is Pamela who makes his self-discovery worthwhile. This deviation from the book, bound up with the addition of the female characters, was one of the most crucial revisions.

The romantic story line was part of a larger conversation going on in Hollywood films at the time, when romantic comedies had become enormously popular. As a result, the Hitchcock team created for the screen one of the sexiest British couples to date. The movie asks the question of what it means to be a romantic couple: at every turn, the pair encounters a different kind of couple—via "couplet vignettes," as Tom Ryall points out. And *The 39 Steps* ends with an exceptional shot, the camera partially framing Hannay and Pamela as they back away from Mr. Memory and clasp fingers in a tender moment, gradually revealing that the handcuff still dangles from one of his hands. This sly, discreet move implies that the couple is now bonded in both the best and worst sense of the term.

Complex (though often lightly treated) gender politics and a modern heroine elevated *The 39 Steps* to a polished gem among Hitchcock's early rough diamonds. These elements became essential ingredients for Hitchcock's seriocomic, romantic spy formula, one to which he would continually return (*Foreign Correspondent, Saboteur, To Catch a Thief, North by Northwest*).

When it came time for *The 39 Steps'* release in June 1935, Gaumont-British showed great confidence in the film. In contrast to the one-page advertisement for *The Man Who Knew Too Much*, the distributor publicized its arrival with an unprecedented five-page spread in *Kine Weekly*. British and American critics bought in, celebrating the film's imagination, pace, and visual virtuosity. The *Daily Mirror* touted it as "the most successful British film of the year." Sidney Carroll, in London's *Sunday Times*, declared simply, "Hitchcock is a genius." In the United States, *Variety* claimed that Hitchcock was "probably the best native director in England," marking a turning point not only for the director but also for the British film industry. *Variety* declared, "They can make pictures in England."

By this time, Joan had adjusted her "Party Party Party" attitude to make room for work, work, and more work. She had come to find story conferences and the behind-the-scenes of filmmaking, in a word, "irresistible." "Time came to mean nothing to me," she later reminisced, "except when hunger drove me to look at the clock. I had no idea whether it was 3:00 in the afternoon or 8:00 at night." When she wasn't sitting in on meetings or performing the work of a personal assistant, she was reading countless books, short stories, and plays and writing summaries of them.

Nearly her entire social life revolved around "Hitchy" and Alma. On weekday evenings, they attended the theater, went to restaurants, or gathered at Cromwell Road. During the weekends that the couple stayed in the city rather than at their country cottage, she dropped by to play tennis on the court behind their flat. There was often a match going, whether singles or doubles, in a variation that might include Alma, Charles Bennett, and his wife, Maggie. Occasionally, Hitchcock would join in—he would stand in one place and wait for the ball to come to him. Tennis was one of his favorite sports, and he would make sure to include Joan as his guest when he attended the Wimbledon finals each year.

Most weekends were spent at the Hitchcock's Tudor cottage in the rural village of Shamley Green. There, the Hitchcocks hosted everyone, from their closest family members to some of Europe's most famous stars. Winter's Grace, as it was called, stood less than five miles away from Guildford, making it convenient for Joan to frequent both the Hitchcocks' cottage and her own family home on the weekends. She discovered that she and the Hitchcocks had much in common—because of her Surrey background, she was familiar with many of the same names and faces, not to mention local pubs and shops. Their cottage and lavish gardens were becoming Joan's second home. And their proximity to Guildford had a mollifying effect on her parents; they were warming up to her new employer.

Her family couldn't necessarily count on her to be local, though. Joan now accompanied Hitchcock and Alma on regular trips to Switzerland, Paris, and the South of France. Just after *The 39 Steps* wrapped, she went to Rome and then Capri with the extended family, including Hitchcock's mother, Emma. Joan and young Pat had become very close. They skied, boated, and read together, and sometimes shared hotel rooms. She soon became like an aunt to Pat.

In her off time, Joan savored a bachelorette existence in the Chelsea flat she shared with Faith. Her sister, now twenty-three, was working in the city as a secretary. They had lived for a short time at 28 Beaufort Gardens, just around the corner from Harrods. In 1935, presumably heartened by the success of *The 39 Steps* and Joan's increased job security, the sisters moved to the Bedford Terrace apartments at 2 Chelsea Manor Court, adjacent to the bucolic St. Luke's Gardens. Their apartment, located in an unremarkable five-story brick building, was not very spacious, but with a fireplace and large windows letting in plenty of light, it had its charms.

Joan wasn't spending much time within its four walls anyway. Her neighborhood was part of the King's Road district, inhabited by artists, writers, actors, and the occasional socialite. Over the years, King's Road had been occupied by scores of literati, including Jane Austen, Elizabeth Gaskell, Oscar Wilde, Bram Stoker, Radclyffe Hall, and Henry James. Like New York's Greenwich Village at that time, the area encompassed its fair share of rough terrain. In the 1930s it was a cobble of artists' studios, squatters, grocers, laundries, shoemakers, tobacconists, bookstores, and cafés.

Though King's Road would become swanker in the 1960s as the epicenter of "swinging London," it bustled plenty for Joan and her sister. If they walked several blocks down Chelsea Manor Court and turned right, she could practically glide into the Chenil Galleries. Previously a hub for modernist artists, Chenil was now renting out space to the Decca record label. Jazz poured forth onto King's Road, and from there to the rest of the country. Duke Ellington, backed by the big-band sounds of his "Famous Orchestra," cut "Hyde Park" and "Harlem Speaks" around this time. If Joan walked down King's Road in the other direction, she might treat herself to a movie at the gigantic Gaumont Palace; Cary Grant had been on hand as the master of ceremonies for its christening in December 1934. Now that she was part of the Gaumont family, she would have been tracking how Hitchcock's films fared at the Palace (renamed the Gaumont Theatre in 1937 and later the Chelsea Cinema). East of there was the Pheasantry Club. Ensconced behind an extravagant facade, the building contained a basement restaurant and bar that attracted bohemians, writers, artists, and celebrities.

At Gaumont-British, the two Hitchcock films that followed offered Joan good training ground. *Secret Agent* (1936), based on the W. Somerset Maugham's short story series *Ashenden, or The British Agent*, is another "wrong man" thriller. During World War I, novelist turned captain Edgar Brodie (John Gielgud) arrives home in London to discover that his funeral has been staged. This is part of a master plan by a British Intelligence agent who identifies himself as "R" (Charles Carson). Brodie is given the alias of Richard Ashenden and an assignment to accompany an assassin known as "the General" (Peter Lorre) on a mission to Switzerland to eliminate a spy known to be working for Germans. A second story line pairs up Brodie/Ashenden with a spy who masquerades as his wife, played by Madeleine Carroll. (Pretending to be his wife doesn't take time away from her flirting with an American hotel guest played by Robert Young.) She has taken the mission "for the fun of it," which irks him (apparently because she is a woman). When it comes time to kill the target, Brodie/Ashenden experiences a crisis of conscience and the General takes over. They soon learn, however, that the General murdered the wrong man. Eventually, the intended mark (who turns out to be Robert Young's character) is located on a train to the Middle East, and an action-packed chase ensues. In the end, "Mr. and Mrs. Ashenden" retire as spies and look toward a brighter future.

Sabotage (1936), based on a Joseph Conrad novel titled, coincidentally, *The Secret Agent*, faced controversy on its release because of a harrowing sequence in which a young boy (the heroine's brother) is killed along with other passengers in a bus explosion. (Hitchcock indicated in retrospect that he wished he'd handled it differently.) Most film critics treat it as a character study of an unlikely villain, the boorish husband Karl Anton Verloc (Oscar Homolka), who proves to be capable not only of terrorism but of setting up the bomb that kills his wife's brother. *Sabotage*, though, pays equal if not more attention to the internal psychology of his wife, Mrs. Verloc (Sylvia Sidney)—a fact that is highlighted by its American title, *The Woman Alone*. Strikingly, the young, sympathetic Mrs. Verloc is spared the narrative fate she receives in Conrad's novel, in which she commits suicide. In the film's romantic, albeit ambivalent ending, along the lines of Hitchcock's 1929 *Blackmail* (and later films like *Shadow of a Doubt*), she is paired with an understanding police detective who comprehends her suffering but, by virtue of his knowledge of her criminal transgressions, will nevertheless maintain a certain degree of power over her.

With *Sabotage* in the can and four films' worth of experience to her name, it was time for Joan to make a bold move. She had read the novel *A Shilling for Candles* by Elizabeth MacKintosh (written under the pseudonym Josephine Tey) and was excited by its prospects. She brought it to Hitchcock in fall of 1936, as he was sulking over an ill-fated John Buchan sequel to *The 39 Steps*.

When Joan and Hitchcock began to discuss it, they arrived at the idea of using the first three chapters as the centerpiece of a film adaptation, which would be titled *Young and Innocent*. Hitchcock was particularly taken with the idea of casting one of his favorites, Nova Pilbeam of *The Man Who Knew Too Much*. Pilbeam was now eighteen, ideal for the role. During preproduction, in the *News Chronicle*, Hitchcock touted the adaptation's twist: "In the book, the girl drifts out of the story. In the film, the girl—who is Nova Pilbeam—*is* the story."

It makes perfect sense that the first film on which Joan began to have major input was jump-started by a female twist, reversing a patriarch's tale into a girl's adventure. *Young and Innocent* registers a shift away from the male authors that had defined Hitchcock's career for the preceding five years. Indeed, it ushers in the beginning of an era dominated by female-generated source material and women's genres, an earmark of the sensibilities that would be associated with Hitchcock for the foreseeable future.

In book form, *A Shilling for Candles* focuses on a Scotland Yard detective's inquiry into the death of a movie actress after her body washes ashore. The film adaptation is about the detective's teenage daughter and her efforts to prove the innocence of the man who discovered the actress's body. It was marketed as "an exquisite study of girlhood verging on maturity, a tender and touching account of the problems of girlhood approaching womanhood."

It is the rack focus from *A Shilling for Candles'* central father figure to the marginal figure of the daughter that signals Joan's influence. The elder man's tale meant nothing to her compared to the escapades of an eighteen-year-old. Harrison was looking to make the kind of movie she herself would be drawn to, and to attract girls who indulged in the same literary fancies she'd had as a teenager.

As she had two years earlier, Joan accompanied Hitchcock, Reville, and Bennett (along with Patricia and Bennett's wife) to St. Moritz for the 1936 holiday season. With the involvement of Bennett and Reville, Joan and Hitchcock began hammering out the treatment. The working vacation began taking some unexpected turns, however. First came the news that Gaumont-British was conducting big layoffs back home. The heads of studio Isidore and Maurice Ostrer faced mounting pressures. The company had overextended itself trying to meet the high demands of the government quota policies. England was on the brink of a severe financial crisis. In what would be later dubbed the

"Christmas massacre," the Ostrer brothers fired Michael Balcon, Ivor Montagu, and a long list of Gaumont employees. Hitchcock's employment wasn't in question, nor was Joan's. But Lime Grove Studios would be shut down and all its operations, including the production of *Young and Innocent*, would move to London's new facility, Pinewood Studios.

Before Joan and the rest of the Hitchcock entourage had a chance to decamp St. Moritz, Bennett received a telegram. Universal was beckoning him to Hollywood. It became clear that *Young and Innocent* would carry on without him.

As the team regrouped, humorist Anthony Armstrong and Edwin Greenwood (who contributed to the scenario for *The Man Who Knew Too Much* and would later play Dandy in *Jamaica Inn*) were brought in, though to what extent is unclear. Comedic playwright Gerald Savory handled the dialogue. Nevertheless, with Bennett gone, the way was clear for Joan to play a greater role in crafting the screenplay.

The writing process was collaborative. It was also feisty. According to Hitchcock, the group "went into a huddle and slowly from discussions, arguments, random suggestions, casual, desultory talk, and furious intellectual quarrels as to what such and such a character in such and such a situation would or would not do, the scenario began to take shape." His description of *Young and Innocent*'s development is a rare instance in which the director gave weight to the complexities of screenwriting. He remarked, "There are few—astonishingly few—people who can write a screen story. There are no chapter headings, no intervals between the acts." This meant that all the narrative action needed to flow logically, because audiences did not have the luxury of assembling disparate pieces as one did when reading. Joan's training had seriously intensified.

At its heart, *Young and Innocent* is about a girl's coming of age, beginning to see herself and the world through adult eyes and, more to the point, standing up to her father's authority as she stakes her claim in the symbolic order. This bears the imprint of what would eventually come to be recognized as a "Joan Harrison" story, patterned by a young woman who knew firsthand what it was like to do the self-calculus in relation to her father.

Erica (Pilbeam) begins the film seemingly identifying with her father. With her mother presumably deceased, the two depend on each other to parent her younger brothers. As she initially tells the suspected murderer Robert Tisdall (Derrick De Marney), "I'm on their side," referring to her father, and the police. However, it soon becomes apparent that for the sake of justice—and love—she will reconsider her position, not merely breaking with her father but usurping him.

The film represents this theme through a compelling series of family meal sequences, in which Erica eventually supplants her father's physical, and hence moral, position at the head of the table. According to the logic of *Young and Innocent*, Erica sees and knows more than the men who are in legal positions of authority. As Maurice Yacowar astutely observes, there's a direct genealogical line from this film to *Foreign Correspondent*, in which a daughter tells her father, "I think the world has been run long enough by the well-meaning professionals. We might give the amateurs a chance now."

There is one crucial party scene that is symbolic on two levels. In a scene in the film that did not occur in the book, Erica and Tisdall go to her aunt and uncle's house for a cousin's birthday party in order to throw the detectives off their track. Their temporary presence ends up creating utter chaos, as stodgy Aunt Mary (Mary Clare) stumbles around blindfolded during a children's game. On one level, the scene signals the film's larger themes of seeing and awakening. It was, according to Hitchcock, "designed as a deliberate symbol—in fact it was the clue to the whole film, but no one got it at the time." On another level, the party scene reveals the degree to which Erica has transgressed the bounds of her family unit, psychologically and socially. Yacowar explains, "As her Uncle Basil (Basil Radford) puts it, 'Something would have to be radically wrong for her to forget Felicity's birthday.' Of course, something is radically different, and from her family's perspective, wrong. The child's mind is lost in the woman's."

Young and Innocent stands out for its attention to a smaller-scale, rural existence in the English countryside, inspired by the Surrey settings with which Joan and the Hitchcocks were quite familiar. It shows a class consciousness that is unusual for Hitchcock films, as Erica and Tisdall move through a truck stop and a homeless shelter, and eventually work to solve the murder with the help of a hobo named Will. Many reviewers celebrated the film's focus on ordinary people on the social margins. *Monthly Film Bulletin* praised its attention to "normal everyday people living a normal everyday life in a typically English country setting." *Cinema* deemed the film an "outstanding example of realism in entertainment." "As you watch the story unfold," *Film Weekly* said, "it comes to you that here, in the best sense of the phrase, is a typical English picture, it has something native in its people, background, humors, and ways of thought, and all of those things unforced."

The opportunity to keenly observe the nuances of the countryside and everyday life—and to play with the contrast between its quaint charms and a lurking threat of violence—may be why Hitchcock considered *Young and Innocent* his personal favorite among his twenty-three British films. It fulfilled his desire to, as he put it in 1937, "commit murder amid babbling brooks." Some of these natural elements were real, though many of the exterior sequences (such as the panorama of the village or the near-collision between the car and train) were actually created through impressive visual effects featuring miniatures and optical printing. The move to Pinewood Studios had ended up benefiting the team, enabling high-end production not possible at Lime Grove. Joan counted the film as a successful first turn at adapting source material she felt closely attached to.

Joan's professional triumphs were mirrored by her brother Jack's successful leadership of the *Surrey Advertiser*. As their father's health declined, he had risen to the position of director and gradually assumed many of Walter's executive responsibilities. The staff respected his determination and vision. Jack was steering the paper's industrial practices in a more modern direction, taking risks and making bold choices. A "new Britain was in the ascendant," according to historian Tom Ryall, bolstered not only by newspapers, movies, and radio but also by consumer goods, electrical appliances, and the automobile; this was a world they trusted the young man to navigate. In something of a symbolic move, Jack convinced the board that it was time for new construction: an eye-catching art deco building on Martyr Road at the edge of town. Creating a sensation, the sleek, modern structure took nine months to erect (and involved twenty-two subcontractors). With reinforced concrete, curved edges, and cream faience-slab facing, it stood out against the town's Norman backdrop. One of the building's most decorative features was a huge clock at its center, announcing that the paper was keeping up with changing times.

Jack had personally overseen the move to Martyr Road and the principal rebranding of the newspaper through the spring of 1937. His parents and the board of directors had vested him with absolute confidence. They fully expected him to take over the reins from Walter once the transition was complete.

Only two months after the new building's doors opened, however, Jack contracted influenza, then pneumonia complicated by mononucleosis. It was at the Grove, the place of his birth, that he gasped his final breaths on June 12. He was only thirty-two years old.

In the wake of losing her brother, Joan was faced with a profound decision. She had the opportunity to accompany Hitchcock, Alma, and Pat on a voyage to New York. This business trip (presented in the press as a publicity tour for several Gaumont rereleases) had been in the offing for a while but was now fast approaching, with the group set to sail in mid-August. To choose to leave her family for America at such a critical time couldn't have been easy. Being quintessentially British in this regard, Joan forged ahead. She helped lay Jack to rest and, as far as any eyes could see, closed off her feelings about losing her only brother. This was the first time that she put her career, and the Hitchcocks, ahead of family. But it would not be the last.

7 | A TEAM OF THREE

ON AUGUST 18, 1937, "Joan Hitchcock" boarded the *Queen Mary*, the flagship of the Cunard Line. She may have intentionally given her name as such, or the attendant may simply have assumed she belonged to the Hitchcock family, but that's the way she was listed on the ship's charter: as Joan Hitchcock, the writer, employed by Pinewood Studios, Iver Heath, Buckinghamshire. Joan was on her way to America. Now part of Pinewood, Gaumont-British was covering all expenses.

Joan shared a cabin with nine-year-old Pat, an arrangement to which she was by then accustomed. Inured to the recurring presumption by strangers that she was the girl's traveling governess, she would simply set the record straight and move on. During this trip, however, she didn't encounter too many people, confronted as she was by a severe bout of seasickness that lasted the entire six-day trip. Pat later remembered that Joan "was not a good sailor . . . [and] belonged nowhere near that ship." She rarely sat for meals. Pat would return from lunch or dinner and regale her with the details, watching her grow sicker with each particular. "I was sometimes a little mischievous, to my parents' delight," Pat joked.

On occasion, Joan would make her way up to the deck to rattle around ideas with Hitch and Alma for the next project. (At the time, they expected to adapt the French short story "False Witness" by Marcel Achard for Nova Pilbeam—a treatment they would generate that autumn only to watch it lie fallow.) When she managed to convey herself to the main dining room, she would join the family while Hitchcock wryly entertained guests and reporters. The Grand

Salon restaurant boasted a set piece that well could have appeared in a Hitchcock movie: it was a large-scale map mural that featured a motorized model of the *Queen Mary*, charting the actual ocean liner's progress across the Atlantic.

Joan and the Hitchcocks debarked in New York City on August 24. Their arrival coincided with the American release of *Sabotage* and revival runs of *The Man Who Knew Too Much*, *The 39 Steps*, and *Secret Agent*. Hitchcock seemed to be everywhere, all the time. Ostensibly, according to Gaumont-British, these screenings were the reason for the director's tour, but his main purpose was to test the waters for an American career move. After the four checked into two adjoining suites at the St. Regis Hotel at Fifth Avenue and Fifty-Fifth Street, Joan enjoyed a front-row view of the apparatus of American publicity, as reporters from every conceivable publication paraded through the couple's door.

On her first night in New York, Joan accompanied the family to the theater and out to dinner. She was captured in a photograph at the unidentified restaurant, seated at Hitchcock's right hand, with a glowing, cheerful smile on her face. Dressed to the nines, bejeweled, with her hair elegantly coiffed, she gazed directly at the camera as though perfectly in her element (and not looking the least bit like someone who just endured a weeklong bout of seasickness). She formed a unique contrast to Hitchcock and Alma, who looked uncomfortable and caught off guard. (Had he just made a joke under his breath? Alma, looking down at her fork, reacted as if in stitches.) Even the precocious Pat, who was a natural in front of the camera and had a reputation as a "little adult," appeared as if she'd been shot out of a cannon and planned to hold her breath until hitting a landing.

Joan's whirlwind junket included shopping at Rockefeller Center, dinner at the 21 Club, and a Rivoli Theater premiere of William Wyler's *Dead End*, starring Humphrey Bogart, Joel McCrea, and Sylvia Sidney (the last of whom was in attendance, accompanied by Norman Bel Geddes; Joan Bennett, Luise Rainer, and Rainer's escort, Clifford Odets, were there too). Joan and the Hitchcocks spent some time in the East Hampton home of Kay Brown, East Coast representative for independent American producer David O. Selznick, who was negotiating a deal to bring Hitchcock to Hollywood. (Brown would soon become a close ally.) They even managed to dart down to Washington, DC, to visit the monuments. On September 4, the group boarded the MV *Georgic* bound for Southampton.

Upon Joan's return, she assisted Hitchcock in all that was necessary for final postproduction on *Young and Innocent*, which went to London screens in November. Next, she foraged around for their next project. (It had become clear that *False Witness* would not pan out.) Though Balcon was gone, making team Hitchcock's position at Gaumont-British more precarious, the director had finagled relative creative freedom under the protection of producer Ted Black.

When Black proposed for Hitchcock's consideration *The Lady Vanishes*, based on the 1936 Ethel Lina White novel *The Wheel Spins*, Joan must have been elated. The material had been developed for American director Roy William Neill. (Adapted by writing team Frank Launder and Sidney Gilliat, an early version by Neill had been partially shot before hitting some obstacles during second-unit filming.) One suspects that if Black had not brought it forth as a preexisting property, Joan might have pursued the prospect herself. This gothic tale, written by a woman author with a female following, was a fitting corollary to *Young and Innocent*. And it fully anticipated the kinds of films that, given the opportunity, Harrison would increasingly choose to make.

Inspired by true-life events at the 1889 Paris Exposition, the vanishing lady tale had appeared in Mrs. Marie Belloc-Lowndes's 1913 novel *The End of Her Honeymoon* and Alexander Woolcott's 1934 book *While Rome Burns* before surfacing in *The Wheel Spins*. White's novel traces the suspenseful journey of wealthy orphan Iris Carr, who boards a train and begins to fear that she is losing her mind when a woman she has befriended goes missing. All of the other passengers declare they've never seen "Miss Froy," insinuating that Iris may be going mad. The stakes run high as Iris sets out to prove that she is right, revealing not only that a crime has been committed but also that a far-reaching cover-up is underway.

Hitchcock was enthusiastic about signing on to the project, in part because the vanishing lady tale had always intrigued him. Once Ted Black was assured of the director's commitment, he dedicated additional funds, ensuring the production quality would be high, even if shooting would take place at Gainsborough's Islington. (That Hitchcock was returning to a studio that had been formative to his development was not lost on anyone.) *The Lady Vanishes*'s increased budget permitted the script to be rewritten so that technical details fell more in line with the Hitchcock team's cinematic interests, such as the differences between what a character sees and what she knows. Writer Launder returned to work, now joining Hitchcock and his inner circle. (Though Gilliat was on another assignment, he came in for some evening sessions.) According to Launder, Hitchcock mostly influenced the beginning and the end of the script, while suggesting only tiny changes throughout to quicken the pace. However, Gainsborough screenwriter Val Guest later recalled a more fluid, collaborative atmosphere in which the writing flowed as if "all in the family."

While Joan may not have written portions of *The Lady Vanishes*, by this point her work went beyond that of a screenwriter. And this is precisely why she mattered more than most of Hitchcock's collaborators. One of her chief responsibilities was to provide continuity of vision and voice, especially where the revision process was rigorous. She was essentially performing the role of a creative producer, a skill she gleaned from Hitchcock himself.

Hitchcock's working methods were similar to that of a producer—and not just any producer but a hands-on creative producer well schooled in the technical aspects of every stage of filmmaking, as Thomas Schatz suggests in *The Genius of the System: Hollywood Filmmaking in the Studio Era*. He had even tried his hand as a solo producer in the early 1930s, taking time off directing to "supervise a number of British International productions" inspired by Irving Thalberg and Erich Pommer—though only one project, *Lord Camber's Ladies* (1932), came to fruition. Indeed, David O. Selznick saw Hitchcock as a variant of himself, apprehending the director's producing skills as a vital asset because this would free Selznick to oversee other productions at Selznick International Pictures. While the executive was attempting to woo the Englishman in mid-1937, he had written to his representative Kay Brown that "what makes the Hitchcock matter so important is that he is a producer as well as a director."

Harrison immersed herself in Hitchcock's unique film preparation system. There was a specific language that Hitchcock had originally developed in concert with Alma, which translated the screenplay into a blueprint for production. In a *Sight & Sound* essay titled "My Own Methods," he described his process: "With the help of my wife, who does the technical continuity, I plan out a script very carefully, hoping to follow it exactly, all the way through, when shooting starts. In fact, this working on the script is the real making of the film, for me. When I've done it, the film is finished already in my mind." The goal was to leave little room for variation in the editing room, in the unlikely event that editing was taken out of his hands. His early drafts came close to resembling formatted screenplays, including scenes, blocking, camera angles, and movement. In addition, one interviewer observed, his scripts tended to be heavily annotated, with notes and even graphics in the margins for each scene, like "a traveling artist's sketchpad."

Harrison had been entrusted with the private code as early as 1937, when Hitchcock asserted her importance to his own agent and potential US bidders for his services. A memo that circulated within the office of Hitchcock's Hollywood agent stated in a separate heading marked IMPORTANT with red underlining: "Hitchcock says it is essential for him to have his secretary and script clerk with him on both pictures. . . . Hitchcock says that this girl has worked with him for years and is invaluable to him in connection with his 'peculiar system' of writing, his shooting schedule, camera angles, etc." Some have painted her as Hitchcock's ideal amanuensis, perhaps misguided by one of the comments Ivor Montagu once made ("You see what happened with Hitch's stories was that he would want an amanuensis. He originally used Alma Reville on a lot of things. . . . He wanted a screenwriter to talk to and the screenwriter would get the credit.") It is true Harrison may have worn many hats—recorder, scribe, muse—but by this time she was also the person who was sharing the film's helm with Hitchcock, seeing it through from start to finish, as any skilled creative producer would.

In the process of adapting *The Lady Vanishes* for the screen, Harrison and Hitchcock were—together and separately—absorbing (as well as applying) literary elements that would emerge again and again in the work that came afterward. The ambivalent bride's railway journey takes a symbolic detour into a psychic landscape filled with lessons about the limits of patriarchy. The riddles associated with a repressed feminine power are made all the more interesting, and suspenseful, because of how well they are woven into a contemporary political plot that allegorically cautions against British complacency in the face of rising fascism.

When *The Lady Vanishes* is placed side by side with *Young and Innocent*, one sees a particular bend in the arc of the "classic thriller sextet" toward young female rite-of-passage stories. Both films feature spirited heroines who seek adventure, truth, and justice and are willing to act on their convictions. Both are adaptations of women's source material, aimed primarily at female readers, engaging in a dance with deeply held beliefs about keeping women "in their place." These are the kinds of movies Joan had always wanted to go see; now, they were the ones she wanted to make.

The film benefited not only from Hitchcock's and Joan's evolving sensibilities but also from expert casting, with the winsome Margaret Lockwood playing Iris and Michael Redgrave (in his film debut) starring opposite her. Dame May Whitty played Miss Froy, the spinster who is revealed to be a spy. Paul Lukas was the shady doctor and Mary Clare (Erica's aunt in *Young and Innocent*) was the malevolent baroness. Caldicott and Charters, the pair obsessed with cricket, were played to the hilt by Naunton Wayne and Basil Radford (the uncle in *Young and Innocent*).

Though Islington's facilities had seen better days, the studio offered all that was necessary to create the hermetically sealed worlds of the European chalet and the cramped train cars. Everything else—mattes, miniatures, optical effects—came from the principle Hitchcock had learned by watching the Germans firsthand: less was more.

The Lady Vanishes succeeded wildly, both critically and commercially. The film performed particularly well abroad, earning effusive praise as the year's best picture in the *New York Times* and winning Hitchcock the Best Director award from the New York Film Critics Circle.

Jamaica Inn was next. At first glance, the film—a gothic tale about a plucky heroine coming into her own and casting light onto a vile world of corruption—might seem tailor made for Joan. Daphne du Maurier had pushed the boundaries of sexual violence in the 1936 novel about young Mary Yellan, who upon the death of her mother moves to her aunt and uncle's tavern in a windy, desolate Cornish coastal town, only to discover that her uncle is a shipwrecking pirate. The book is edgy and uncomfortable, containing sadomasochistic scenes and a torturous moment in which a pirate gang forces Mary to watch as they murder the group of survivors whose ship they've just "wrecked." She eventually discovers the true mastermind behind the criminal ring is someone she has trusted most deeply, the town vicar, though her realization comes too late to spare her beloved aunt from death.

In reality, the Hitchcock team had been practically cornered into making *Jamaica Inn* after entering into a short-term partnership with German producer Erich Pommer and coproducer Charles Laughton. Pommer and Laughton had formed the new company Mayflower Pictures, intending to produce star vehicles for Laughton, and Hitchcock had long wanted to work with the actor. Now that his Gaumont-British contract was up, the director was growing ever more serious about Hollywood. But given the degree to which his American studio prospects were out of his hands, the timing for a collaboration with Mayflower looked good. Plus, Hitchcock had ulterior reasons for entertaining du Maurier's novel. She was the daughter of longtime friend Gerald du Maurier, who had worked with Hitchcock on the 1932 *Lord Camber's Ladies*. On June 1 the trades announced that Hitchcock would direct *Jamaica Inn*; preproduction would begin within weeks.

It's hard to imagine that Joan was very concerned about *Jamaica Inn* when there were much more important proceedings underway which might finally take the Hitchcock family—and Joan with them—across the pond to Hollywood. Hitch and Alma embarked on an extended trip to America in June 1938, leaving Pat in Joan's care. The expedition was the culmination of Hitchcock's yearlong effort to negotiate a deal with producer David O. Selznick, one that brought with it hopes of bigger budgets, more creative control, and access to American stars, all of which could cement his stature around the world.

Hitchcock had identified Selznick as his best bet to facilitate his climb. The producer was the son of Lewis J. Selznick, a Russian Jewish immigrant who had built his own film company from the ground up. The younger Selznick inherited his father's entrepreneurial spirit and natural instincts for moviemaking, which had led to a position as a story editor with his father's company while he was still in his early twenties. Described as possessing a "rough attractiveness" and known for all-night work binges, David O. Selznick also had daring and vision.

Selznick had worked at three of Hollywood's Big Five studios—Paramount, RKO, and Metro-Goldwyn-Mayer—flourishing at the latter, where he oversaw his own production unit for studio chief Louis B. Mayer (and he had shown the good sense to marry the boss's daughter, Irene Gladys Mayer). In 1935 he struck out on his own, founding the independent Selznick International Pictures, which specialized in expensive, lush star vehicles. By 1938 he was already deep in preparations for what would become the highest-grossing film of the classical era: *Gone with the Wind*. Selznick's record of backing big-ticket prestige pictures appealed to Hitchcock. So did the capital he had cultivated from New York investors. Hitchcock had already signed on with Selznick's older brother, Myron, head of Hollywood's most powerful talent agency, as a tactical move.

David O. Selznick had been wooing Hitchcock even before their trip to America the previous year. They had entertained big ideas via long-distance telegrams and emissaries, starting off with an epic screen treatment of the sinking of the RMS *Titanic*. Though the alliance seemed natural, the producer and director had been able to agree on very little. Hitchcock had named a salary minimum of $40,000 per picture. Hitchcock saw it as a necessary figure owing to the tax hit he would take as a non-US resident, but Selznick found it bafflingly high, especially since Hitchcock had yet to prove himself as a viable Hollywood property. For this reason, the producer seemed to run hot then cold on the partnership. Preoccupied with his search for the ideal actress to play Scarlett O'Hara and frantically overseeing *Gone with the Wind* script revisions, Selznick had for months deferred contract negotiations with Hitchcock, at one point even advising the director to sign with another studio. But now Hitchcock and Alma were back in the United States hoping to finally seal the deal.

While the Hitchcocks were overseas, Joan and her family received some stunning news about her older sister, Muriel. For the past several years, Muriel's oscillations had bedeviled the Harrisons. Having found her métier in teaching, assuming appointments at Wycombe Abbey in Buckinghamshire and the Cheltenham Ladies' College (following her time in Exeter and Harrogate), she couldn't seem to settle into a stable position. There was no questioning her intellect, which was wide ranging and showed a special aptitude for early nineteenth-century European history. But she seemed unable to fit into the stringent requirements of the British educational system.

And then there were Muriel's ill-fated romantic choices. She had at one point announced her intention to marry an army captain. The man, perhaps believing the Harrisons to be wealthier than they were, might have had his eyes on the family riches, but he broke off the engagement. The officer's rejection caused such dismay that Muriel ran away to a convent, intending to become a nun. She spent six months there before she called her mother, asking to be "rescued." Joan reluctantly accompanied Millie on the trip to bring Muriel home. By this time, she had tired of her sister's antics.

Not particularly religious herself and often irritated by piety, Joan was bothered by Muriel's experiments in theological devotion. On a deeper level, Joan simply disapproved of Muriel—her vocation, her interests, and her personality. She looked down on her because she was "only a teacher" and hadn't chosen a more ambitious or glamorous profession. Joan was prone to an elitism that supposed certain jobs and people were "below her station." This had been bred in her since infancy, and she resented her sibling for not adhering to the family doctrine. Teaching was no job for a "lady."

Though she may not have felt an emotional bond with Muriel, the news she received on June 23, several days after her thirty-first birthday, must have come as a shock. Muriel had been in a terrible car crash. She had been driving her Baby Austin on the northern bypass five miles outside Oxford, where she lived at the time, when she collided with another vehicle. Her passenger, Rev. Eric Burrows, a fifty-six-year-old Jesuit priest and respected scholar in Near Eastern studies, died within a few hours. Muriel would linger in unstable condition at Radcliffe Infirmary for over two weeks before succumbing to related infections on July 9. She was just shy of thirty-six.

Losing two siblings in less than a year was a severe blow. Going forward, the months of June and July, which had always been marked by celebrations of wedding anniversaries (not only Millie and Walter's but also Millie's parents'), her own birthday, and the birthdays of Faith and Muriel, would be marred by the sad fact that two bright people were simply gone. They had been in their prime. The Harrison family was broken.

Joan did what was typical in British upper-middle-class circles at the time: she cordoned off her feelings and forced herself to keep going. Her family likewise didn't dwell on the losses of Jack and Muriel. In later years, Joan's niece, Faith's daughter, Kate, asked her grandmother Millie about the older siblings, but "Millie really didn't want to talk about it. The attitude people had to bereavements back then was, people have to get over them. They all put it to one side."

But that wasn't easy for Joan with her surrogate family a continent away. She had been fielding reports of Muriel's deteriorating condition from her father in Oxford while reading a panoply of headlines trumpeting the Hitchcocks' every move from New York to Los Angeles. The director had been actively working for Joan's salary to be included in his next contract, telling studio executives that she was "indispensable." She'd hoped to be Hollywood-bound with the Hitchcocks as soon as a deal with Selznick went through. But her sister's accident had thrown everything off axis.

One work-related enterprise provided a diversion: Joan was attempting to acquire the film rights to *Jamaica Inn* author Daphne du Maurier's next novel, *Rebecca*, set to be published in early August. Joan had read prepublication galleys of the book and proposed it to Hitchcock immediately. He now hoped that an adaptation would be one of his first American films; his only reservation was that the author, despite her newly minted professional relationship with the director, might demand a high price for the rights. The highly anticipated gothic story, about an orphaned young woman who marries a wealthy, brooding widower and immediately begins to question her choice, was currently enjoying an advance publicity campaign that gestured toward *Gone with the Wind.*

Joan had initiated clandestine communication with du Maurier in the spring and early summer of 1938, under the pretense of doing research for *Jamaica Inn.* It didn't seem out of the ordinary for the women to correspond, writer to writer. But Joan had her work cut out for her. She had dual objectives: convince du Maurier that Hitchcock was the most suitable filmmaker to handle her cherished material while bargaining her down to her lowest price. This was no easy task, considering that du Maurier harbored serious concerns about the way *Jamaica Inn* was being treated by all involved. Through her literary agent, she'd learned that the adaptation had considerably altered her book, and not for the better. From her sideline view, she was dubious about anything Joan said, knowing her to be one of *Jamaica Inn*'s principal collaborators.

Nevertheless, Joan knew that anything she could do to advance the *Rebecca* project could potentially provide Hitchcock with leverage as he tried to clinch a deal with Selznick. The desire of the Hitchcock camp to obtain the du Maurier property on their own had not gone unnoticed by Selznick's representatives. As the director's meeting with the producer approached, Selznick's London agent, Jenia Reissar, reported to her boss, "Joan Harrison is Hitchcock's mouthpiece. . . . I think Hitchcock wants to make that picture, and by buying it he would like . . . to ensure that he could in fact direct it himself." Selznick advised Reissar to keep a close eye on Joan and du Maurier's dealings, with the intention of scooping up the property himself if it would help him lock in Hitchcock. In the meantime, Joan continued to lobby Selznick's New York rep Kay Brown on the merits of the novel; Brown, after all, had convinced Selznick to acquire *Gone with the Wind.* This series of back-channel conversations among the three women—Harrison, Reissar, and Brown, all of whom saw the book's screen potential—had been going on for months.

Neither Hitchcock nor Selznick had secured the literary rights to *Rebecca* when the Hitchcocks alighted the train in Los Angeles on June 15. The director arrived with the galleys under his arm, hoping that Joan was making headway with du Maurier at home. Selznick, meanwhile, had read a short synopsis of the book that hadn't won him over. He knew, though, that he wanted Hitchcock at Selznick International Pictures. Finally, after weeks of prolonged dickering, the producer sat down at the Beverly Wilshire Hotel with his brother Myron and hammered out a deal for whatever the first venture would be. Hitchcock was content enough that most of his terms had been met.

As for Joan's part of the agreement, Hitchcock pushed to get her $200 a week, but had to settle for $125—"for a maximum of twenty weeks only," regardless of how long the project required. At a time when the median weekly income for a Hollywood writer was $120, these weren't bad terms. And the contract did ensure that she would continue on for the director's next films, so long as her work was satisfactory. Selznick also consented to a last-minute perk, agreeing to pay Joan's moving expenses.

On July 2 the studio contract between director and producer—which Joan had quietly yearned for—was secured. That week, Joan helped her family contend with her dying sister while the Hitchcocks celebrated at Myron Selznick's house with Hollywood royals Carole Lombard and Clark Gable, beheld the heartland of their new home country aboard a New York–bound train, and took in a Yankees game. On Friday, July 8, the day before Muriel's body gave way to infection and associated blood poisoning, the Selznick-Hitchcock deal was announced in the United States and Britain.

Joan knew that if she wanted it, a Hollywood career was hers for the taking. There was one piece of information to which she was not privy but that could help tip the scales. If Hitchcock's many exchanges with Selznick during his Beverly Hills stay had had any effect, they'd mobilized everyone at the Selznick International Pictures offices to take *Rebecca* seriously. On July 15, as the Hitchcocks sailed home aboard the SS *Normandie*, story editor Val Lewton sent Selznick a message: "The more I think of it, the more I feel that we have got ourselves a tiger. [*Rebecca*] is as good as *Jane Eyre* and I think the women will be wild about it."

Selznick was finally spurred into action: he read the manuscript. On August 4, the day before du Maurier's book hit London bookstores, he gave Kay Brown permission to close the deal. In an interesting twist, Jenia Reissar conceived of a strategy that might capitalize on the goodwill that Joan had been working to build up and would hopefully land the property safely—and affordably—in the hands of both Selznick and Hitchcock. Reissar proposed to act as a straw buyer of sorts, putting forth an offer, backed secretly by Selznick, on behalf of Harrison and Hitchcock. If du Maurier bit, Selznick and Hitchcock would have their property. If she didn't, Selznick could still come in with a better offer.

It worked. Selznick authorized Joan and Hitchcock to make a bid of $40,000. Du Maurier balked at Hitchcock's price. But when Selznick came in at $50,000, with the added promise that he would treat du Maurier's novel with fidelity, she agreed. By late September, Selznick (and Hitchcock) had *Rebecca*. And Joan had the chance to adapt a pet project, and a novel that was well on its way to bestseller status. She judged it best to wait for the opportune moment to discuss her decision with Millie and Walter.

Meanwhile, *Jamaica Inn* was slated to begin production in September and end in October, under the assumption that the Hollywood move might occur as early as January. In fact, *Jamaica Inn*'s production ended up running through January; nothing about the production process came easy. Laughton had an enormous ego, and his producing partner Pommer, the former head of Germany's UFA, was overly hands-on. For Joan, the script development process had been difficult. Clemence Dane (a pseudonym for Winifred Ashton) had written a screenplay in 1937 when the project had a false start. Now that Hitchcock was commissioned, Dane's script went by the wayside and Sidney Gilliat came on board, along with novelist and playwright J. B. Priestley (brought in by Laughton to pen additional dialogue for his character).

Before Harrison and Gilliat's involvement, Laughton had sent Dane's draft to the Production Code Administration in anticipation of a successful American release. He heard back that there was an essential problem; they needed to alter the fact that the villain was a man of the cloth so as not to offend religious groups. (After hearing this, Laughton nearly wanted off the picture.) Upon deciding to change the vicar into the town squire, Gilliat recalled, "We evolved (Hitch and Joan and I) a fairly satisfactory Jekyll-and-Hyde-character." Then there was the challenge of how to handle the big reveal. In the book, the reader doesn't arrive at the mastermind's identity until nearly the end. In the film, the *aha* moment occurs early on, partly because of narrative necessity—the villain is now a legal authority and an integral part of the community—and partly because Laughton wasn't about to be confined to the finale.

Hitchcock found it troubling that the "surprise story" now became "a suspense story" (structured around the question of *When will Mary and the others discover that which the spectators already know?*). Hitchcock once said, "It's very difficult to make a who-done-it. You see, this was like making a who-done-it, and making Charles Laughton the butler." With the director "truly discouraged," each script meeting was filled with stress. To him, "it was completely absurd, because logically the judge should have entered the scene only at the end of the adventure."

On top of this, writer Gilliat, who had a well-earned reputation as a quirky and fun chap, had gone sour on Hitchcock in recent days. He did not appreciate that the director had recently dismissed the importance of screenwriters in an interview he gave to the *New Yorker*. Gilliat felt that Hitchcock had overstated his own role in the writing of *The Lady Vanishes*, which was due in theaters in December. Why steal his enjoyment of what rightly should have been a terrific triumph? A simple correction or apology would have gone a long way. But in this case, the director's pettiness prevailed.

During the shooting of *Jamaica Inn*, there was also Laughton's histrionic personality to contend with. As he struggled to find his character, he demanded numerous takes and more than a little hand-holding. According to Hitchcock, the actor's "mercurial" personality was so confounding that the director "tried to duck out of the picture two weeks before we started shooting," but little could be done once the contract was signed. Joan's role throughout it all was to serve as the buffer, doing the best she could to smooth out the tense back-and-forth among Hitchcock, Laughton, Pommer, the writers, and the actors.

Eighteen-year-old Maureen O'Hara, a relative newcomer from Ireland, played the female lead. Luckily, O'Hara enjoyed Laughton. She was riding high as a recent Mayflower Pictures discovery and had just signed a seven-picture deal. What she may not have realized was that if the adaptation had remained more faithful to the novel, she would have enjoyed more screen time. As difficult as it was to compete with Laughton's on-screen mugging, she turned in a respectable performance as a courageous, precocious, and self-possessed heroine.

Upon *Jamaica Inn*'s release, du Maurier was so disappointed that she demanded her name be removed from the opening titles. The film's reputation has not improved much with age, and the struggles that Laughton, Pommer, and Hitchcock's team had over creative control are evident on the screen. The movie suffers from Laughton's overblown performance and a decided lack of suspense, based on the fact that his character is revealed to be the villain so early on. Several decades later, it was named one of the "fifty worst films of all time" in Harry Medved and Randy Dreyfuss's book of the same title.

There have, however, been efforts to rehabilitate the film's reputation and reclaim it for Hitchcock's canon. Maurice Yacowar, author of *Hitchcock's British Films*, concludes, "[Laughton's] dominance over the director hurts the film. But the film remains a Hitchcock."

The case can be made that the film is also thoroughly "a Harrison," given the ways it anticipates her later work. *Jamaica Inn*'s domestic gothic themes and disturbing psychology are reminiscent of those found in *Phantom Lady*, *The Strange Affair of Uncle Harry*, *Nocturne*, and *They Won't Believe Me*. Its perverse textures and pathological violence speak directly to Harrison's preoccupation with what lies hidden beneath romantic, marital, and familial relations. Moreover, the scene in which Mary is trapped in her bedroom with her uncle may be viewed as a predecessor to *Phantom Lady*'s finale, in which Carol Richman is cornered by the murderous Marlow. (Women's fearlessness in the face of jeopardy would become a recurring theme.) There are additional distinguishing marks of Harrison's signature: Mary's investigative gaze, her rescue of the hero, and the idea of women saving women. *Jamaica Inn* sits neatly beside *The Lady Vanishes*, as these signature marks come into focus and a shift away from light seriocomic thrillers becomes more obvious.

Harrison scored her first official screen credit on *Jamaica Inn*—as one of the writers. Some, even Hitchcock in one instance, have suggested this was chiefly a tactical maneuver, his way of ensuring her entrée into Hollywood. However, there is a good deal to indicate that she bore a significant influence on the film. Her day-to-day involvement in the writing sessions, her presence on the set, and *Jamaica Inn*'s close affinities with her other films authenticate this. Hitchcock's passing pronouncement notwithstanding, Joan earned her *Jamaica Inn* writing credit.

In November 1938, as production on *Jamaica Inn* ground agonizingly toward a conclusion, *The Lady Vanishes* opened to resounding acclaim. London critics hailed it a smash success, as American reviewers would the following month. Kay Brown and Selznick's investment partner John Hay "Jock" Whitney immediately flew to England to finalize the terms of Hitchcock's agreement. As they dined and celebrated their two-picture deal, Hitchcock agreed to generate a treatment of *Rebecca* for a $5,000 flat fee.

All that was left was for Joan to decide, once and for all, whether to join Hitch and Alma as the "third Hitchcock." The biggest hurdle was the idea of leaving her family, given all they had been through. She worried most about her mother. The burden was made worse because she knew she would be saying good-bye indefinitely, as it was becoming increasingly clear that war was on the horizon. In the fall of 1938, key territory in Czechoslovakia was ceded to the Nazis. Adolf Hitler's war machine was advancing. Who knew what lay ahead?

It gave her comfort that she could trust Faith to tend to Millie and Walter—and even the business, Faith having taken on a more active role at the *Advertiser*. Faith had also fallen in love with a doctor, John Murray, whom she planned to marry within the year. This seemed freeing for Joan, knowing that Faith had found her path. In truth, there was little reason for Joan to remain behind. To stay in England would mean hitting a ceiling, staying forever consigned to an undercapitalized, ever-struggling film industry. And she was unlikely to ever work with another director as important as Hitchcock. She was unwilling to part ways with him.

The feeling was mutual. Much to Joan's surprise, Hitchcock made a visit to the Grove. As if this were a studio deal that might fall through, he feared an unexpected snag: What if Walter and Millie objected to Joan leaving? The director sat down with the family and painted a rosy picture of California. He implied there was a difference between "Los Angeles" and "Hollywood," which was where all the gossip and scandal came from. Promising to keep their daughter away from the "Hollywood" side of things, he vowed to look after her. The encounter played out a little bit like a marriage proposal, Hitchcock asking for Walter's permission to take his daughter to a foreign land. Won over by his charm, Joan's parents gave their blessing.

Joan knew that Hitchcock was misrepresenting the life that awaited her. Her niece, Kate Adamson, explains, "She didn't encourage the idea [of Hitchcock coming to the Grove], because she knew it was going to be a tremendously exciting life. She knew what she was getting into." On March 4, 1939, less than two years after her first trip to America, she was back on board the *Queen Mary*, sailing fearlessly toward her future.

8 | GOING HOLLYWOOD

THOUGH PASSAGE ON THE RMS *Queen Mary* meant the height of luxury, with two indoor swimming pools and a plethora of entertainments amid elaborate art deco decor, Joan couldn't have been happier to dock in New York City on March 10, 1939. No matter how many times she sailed, she was never going to get her sea legs. A big welcome was orchestrated by Myron Selznick and Albert Margolies, Gaumont-British's East Coast publicity director. After the usual press huddle, reporters followed the group to the St. Regis Hotel, where Joan and the Hitchcocks would stay for the week.

Hitch, Alma, and Pat then ventured south by train to enjoy the weather and the late horseracing season in Florida. Joan stayed for a few extra days in Manhattan, then joined them at Palm Beach's palatial Whitehall Hotel before the four took off for an excursion to Havana. Eventually, they boarded a train back to New York and then on to California, arriving on April 5.

Upon reaching Los Angeles, Joan made her home at the low-rise Wilshire Palms Apartments at 10331 Wilshire Boulevard in Westwood. Her one-bedroom, ground-level apartment featured pastel carpet and drapes, along with exquisitely appointed furniture. In a cozy arrangement, the Hitchcocks resided on the top floor, in a three-bedroom penthouse that, though still small, afforded a sensational bar and a glorious view of the mountains, ocean, and even the Culver City complex where David O. Selznick's studios sat five miles away. Because they had arranged to do script preparations away from the office as usual, Hitch and Alma would go downstairs to Joan's each morning to work on their treatment for *Rebecca*. They preferred her space to the sparse white walls and monochromatic furnishings of their penthouse, which made them feel decidedly not at home.

The Wilshire Palms couldn't have been more perfect as a residential launch-pad for Joan. The building played home base to a steady stream of Hollywood newcomers, as well as marquee stars in between marriages and romances. Franchot Tone, nursing his wounds from a highly publicized breakup with Joan Crawford, had recently moved in. Soon afterward, Billy Wilder would find himself there. Pat Hitchcock fondly remembers a couple of the Ritz Brothers, the Twentieth Century Fox comedy team. Mobster John Rosselli had recently married Fox actress June Lang, and moved her into one of the pricier units. If the soirees or "pinch me" moments ever slowed down at home, Joan could turn her attention next door to the Chateau Colline, the French Normandy castle-style apartment building that turned the same kind of business for oil-men, playboys, ingenues, and stars such as Bette Davis and Gable in their early Hollywood days.

In another sense, the Wilshire Palms location eased Joan's transition from England to Los Angeles. Though technically in Westwood (with its shops, restaurants, and movie theaters only a short drive away), it was tucked up against Holmby Hills, one leg of the "Platinum triangle" (along with Bel Air and Beverly Hills). Initially developed by Arthur Letts Sr. and his family as a monument to his birthplace, a small English hamlet called Holdenby, the neighborhood boasted streets named after British towns, custom-made streetlamps, and a swath of Tudor-style homes. The grand, picturesque estates—amply spaced out—created an old-world ambience, against the green backdrop of lavish lawns and plentiful luxurious country clubs.

Joan and the Hitchcocks, like so many other transplants, had found a way to recreate an enchanting version of their native homeland. They were drawn to the "village life" of the Westside enclaves and the small, refined town center of Beverly Hills, which filed along Wilshire Boulevard, a gigantic corridor originated by anglophile Gaylord Wilshire. The British mystique of Beverly Hills and its surrounding area ran deep, according to David Niven, who later became one of Joan's closest friends. It went beyond the English Renaissance architecture, bridle paths, and patchwork patterns of open countryside, all the way back to its early landscaping. Niven explained, "When the Rodeo Land and Water Company decided to develop its gently sloping acreage, it had the great good taste and foresight to send for an expert from

Kew Gardens, London, who planted a different species of tree for every street, and thereafter a fascinating variety of architecture proliferated beneath maples, magnolias, palms, corals, pines, sycamores, flowering eucalyptus, elms, olives, jacarandas, and oaks." Wilbur Cook, who had worked with the esteemed Olmsted Brothers, was responsible for Beverly Hills' landscape architecture, designed with curvilinear streets and triangular parks that differed from the monotonous grid-like patterns dominating American cities. As British expats arrived for the first time, the neighborhoods, houses, flats, and gardens oddly felt a bit like home.

There were additional perks to Joan's residing in the Wilshire Palms. By living just west of the Beverly Hills boundary, she could not only savor the Beverly Hills ambience but also enjoy carte blanche when it came to gratifying her more superficial impulses. Its downtown core was home to high-end boutiques and luxury department stores, including Saks Fifth Avenue and I. Magnin. Whereas some in her position would have been consigned to mere window shopping, her family account afforded her some comfortable room to splurge. Pesterre's was a tailor shop on Beverly Drive specializing in women's and men's British tweeds. Not only did Arthur Pesterre fit top stars like Laurence Olivier and Greta Garbo, but he was also a chief supplier of British riding costumes to the major studios. The haberdashery offered Joan another little taste of home, and helped her maintain the strong fashion sense she had formed years earlier.

Beverly Hills also had gorgeous movie palaces and stylish restaurants, including the Brown Derby, housed in a giant, cocoa-colored dome, and Lawry's (where chefs came to each table to personally carve each steak). Then there was of course Chasen's on Wilshire, which at that time was "the hub of the movie social wheel," according to Niven. The biggest stars and most powerful people from around the world came to try the famed cuisine—the barbecue ribs, deviled beef bones, chicken curry, creamed spinach, and for dessert, banana shortcake—amid green and red leather booths and warm wood interiors. Filmdom's reigning star couple, Clark Gable (the "king of Hollywood") and Carole Lombard (the original screwball comedienne), embraced Hitch, Alma, and Joan when they first arrived and introduced them to Chasen's. The Hitchcocks began making dinner at the restaurant a Thursday-evening ritual, often adding a second night of the week. Their allegiance to the restaurant earned them their own booth, decorated with Patricia's photo above the table. Each Thursday, Dave Chasen knew to set a place for Joan.

Joan was also partaking in the "buffet-style supper-party circuit" enjoyed by Myron Selznick's agency clients. He had added her and the Hitchcocks to the list, which included not only Gable and Lombard but also the screwball queen's former husband William Powell, Loretta Young, and director Leo McCarey. As a result, Joan found herself seated at intimate dinners with some of the biggest names in the business. Soon, her social calendar would include the occasional weekend stay at the luxurious Arrowhead Lodge. She thoroughly enjoyed this kind of rubbing elbows, viewing it not merely as an obligation but as an added dividend for someone aspiring to a Hollywood screenwriting career.

After two months of work around Joan's cramped dining room table, she and the Hitchcocks had a forty-five-page outline for their *Rebecca* adaptation. The blueprint was in fact the culmination of six months of work over the course of their travels, at times with the help of British actor turned writer Michael Hogan, but now it was finally ready to submit for Selznick's approval. So off Joan and Hitchcock went to Selznick International studios. Leased by Selznick from neighboring Metro-Goldwyn-Mayer, the fourteen-acre site included more than a dozen soundstages and a host of bungalows and dressing rooms. Originally the Triangle Film Corporation, built to showcase the productions of Thomas Ince, D. W. Griffith, and Mack Sennett, it boasted at its impressive entrance the signature Mount Vernon–style estate that appeared as the logo on all Selznick pictures. With its white colonial facade and tall white columns, the building—which housed the administrative offices of the studio—had come to be known simply as "Tara," after the plantation house in *Gone with the Wind*. (There were retakes occurring into the summer, so it was not odd to see cast members in antebellum costumes parading between the main soundstages.)

Selznick provided Hitchcock and Joan with a shared suite—including kitchen and bath—in a bungalow toward the back of the studio property. To drive himself and Joan to the studio each day, the director acquired a Baby Austin. The British compact was a touch of home, even if somewhat out of place among the Cadillacs and Packards commonly seen in Hollywood.

By the time they arrived on the lot, Daphne du Maurier's source novel had become a smash hit. *Rebecca* had been deemed a literary masterpiece upon its release, and serialized in the London *Daily Express* and the *New York Daily*

Mirror. (Delivery trucks for the *Daily Mirror* advertised it on their side panels.) Sales of the book had already surpassed one million; it had been broadcast in the US as an Orson Welles radio program, and it was soon to become a play.

After Selznick reviewed the adaptation's outline, it was time to receive notes and bring in some reinforcements. In early conversations with Hitchcock, Selznick had ideas about which writers might be hired to write the final screenplay, proposing Clemence Dane and two highly successful Americans, John Balderston and Ben Hecht. But the director overrode these suggestions. Selznick, who was in a position to cast a final veto, gave him room to choose on this first project.

Hitchcock went to bat for Hogan (recently imported to RKO), whom the director had been paying out of pocket to help with the treatment. Hogan would work on individual scenes. He also brought on Scottish (London-born) Philip MacDonald, a successful writer of whodunits, to work on overall structure.

Du Maurier's novel tells the story of a plain, insecure woman employed as a companion to a demanding American matron on a trip to Monte Carlo. The heroine, who remains unnamed throughout the story, eventually falls in love with the attractive, moody widower Maxim DeWinter. He proposes marriage and promptly installs his new bride in his ancestral home. Ill-equipped to run a large household or manage its staff (led by the ominous head maid, Mrs. Danvers), the heroine is further plunged into self-doubt by daily reminders of Maxim's first wife, Rebecca. The deceased Mrs. DeWinter appears to have possessed all the beauty and sophistication that the heroine lacks.

After a prolonged and heart-wrenching ordeal, the heroine comes to realize that Rebecca was a wicked adulteress whom her husband hated and eventually killed. Realizing that Maxim loves her as he could never have loved Rebecca, she stands by his side through a trial in which Rebecca's death is wrongly determined to have been a suicide. The book ends with Maxim and the heroine recommitting to their romance, which will always be clouded by the second Mrs. DeWinter's knowledge of her husband's crime.

When writing, du Maurier had conceived it as a "rather grim" portrait of how humiliating marriage can be for a woman, "trying to explore the relationship between a man who was powerful and a woman who was not, just as she had done, in a different way, in *Jamaica Inn*." The novelist feared that the publisher's promotional tactics would lead readers to misinterpret the story as a watered-down version of Charlotte Brontë's *Jane Eyre* or "an exquisite love story." But the purity of her craftsmanship meant she needn't have been concerned. She had hauntingly evoked her character's personal sympathy and interior subjectivity by looking into her own deeply disturbed heart. The story stemmed from her own jealousy over her husband's one-time fiancée, who figured in du Maurier's mind as an exotic, restless first love.

Readers in both America and Britain were as hungry to consume a story that conjured up the humiliations of "a marriage that had failed" as du Maurier had been desperate to concoct one. *Rebecca* touched a nerve with female readers in particular, at a time when women in Europe were entering hasty marriages with men preparing for active military service. Many women, like du Maurier's character, were left fretting over what it would be like to forge a marriage with a stranger, one who might never return from war. Or perhaps a worse fate, wedding someone who, in coming home, proves to be deeply troubled.

The book also tapped into women's more general anxiety over changing gender roles. Here was a ghost story in which the phantom lady of the title was pictured first as a feminine ideal and ultimately as a monstrous whore. As the heroine attempts to navigate the imposing walls of Maxim's mansion, she is haunted by an image that represents simultaneously all that she longs to be and all that she—in her purity and simplicity—is not. Many women related to the heroine's identity crisis, caught between the traditional expectations of the Victorian era (and its elevation of the "domestic angel") and a modern world where women were reimagining their place as social and economic agents.

Selznick's East Coast representative, Kay Brown, a talented and shrewd judge of material, had declared the novel to be "the most fascinating story I have read in ages." Selznick, who envisioned himself as a proprietor of women's tastes (and usually correctly so), believed he understood the appeal. As his story department put it, the main character "probably exemplifies the feeling that most young women have about themselves."

Selznick's gift was adapting literature written by women for women, taking advantage of already-successful books that were essentially "presold" as film commodities, or seizing on work in the prepublication stage that seemed destined to hit big. Selznick was also a star maker, and casting the heroine in *Rebecca* would provide him with an opportunity to replicate the success (and mountains of publicity) he had achieved tapping little-known Vivien Leigh to play Scarlett O'Hara in *Gone with the Wind*.

For the Hitchcock camp, *Rebecca* was a great story—a Cinderella ghost story. There were rich layers in such a tale. The protagonist is not merely an insecure bride who feels she cannot attain the level of beauty and sophistication of her predecessor. She is a woman who feels like a girl, a mansion mistress who feels like a maid.

The Britishness of *Rebecca* also made it ideal for the Hitchcock camp. All the action takes place in an unspecified and ambiguously British province. Almost all the characters are from England, which meant they would be played by British actors already well known to Hitchcock and his writers. This smoothed everyone's transition to the American studio system: they could create a small island that did not seem so far from home.

The baroque ambience and atmospheric mood of the gothic novel would translate well to the medium of cinema, especially as a "Hitchcock picture." The stage was set for those Hitchcock touches by which seemingly trivial objects occupying the domestic sphere—a teacup, a hairbrush, a fork—could take on terrifying and violent dimensions. The screen version of *Rebecca* would, in fact, become a consummate Hitchcockian example of how "things" could assume psychological, almost human characteristics. The film would display its creators' superior ability to transform the camera into a body, that of a nameless woman, known only as the second Mrs. DeWinter, or "the Girl," who begged for the audience's identification.

Better than any other filmmaker, Hitchcock cultivated a distinctive style of first-person, subjective cinematography—moving camera shots, detailed framing, and carefully choreographed editing—all of which pushed the boundaries of existing film grammar and helped establish his status as an auteur. Even those shots that appeared objective often gave the viewer a strong sense of being inside the mind of the character. With *Rebecca*, Hitchcock was about to hit a certain stride.

Joan was hitting her stride too. She was realizing that the "woman's angle"— the persistent search for filmic ways to penetrate the mind of a sympathetic female character—was her greatest motivation. *Jamaica Inn* had presented her with the opportunity to test herself as a writer in this regard, as had her involvement with *The Lady Vanishes*. But *Rebecca* fed her avid interest in mystery novels and female true crime stories going back to her younger days. She *was* du Maurier's target audience.

Joan still considered herself a protégée, a writer honing her craft, but she knew one thing for certain: the female protagonist needed to be stronger and more independent. Du Maurier may have written the heroine as an insecure naïf, but Joan believed the Brontë-esque undertones would benefit from a touch of Jane Austen. Hitchcock would put up no resistance; it was common for him to embellish his female characters.

When Kay Brown and Jock Whitney had visited London in November 1938 to discuss the project, they were particularly enthused to hear the plans for a more self-assured heroine. Joan and Hitchcock's desired tack was to make her "much less passive." At the very least, she was to appear "fairly bright, attractive and amusing" in the early scenes, before she marries Maxim. Then, once she arrives at Maxim's estate of Manderley, she would be overwhelmed somewhat by the larger-than-life reminders of the first wife. This would create a noticeable contrast, "a change in the Girl," upon her assumption of the new role as mistress of the house. Her assertiveness would fade like a "smile that drain[s] away from the face." To adapt a novel for the screen required such visible changes to convey the heroine's lost confidence, Joan and Hitchcock contended, as a substitute for the book's interior monologues.

Selznick, however, objected to the idea of a more assertive heroine. He held to his belief that audiences would bristle if the character strayed from the novel. Just as he felt that readers identified with the heroine's insecurity because "this is how most young women feel," he supposed that female viewers would relate to all "the little feminine things which are so recognizable and which make every woman say, 'I know just how she feels. . . . I know just what she's going through,' etc." Even once she had been taken down a notch at Manderley, the character remained too spirited for Selznick. "We bought *Rebecca*, and we intend to make *Rebecca*," he exclaimed in a lengthy memo to Hitchcock, upon reading the team's work in June 1939.

Selznick's reaction was a devastating blow. Joan would have to water down some of the heroine's moxie. This went against her better instincts, but in acquiescing to the producer's demands, she discovered her talents for added touches. With each writer bringing certain strengths to the project, Joan focused attention on minute details that would bring into focus the heroine's identity crisis, such as the character's "reactions of running away from the guests, and the tiny things that indicate her nervousness and self-consciousness and her gaucherie." She drew on her literary instincts, using women's domestic rituals and feminine accoutrements to heighten the importance of seemingly inconsequential items, such as personal correspondence, address books, and monogrammed pillows. Many of her rewrites—a scene here, a line there—did not make it into the final screenplay, but they nevertheless influenced the construction of "the Girl" and gave Joan practical experience in thinking about how sets and props could reveal character. They underscore a sensitivity to class distinctions, looking closely at the maids' interactions in Manderley and highlighting themes of female bonding in ways that the final version of the film does not.

By late June, she, Hitchcock, and MacDonald boarded Selznick's boat to discuss their revised treatment. Thankfully, the producer was heartened overall; they were moving in the right direction. He still harbored concerns that the second Mrs. DeWinter was too spirited. Perhaps by the time all was said and done, he didn't notice that Joan ignored his notes to remove such remarks as the heroine's "uncued and unjustified" displays of disrespect to her employer, Mrs. Van Hopper. There were plenty of other story details to attend to.

Another central concern when it came to scripting *Rebecca*, which had controversial elements of sex, scandal, suicide, and murder, was how to forestall the censors. In the book, Maxim is responsible for his first wife's death. Having discovered that she is committing adultery with her cousin, Jack Favell, Maxim goes to the boathouse (the location of their trysts) intending to frighten him away. Instead, he finds Rebecca and demands a divorce. She laughs at Maxim, taunting him with the news that she is pregnant by Favell and telling him, "If I had a child, neither you nor anyone in the world could ever prove it wasn't yours."

An incensed Maxim shoots Rebecca and then places her body in a sailboat. After driving spikes through the boat's hull, he pushes it off into the water, sending Rebecca to a watery grave. When her corpse materializes, no bullet wounds are found—Maxim believes the bullet must have passed through Rebecca's body—and investigators are left to speculate as to the cause of death. What role did those holes in the boat's hull play? A series of courtroom scenes and several rounds of detective work lead them to conclude that she committed suicide. She, they deduce, made the holes herself after discovering on the day of her death that she had a malignant tumor. The book ends on an unconventional note: no one will ever know that Maxim murdered his first wife, except for Maxim and his new bride.

Given the regulations of the Production Code Administration (PCA), which governed the moral content of Hollywood films, there was no way that the husband could get away with murder in the movie adaptation. Joseph Breen, head of the PCA, proposed a rather ridiculous narrative solution: turn Rebecca's murder into an accidental death, the result of a skirmish during the boathouse confrontation. This was so irksome to not only the writers but also Selznick that the producer considered revolting against the PCA with as many writers, directors, and actors as he could rally behind him ("I think we would become heroes with them for having won the fight against so insane and inane and outmoded a code," he wrote to Jock Whitney.) Everyone quickly regrouped, deciding to cut their losses and go with Rebecca's "accidental death," partly to smuggle through some other censorious details. The result was a highly contorted narrative logic. As Selznick lucidly lamented, "The whole story of *Rebecca* is the story of a man who has murdered his wife and now it becomes the story of a man who buried a wife who was killed accidentally!"

It was one thing for Breen to concoct the "accidental death" scenario; devising an elegant strategy for carrying it out was another. With the production start date only weeks away, Joan experienced for the first time what it was like to work in the Hollywood trenches. Selznick imposed a new writer on the team, Robert Sherwood, claiming he was needed both to solve the last-minute story problems caused by the censors and to polish the dialogue. Sherwood, one of the original members of the Algonquin Roundtable, had parlayed his playwriting into a Hollywood career. Though he would ultimately be responsible for only the last 10 percent of the screenplay, he would receive top writing credit—as well as the highest paycheck, $15,000. Sherwood joined Hitchcock and Joan at Selznick's home for all-night brainstorming sessions around the pool that looked more like a seventy-two-hour bender. Joan transcribed anything useful as the producer rode high on injections of speed and vitamin B12 while the others fortified themselves with mere alcohol.

But through the fog and fury, they began to craft the specific contours of the flashback: Maxim would not shoot Rebecca, per Breen's wishes. Instead, blinded by rage, Maxim would shove her and she would clumsily fall onto an anchor, which would pierce her skull. Adhering to the novel, the ensuing investigation would bring to light that she wanted to die, having just learned of her terminal illness. Authorities would determine that she goaded Maxim into attacking her—in essence, committing suicide, but not before implicating her despised husband as her killer.

The central issue for the censors, as the script changes indicate, was character intention. As long as Maxim did not deliberately cause Rebecca's death, the production code would not be violated. The revisions gave Maxim a moral makeover, and Rebecca was now pure evil. A story filled with moral ambivalences was now painted in broad strokes of black and white. The only character left who saw the world in all its shades of gray was the female protagonist. Despite the flattening of the other characters, the adaptation process did manage to produce an even more complex portrait of the heroine. Skirting the censors—and measuring the costs and the benefits of changing source material—would become a career-long struggle for Joan, as she was increasingly drawn to provocative material.

As script revisions on *Rebecca* rolled through the summer of 1939, Joan also involved herself in the casting process. It had actually taken months to determine who would play the unnamed heroine. Selznick wanted another Scarlett O'Hara publicity roar, even if at a lower decibel. This was a difficult part to cast, given that the second Mrs. DeWinter needed to be notably youthful, as her nickname, "the Girl," implied, but everyone agreed the actress could not be *too* young, at least not scandalously so. In an era when audiences liked their actresses tough (Bette Davis), independent (Barbara Stanwyck), and even cocky (Carole Lombard), delicate, insipid women were hard to come by.

Meanwhile, Hitchcock's team debated with Selznick about the best actor to play the aloof and sensitive Maxim. Actually, all were in agreement on their first choice: elegant Englishman Ronald Colman (star of *A Tale of Two Cities* and *The Prisoner of Zenda*). Hitchcock tried to woo the actor, who displayed sincere interest. But Colman had concerns that playing a murderer (even an accidental one) would damage his image, so he declined. The suave (and British) David Niven, in the midst of a string of hits at Samuel Goldwyn Productions, was also an option. For this role, Hitchcock decided he was "too shallow."

After Colman, Selznick had a short list of favorites: Walter Pidgeon, Leslie Howard, Melvyn Douglas, and William Powell. Of these, Powell most interested the Hitchcock team. Joan, Alma, and Hitchcock had become fast friends with him upon their arrival in the States. The cultured, debonair image he had cultivated in the Thin Man series and other comedies positioned him well. But would he be believable as the tortured husband? Doubts persisted.

Finally, everyone arrived at Laurence Olivier, the classically trained English actor whose debut Hollywood performance as the brooding Heathcliff in William Wyler's *Wuthering Heights* had been a huge success. Olivier would make for a convincing Maxim—romantic, troubled, tragic. For Selznick, this choice came with the added benefit of pleasing Vivien Leigh. Olivier and Leigh had been having an open affair for several years, providing fodder for the British tabloids but remaining under the radar stateside. Leigh wanted him close by while she waited out postproduction on *Gone with the Wind*.

Moreover, Leigh passionately desired to play the principal part in *Rebecca*, so much so that she agreed to audition, a concession on her part given her newly empowered position. But the screen test was miserable, even with Olivier feeding her lines. She managed to be both too dull and too fiery at the same time. She could not shed her Southern belle act, let alone replace it with mousy reticence. Everyone concurred that "she doesn't seem at all right as to sincerity or age or innocence." Leigh was devastated. Olivier was relieved. He later reflected, "It was perhaps better for us to have a little vacation from constant togetherness."

Through July and August, Joan, Alma, and Hitchcock, sitting through endless screen tests, considered more than fifty actresses. But they knew all along that Selznick had a favorite for the female lead. It was Joan Fontaine, the skinny younger sister of *Gone with the Wind*'s Olivia de Havilland. The twenty-one-year-old ingenue had begun her rise to stardom with small roles in *Gunga Din* (1939) and *The Women* (1939), but she first caught Selznick's eye in the summer of 1938 after being seated next to him at a dinner party hosted by Charlie Chaplin. It has been speculated that the producer fell in love almost instantly with Fontaine, keeping in near-daily contact with her over the next year. But even Selznick knew she was a long shot for the role in *Rebecca*, a concern that was confirmed by a less than spectacular screen test.

Upon viewing that initial audition, Joan and Alma reported that "Fontaine was just too coy and simpering to a degree that it was intolerable." She was fidgety, with a breathy hush of a voice that both women found "irritating." They much preferred the New England–bred Margaret Sullavan, whom they deemed "far ahead" of the others. Joan proposed that "Sullavan, if she enacted the part, would help to relieve the monotony which might arise through the terrific number of scenes 'the Girl' has to play." The writer was keenly aware not only that the character appeared almost constantly on screen but also that her scenes were generally static.

The luminous Anne Baxter came in a close second in Joan and Alma's book. She was "much more moving" than the others, they thought. Though only sixteen years old at the time, she had strong command over her naturally deep voice, a refreshing change from Leigh and Fontaine. They believed "her voice has a quality that could be taken easily for either English or American," a plus for a film that would attempt to straddle the two cultures. They did have a fear, however, that the teenager "would not be able to play love scenes due to her age and lack of experience."

The grueling casting process was not without its moments of levity, infused no doubt with Hitchcock's caustic wit. Joan and Alma's notes indicated that the unknown Miriam Patty was an ideal candidate to embody not a character but a prop. Patty was "too much Dresden china," they wrote. "She could play the part of the Cupid that is broken—she's so frail." And they found newcomer Audrey Reynolds "excellent for [the part of] Rebecca, who doesn't appear." Her screen presence was apparently lacking.

The notion that Rebecca might appear in the film had actually been considered and then dismissed. In the process of adapting the novel into a movie, the writers had faced a giant creative problem translating the character's looming invisibility, which gave her so much power in the mind not only of the protagonist but also of the reader. For most of the film, Hitchcock's camerawork and editing would exploit this same power, conveying the sense that Rebecca was on the verge of entering the frame from all sides. But how to adapt the climactic confession, in which Maxim recounts to the protagonist just how, where, and why he killed Rebecca? Surely Rebecca would have to make a grand appearance in a flashback, wouldn't she? Yet by materializing, her magic would be lost.

Joan and Hitchcock finally decided against putting the character on-screen, partly because they questioned whether any actress could match the audience's outsized expectations. It was in their eleventh-hour story sessions with Robert Sherwood (which in truth extended well beyond the "midnight deadline" of the production's start date) that they arrived at a concrete cinematic device for handling the confounding confession sequence. The camera would follow an imagined Rebecca—tracing empty space as it panned across the room—as though "etching" her prior movements from Maxim's point of view.

As for "the Girl," the casting decision was ultimately up to Selznick. To the surprise of few, and with no argument from the Hitchcock camp, he chose Fontaine. Three weeks before filming began, on August 19, the actress was suffering through an Oregon honeymoon (including, in her words, "a wedding night *not* to remember") with the British stage and screen actor Brian Aherne. She received a telegram confirming that she would star in *Rebecca* and instructing her to report to the set after Labor Day. Cutting her trip short, Fontaine immediately drove back to Los Angeles.

Principal photography began on Wednesday, September 6, 1939. It was far from a jubilant occasion, however. Just five days prior, Hitler had invaded Poland. England and France issued declarations of war against Nazi Germany. Though the US remained neutral for the moment, so many members of the cast and crew were British that focusing on the production proved difficult.

That same month, Joan's sister Faith held her wedding in Kensington. If Joan felt a slight tugging to return to England then, she didn't act on it. Nor could she. "We realized during the war how much of a small town Hollywood was," said Joan Fontaine, "because we weren't going anywhere." For her part, Alma was able to convince her mother and sister to move to Los Angeles and would soon bring them over.

As if tensions weren't high enough, September brought a deadly heat wave to Los Angeles. Four days in a row, records were broken, as temperatures hovered between 103 and a blistering 107 degrees. The vicious spell was punctuated on September 25 by a tropical cyclone—the only tropical storm to hit California in the twentieth century—which made landfall in Long Beach but proceeded to flood the Los Angeles River and take down houses from Malibu to Huntington Beach. Nearly one hundred people were killed and thousands were left without electricity.

During production, Joan's days were intense, between the "crisis-prone rhythm" of Selznick's working environment and the enormity of Hitchcock's learning curve in the American studio mode of production. Except for Sundays, her days began before 7:00 AM and lasted a minimum of fourteen hours. She was rewriting critical scenes (such as Mrs. Danvers's tour through Rebecca's room, the boathouse confession, and the Monte Carlo scenes) well into October, six weeks after filming began. The shoot, which had been slated for thirty-six days, ended up going for sixty-three days, wrapping up on November 20. Everyone's nerves were frayed, if not seared, by exhaustion.

As 1939 came to an end, so did the production phase of *Rebecca*. Joan closed out the year by spending Christmas Day with Lombard and Gable at Lombard's former Bel Air home on St. Cloud Road, which the Hitchcocks had purchased for their first home in America. Raising a glass of eggnog to the holiday season, Joan had much to celebrate.

As the new year began, Selznick commandeered Joan to serve as Hitchcock's representative during *Rebecca*'s final stages. (The director was making a segue into the next project.) She sat by Selznick's side as he filmed additional scenes that he and Hitchcock agreed would bolster the film (such as strengthening Mrs. Danvers's presence and recalibrating Fontaine's narration). The picture was redubbed, and its running time was shortened through careful trimming. Joan later remembered "shedding quite a few tears" over the scripting of *Rebecca*. But "even that was a good experience," she recalled. "I learned the hard way, but by the time I was through with that job I knew exactly what the American motion picture industry was all about."

The original plan was to release *Rebecca* on January 10, when it would still be eligible for 1939 Oscar consideration. Selznick sought to capitalize on the timing of *Gone with the Wind*, which had premiered in mid-December and would see wide release in March 1940. Once it was clear *Rebecca* would miss the target date, the producer felt strongly that the film's test screenings should be engineered in a strategic fashion. Breaking with the tradition, whereby the studio surprised audiences with an unexpected preview screening, in this case viewers knew to expect *Rebecca* in advance. The goal was to gather more thoughtful—and useful—responses.

In yet another alternative move, Selznick chose to hold *Rebecca*'s grand premiere not in Los Angeles or New York but in Miami Beach, Florida. On March 21 the film opened at the art deco Lincoln Theatre, the flagship of local Wometco Enterprises and a magnet for glamorous snowbirds. Al Jolson, Sophie Tucker, and William Wyler turned out, among scores of other Hollywood names. The one-week interval before *Rebecca*'s New York City premiere on March 28 provided a window for ad copy to circulate and word of mouth to build.

Rebecca opened to rave reviews. The *New York Times* deemed it "an altogether brilliant film. Haunting, suspenseful, handsome, and handsomely played." According to the *New Yorker*, the film was "more stirring than the novel." *Film Daily* noted its "mark of quality in every department—production, direction, acting, writing, and photography." It was named best movie of the year in *Film Daily*'s poll of national film critics.

The film enjoyed wide success in London, and though Joan wasn't there to bear witness, St. Hugh's students flocked to view it when it premiered at their local cinema, where Daphne du Maurier personally promoted it. It was a picture close to Joan's heart; later in life she would name it as the one she was most proud of. *Rebecca* would go on to earn eleven Academy Award nominations. Joan, sharing credit with Robert Sherwood, was nominated for Best Adapted Screenplay. Joan had come to Hollywood to make a name for herself and had done it on her first try.

9 | OSCAR CALLS

BY THE START OF 1940 JOAN was already knee-deep into the screenplay for Hitchcock's next project, *Personal History*, which would ultimately become *Foreign Correspondent*. Producer Walter Wanger had arranged to borrow the director's services to turn a B-grade story about a wartime reporter into a lavish action picture. This mean that Joan too was on loan-out from Selznick, commissioned to come up with a timely tale that would speak to contemporaneous political events. Wanger liked his films to make statements, and he encouraged the team to push American audiences to rethink their country's neutral stance toward the war.

In early fall 1939 Wanger had paid the Hitchcock triumvirate to begin brainstorming, including a sum of $2,300 that went to Alma. By November 20, however, Joan and Hitch were on their own, having completed a twenty-five-page script for *Personal History* "based on an original story, suggested by Vincent Sheean's book of the same name." They had scrapped the source material, encouraged by Wanger, who had tried unsuccessfully for five years to adapt the novel.

A *Los Angeles Times* article conveyed the early stages of development the following way:

> When the producer Walter Wanger employed Hitchcock to direct *Foreign Correspondent*, Hitch said: "Don't tell us the story—just the general idea and the principal characters." Wanger complied. Hitch recalls: "We—Miss Joan Harrison and I—decided at once

we would have terrible people and events menace this American newspaperman—worse than any gangster practices at home. Where would we start the story? We closed our eyes and let our minds travel: Italy, France, Belgium, Holland.

The initial treatment showed that their minds had wandered sufficiently to arrive at the basic premise, spelled on a title card as a written foreword:

This is the story of a young American newspaperman who goes to Europe with certain ideas about what is right and what is wrong. In his opinion, Europe in the year 1939 has only itself to blame for its political trouble and the rapidly approaching war crisis. He learns, however, through bitter experience, that European life is more complex than he had imagined. . . . He learns, too, that an enemy may not always adopt an expected guise.

A surrogate for American audiences, the main character was to undergo a wartime conversion. In Joan and Hitch's formulation, a crime reporter is plucked off his beat by his boss, who expects that he will outperform even the best foreign war correspondents. After all, says the editor, the war is the worst crime imaginable. The finished film puts a fine point on his moral and political transformation, in journalistic language that Harrison surely reveled in.

By the time it reached the screen, *Foreign Correspondent* featured Joel McCrea as American reporter Johnny Jones, who travels to London masquerading as foreign correspondent Huntley Haverstock in order to interview a Dutch diplomat named Van Meer. Jones soon meets Stephen Fisher (Herbert Marshall), an organizer for the pacifist movement, and his pro-peace daughter, Carol (Laraine Day), for whom he falls head over heels. When Van Meer is assassinated (or so it appears), Jones joins Carol and another correspondent, Scott ffolliott (George Sanders), to track down the Nazis who are out to sabotage the peace process. In the course of this, Jones realizes that Carol's father is actually a Nazi and that Van Meer—the real Van Meer—is still very much alive and being held captive, and sets out with ffolliott to free him. Jones and ffolliott eventually wind up aboard an airliner (a monoplane flying boat) bound for America, with war having been declared between England and Germany. Fisher and Carol are on the same flight. After the aircraft is shot down by

German antiaircraft fire, everyone struggles to stay afloat in the ocean until an American ship comes to their rescue. Carol's father, confronting the certain prospect of arrest, sacrifices his life for the other passengers.

One notable feature of *Foreign Correspondent*'s screenplay is the figure of Carol, who serves primarily to accelerate the reporter's moral awakening. Fully committed to the peace cause, she stands in marked contrast to both Jones (who boasts "unoriginal" opinions) and her father (a political villain). A series of humorous reversals are written into their early encounters, which depend on the reporter being confounded by the daughter's "exceeding brilliance" and high stature. In other words, even at this stage, the script was structured by the narrative "surprise of the woman," someone who could be counted on to produce unexpected wit and strategy. This is Joan's handiwork, early traces of an imprint that would soon show more forcefully. Though Laraine Day's performance is somewhat lacking, *Foreign Correspondent* provides the female character with complex dimensions, including her own moment of moral insight as she struggles for her life on the crowded lifeboat after the plane crash and suddenly, according to the screenplay, "becomes convinced of the real truth about her father."

Joan had already committed much of the film's architecture and many of its scenes to paper in rough form when Charles Bennett came on board in January 1940. For approximately six to eight weeks, Bennett worked with Joan and Hitchcock in intense sessions to fill in the missing elements. After Bennett, James Hilton—author of the novels *Lost Horizon* and *Goodbye, Mr. Chips* and a scripter of the Greta Garbo classic *Camille* (1936)—followed. Robert Benchley was also conscripted, as a dialogue specialist. All told, fourteen writers worked on the screenplay. A central challenge was the need for up-to-the-minute rewrites; the hope was to make the most politically current film possible. The shooting script was submitted on June 5, 1940.

Not surprisingly, *Foreign Correspondent* became part of a larger cultural debate about credits—who deserved them and how they were parceled out. Film critics in the *New York Times* wrangled over whether directors or writers made more of an impact on a film, which generated further discussion on scripts involving multiple authors. In "Credit—Where is it Due?" Bosley Crowther pointed specifically to Harrison and her collaborators as the central illustration, hazarding random guesses at what the five credited writers may have contributed before concluding, "Frankly, we don't know." The *New York Times* settled the question by determining the pursuit of an answer to be futile.

The truth is that Joan's primary function on *Foreign Correspondent* is easy to pinpoint: she was there to maintain continuity of vision and voice. This was essential precisely because of the number of writers assigned to the project, rotating in and out in quick procession. Joan was the only writer on the project from beginning to finish. This was one aspect of the creative producing role that was now clearly defined. As the crucial figure entrusted with Hitchcock's "peculiar system" of script development, Joan's job was to keep the big picture in sight, and oversee film preparation.

Joan had inherited more and more of the workflow by now, increasingly assuming more of the responsibilities that had once been Alma's domain. Though Alma continued to play an important role, especially at a project's start and finish (or when a project proved particularly difficult), Joan was now on equal creative footing with her. This new reality complicated the Hitchcocks' working lives. They were a devoted couple; the director respected his wife's opinion. (Alma was his "Rock of Gibraltar," as biographer Patrick McGilligan puts it). But Harrison had become less a helper than an official "work wife," to use a phrase of the period. She was also their constant traveling companion and de facto family member. What would this mean for Alma?

Alma had been tending to the business of relocating their household from one country to another, including making all the necessary arrangements for travel, furniture shipments, rentals, and a school transfer for Pat. She had then devoted time to getting acquainted with her new surroundings, caring for Pat (happily adjusted to school), and preparing gourmet meals (after the cook they brought along departed to become a chiropractor). The Hitchcocks purchased their home in Bel Air and then a Northern California getaway, which drew her toward interior decorating and gardening—activities she loved. Still, Alma was very much involved in her husband's career. Joan Fontaine remembers her being on the set of *Rebecca* every day. Harrison, Reville, and Hitchcock "were a triumvirate, always conferring," according to Fontaine. Alma's approach was to be there as Hitchcock needed her. But the truth was, with Joan by his side, he relied less and less on Alma.

If Alma nursed growing apprehension about her husband's relationship with his chief collaborator, she kept it mostly to herself. Some associates, though, detected at least a hint of misgiving. When Bernard Herrmann met Alma for the first time (a decade later, in the 1950s), he spotted trouble, saying, "That woman is consumed with jealousy."

Not only was Joan as lovely—and unattainable—as ever, but she took center stage, especially where Hitchcock was concerned. At public events, Hitchcock would stand close to Joan as if he were escorting a movie star, shunting his wife to the margins. When they went to dinner, he preferred to sit next to Joan, leaving Alma off to the side—on the other side of Joan, that is. There are enough candid photos from the late 1930s and early 1940s that repeatedly capture this arrangement that it appears to have been the norm. As a director whose films obsessed over reconstituted families, could Hitchcock have been unaware of the manner in which he was presenting his own family and what this implied about his own desires?

There are no sources to support a claim that Joan and Hitchcock ever entertained a physical relationship, though Charles Bennett did make a veiled allusion to an affair in his memoir, published posthumously in 2014. "I believe Hitch's married life was a happy one—until a second woman became a disruptive part of it," wrote Bennett. "She was a lady whose for-a-while sensational film career was built on nothing but Hitchcock's sexual interest in her. . . . It's a revelation that could sell books like hotcakes, but none of us wants to be sued." Though he mentions no one by name, and the "sensational film career" could have belonged to an actress, the snippiness of Bennett's prose suggests he is writing about a fellow screenwriter, one whose talents he was known to dismiss.

When Peggy Robertson took up the role of Hitchcock's right hand a decade after Joan, she reportedly asked Hitchcock if Joan's rise had begun on his couch. According to Hitchcock biographer John Russell Taylor, the exchange went something like this: "Hitchcock responded, 'I can say with complete conviction that I was never between the sheets with Joan.' 'Well, that's not saying much,' said Peggy. 'What about on the hearth-rug, in the haystack, over the kitchen table?' Hitch gave a convincing look of horror. 'Do people really do things like that?'"

If there were suspicions about Joan and Hitchcock, they were undoubtedly fueled by how easy it was, for some observers, to disregard or at least underestimate Alma because she was self-effacing. "Alma was so petite," Joan Fontaine remarked, "it was possible if you looked quickly, to overlook her. She was quiet as a mouse." At the same time, Alma was alluring and possessed a secret flair.

As a young woman, she had cross-dressed to scandalous effect, and to work she had worn men's suits tailor made for her at Austin Reed. Screenwriter Whitfield Cook observed, "Alma was very short but very attractive, and part of her attraction came through her intelligence and her warmth."

What's more, she was the first romantic relationship, and possibly the only consummated sexual partnership, Hitchcock had ever known. He had been confined to a rather stifling Victorian existence of separate spheres, psychologically speaking, before their work and travels together opened up his world. Reflecting on initially encountering her at Famous Players–Lasky British Producers, he explained, "Alma was different than any girl I'd ever met. Until then, I never understood what women wanted. I only knew it wasn't me."

Alma was stronger and shrewder than most people gave her credit for, according to Norman Lloyd, who viewed the dynamic among the three for several decades. There were things that Alma understood about Hitchcock better than he understood about himself, and she knew that to be productive creatively, he fed on an active fantasy life. "If it ever appeared that Joan and Hitchcock were closer than they should have been, such as at public events, you have to realize, that was Alma's staging," Lloyd said. "She knew exactly what she was doing, and didn't mind Joan being at the center." Alma seemingly allowed a certain amount of room for the mentoring relationship between Joan and Hitch to play out so as to give Hitchcock's desires free rein inside his head.

All of which is to say that while the evidence would suggest that Hitch and Joan's relationship never ventured into the physical realm, it was not an uncomplicated—or tension-free—arrangement. It was, in fact, more complex than most.

Only Alma knows the degree to which she may have been bothered when Joan traveled alone with Hitchcock to England in late June 1940, just after Joan's thirty-third birthday. They stopped first in New York to sign contracts for two films with RKO. Though a major studio since its inception in the early stage of talkies, RKO had experienced continual turnover in leadership and ever-shifting governing policies. Individual movies and filmmakers occasionally thrived, but, unlike its competitors, RKO had not developed an overarching personality or house style. Successes like *King Kong* (1933), *Swing Time* (1936), and *Bringing Up Baby* (1937) made noise at the box office, but the studio could never seem to build any momentum. Under newly appointed president George Schaefer, RKO was narrowing its focus to prestige pictures, helmed by ambitious talents such as Hitchcock.

His two films for RKO were *Mr. and Mrs. Smith*, a romantic comedy from which Joan would soon beg off, and *Before the Fact*, the Francis Iles novel adaptation that would become *Suspicion*. Both features were loan-outs from Selznick, for which everyone was grateful—especially Selznick, who earned more than double the director's salary on the deal.

Next, Joan and Hitchcock went to Ottawa. After a series of frustrating delays, they caught a Canadian merchant ship in convoy to England. The war had brought them there—or, rather, the newly formed British Ministry of Information and its film adviser, Sidney Bernstein, had. Having resigned as chair of Granada Theatres to serve the British war effort, Bernstein hoped that Hitchcock would also heed the call to service. The director needed little coaxing. In fact, he'd already joined a small group of British expatriates in Hollywood that included Cedric Hardwicke, Victor Saville, and Herbert Wilcox who were helping to hatch the propaganda anthology series *Forever and a Day*. These artists were as organized as any political faction, having been agitating against isolationism for more than two years. Hitchcock informed Bernstein of his plans to direct an installment of *Forever and a Day* and pledged to produce additional war propaganda.

During this trip, Joan visited the Grove with Hitch in tow, bearing gifts and goods for Millie and Walter. The Harrisons toasted their guests with warm champagne, which Hitchcock found irksome. The reunion was bittersweet. Walter's health was failing, having deteriorated over the past several years. This would end up being the last time Joan would see her father; he would die in November 1942 before she could manage safe passage back.

It was a grim time to be in London, as men practiced their drills for the Battle of Britain and women and children evacuated the city. (Winston Churchill had just made his "We Shall Fight on the Beaches" speech to the House of Commons several weeks prior.) As Joan and Hitchcock left on July 3, a week before the German bombs began to fall, they committed to doing all they could for the sake of the war effort. On their layover in Ottawa, they made the necessary arrangements to expedite the evacuation of sixty children from the London-based British Actors Orphanage to America, cutting through red tape with the Canadian government.

Once back in Los Angeles, they determined that it was imperative to find a more resonant closing scene for *Foreign Correspondent*. By this point, the film was already in the can, having gone over budget and past schedule. Yet no one was satisfied with its conclusion, which had Jones, Carol, and ffolliott being rescued from the plane crash but then jokingly wondering if the Germans had staged the incident to pull the US into war. The decision was made to bring in Ben Hecht (writer number fourteen), who, overnight, turned out a new final speech for Jones, a rousing radio address broadcast live to the US from London as bombs fall all around. "Hello America, hang on to your lights! They're the only lights left in the world," he urges as the power goes out in London. Darkness envelops Jones and Carol.

Jones's monologue gave the Hitchcock team the precise beacon they had been looking for—a frantic, swirling mix of caution and urgency they hoped would stir America from its isolationist slumber. The film answered the open criticisms from British colleagues, who resented the Hitchcocks for "abandoning" the country during wartime (though many would continue to hold this against Hitchcock and his collaborators for years to come). And it provided Wanger with the message movie he'd long sought. Upon its release, the producer named *Foreign Correspondent* as the film of which he was proudest.

In its final iteration, *Foreign Correspondent* told American audiences a story they needed to hear ("This is a big story, and you're a part of it")— a story many of them *wanted* to hear, judging by the film's box office success. In its first four months, it grossed $1.8 million. Deemed by *Time* magazine "easily one of the year's finest pictures," it went on to earn nominations for six Academy Awards, including Best Picture. As with *Rebecca*, Joan was nominated (with the other credited screenwriter, Charles Bennett) for an Oscar for Best Screenplay.

Foreign Correspondent and *Rebecca* were both released in 1940. This was the first year that the Academy divided the screenplay awards into two categories: Best Original Screenplay and Best Adapted Screenplay, which meant that Harrison had a script nominated in each one. On Thursday evening, February 27, 1941, at the Biltmore Bowl of the Los Angeles Biltmore Hotel, Joan was basking in the glow of her success. She had written two films that had garnered seventeen nominations between them. A newsreel camera panning across the Selznick table captured a luminous Joan, holding a cigarette in her white-gloved hand and throwing her head back in a carefree laugh. No matter that Best Original Screenplay went to *The Great McGinty*, or Best Adapted Screenplay to *The Philadelphia Story*. Or that Hitch went home without winning Best Direction for *Rebecca*, having lost out to John Ford for *The Grapes of Wrath*. She was now a two-time Oscar nominee (the first screenwriter to be nominated twice in the same year), and she had made a name for herself in the industry. And, to cap off the evening, the epic suspense story that she had considered "hers"—*Rebecca*—walked off with the award for Best Picture.

It wasn't only Joan's professional horizons that were expanding. By this time, her intellectual and social circle had moved beyond the Hitchcocks. She was well known in the European émigré community. She gravitated to the transplants she knew from Gaumont-British, most of whom were now heavily active in grassroots antifascist campaigns or loosely formed organizations such as the European Film Fund and the Hollywood Anti-Nazi League. This meant that she spent much of her spare time immersed in the political and creative conversations of European expatriate writers and actors and their friends who had spent the 1930s warning about the rise of Adolf Hitler in Germany and Benito Mussolini in Italy and trying to unionize the Hollywood studios.

Her weekends and evenings included cocktail parties and dinners with Fred Zinnemann, Billy Wilder, Robert and Curt Siodmak, William Dieterle, Fritz Lang, Ernst Lubitsch, Walter and John Huston, Franz Waxman, Claude Rains, and Marlene Dietrich. Parties and politics flowed together; everyone organized activities around an early-evening clock, making sure guests arrived safely home—in advance of wartime Los Angeles' eight o'clock curfew for Central Europeans, who were seen as threatening "alien immigrants." Money was donated to organizations dedicated to rescuing political refugees.

Soon, Joan's closest friends were two couples: Lewis Milestone and his wife, actress Kendall Lee Glaenzer, and Paul Henreid and his wife, Lisl (previously, a fashion designer). The Moldavian-born, Jewish Milestone ("Milly") had already accrued a long list of credits, including *Two Arabian Nights* (1927) and *All Quiet on the Western Front* (1930), which won him Oscars, and *The Front Page* (1930), which earned him a nomination. His rugged, temperamental personality made for an oddball pairing with Glaenzer, who came from Virginia society and was celebrated the town over for her skills at entertaining. (At Glaenzer's wake, the couple's butler would come to pay his respects; upon raising a glass, his only words were "She gave the best parties." Her husband took this as the highest of all compliments, coming from the butler.)

Joan met the Henreids soon after they emigrated. Paul Henreid, an Austrian-born actor who distinguished himself in the German theater, had fled to England to escape the Nazis, only to be blacklisted by the British as a possible collaborator. This made America his last resort. The actor was on the cusp of a double breakthrough with *Casablanca* (1942) and *Now, Voyager* (1942). According to Monika Henreid, Paul and Lisl's eldest daughter, her parents' home felt like a "Viennese island" in the middle of Brentwood. "Joanie was around the house all the time," remembers Monika, who was Joan's goddaughter. "She was a terrific storyteller. My parents loved good conversation."

There is little mystery to Joan's attraction to the European émigrés, and little doubt that she was moving closer to that epicenter that would soon give full rise to her special brand—war-weary noir films, gothic mysteries, and crime thrillers. The "diasporados," as screenwriter Curt Siodmak described them, offered her an intellectual home—a space to share her love of literature, music, art, language, and ideas. Norman Lloyd, who remembers Joan from that circle in the early 1940s, recollects the mesmerizing conversations with Bertolt Brecht, Thomas Mann, Hanns Eisler, Igor Stravinsky, and Arnold Schoenberg: "I rarely spoke, I mainly listened. It was breathtaking," he muses. Such dramatic philosophical and political displays would have riveted Joan more than any Hollywood movie.

Salka Viertel's Sunday afternoon salons afforded the most regular opportunities for such reverie. Salka was an actress and screenwriter, and her husband, Berthold, was a screenwriter and director. They had come to Los Angeles from Austria in the late 1920s, when Berthold was offered a long-term contract with Fox, and decided to make the United States their home after the political situation in Europe deteriorated. (Berthold Viertel continued to travel to Europe for work, as when he directed the British *The Passing of the Third Floor Back*, cowritten by Alma, in 1935.)

Salka, whose Hollywood work included scripts for her friend Greta Garbo's *Queen Christina* and *Anna Karenina*, became a popular hostess among the European expats. She served up soup and *Sachertorte* (a Viennese chocolate cake) most weeks at her Santa Monica beach house on Mabery Road. The Viertel home was a refuge where recently arrived Europeans and famous movie stars mingled as if they were literati gathering at a roundtable in a prewar Berlin café. At any given moment, Joan might encounter enthralling talks between Thomas Mann and Charlie Chaplin, or Bertolt Brecht and Billy Wilder, or Stravinsky and Hedy Lamarr. Lloyd says, "I remember Joan being there, taking it all in. Joan and I never talked politics, but I knew where she stood." Years later, when a conservative backlash in the country resulted in left-leaning writers, actors, and directors being blacklisted, Lloyd would watch as Joan came to the rescue of many from Salka's circle, including him, by hiring them when she had the chance.

In gatherings such as the Sunday salons, Joan preferred to listen. Chris Coppel, who came to know Joan after she befriended his parents, Alec and Myra Coppel, describes her approach to parties and dinners: "Joan would think before she spoke. She didn't like to talk just for the sake of talking. She was a quieter voice in a crowd." Still, she made a lasting impression. At Salka's, she was forming friendships and alliances that would help propel her solo career, most importantly with Andre de Toth, Zinnemann, Huston, and the Siodmak brothers.

Joan was also gaining an increased sense of urgency when it came to the war effort. Her return trip to England in the summer of 1940 likely signaled her own growing commitment to anti-isolationist propaganda efforts—and to Sidney Bernstein's cause—as it did Hitchcock's. Given how grueling travel on the mostly male convoy trip would have been under those conditions, Joan's reasons for making the trek must have gone beyond seeing her family. It was time to take action, even if that simply meant supporting Hitchcock's endeavors.

Joan's Hollywood life was full. When she could take a respite from her seventy-hour work week, she spent Saturday mornings playing tennis at the Beverly Hills Tennis Club—Charlie Chaplin was a favorite mixed doubles partner because, as she was fond of joking, "he liked to win"—followed by a gin martini to cool down. After lunch, she headed to the center of Beverly Hills for her weekly manicure and hairdresser's appointment. Saturday evenings took her to Ciro's, Café Trocadero, or the Mocambo. On Sunday afternoons, when she wasn't with the Hitchcocks working on a script, she would spend time at Salka's or another soiree.

Joan was in the middle of it, where the action was. Her romantic life, too, was in full swing. Some of her beaus were little more than chaperones, such as the dates she had with RKO publicity agent Danny Winkler in the spring of 1941. (Winkler's marriage with serial star Jean Rogers was temporarily on the rocks; meanwhile, he was trying to steer Joan toward an RKO contract.) Other relationships were rumored to be more serious, such as with Billy Wilder. "Proximity brought forth romance" between Wilder and Harrison, according to Norman Lloyd. "Billy moved around a lot in this regard, until he married Judith [Iribe]," he acknowledges, "and then after he got married, he moved around a lot." Judith, who shared many of Joan's qualities—she was cultured, glamorous, and fluent in French—was aware of the "rumors of affairs with actresses and screenwriters" but looked the other way. (Wilder and Iribe divorced in 1947.) With Wilder, Harrison would have known the arrangement was a temporary stop and not a love that ran "straight down the line." She entertained few feelings of sexual guilt in general, and kept herself grounded when it came to extramarital affairs. She felt that "if you loved someone or had strong feelings for them, then it's okay to sleep with them."

When a platonic friendship came along, Joan also welcomed it. Joan had met Franchot Tone when they were Wilshire Palms neighbors and he was waiting for his divorce from Joan Crawford to finalize. Born in Niagara Falls to an affluent industrialist family, the stage-trained actor had racked up a string of successes in the 1930s, including *Love on the Run* (1936), *The Bride Wore Red* (1937), with his then wife, and his Oscar-nominated performance in *Mutiny on the Bounty* (1935). An "idea man" going back to his days with the New York–based, progressive Group Theatre collective, Tone was a glutton for good conversation.

Franchot had a high regard for women who were independent and successful, qualities he admired in his mother, Gertrude Franchot Tone, who had led the suffragist movement in Niagara Falls, a cradle of early nineteenth-century feminism. "He would have picked up on these attributes in Joan; it doesn't surprise me that they would have been good friends," says Franchot's son Pat. He was a loyal supporter, plus she appreciated men who turned themselves out in a stylish yet relaxed way. "He felt as comfortable wearing 'white tie and tails' as jeans and a sweater," according to Pat. The two got on well, laying the groundwork for a personal and professional friendship that lasted for decades.

In summer 1940 an idea had been hatched for a weekly radio anthology series that would further extend the Hitchcock brand (though no one called it that then). Team "Hitchy and Joanie" would work with radio producers to pitch a program called *Suspense*. With Hitchcock as the host, big-name stars would populate the dramatic mysteries. At the time, radio producer Joe Graham was fielding interest from CBS, though NBC threw its hat in for consideration. Myron Selznick saw the financial benefits, as did Walter Wanger, who was hoping for a long-term relationship with the director. It would be a way to increase Hitchcock's value as a property, and spotlight whatever film he had on the way.

Hitchcock saw the weekly production schedule as viable, since his role would be limited to a one-hour story conference per week, one hour of rehearsal, and the evening broadcast. The person to fill in the gaps—to operate as a go-between among the director, the writers, and the network—would be Joan. He noted that she would be paid out of his $1,000 weekly salary, with the implication that she was running his side of things. This was a rare concession.

Hitchcock's series was not meant to be. David O. Selznick blocked his brother and the Hitchcock team from moving forward with the idea, fearing that it would be a financial and creative drain on his prized asset. *Suspense* eventually took to the radio airwaves without Hitchcock in 1942.

But the idea of an anthology series—and how to run it—would stay with Hitchcock and Joan.

For the moment, however, Joan's attention would turn to the script that lay in front of her: *Suspicion*, which had all the makings of a stunning follow-up to *Foreign Correspondent*. At least it seemed that way at the time.

10 | BUILDING SUSPENSE

JOAN'S NEXT PROJECT looked to be a pleasant and straightforward assignment, but *Suspicion* would prove deceptive. Published in 1932, *Before the Fact: A Murder Story for Ladies* was a celebrated British novel written by Francis Iles (a pen name for Anthony Berkeley Cox). It was a tale the Hitchcock team had sought to make since their Gaumont-British days: an unsuspecting wife becomes an amateur detective in her own murder as her cheating cad of a husband slowly does away with her. Like *Young and Innocent*, *The Lady Vanishes*, *Jamaica Inn*, and *Rebecca*, the book played to Joan's literary instincts. RKO had considered it for its B-roster but kept it on the back shelf. The Hitchcock team pitched the studio what would become *Suspicion*: a glossy, gothic A-picture told "through the eyes of the woman," though less tragic than the novel, because the husband would "be the villain in her imagination only."

With enthusiastic support from new RKO exec Danny Winkler, all the ingredients for a star-studded, romantic mystery were lining up. Hitchcock's terms with RKO gave him relative autonomy, free from Selznick's purview. They settled on a robust $550,000 budget. RKO secured Joan Fontaine from Selznick for the lead role, which was a coup. Coming off a string of RKO hits, the suave box office prince Cary Grant agreed to play the husband.

This time Joan would write the initial treatment solo. She commenced work in August, just after postproduction on *Foreign Correspondent* concluded. She submitted the outline in late October and celebrated the occasion by attending with the Hitchcocks the grand opening of the "world's largest dining and dancing palace," the Hollywood Palladium, on Halloween eve. Tommy Dorsey and his orchestra played. The band's "boy singer" and rising talent, Frank Sinatra, serenaded an estimated crowd of ten thousand.

Next, Joan and Alma teamed up to produce the full screenplay. After two pictures that had employed roughly twenty writers in total, a pared-down family affair would be a welcome relief. RKO had granted the women permission to work off premises, so Joan and Alma spent their days hashing out initial drafts, in comfortable conversation, while seated on the Hitchcock family sofa.

In a nationally syndicated article, Joan and Alma's collaboration was highlighted as the only female screenwriting partnership in Hollywood (not true, but it made for good copy), and as a cozy domestic arrangement that thrived. "Arguments?" said Alma. "Of course. But no bad feeling. I'd just as soon work with a woman as a man, just so long as she's good." Hitchcock was tied up most days prepping and shooting the romantic comedy *Mr. and Mrs. Smith* (1941), starring Lombard and Robert Montgomery. When possible, he joined Alma and Joan in the mornings for story sessions, leaving them to produce pages in the afternoon. Occasionally he treated them to a working lunch at Romanoff's.

By November's end, Joan and Alma were ready to bring in fine-tuner Samson Raphaelson. A born-and-bred New Yorker, Raphaelson had worked in advertising, journalism, and theater before turning out impressive screenplays for Ernst Lubitsch and others. He was amiable and focused on the job. RKO flew him in from the East Coast and housed him at the Riviera Country Club, from which he ground out pages and messengered them over to St. Cloud Road by limousine each day.

Raphaelson remembered his writing stint in Los Angeles as rather bleary-eyed. "I drank more than I ever drank in my life," he recalled. "[Hitchcock] was drinking a lot then. He was very fat. I would come to his home in Bel Air, he would be behind the bar, shaking orange juice and gin, and he'd say, 'Have a drink, Rafe. Got it with you?' I'd put some pages of script down and while I was having the drink, he would lean over the edge of the bar and turn the pages." This nontraditional approach doesn't appear to have hindered the work. "That story broke more easily than anything I have ever written," Raphaelson claimed. He had lots of ideas of his own that didn't necessarily agree with the women's approach, and Hitchcock gave him room to try them out, only drawing in the reins where he felt censors or studio executives might intervene.

In Iles's novel, Lina McLaidlaw, a wealthy woman with few prospects for marriage (nearly thirty, she is already a "spinster"), falls in love with and marries the charmer Johnnie Aysgarth. She soon realizes her husband is a philanderer and a thief, scheming to kill her for the insurance payout. *Before the Fact* takes an experimental approach, deviating from most domestic gothic tales by signaling to the reader that Johnnie is a murderer within the first paragraph. The novel states, "Some women give birth to murderers, some go to bed with them, and some marry them. Lina Aysgarth had lived with her husband for nearly eight years before she realized that she was married to a murderer." The governing mystery posed by the book is, Who will be Johnnie's victim (or victims) and what are his motivations?

The book's unconventional narration—which keeps the reader grounded almost entirely in Lina's perspective—is made even more subversive by the ending, in which the reader is allowed to eavesdrop on Lina's dying thought. "It did seem a pity that she had to die, when she would have liked so much to live," Iles writes in a haunting passage after Lina drinks a glass of poisoned milk administered by Johnnie. The book reads like a prolonged suicide note in prose form, film critic Bill Krohn astutely points out.

Given Joan's interest in the "woman's angle," *Before the Fact* was an ideal property. The book's entire emotional architecture was structured to bring readers into the mind of a woman who is so passive that she willingly accepts her own annihilation rather than question her husband. Why does she embrace her position as victim so easily, humbly, lovingly? As Lina dips into a mystery penned by her neighbor, acclaimed writer Isobel Sedbusk, she delves into her own psyche. Iles writes, "Analyzing her subject, the authoress had suggested that just as there are born murderers, so there are born victims . . . persons who, even as they see murder bearing down on them, are incapable of moving out of its way. Lina laid the book down on her lap, and stared into vacancy. Was she a murderee?" Part of the impact of Iles's tale, as Patrick Faubert observes, is that the wife plays both accomplice and "unwitting detective" in her own murder.

A Hollywood movie would need to approach this a little differently, of course. Between Hitchcock's desire to lighten the material through a final twist that questions the heroine's mind and RKO's concerns over having their leading romantic comedian cast as a murderer, the script called for a new ending. This required a delicate dance on the part of the writers. Even if Johnnie was redeemed or proved guiltless in the end, he would look guilty through the bulk of the movie, which meant that Grant would too. Would audiences embrace him in such a role? Grant's magnetic, seductive personality and box office power gave him top billing, but in truth he would take second place to Fontaine's psychological neurosis. According to Fontaine, this became apparent to Grant halfway through filming, which began in February 1941: "The only mistake he made on *Suspicion* was not realizing that the part of Lina was the major role. It was through her eyes that the story unfolded. She had all the sympathies. He was the villain."

Actually, it didn't become clear to anyone—writers, producers, or director—how the plot would progress until after principal photography had wrapped. Fundamental questions typically decided in the script stage had not been resolved: Whose story is this (Lina's or Johnnie's)? Will the protagonist die at the end? Is the husband a murderer?

Joan and Alma continued to turn out revisions through February and March, consulting occasionally with Raphaelson long distance. They picked up the pace in April, working frantically through June. The central dilemma was how to end the story. Though they were concerned about Joseph Breen's office, of course, it was the heads at RKO who were foremost in mind. President George Schaefer and producer Harry Edington, acting as self-censors in antic- ipation of the PCA, feared the novel's plot bends of adultery, pregnancy, suicide, and unpunished murder. Every narrative solution created a new problem; every twist led the writers down a new turn.

By May, Joan and Alma were toying with two potential endings. In the first, Johnnie grasps that he is a murderer in Lina's eyes after noticing her odd reaction to the milk. (She believes the milk to be poisoned and drinks it while eyeing him, strangely.) He responds to this realization by running off to join the armed forces, in a bid to redeem himself in her eyes. There is an implicit happy ending as Lina watches him board a bomber headed to Berlin on a heroic mission. The second version concludes in the couple's bedroom. Once Johnnie deduces that his wife believes he is about to poison her with a concoc- tion suggested by their neighbor, the mystery-writer Isobel, he drinks it down himself, confesses his caddish behavior, and collapses into Lina's embrace. Lina quickly calls Isobel, who reveals that there is no poison; it had all been a ruse to enable the couple to work out their problems.

By mid-May, Hitchcock had filmed both these endings, along with an additional scene that offered a third emotionally downbeat conclusion: while in Lina's arms, Johnnie admits that he is a cad and promises to reform, but according to the script, "we know we cannot believe him." Meanwhile, at the financially beleaguered RKO, both Edington and Winkler had been fired, with *Suspicion* being cited as a production in supposed disarray. Hitchcock had little protection. In an unpredictable turn of events, RKO's president made Joseph Breen chief of production. This added to the concern surrounding the film. Still unhappy with the ending, Hitchcock conferred with Raphaelson in New York, who proposed writing an ending with some comic relief; in this iteration, the couple feeds the milk to the dog, and Lina laughs off Johnnie's bad behavior.

The director later told François Truffaut that, if given his way, he would have had Lina write a letter to her mother implicating Johnnie just before he poisons her. This way, she would have the last word, so to speak, sealing his fate by asking him to post her mail in the morning. "Fade out and fade in on one short shot: Cary Grant, whistling cheerfully, walks over to the mailbox and pops the letter in," Hitchcock remarked. The husband is punished, the censors and studio are satisfied, the novel retains some fidelity, and the film-maker gains some perverse pleasure in killing off both central characters. The "letter-in-the-mail" ending was never a real possibility. Though he lured Grant to the project with the delicious prospect and may have continued to tease the actor with its promise, RKO never wavered on this point. Like many of Hitchcock's impulses, however, it hovered in his mind, as suggested by the film's many references to letters, stamps, and mail.

By mid-June, any hopes that *Suspicion* would soon be completed were fading fast. RKO conducted two sneak previews of the version featuring the "bedroom confession" scene, one in Pasadena and one in Inglewood. Audience reaction varied, but clearly the movie wasn't working. There were comments that the tone shifted too abruptly, the picture didn't suit Cary Grant, and the genre wasn't clear: Was this supposed to be a thriller, a romance, or a comedy? The Hitchcock team didn't need audience response cards to tell them the picture had problems. They had already requested more time to sort through the tangle of scenes and try to fix the film in postproduction.

Joan and Alma experimented with more script variations on the West Coast, while Hitch and Raphaelson did the same in New York. (Hitchcock was doing a radio appearance while Raphaelson's wife, actress Dorothy Wegman, was tied up in summer stock, keeping him anchored in the East.) Suddenly, Hitchcock was notified that producer Sol Lesser, Breen's second-in-command, had cut the film himself, eliminating all potentially offensive material. Lesser's version was fifty-five minutes. On July 2, the director rushed back to RKO to stem the bleeding.

Raphaelson remembers receiving a phone call a little later in which Hitchcock announced, "Joanie and I have written a new ending." In this version, the film fades out after Johnnie deposits the milk in question at Lina's bedside, gives her a slow kiss, and says, "Good night, Lina." As he leaves the room, the camera tracks forward to a close-up on her face, panning left to the milk. Will she drink it? Fade to black. Fade up. It is the next morning and the glass of milk remains untouched. Packing her suitcase, Lina has decided to visit her mother. She is hastily taking leave of a confused Johnnie, who insists on driving her there. During the trip, her car door opens and it seems as though Johnnie is trying to push her out, down a rocky cliff. They pull over to calm down and during their conversation, he reveals that he had asked Isobel about the poison because, owing to her suspicions about him, he had planned to kill himself. Lina realizes she has been blind to his love. As he starts the car, their future is uncertain. From a bird's eye view, we watch the car make a U-turn, heading for home.

This conclusion relieved the script of many of its thorns, smoothing over the adultery, pregnancy, and murder—and to a degree, even the suicide. It allowed both characters to live and offered them the possibility, however ambiguous, of a future together. Given that any narrative strategy would leave the audience dissatisfied—as the preview response cards had shown—this seemed like the least worst choice.

The new path out of the film that Joan helped carve was achieved by rearranging two existing sequences and writing and shooting several new scenes. Inspiration came in part from a previously filmed dramatic beat in which Johnnie's reckless driving frightens Lina. In order to reconfigure this into a climactic confrontation, a "suitcase packing" scene was needed. Because Fontaine was not available, a double took her place (which is why Lina has her back to the camera as she packs to go to her mother's).

Once the basic approach emerged, the nuts and bolts of assembly still needed attention. Alma's expertise as a cutter likely paid off here. It's logical that Reville would have been involved in the editing of *Suspicion*, especially its last ten minutes. She offered her practical expertise during troubled times, and this would certainly have qualified. Krohn postulates, "You could not take the film we have and simply switch last scenes. . . . [The] 'editing trick' required extensive re-shooting of the wild ride and what goes before and after it."

Joan, Alma, and Hitchcock had put their heads and hands together to pull off an ending. Joan, meanwhile, had gotten a crash course in how to "write" and "rewrite" a film through the editing process. *Suspicion* was Joan and Alma's most in-depth collaboration. Did the pair of women recognize the irony that they were collaborating—and apparently without much friction—on the story of a suspicious wife contemplating "the series of pictures that composed her married life" and the ambivalent, fatal places that a marriage can go? As gothic femme tales go, this was as bleak as a Joseph Conrad novel. The pair had plumbed its depths together over tea on Alma's sofa.

Even with all its headaches, upon its release in mid-November 1941, *Suspicion* performed well at the box office. And while some reviewers grumbled at its flaws, the film generally received high marks. The *New York Herald Telegram* declared it "a far finer film than *Rebecca*." In the *New York Times*, Bosley Crowther called it "a tense and exciting tale, a psychological thriller which is packed with lively suspense." *PM* deemed it "a cinema masterpiece," and *Harrington's Reports* said, "The closing scenes . . . are so tensely exciting that one is left trembling at the conclusion." *Suspicion* was nominated for three Academy Awards, including Best Picture. Joan Fontaine won in the Best Actress category.

But Harrison's most significant contributions to the film have gone largely unacknowledged. Not only did she deepen *Suspicion*'s thematic tensions, but she also contributed the lesbian subtext between Isobel and her friend Phyllis Swinghurst (Nondas Metcalf). When Joan turned in her initial treatment in late October, it contained the new character of Phyllis, who didn't exist in the novel. Isobel and Phyllis, who appear together in two scenes (the foxhunt and the dinner party), were presented as a butch-femme couple through implicit subcultural codes recognizable at the time. At Isobel's house, her brother, the coroner Bertram Sedbusk (Gavin Gordon), Johnnie, Lina, Phyllis, and she gather around the dinner table. The script notes that Phyllis wears a "mannish suit," which Johnnie obviously perceives as keeping with her overall lesbian appearance. For example, as murder plots are discussed, Johnnie says, "It's too complicated, old boy."

Phyllis reacts, "Don't call me old boy."

He replies, "All right, then . . . young fellow."

Joseph Breen bristled at this scene upon reading the first submitted script to the PCA, stating, "This certainly seems suggestive of lesbianism and hence is entirely unacceptable." He insisted that they "remove this flavor entirely," including Phyllis's masculine costuming. Breen also objected to the fact that Phyllis treated Isobel's home as her own, another hint of lesbian "flavor" in his view.

The writers removed the "old boy/young fellow" exchange but kept Phyllis's suit and tie despite Breen's objections. They also retained the following interaction from the script:

> Isobel glances around the table, then to Phyllis.
> ISOBEL: Phil—
> PHYLLIS: Yes—Issie?
> ISOBEL: Do the wine, will you?
> Phyllis rises and crosses to a side table, showing complete familiarity
> with the house. She returns and starts to pour out the claret.

Thus, in the end a compromise version of the lavender relationship made it to the screen.

But given how minor Phyllis's role is—she plays no part in the plot—what precisely was the thinking behind this back-and-forth between the filmmakers and the censors? Perhaps it was a strategic decision: Under the PCA, writers were adept at adding scenes they knew would cause rancor with the censors in the hopes that other elements would slip by unnoticed. Maybe the point was to distract Breen with the lesbian subtext in hopes that he wouldn't object to Cary Grant's character being portrayed as villainous. Or perhaps Joan wanted to make a point about the unspoken perversity of heterosexual relations and institutional marriage. After all, don't Isobel and Phyllis appear far happier than Lina and Johnnie? This latter possibility is particularly interesting in light of the implied erotic desire, often noted by critics, of Mrs. Danvers for the first Mrs. De Winter in *Rebecca* and the female homosocial or homosexual overtones that would emerge in Harrison's later films.

Whether it was the tactical smuggling of certain sexual themes past the censors or the rigorous rewrites of *Suspicion*'s ending, Joan had earned a wealth of experience in short order. She was also learning the limits of her own patience. Growing restless with the system and the impositions of studios and the PCA, she began to conceive of going in a new direction. It was a question mired in its own suspense: Who might she be if she weren't Hitchcock's right hand?

11 | HITTING HURDLES

JOAN SPENT THE FALL of 1941 working on a script about a Los Angeles munitions worker falsely accused of setting fire to the aircraft factory where he's employed, then proving his innocence by tracking down the man responsible. By mid-October, the elements for what would become *Saboteur* had come together into a very detailed 129-page treatment, which Harrison and Hitchcock submitted to David O. Selznick. The producer had involved himself in the early stages of development, participating in protracted story meetings that also included Alma. Writing *Saboteur* proved to be an intense process, even once Selznick extracted himself, with Alma staying on to bandy about scenarios and strategies under a looming deadline. A reporter who called on St. Cloud Road in November 1941 observed the Hitchcocks and Joan "rushing into different rooms with typewriters and manuscripts, taking over tables, chairs, and lounges, and at once starting to work feverishly."

In truth, it was no more racking than any of the previous films. But Joan didn't know how many more light "double chases" she could muster. Her heart wasn't in it anymore. She asked to be replaced on *Saboteur* midway through development.

For Joan, this was the first step in her break from Hitchcock. The director had to know that such a day would come—indeed, in so many ways, he had been grooming her for this moment—but now the reality of it felt grim. He went immediately to David O. Selznick and urged him to increase Joan's salary as an enticement for her to stay on. When Selznick refused, Hitchcock became irate and stormed out of his office.

Fortunately, there was someone on scene to calm the hostilities between the two men. John Houseman, best known at that time for his work with Orson Welles and the Mercury Theatre and fresh off a successful Broadway adaptation of Richard Wright's *Native Son*, had been brought in to produce films for Selznick. Houseman had been assigned to *Saboteur* and had helped find it a good home at Universal. Now Houseman exercised his fine skills in diplomacy to quell the argument.

It may have been that Houseman had a personal interest in smoothing over the office tensions. If he and Joan were not at that precise moment romantically involved, they soon would be. ("For some time, she was mine," as he put it.) John was Joan's type. Well cultivated and posh, he had great stage presence, which made him the life of the party. (Norman Lloyd remembers his booming voice.) By the time he joined Hitchcock's team, he had lived a life of adventure. Born in Romania to a French Jewish father and an English mother, he had grown up in the British education system and tried his hand in the Argentine grain trade. He had proven himself as a writer, director, and producer in theater and radio, and was then in the process of releasing the controversial *Citizen Kane* (1941). Like so many of Joan's paramours at this time, he was a political progressive, feeling restless and agitated by war in Europe and America's neutrality in the face of the nonaggression treaty between Germany and the Soviet Union. Houseman was eager to confront the spread of fascism in the world, and indeed would join the war effort and leave Los Angeles within months.

At this point, however, neither Houseman nor Selznick nor Hitchcock could prevent Harrison from striking out on her own. She felt the need to prove that she was more than Hitch's assistant. "I would have to try my own wings," she believed.

Writing duties on *Saboteur* passed to Peter Viertel, the son of Salka and Berthold, who was then a twenty-one-year-old junior writer under contract at Selznick International. Having left Dartmouth after his first term, the cultured and athletic Viertel had recently published a successful first novel, *The Canyon*, and spent most of his time playing tennis. Unlike Joan, he was not a member of the Beverly Hills Tennis Club, but he knew how to get himself invited there whenever he wanted. (Billy Wilder could always be relied upon in this regard.) Harrison and Viertel ran in the same social circles.

As for Joan, her only question at the moment was where she would land. She had been making the rounds, interviewing at studios.

Then, on Sunday, December 7, 1941, hundreds of Japanese fighter planes attacked the US naval base at Pearl Harbor. At around noon in Los Angeles, word of the air strikes began to filter in, with initial statements estimating that a hundred military personnel had been killed and several hundred more wounded. Soon, the numbers grew exponentially. For the United States, there was no turning back. On Monday, December 8, FDR delivered his "Day of Infamy" address to Congress, and the US officially entered into World War II. Studios were in a general state of anxiety, with questions about whether pay would be frozen or productions put on hold.

That same day, Joan signed a contract with Paramount Pictures. She was promised $600 per week for "an indefinite period commencing immediately to perform general writing services." This put her in the upper echelon of the pay scale. (Junior writers might hope for $50 a week.) Her first assignment was a plum one: a Charles Boyer vehicle called *Hong Kong*, supervised by Arthur Hornblow Jr. Boyer epitomized the European romantic lead and was well positioned by a string of successes, including *Love Affair* (1939), *All This, and Heaven Too* (1940), and *Hold Back the Dawn* (1941). In addition to having Boyer as the film's star, Harrison was equally fortunate to be matched with the savvy Hornblow, who had coaxed great results from the likes of Preston Sturges, Virginia Van Upp, Charles Brackett, and Billy Wilder.

She completed the screenplay in five months, feeling "tremendously enthusiastic" about her first assignment. Suddenly, Hornblow announced he was leaving Paramount for Metro-Goldwyn-Mayer (MGM). Boyer took the opportunity to make a move to Universal and launch his own production company. Without Boyer, the *Hong Kong* property was dead. "And there was my beautiful scenario, with nobody to produce it and nobody to act in it," Joan remembered. Her script never saw the screen, a not-uncommon occurrence in the studio system, but a foreign experience for someone who had written only for Hitchcock.

All was not lost. Following Hornblow's lead, Joan signed with MGM. This was a big step up. MGM had been the reigning studio in Hollywood for a decade. Home to Clark Gable, Joan Crawford, Spencer Tracy, Katherine Hepburn, and Judy Garland, the studio famously boasted "more stars than there are in heaven." Joan was attached to the adaptation of *The Sun Is*

My Undoing, a twelve-hundred-page epic by Marguerite Steen published in June 1941. Steen had just sold MGM the rights for $50,000, in a deal that the trades were comparing to that for *Gone with the Wind*. An absorbing tale of shattered romance set against the eighteenth-century African slave trade, the book presented a number of narrative and censorship dilemmas. It featured concubinage and interracial romance, including a revelation that the female lead (a "negress" in the book) turns out to be Arabian. In spite of these elements—or perhaps because of them—many writers in the building were champing at the bit to tackle it.

Joan adapted *The Sun Is My Undoing* with two of the studio's most prestigious stars in mind: Clark Gable and Hedy Lamarr. Dubbed by MGM as "the most beautiful woman in the world," Lamarr was a ravishing Austrian who had already held her own opposite Gable in *Boom Town* and *Comrade X* (both released in 1940). Gable was one of Hollywood's highest paid and most popular stars, having come up through the 1930s playing rugged, no-nonsense types, romancing the likes of Jean Harlow, Joan Crawford, and Claudette Colbert. And, of course, there was the unprecedented success of David O. Selznick's *Gone with the Wind* in 1939, which had confirmed Gable's status as "the king of Hollywood."

But now Gable was nursing heartbreak. Only months earlier, on January 16, his beloved wife, Carole Lombard, had been killed in a plane crash during a war bond tour. Newspaper headlines of her death had rocked Hollywood, bringing home the fact that tragedy could befall anyone at any time, a sad, absurd truth magnified by the illogic of war. "Without her, this place changed permanently," explained Wesley Ruggles, who had directed Lombard and Gable together in *No Man of Her Own* in 1932. "We couldn't comprehend losing Carole and we never adjusted to it, either. She was irreplaceable, and we just kept on missing her."

His wife's death had a profound effect on Gable. Those closest to him later reflected that he never did fully recover. When Joan joined MGM in March, Clark had started back to work after a four-week hiatus, in order to finish out the war romance *Somewhere I'll Find You* (1942) opposite Lana Turner.

Harrison had come to know Gable well, sharing many a casual evening with him and Lombard around Alma's dining room table (and on more relaxed occasions, gathering in her kitchen). Now, perhaps, she thought work would be the best remedy for him. Gable had other ideas. He announced in August that he would enlist in the US Army Air Forces as a show of his loyal love for Lombard and out of a duty for his country. *The Sun Is My Undoing* was shelved, and it never again saw the light of day. For Joan, that was another six months' work down the drain.

It also might have signaled the end of a fledgling love affair with the grief-stricken Gable. No one can say for sure whether a romance between Joan and Clark was consummated during preproduction on *The Sun Is My Undoing*. John Houseman has speculated that they may have dabbled in an affair *before* Carole died. Though it's unclear when it developed, the attraction between them would last much longer than either might have expected. After the war and Gable's return to civilian life, they would be seen together frequently.

With Gable off to the army, if Joan's attention was focused on any man, it was the literary demigod Irwin Shaw. He was a ruddy-looking, barrel-chested former football player with a thick Brooklyn accent whose plays and short stories had recently catapulted him into the New York limelight. Sporting a mane of dark curls and always impeccably attired, Shaw was larger than life. He "always seemed delighted with the people he'd just met, the food he was eating, the places he was seeing." By spring 1941 he had been hired by Columbia Pictures to write the A-list comedy *The Talk of the Town* for Cary Grant and Jean Arthur.

Joan met Irwin playing tennis. The connection likely happened through Shaw's new friend Peter Viertel. Shaw's love for tennis was compulsive, and so was his eye for the ladies. On the sun-drenched courts of the Beverly Hills Tennis Club, Joan was difficult to miss. "She wore a skirt as short as a bib, so high that it was barely there," says Norman Lloyd, who had temporarily come to Los Angeles from New York to play the title role in *Saboteur* (the villain who falls to his death from the top of the Statue of Liberty).

Norman had a front-row seat as the love match between Joan and Irwin unfolded. Irwin was, for the moment, unattached. His wife, Marian Edwards, was in New York City performing in a play, and they were essentially separated. (She had recently upset him by letting on about her fling with Hume Cronyn.) Joan had the kinds of qualities Irwin most admired in a woman; she was stylish, witty, and coquettish. "It was not flirtatiousness precisely, but a wonderful femininity," according to Lloyd.

Meanwhile, the East Coast writer had many qualities that appealed to Joan, not least of which was surely his animal charms. Mary Welsh, who dated him in London during World War II while working as a *Time* correspondent confided to a fellow reporter that "Irwin was the best lay in Europe."

But another part of the attraction must have been Irwin's literary talent. At that time, the esteemed writer was pushing the bounds of story form and naturalism. He was a complicated man, someone who kept parts of himself locked away—the poor Jewish kid from an immigrant family who was always striving to succeed in blue-blood society. This deepened his perspective on the troubled, seemingly irresolvable ways that women and men related to each other. Joan shared his preoccupations with the silent pacts that kept couples together and what happened when they came out in the open.

One of Shaw's best-known stories, "The Girls in Their Summer Dresses" (published in the *New Yorker* in 1939), turns a Sunday-morning stroll down Manhattan's Fifth Avenue by a young married couple, Frances and Michael, into a perverse look into the gendered psychology of a seemingly ordinary husband (and therefore, any man, *every* man). When they pause at a bar for a drink, she confronts him about the way he's been ogling the attractive young women they've passed. ("'You look at them as if you want them,' Frances said, playing with her brandy glass. 'Every one of them.'") He admits that it's true, though he doesn't "do anything about it." ("I like to sit near the women in theaters, the famous beauties. . . . And when the warm weather comes, the girls in summer dresses.") As Frances nears tears, she has come to understand that one day Michael will act on his desires. As she walks away from the table to make a phone call, exasperated and resigned, the story delivers a devastating final line: "Michael watched her walk, thinking, what a pretty girl, what nice legs."

The writer captures perfectly the sense of male desire as eternally outward looking. An idealized, inaccessible woman, Shaw seems to be saying, will always be more attractive to a man than the one at his side. In this way, Michael's objectification of his wife at the end of the story is meant as a compliment. If women, Frances included, simply can't understand, that is their problem.

Shaw's talent as an author was that he conveyed a certain self-consciousness; he also saw the husband through Frances's frustrated lens. But it seemed that the writer wasn't always so attuned when it came to his own personal life, according to his biographer Michael Shnayerson. The story surely troubled the women who saw how closely the everyman Michael resembled Irwin. It wasn't long before Shaw moved on, and so did Joan.

Joan's career took an interesting turn when she was hired by Columbia to write for the only woman director in Hollywood at the time, Dorothy Arzner. Having gained considerable clout in the industry, with contractual powers that came close to those of a producer, Arzner had a reputation for making "women's films" featuring working girls, female friendships, and melodramatic spaces. She was provocative in her personal style, brandishing a "butch" appearance at a time when codes of lesbian fashion marked her as different. Her work has offered rich ground for present-day feminist and queer scholars.

Joan would work on Arzner's project *First Comes Courage*, an adaptation of Elliott Arnold's novel *The Commandos* (1942). Set in occupied Norway, the novel traces the stories of two members of the Norwegian underground, Lieutenant Alan Lowell and Nicole Larsen, as their romance takes twists and turns under escalating political pressure. As part of the resistance effort, Lowell is sent to the home of Captain Dichter to rescue the Nazi officer's new bride— Nicole, who has married the captain as part of an underground spy mission that is running afoul. Alan's assignment is complicated by the fact that Nicole is his former lover. He contends with renewed feelings for her, while questioning whether she remains loyal to the underground.

When Harrison joined the project in fall 1942, Arzner had been working on the screenplay for at least six months. (It was typical for her to hold a script for a year or more before beginning production.) In the final version, it is evident that Dorothy and Joan lasered in on a few key story and character elements. The adaptation (working title: *Attack by Night*) shifts the anchoring subject from Alan (who becomes Captain *Allan* Lowell in the script) and his mental and physical trials to the character of Nicole. Her moral and ethical dilemmas take on greater psychological importance than in the book, indicating that Harrison and Arzner were interested in the more mythic levels of her nearly impossible quest to define heroism—and feminism. This is because Nicole assumes a very active role in the story, while Allan makes weak, self-serving choices.

The ending of *First Comes Courage* has been compared to the final scene in *Casablanca* when Rick (Humphrey Bogart) makes a speech to Ilsa (Ingrid Bergman) after having done "the thinking for both of them," and sends her on a plane with her husband to keep the resistance alive ("The problems of three little people don't amount to a hill of beans in this crazy world," Rick says). In *First Comes Courage*, by contrast, Nicole is given the clear-eyed final pronouncement. After Allan holds her up as a specimen of fearlessness and nobility, he insists he can never leave her. She responds, "Oh, but darling, it isn't that kind of world any more. People don't dance and laugh and ski, as we once used to." In this instance, Nicole has "done the thinking for both of them," and she makes the choice to carry on her struggles on behalf of the underground resistance.

This is not to say that *First Comes Courage*, which was produced at the same time as *Casablanca*, rivals the latter film in quality, but the difference in gender politics between the two is notable. It's obvious by the way that Nicole's character evolves from the novel to the film that Harrison and Arzner sought out ways to make her more decisive, knowing, and shrewd. By contrast, in the book Nicole's physical attraction to Allan is a driving force. The closest she comes to the heroic speech in the film is to say, "We can't have this anymore. . . . It's not for us, darling. . . . It's all right for some people. But we mustn't give in to this."

Harrison's partnership with Arzner was momentous—it was the only time she would pair up with a female director in the studio system—yet there is little record of Joan's specific contribution to the film. Given how highly Dorothy valued the input of her writers, and her long track record with women scriptwriters (such as Mary C. McCall Jr., Tess Slesinger, and Zoe Akins), Joan's opinion would have been crucial during writing and production. The director was atypical in that she kept her writers on set for counsel and rewrites. When McCall wrote *Craig's Wife* for Arzner in 1936, she was surprised at the degree to which she was included in the decision-making process. "At the end of every rehearsal she turned and said, 'How was that for you?'—and I couldn't believe it!" McCall reflected. It was uncommon for directors in the studio system to keep the lead writer by their side, and rarer still for them to actively consult them during takes. This was Arzner's usual method, and there's no reason to believe she deviated from it with Joan.

The production launched well. The part of Nicole Larsen went to Merle Oberon, who had beguiled audiences in *The Private Life of Henry VIII* (1933) and *Wuthering Heights* (1939). Brian Aherne, appreciated for his versatility (and still married to Joan Fontaine), would play the part of Captain Lowell. Carl Esmond would play *Major* Paul Dichter.

Soon into filming, however, *First Comes Courage* began to run into problems. Some of the very attributes that had won Arzner respect just a few years before, such as her fastidiousness and her ability to "make" great female stars, began to be seen as liabilities by the ornery studio head Harry Cohn. He worried about the bottom line. The director was blamed for paying too much attention to the film's every shot. (*First Comes Courage* did not have the benefit of a second unit, which means she directed all location filming, military maneuvers, and stunt scenes on her own.)

One major slowdown had to do with lead actress Oberon, an acquaintance of Joan's from the tight circle of Hollywood British émigrés (she was married to famed producer and recently knighted Alexander Korda at the time). Oberon always needed a certain amount of handling; she required special lighting owing to facial scars caused by a 1937 car accident, and she was constantly battling skin problems as a result of overtreatment. She had arrived the first day with a severe facial rash (later determined to be permanent allergic reaction to cosmetics and sulfa drugs). This called for meticulous cinematography and direction, not to mention a lot of confidence boosting on Arzner's part.

Oberon's crisis deepened when she received the news that Richard Hillary, a young Australian war veteran with whom she'd fallen deeply in love only several months before, had died. *First Comes Courage* was four days into production when, on January 8, she learned that he had crashed to his death in England while flying a personal plane on an icy winter night. Some conjectured it was suicide, but the high-strung romantic (who claimed him as her soul mate and believed to know him better than anyone) cursed the only possible cause: divine providence. Oberon went into seclusion for several days, and when she finally emerged, she had trouble focusing. Add to this the fact that Arzner felt the story was weak to begin with, according to cinematographer Joseph Walker, and *First Comes Courage* was in a precarious position.

When Arzner was struck with pneumonia, which brought her so close to death that her health suffered for a year, Harry Cohn seized the moment. In mid-February, director Charles Vidor charged onto the set and announced, "Arzner's off the picture. Cohn thinks this thing's a dud." Vidor, who was not the most well liked of Columbia's directors, said that upper management had decided not to spend any more money on *First Comes Courage* and "to finish it in fast order. And that means no more babying Oberon—we're showing both sides of her face from now on." (*First Comes Courage* would be Arzner's final film, and she would go uncredited.)

If Cohn cared little how his leading lady looked on screen, he cared even less about pulling together a good story. He did, however, see Arzner's departure as a way to tilt the script in a more masculine direction. The studio brought in new writers. Harrison was replaced by George Sklar, a luminary in proletarian theater with little Hollywood experience. Added to the team were Lewis Meltzer, a genre scribe who had just completed the war picture *The Destroyer* (1943), and New York stage transplant Melvin Levy. Hedda Hopper summed up the fate of *First Comes Courage* in spring 1943: "The studios didn't think that Arzner knew much about 'action stuff' and she was taken ill. So somebody else re-did the story."

Joan saw the final cut in May. "What came out on the screen didn't even vaguely resemble what I had written," she recalled. "I was heartbroken." Not only had it been mashed up, but its pace was uneven and slow. In actuality, the big picture of *First Comes Courage* may not have changed very dramatically, given how closely story, character, and theme elements adhere to the Arzner films that had come before (and Harrison's to follow). It was the particulars that apparently irked Joan, the liberties taken by the new team and the way Cohn pushed her off the project. She was left "wondering whether there was something wrong with me, or with Hollywood." Her only recourse was to remove her name from the script, which itself was a battle. When she confided her woes to Hopper before the theatrical release, she said with relief, "And I've just this minute been able to get my name taken off the credit list."

Joan next signed on for an assignment with MGM. Based on an Anna Seghers novel published in September 1942, *The Seventh Cross* was a tense social drama tracing the journey of seven men as they escape from a Nazi concentration camp, headed for the Dutch border. (One of the first and only literary depictions of a concentration camp written during the war, Seghers's book was so well received that it was translated into five languages, including German, within a year.) The camp commandant captures the fugitives one by one and strings them up on makeshift crosses for all the prisoners to see, until only the last man, George Heisler, remains free. The commandant vows to capture him and hang him on the seventh cross. The film thus follows George in a story of underground resistance, including his encounters with many ordinary Germans who show a willingness to risk their lives to help him.

With Pandro Berman attached as producer, MGM chose an up-and-coming director whom Joan already considered a friend: Fred Zinnemann. The Austrian-born filmmaker had trained in Paris, Vienna, and Berlin before apprenticing at the studio in the division that made short dramas and historical mysteries. This was his first A-level feature. He aspired to give authenticity to a struggle he deeply cared about. (Tragically, he would learn only after the war that by this time both his parents had already died in concentration camps.)

Joan was paired with Barnard College graduate Helen Deutsch. Having thrived in the world of theater publicity and criticism, Deutsch had one Universal romantic credit to her name (and would soon write *National Velvet* for Elizabeth Taylor). Joan and Helen had actually collaborated once before, turning in an original story titled "Jackpot" to Paramount for purchase consideration in December 1941, as Joan was parting ways with Hitchcock. Nothing ever came of it. Now they set about adapting *The Seventh Cross*.

As the women worked, they kept a *New York Times* review of the Seghers novel in sight. Carrying the headline REMEMBERED AFTER DARKNESS: THE GREATEST HORROR IS THAT THE HORROR IS TRUE, the article had a section highlighted: "He is not only an enslaved symbol of the free spirit in an enslaved state, he is also a challenge, a test, causing all the people with whom he comes in contact to ask themselves where they stand, to examine their beliefs, to discover the remnants of their humanity."

The quote offered clarity when Joan and Helen risked losing focus; whether one individual escaped mattered less than the mirror that the protagonist held up for "all the people"—and for the audience—to examine their own moral stance. The multiple drafts that Harrison and Deutsch generated between March and April 1943 indicate that they were wrestling with a number of dilemmas related to plot and theme. A great deal of their time was spent adding dimensionality to the various female characters George encounters. They experimented with moral and ethical decisions for them, especially George's wife, Ely (changed to Leni in the film); many of the changes (like the characters) were discarded along the way.

The Seventh Cross received top-shelf treatment. MGM cast Spencer Tracey as George, supported by Herbert Rudley, Agnes Moorehead, Hume Cronyn, and Jessica Tandy. (Cronyn and Tandy rehearsed scenes with Zinnemann every evening to boost his confidence for the next day's shoot.) The illustrious Karl Freund served as cinematographer. Cedric Gibbons provided art direction. When eventually released in New York in September 1944, the film bowled over reviewers. This marked the beginning of Zinnemann's rise in Hollywood, not to mention a milestone in cinema history, a film made "at a time," the director reflected later, "when we were fighting Germany, and every German in the eyes of the American people was a monster. . . . [We] made the point that even in Germany there were people who had the courage to go their own way and stand up against what was happening." The group had a made powerful contribution to European exile cinema.

Given how much energy Joan devoted to the fine textures of *The Seventh Cross*, it's curious that she never made mention of it in later years when listing her achievements. *The Seventh Cross* was not a point of pride. For one, she vehemently disagreed with the casting of Spencer Tracey. Without ever referring to the film by name, in several interviews she alluded to what can only be *The Seventh Cross*, complaining, "The script was so unsuitably cast that the characters were not recognizable." But the bigger disappointment for Joan was undoubtedly being left off the film's credits, possibly because MGM deemed that the script had undergone significant enough changes following her departure from the project in April 1943.

At that point, it had been a year since her name had appeared on the screen (on *Saboteur*, her final collaboration with Hitchcock). It had been nearly eighteen months since she'd put her name on a solo writing contract. After trying her hand at costume dramas, romances, and, finally, a Holocaust film, she'd begun to second-guess her career choice altogether. Had she indeed been riding on the master's coattails, as some in Hollywood had speculated? She wondered if she had been spoiled as part of Hitchcock's team, where most of his proposed projects saw a green light. Certainly, life without Hitch was proving harder than she had envisioned. "Everything I wrote was either shelved or turned out so badly I asked to have my name taken off it," she explained later, saying, "A writer can stand just so much of that before going mad."

At the heart of it for Joan was creative freedom; she wanted some guarantee that what she wrote would resemble what turned up on the screen. Entering into another writing assignment—any writing assignment—seemed like a recipe for disappointment. "I had no desire to write another script I would be ashamed of on the screen, however much money was offered," she declared. So she took the time to adapt a book that really intrigued her: the newest murder mystery by William Irish (the pen name of crime writer Cornell Woolrich), titled *Phantom Lady*. She devised a twist that would move the crime story at the book's heart from the male protagonist's point of view to that of his secretary, a girl Friday turned detective.

Joan's agent shopped the script around to a couple of studios, but the answer was always no. She told her agent that she was thinking of leaving the business. He convinced her to let him knock on one last door. He took the script to Universal and came back with the same response: the studio would be delighted to hire Harrison to adapt Woolrich's novel, but not *her way*. She had been here before. As a young woman eager to try journalism, she had been told by her father she should aspire to find a husband instead. But this was not her way. As a rookie secretary, she had proven she had the drive and determination to learn the craft of filmmaking, and to make movies her way. By going solo, she had mastered a lot about the American studio system, but it was time Hollywood learned something about her. She was a woman who liked to be in control.

When she declined the offer, the studio made a surprising counter: *If you feel so strongly about the script, then why don't you produce it yourself?* And with that, in spring 1943, Joan Harrison became the first woman producer at a major studio. Instead of walking away from the table, she'd been given the chance to double down.

12 | PHANTOM LADY

OVERNIGHT, Joan became a star property at Universal. On April 30, 1943, the *Los Angeles Examiner* announced that she had joined the studio as the "first woman producer since [famed silent movie studio head] Lois Weber of more than a decade ago, and the only woman to hold such a position in the industry." She made headlines in the *New York Times* as HOLLYWOOD'S ONLY FULL-FLEDGED WOMAN PRODUCER, where she was heralded as the only producer "anywhere, with dimples and a twenty-four-inch waistline."

Universal itself played up Joan's beauty and charm. The studio rolled out the red carpet, granting her the kind of star treatment typically reserved for their A-list actresses. The press ate it up. To Hedda Hopper, the "golden-haired ball of fire" was "Glamour Girl Number One." *Collier's* trumpeted her as "Hollywood's only femme producer." The *Los Angeles Times* claimed that Harrison was more a "blonde, blue-eyed babe" than a lady executive. She was singled out as one of a kind: a powerhouse with looks that could kill.

Joan, having been schooled in the art of self-promotion by Hitchcock, conspired with the publicity department at Universal to craft a mutually beneficial public persona. In an interview with *Time* magazine, when asked how she differed from other producers, she coquettishly "tilt[ed] one blond eyebrow, grinned, and replied, 'I use my sex.'" Then, when a press photographer began to take his leave, she brandished a disappointed look before changing the mood by striking a sexy pose and coyly burying her nose into a file folder. She called out to all the snappers in the room, "Well, want any leg art, boys?"

The world saw quite a lot of Joan in 1943, as a bevy of dazzling studio stills cut a wide swath across the pages of newspapers and magazines. She was posed peering at shelves lined with scripts, poring over mock-ups of set designs, consulting an art director as they examined a miniature set, overseeing a musical session in a sound booth, and on and on. The accompanying message was that though she might have become a movie star, she chose instead a professional career. She was "small, and hoydenish, and [wore] an evening gown with the same eye-filling éclat as Lana Turner," according to *Collier's* columnist Jerry D. Lewis, but she much preferred to roll up her sleeves and get down to business.

To assume new "glamour girl" dimensions, Joan inaugurated a style that soon became her trademark. She wore her hair, newly lightened, gorgeously coiffed into tight platinum ringlets atop her head (attained by hundreds of bobby pins seamlessly tucked into place). She also made a point of losing weight. With every detail pulled together perfectly—manicured nails, simple jewelry, and Italian shoes—she donned designer women's work wear. Though she was still stocking her closet with the help of Beverly Hills boutiques, she also relied heavily on the generosity of Universal's wardrobe department. Designers like Vera West and Adrian outfitted her in structured jackets, suit separates, and tweed, mirroring professional menswear but maintaining hints of femininity. Sporting a gingham checked blazer with a high hem and towering far above the ground in a picture taken by famed photographer George de Zayas, Joan made a first and—for many—lasting impression in the *Collier's* spread. Katharine Hepburn may have played ambitious, accomplished professional women in the movies, but Joan was the real thing—*Woman of the Year*'s Tess Harding come to life.

Joan Harrison's star power—meant to distinguish her from all other producers, she had decided—was derived from the fact that she was going to make mysteries "from the woman's angle." She would be the "Mistress of Suspense"— a female Hitchcock. (*Collier's* rhapsodized, "If you think [she] sounds like some fantastic character dreamed up by Alfred Hitchcock—you're right.") The *Hitchcock's girl Friday makes good* marketing campaign was a natural move, as she stepped away from the grand silhouette of the master. But it was also a coordinated strategy to draw attention to her as a new force in the studio system, and to differentiate her brand of production. As Universal began to promote her debut, the press book announced it would be "a formula which has never before been translated for the screen . . . [a] mystery film, based on feminine psychology for its essential appeal." Joan would make female suspense the new "it."

Joan knew better than anyone that the silver screen had already seen at least a few mysteries with women at the center. As Hitchcock's writer, she had been responsible for some of the best. But this was no time to quibble; emphasizing the woman's angle made good business sense. Besides, if she had her way, the pictures she produced would carve out an even larger, more sensational niche for gothic femme noire. She intuited that there was a female demographic for her movies, waiting in the wings. "Women need something to pull for, you know," she mused to the *New York Times*, "whether it's a dog, a horse, an old beggar—or even another woman!"

Among those pulling for Joan were the executives at Universal. Her fanfare was not mere lip service. The studio was making a tactical move to draw in more female fans—in particular, women who had entered the wartime economy—who might see Joan as a surrogate, someone who reflected their own increasing prominence in public life. It was a smart business decision for Universal, and for Joan.

As a "minor major" studio, Universal had been rebounding economically since the late 1930s, following the ousting of the Carl Laemmle leadership. Now helmed by Nathan J. Blumberg and vice president of production Cliff Work, the company aspired to make fewer films with higher production values. The Abbott and Costello series was a steady source of income, and vehicles starring Deanna Durbin, Maria Montez, and Basil Rathbone (as Sherlock Holmes) were consistent crowd pleasers, but Universal now aimed to distribute more A-movies and diversify its brand. René Clair's *The Flame of New Orleans*, starring Marlene Dietrich, and Hitchcock's *Shadow of a Doubt* were early pieces of the strategy.

This aggressive move toward quality was part of the studio's attempt to bid for attention from exhibitors, who previously had shut out its films from the first-run market. The way was clear now that the US Department of Justice had challenged the major studios' block-booking practices, whereby they would require theaters to program their films in blocks, rather than single out the movies they wanted to screen according to quality. Universal looked to be on the move as Joan set up shop in a couple of offices in Building H.

Joan's launch would be *Phantom Lady*, based on a Cornell Woolrich novel that had met with extraordinary commercial success a year earlier. Woolrich, a prolific pulp writer, was churning out so much material that by the time of *Phantom Lady* he was using the nom de plume William Irish, a second legally registered name that he had spun off and sold to J. B. Lippincott with the permission of his publisher Simon & Schuster. Almost anything associated with Woolrich was a good bet for a producer. And for Universal, *Phantom Lady* was to be the studio's first noir film (the common ideas and aesthetics of which were understood at the time, though the term *film noir* wasn't coined until later), allowing it to rise above its monster movies and westerns and to compete with *Double Indemnity* (Paramount) and *Laura* (Twentieth Century Fox).

In Woolrich's tale, New York businessman Scott Henderson goes out alone on the town after a marital squabble, spends a rather harmless evening with a "woman in a hat" he meets in a local bar, and returns home to find his wife strangled to death in their apartment. He sits in a prison cell awaiting the gas chamber while his best friend, a girlfriend, and a sympathetic detective race against the clock, fanning out across the city to search for the woman in a hat—Henderson's potential alibi—while gradually realizing that their lives are at risk. The deranged killer has it out for them too. In a dramatic ending, it is revealed that Henderson's best friend is actually the murderer (and a philanderer, who murdered Henderson's wife when she refused to run away with him). He has been paying off, and killing, the witnesses whose testimony could set Henderson free.

Joan had convinced the studio to hire her by pitching an unusual adaptation: as the mystery intensifies, place the point of view, which the book roots in multiple characters, with the girlfriend—now Henderson's girl Friday. The book's third-person narration had deftly moved in and out of the perspectives of the murder suspect, detective, friend, and love interest, but held to a "hard-boiled" voice. In Joan's equation, the film, while capitalizing on Woolrich's name (and many assets of his story), would attempt to reach a more expansive audience of wartime working women. Harrison's *Phantom Lady* would follow an innocent young woman down a garden path and into danger as she tries to track the whereabouts of the vanished lady who was wearing the hat.

It was a stroke of inspiration on Harrison's part to place the character of Carol Richman at the story's center, and to stress her role as secretary over that of love interest. Carol's nickname, "Kansas," identifies her as an easily relatable type: a newly arrived transplant from the Midwest. She was a "shiny-faced American babe," according to studio press materials, who wore "clever clothes, show[ed] aggressiveness and initiative in dealing with a man," and was "honest and straightforward." Carol could have easily stepped off the screen and into the seat next to any of the millions of women who were the intended audience for *Phantom Lady*. These were wartime workers caught in between, and largely rejecting, two glorified ideals of womanhood: Rosie the Riveter and the cheesecake pin-up girl. Instead, they were reimagining themselves as resourceful, resilient, and self-consciously modern. They were Carol in the flesh.

Carol was also a counter to the demonized version of femininity that was teeming on Hollywood screens: enigmatic femme fatale figures such as *Cat People*'s killer Irena Dubrovna or *The Maltese Falcon*'s dubious Ruth Wonderly. Indeed, Carol's virtuous moral character promised to be *Phantom Lady*'s biggest plot twist. In most early 1940s noirs, even if the "good" girl wins, according to film critic Imogen Sara Smith, "she turns out to be a nightmare." However, as Smith observes, the "smart, tough, wisecracking" Carol is more akin to the great fast-talking dames of the 1930s.

These two changes—deepening the character of Carol and recontouring *Phantom Lady* for a female audience—were only two of Harrison's many ideas. She was fortunate to have landed at a studio where producers enjoyed relative creative freedom. Such free range was one of the reasons Joan had chosen Universal. By the time she arrived, the old vertically integrated central producing system (established by Carl Laemmle) had been replaced by a flexible producer-unit system. This decentralization gave her room to roam, so long as she didn't go over budget, met the deadline, and avoided major run-ins with the Production Code Administration. Calling the situation "swell," Joan appreciated that "they gave me a free hand, within restrictions."

The producer-unit system went against the factory mode of classical Hollywood studio production, typified by an ensemble of units working in tandem (via rigorous preparation and fixed timetables). Instead, Universal's machinery was greased by a less formal collaboration within the producer unit; according to film scholar Thomas Schatz, it was "the familiarity of the collaborators with one another and with certain star-genre formulas [that] enabled them to somehow pull things together."

Someone helming a film at Universal would develop material with one or two writers. Once a green light was given to a project and a start date assigned, the producer had a short window to decide on casting and crew lists. With minimal preparation time, the creative team would launch with "only a sort of vague conception of both the production and the finished product," according to Schatz. Much of the story and design would come together during production.

At Universal, Joan could count on having a lot of room to develop the script and, from there, advancing the film through the production process with little interference from the executive level. Though her title was associate producer, she was in fact the top producer on the project. (Universal had been reticent to give her the full title on her first picture.) The only person above her was executive producer Milton Feld.

The studio assigned a novice, Bernard C. Schoenfeld, to serve as *Phantom Lady*'s official screenwriter. Though Schoenfeld had written radio episodes for the *Suspense* series, he had no experience in film. To the press, Joan explained that he may be new, "but I believe a new writer can be taught quickly" (using herself as an example). On a personal level, she had to have been pleased with the choice, which placed her in the driver's seat—or, in this case, the writer's seat. She knew full well that the apprentice was not likely to question his master, especially on critical decisions like structure and character. And Schoenfeld's radio skills came in where Joan needed them most—writing dialogue. Given her degree of input, Joan had justification to assume a writing credit on the film, but industry guild policies required her to make a choice between producing and writing credit. She chose the former.

Joan joined forces with Robert Siodmak, who would become an important ally. The German-born director had come to Universal after making several low-budget films at Paramount but had stalled out in Universal's B-movie division. He was a workhorse and a true craftsman, with ten years of film-making experience in Europe. Now he found himself stranded in a world of over-the-top special effects romps beset by vampires and snake dancers.

Harrison first met Siodmak at Lucey's Restaurant, a favorite lunchtime hangout among Universal's writers and directors, particularly those émigrés seeking a midday reprieve from the studio bosses. She was aware of his work. It was his 1942 low-budget Paramount thriller *Fly-by-Night* that first caught her attention, no doubt because of its Hitchcockian "wrong man" plot. Siodmak's French thriller *Pièges* (literally *Traps*, but released in the United States as *Personal Column*), completed a few years earlier and featuring a taxi dancer turned detective, would also have piqued her interest. Though it's unknown whether she'd seen it, she would have at least heard about it through the grapevine. (When *Pièges* was banned in Germany in 1939, the director hand-carried a print with him during his and his wife's perilous escape from Europe.) Joan took an instant liking to Robert; his tireless work ethic, dry humor, and artistic sensibilities squared with her own.

In truth, however, Siodmak had not been her first choice for *Phantom Lady*. She had first proposed another German expatriate, Max Ophüls, who had enjoyed a successful career in France until Nazi occupation forced him to flee to the United States. Hollywood was not panning out for him either. Harrison had met Ophüls informally—they had a mutual acquaintance in the agent Paul Kohner—and she'd been familiar with his films when in London. She made the case to Universal executives that they "would be fortunate to have a director of his caliber" and, without an official green light, she began developing the project with him. "Max came to the studio and we discussed several approaches to the novel," she recalled. "We then met again at Max's house, but Universal then stepped in and stated firmly that they had a foreign director, Robert Siodmak, under contract and would prefer to use him." It was standard practice to go with a contracted employee before reaching outside the stable. "Under the circumstances," Joan added, "I don't blame them. I was a novice producer and Ophuls' work was not generally known in the States."

Once Harrison and Siodmak settled into a preproduction workflow, they put concerted effort into planning *Phantom Lady*'s look and visual tone. There would need to be a contrast between the bright, well-organized business world inhabited by Carol and her boss (an engineer in the adapted script) and the city's distorted, menacing underworld, as Carol slides ever further down the rabbit hole. They knew from the start that they wanted to create the nightmarish atmosphere through highly stylized moments, rich textures, and claustrophobic settings. They envisioned a film filled with night exteriors, slow pacing, and long segments, with little to no dialogue, that at times took on silent movie contours. Siodmak favored low-key lighting, which would lend itself to sharply contrasting shadows and large areas of black.

These were Siodmak's preferred techniques going back to his amateur days at the German studio UFA, where he had self-trained among some of the most talented filmmakers in the world. He and his brother Curt had met Fred Zinnemann, Edgar George Ulmer, Eugen Schüfftan, and, most crucially, Billy Wilder in Berlin. They had forged a mighty collective they called Filmstudio 29 and, over the course of six months, made an experimental, pseudodocumentary feature, *People on Sunday* (*Menschen am Sonntag*), that proved to be a tour de force upon its release in 1930.

By the time of *Phantom Lady*, Siodmak had professionally mastered the art of expressionism, an approach inspired by ideas of *squeezing out* the unstable inner lives of characters and society onto the external world of the film. For *Phantom Lady*, the director took under his wing British cinematographer Elwood "Woody" Bredell, then still coming up in the ranks. He tutored him in the art of light and dark, advising him to study Rembrandt's paintings as an example of how dark shadows could attract the eye of the viewer toward a certain portion of the composition. *Phantom Lady* became a training ground for Bredell and Siodmak working together, as they tested the limits of stark black-and-white photography and worked up realistic backdrops. The film's production space became something of a laboratory, in which Siodmak's French poetic realist sensibilities and burgeoning ideas about social documentary also came into the mix, leading to fascinating visual tensions between realism and artifice.

While Joan's director and cinematographer were critical to *Phantom Lady*'s style, her selection of art director was also crucial. She was responsible for securing John B. Goodman, who had over sixty credits (beginning at Paramount, before moving over to Universal). He had recently earned an Academy Award for the Technicolor prestige picture *The Phantom of the Opera* (1943). And she had seen Goodman's sensibilities up close as he concocted the vivid, dualistic designs of *Shadow of a Doubt* for Hitchcock, an association that may well have smoothed the way for Goodman's attachment to the project.

Joan knew that by choosing a smart art director, she could keep her budget of $350,000 under control. She had to prove that she could bring in a picture under cost if she entertained hopes of making the next one. America's entrance into the war had yielded additional constraints, including limited location shooting, energy shortages, and blackout regulations. The War Production

Board had put a spending cap on Hollywood's new construction, mandating that no more than $5,000 per film could be expended on new materials (when previously $50,000 had been standard).

Harrison worked alongside Goodman, coming up with an approach that would minimize new set construction for the film's many nighttime city street encounters. They would shoot day-for-night on the Universal backlot, recycling an elaborate prewar rig—an 810-square-foot black tarpaulin—to serve as the night sky. The tarp, which publicity called "the largest in the studio's history," towered forty-two feet over the expansive set, the center of which consisted of two intersecting streets of brownstones and storefronts. Joan employed other cost-saving measures too, such as forgoing the tarp and shooting the backlot as an "open street" when possible, cutting down on the number of camera angles. This saved both time and expensive film stock.

For all the attention on preproduction, Joan knew that it would be casting that would either make or break *Phantom Lady*. She was keenly attuned to the fact that the film's featured role was neither the hero nor the heroine but the villain, artist Jack Marlow, who comes to the aid of his best friend only to slowly and dramatically reveal himself to be a psychotic murderer. Joan had in mind an unlikely choice for the part of Marlow, someone she had known since her very first days in Los Angeles: Franchot Tone. The well-regarded actor wore the patina of his early New York theater career like a comfortable suit, having played mostly romantics and idealists in films such as *Dancing Lady* (1933), *Gabriel over the White House* (1933), and *Mutiny on the Bounty* (1935). Hitchcock had given Joan only one piece of advice so far as *Phantom Lady* was concerned, and that was to look for an actor who went "against the conventional image." Harrison believed that casting Tone as a murderer would make for a radical turn—and she had "always thought of him as the heavy more than the hero."

Plus, the timing was good. Tone had rejected the grinding schedule of the studio system. Having greeted the end of his MGM contract in 1940 with relish, he had taken some time off for his true love: the stage. Now he was making movies only sporadically, such as Billy Wilder's searing *Five Graves to Cairo* (1943). Tone was looking to experiment. "Mentally," says the actor's son, "he was turning away from the majors and the star system, hoping to do more independent productions."

On the other hand, Tone had to be willing to take a chance on a B-grade thriller in which his character wouldn't appear until the forty-fifth minute, and then only to be revealed as a disturbed killer. When Joan sent the script to his agent, the actor reportedly passed.

Later, Joan would recall having taken the script over to Tone's home and personally acting out the final scenes of the killer's unraveling. "I stayed up all night just to rewrite that scene," she recounted. "I went to Franchot's house the next morning and read it to him. It was the final, big scene, and I wanted him to like it. Suddenly Franchot said, 'Okay.' I was so tired I couldn't believe it. I felt as if I'd found a million dollars." For a mere $60,000 (a relatively small sum for an actor of Tone's stature), she had acquired a bankable star. This was a shrewd business calculation. Once Tone was attached, Universal upgraded *Phantom Lady* to an A-list picture.

Casting Carol "Kansas" Richman gave Joan the opportunity to make a star out of someone. The girl Friday role would open the door for an ingenue to prove she had the chops to play alongside any of the great leading ladies of the day. Joan's superior instincts, reinforced by a decade of practical casting experience with Hitchcock, led her to an ideal match: Ella Raines.

Newly signed to Universal, Raines was ravishing, with glassy green eyes, high cheekbones, and a thick mane of black locks. Growing up as a tomboy in the small town of Snoqualmie, Washington, she'd been raised on fishing, shooting, mountain climbing, horseback riding, and music lessons. Raines didn't hide her fiery temperament, but director Howard Hawks and agent Charles Feldman tried to soften her edges as they groomed her for the new production company that Hawks was setting up with Charles Boyer. (Feldman had stolen her out from under David O. Selznick when, while watching her screen test in the company of Selznick one afternoon, he exited the room to sign the actress before the screening even ended, leaving Selznick to stew over his losses.)

Raines was in fact the first star signed by Hawks and Boyer for their joint venture, B-H Productions, in January 1943. She was only twenty years old. In an instant, she went from a New York stage production of *Away We Go!* (which would become *Oklahoma!*) to a five-month contract at $300 per week and an option for six and a half years. Hawks prepared her for her debut part in the war film *Corvette K-225* (1943), in which she played the sister of a fallen officer, by teaching her how to pose for the camera and take advantage of camera angles and lighting, and in the course of this transformed her into the Hawksian female type: a sleek, sexy tough-talker. Hawks fell for the persona he'd helped to create, whisking Raines away to a ranch in the Santa Monica Mountains while his wife, Slim, was away for "rest," as he put it. At the time, Raines was married to her high school sweetheart Kenneth Trout, who was flying bombing missions in the US Army Air Forces. But she had made the tactical decision that career came first. Besides, she later disclosed, "I loved [Howard] and adored him. . . . He was very charming, very thoughtful, very kind." The affair broke up Hawks's marriage.

By the time she was up for *Phantom Lady* consideration, Raines's B-H contract had been sold to Universal for $1 million. *Life* magazine, sporting her on the cover in a demure peek-a-boo wave, touted the headline PRETTY YOUNG STAR BEGAN HER CAREER BY BEING INCORPORATED FOR $1,000,000 BY A PRODUCTION FIRM. This had been Boyer and Hawks's plan all along: they aimed to launch new stars, then turn them around for quick profit.

Joan had looked at the rushes (unedited film footage) of Raines's previous performances, since *Corvette K-225* (produced at Universal) and her follow-ups *Cry Havoc* (1944) and *Hail the Conquering Hero* (1944) all had yet to be released. Even the uncut footage made it clear that the actress had the mix of attractiveness and sauciness that the role of Carol called for. Raines admitted that initially she had done "a bit of an inward groaning. The picture's name made it sound like a whodunit, and generally screen mysteries don't offer good roles for leading women." But upon reading the script, she was won over. Raines was ready to invest everything she had in the role, seeing that her character appeared in almost every scene. She recognized that many involved in the production were newcomers like herself and was attuned to the fact that everybody "felt that this was our big chance."

Harrison steered Raines to make her more relatable to those young working women who were experiencing wartime austerity. She wished to portray Carol as a realistic secretary, not a movie version of a secretary, going shopping with Ella to choose clothes appropriate to the role: "The usual studio designer would have put her in a little outfit which every forty-dollar a week secretary yearns for but could never afford," Harrison told the *St. Louis Post-Dispatch*. "I ought to know. I was one myself." Joan's instincts that Ella was ideal to play Carol were confirmed when the producer first let the actress know "that her clothes would be ordinary, some of them downright shabby." Raines responded,

"Goodness, Miss Harrison, I didn't work so very hard for years and years just to come to Hollywood and look pretty. I want to be a really fine actress. I don't care how I look."

Once Tone and Raines were locked, casting the remaining roles was a cinch. The part of wrongly accused engineer Scott Henderson was not insignificant, though the "leading man" spent a disproportionate amount of time off-screen, imprisoned and ineffectual. Harrison selected Alan Curtis, who had been typed as a tough guy. Curtis had recently romanced Michèle Morgan in *Two Tickets to London*, proving he could stretch to play Henderson as both sympathetic and inscrutable. Joan was particularly astute in envisioning Thomas Gomez as Inspector Burgess. The veteran Spanish American stage actor had been relegated to the background—in villain or comic relief roles—since breaking into the movies the year prior. He was perfect to portray the methodical detective, the moral center who quietly knows more than the other characters realize.

Fay Helm was chosen to play Ann Terry, the titular "phantom lady" whom Henderson stumbles across in a bar and takes to a show while his wife is being murdered. Having worked for seven years at multiple studios, Helm had more than enough experience to play the elusive "woman in a hat" who appears only at the film's beginning and end. (Raines once noted that Helm, who hailed from a wealthy oil family, thought a little too much of herself, when weighed against the size of her part.)

Brazilian singer and actress Aurora Miranda was selected for the role of Estela Monteiro, the nightclub performer who supports Henderson's alibi by remembering the phantom lady's outlandish hat (a style of hat the two women shared). Miranda, whose sister Carmen had a more extensive career in film, sang and danced to "Chick-a Chick" in one of the film's sequences. Rounding out the cast were Elisha Cook Jr. as the demented jazz drummer Cliff Milburn, Andrew Tombes as the bartender, and Regis Toomey and Joseph Crehan as police detectives.

Production began in mid-September 1943 and ran through late October. The shoot went smoothly, not even pausing for a record-breaking four-day heat wave in which temperatures rose as high as 106 degrees. The extras in that week's courtroom scenes sweated it out in what amounted to hothouse sets.

From the perspective of narrative structure, *Phantom Lady* has an unusual arc, starting off as a "wrong man" film, then turning into a female investigative thriller once Scott is convicted. (With a total running time of eighty-seven minutes, this story shift occurs at the thirty-minute mark.) On some level, this can be understood as Harrison incorporating genre conventions she had helped develop during her time with Hitchcock. But the film's bifurcated structure also has a symbolic function, in that it suggests Joan's turning of the page. Once Carol's investigation launches, with Henderson immobilized in his jail cell and the wrong man formula summarily set aside, the woman's story begins.

What sets *Phantom Lady* apart from other noirs is its female-centeredness. Because its structure is rather loose and episodic, it's easy to overlook the tight focus on Carol's obsession with finding Ann Terry. *Phantom Lady* shuffles the deck of story formulas when Carol begins to take on a lead detective role (upsetting hard-boiled genre expectations that Henderson or Inspector Burgess would do so).

What's perhaps more extraordinary is that the phantom lady turns out to be more than just a funhouse reflection on Carol's shiny-faced modern girl, a version of the "monstrous feminine" archetype that was common to the movies of the 1940s. Though Ann Terry is an inconsolable bride who has lost her sanity, stowed away upstairs, she is not a devious seductress or a deranged "madwoman in the attic" à la Bertha Rochester in *Jane Eyre*. Instead, she is an emotionally despondent bride-to-be who went off the rails after losing her fiancé to an unexpected illness. She has simply been too incoherent to notice the news of Scott's imprisonment and come forward.

Moreover, *Phantom Lady* has a distinctive spatial movement and momentum because it follows a feminine logic. Even as Carol's investigation leads her toward reconciling patriarchal law and order (she serves as a surrogate for the police) and eventually into marriage with Henderson, she journeys through a series of female spaces, aided repeatedly by women, in a feminist odyssey that ultimately sees her transcend what she thinks she is capable of.

For example, before going upstairs to Ann Terry's bedroom to ask for assistance, Carol expresses trepidation to Marlow, whom she still thinks is her ally. The upstairs space is presented as an insurmountable threshold, yet Terry's doctor (notably, a woman) emerges to encourage Carol to follow her up to the woman's room, going out of her way to confine Marlow to the downstairs space ("It's better if Miss Richman goes in alone"). This scripting and blocking set the stage so that Carole and Ann might relate to one another "female to female" and finally resolve the question of the alibi.

Compounding this feminine logic is the fact that the plot turns on a woman's accessory—the vanished lady's hat. Unlike the typical phallic objects obsessed over in noir (guns, knives, or cigarettes), a large, round, feathered hat assumes symbolic significance as the key to Henderson's freedom. The hat takes Carol (accompanied by Marlow) on a hunt for clues into the backstages of female performance (e.g., Estela Monteira) and the backdoor worlds of millinery. As a prop, it made for great promotion, with such designers as John Frederics, Sally Victor, and Florence Reichman competing to score the assignment; Kenneth Hopkins won out in the end. As a gimmick, it also offered endless marketing opportunities, such as the "hat of horror" that Universal advised local shops to sell in display windows, or design contests held at neighborhood theaters.

All this attention to feminine detail and women's spaces is punctuated by the keen sense of Carol's characterization. The multidimensionality of this female protagonist points to Joan's own obsession with character (which always mattered more to her than plot). Carol was Ella Raines's favorite role precisely because "it really was four characterizations in one," according to the actress. Raines explained, "At first, Carol was a prim, severe-looking secretary; then she fell in love with her boss, and, blossoming out, became almost a glamour girl. Finally, when the man she loved was convicted of murdering his wife, Carol posed as a barfly, a woman of loose morals and 'hepcat' in order to collect the evidence that would prove his innocence." In Raines's performance, she masters the challenge of embodying the fourth character implicit in the script—someone who was none of these women but capable of masquerading as all of them. Raines remarked, "The audience had to feel that Carol was not like any of the types she impersonated."

One of the film's central questions becomes, just how far will Carol go to solve the mystery, in order to save a man who doesn't even know she's in love with him? Where is her moral line and how close will she come to crossing it? Some of *Phantom Lady*'s most visually powerful sequences dramatize these questions about transgression. For example, when Carol attempts to intimidate a lying bartender into a confession, she sits at the end of his bar quietly glaring at him, night after night, aiming her stare like a weapon. Finally, one evening, she stalks him through the darkened, rain-slicked streets of the city, causing him to panic as he hears the relentless sound of her heels on pavement.

A game of cat and mouse ensues; first he gains the upper hand on an elevated subway platform, nearly pushing her into an approaching train, and later the pursuit ends in confrontation on a sidewalk curb. The bartender makes a move to lash out at her, and suspense builds as several male bystanders attempt to hold him back. The tension is amplified by the fact that the young men misread the situation, perceiving Carol as a victim in need of protection (which, as Michael Walker points out, constitutes a shrewd break in gender stereotype). The man panics and he runs into the street, only to be struck by an oncoming truck. Carol is left alone in the frame, looking down at the man's rumpled hat in the gutter, presumably forced to come to terms with her own guilt and complicity in the accident.

The most vivid example of Carol's moral transgression occurs in what Universal's marketing machine called "one of the wildest scenes recently put on screen." This is the jazz jive sequence, which starts as Carol poses as a hepcat (calling herself Jeannie) and enters the music hall where Scott had taken the phantom lady. Decked out in garish black satin and fishnet, she provocatively captures the attention of orchestra drummer Cliff Milburn in hopes of pumping him for clues. The hopped-up musician escorts her to an underground jam session. Obviously in over her head but sensing that it's time for her to turn up the heat, Carol knocks back shots of hard liquor, dances frenetically, and endures the hard kiss Cliff plasters on her lips, all the while wearing an exaggerated smile. As she steps back to reapply her lipstick, she takes a close look in the mirror. The film pauses with her for a brief somber moment of reflection as Carol stares at herself and shakes her head, as if trying to shake herself out of a nightmare. For such a highly theatrical scene, it is an intensely private moment in Raines's performance and a pivotal point in Carol's story. The self-confrontation raises the question, according to Imogen Sara Smith, of "how far the sheltered Kansas will let herself go in the interests of justice."

Of any scene or theme in the film, this extended passage of musical and sexual furor had been the chief concern of the censors during development and writing. Joseph Breen's notes to Universal included a directive that "the relationship between Carol and Cliff should be handled carefully in this sequence, especially the business of Carol dancing, to avoid any offensive suggestiveness"—a warning that went unheeded. Breen actually expressed deeper concerns over the portrayal of Cliff and his fellow players as junkies than the sexual excess, instructing that the film should "avoid any intimation that Cliff and the rest of the musicians are dope addicts."

Although Harrison did capitulate somewhat when it came to how the drummer's drug consumption was treated, she forged ahead with the lascivious interplay between Carol and Cliff. Pushed to the hilt by Arthur Hilton's rousing editing, it stands out as one of noir's most frenzied and excessive scenes. (The Production Code Administration may have let it slide, but some localities took their own measures; a Pennsylvania theater cut out all the close-ups of Cliff's supercharged beating of the drums during "Jeannie's" dance.) Most film critics were wise to the scene's symbolism at the time, though it was the *Nation*'s James Agee who best summed it up, observing that the "jam session [is] used as a metaphor for orgasm and death—which in turn becomes a metaphor for the jam session."

Phantom Lady is resolved when Carol is confronted by Marlow in his studio apartment. He is about to strangle her when Inspector Burgess and police break down the door, which motivates Marlow to end his life by jumping from a window. In the film's coda, Carol joins Burgess and the now-exonerated Henderson at the engineering firm for a celebratory toast, neatly bringing the story full circle (and seemingly returning her to her secretarial role). Burgess and Henderson scurry out, leaving her alone in Henderson's office, listening to his voice on the Dictaphone and taking notation. A surprise "cute" ending hits a romantic comedy note when she hears him interrupt a mundane memo to propose marriage. The film fades out as she listens to his voice repeat (with the needle stuck, skipping on a groove), "and every night, every night, every night . . ."

Some film analysts have questioned whether *Phantom Lady*'s feminist logic is overturned by its ending. The implication, critics suggest, is that she will now set aside her detective skills (and probably her day job) in order to become Scott's wife, a role that brought little happiness to the previous Mrs. Henderson. (An adulteress whose bad choices left her husband to hang, she hovers outside the film's frame not unlike Rebecca of Manderley.)

While this interpretation certainly has merit, *Phantom Lady* is purposely constructed to encourage an alternative view of Carol's future. For one, Carol's resourcefulness and tough independence—exhibited throughout the film—are not undone simply because the ending has her contemplating marriage. Second, the marriage proposal is treated in a completely nontraditional way, with Scott absent and Carol alone in the room. This twist thwarts romantic convention in a way that is in keeping with the modern, self-conscious characterization of Carol in general.

Released in January 1944, *Phantom Lady* enjoyed commercial success, as a sleeper that built its audience gradually. The film proved to Universal that Harrison's instincts about the wartime women's market had been correct.

She may have been more attuned to growing cultural trends of "haunted women" than even she knew. Between February and June 1944, a department store in New York City reported that fifty thousand Ouija boards had been sold to customers who were mesmerized by their movements and hoped to receive messages about soldiers abroad. The store saw this female preoccupation with the occult as an attempt "to engage with the emotional and epistemological uncertainties of wartime." Joan was speaking directly to this burgeoning demographic by invoking the figure of a modern, working woman whom she had essentially handcrafted: the secretary who can't stay away from a good mystery.

Harrison was widely celebrated for moving the horror genre out of the B-class and saluted for turning "a womanly experiment into a box-office bonanza." The picture proved a positive test case for Universal. With its stylish look and artistic flourishes, it helped elevate the studio's image. It even marked a turning point in Woolrich's career, raising his books into the A-list as well.

Joan was part of a new vision for Universal, providing a benchmark for the original, offbeat film noirs that were to come. Over a series of articles in the *New York Times*, critic Fred Stanley cited this trend of Hollywood shelving war projects while "a new horror cycle is being launched on a far more ambitious level than the forerunning vampire, werewolf and Frankenstein chillers." Universal, in fact, showed early foresight by putting its resources into this cycle and producing, according to Schatz, thrillers and crime pictures that were "the only wartime product that did not lapse into utter predictability."

Joan's success not only jump-started a new storytelling phenomenon, it also helped open doors for other women in Hollywood. In August 1943 RKO signed a feature-producing contract with Harriet Parsons, daughter of powerful gossip columnist Louella Parsons, which was a lifeline out of her job writing, directing, and producing shorts for Poverty Row. In February 1944 scenarist Virginia Van Upp was hired as a producer by Columbia, where she would soon promote Rita Hayworth's career while making herself invaluable to Harry Cohn. Harrison, Parsons, and Van Upp could be spotted at cocktail parties putting "their heads together and talking [things] over"—a sign of the power and influence they shared. Though less visible, there were many more "organization women" working throughout the system, in an array of positions and at all levels.

At the time, trendspotters speculated that the promotion of women at major studios was a wartime phenomenon, a result of the "man shortage." This was temporary, they said, not unlike the way that certain movie genres came and went out of style. It would be up to Joan and her compatriots to prove them wrong.

13 | NEW ASSOCIATIONS

BY THE TIME *PHANTOM LADY* arrived in theaters in January 1944, Joan had debuted another passion project: a new house. She had commissioned esteemed Hungarian architect Paul László to design a California home boasting one of the most coveted (and hardest-to-acquire) views in Hollywood: the Los Angeles Country Club. The new home would be located only a block away from her Wilshire Palms apartment in Westwood, at 874 Birchwood Drive, near the intersection of Wilshire Boulevard and Comstock Avenue.

László, who had established himself in Germany before emigrating to the United States in 1936, created a modernist, Miesian box-style house meant for, he mused, "an intellect, a lady, . . . [a] bachelor." With redwood exteriors, it sat perched atop a steep hill surrounded by tall maples and oaks, imparting a panorama of the golf course (too exclusive to grant membership to movie people) as well as Beverly Hills and Culver City. The house was U-shaped, with a garden courtyard at the center. This created two symmetrical wings extending out from the foyer. The kitchen, dining room, and living room occupied the north wing, with the master suite and an office bedroom in the south wing.

The house's interior played with contrasts. The walls and carpeting were light gray, with just a few drapes in creamy yellow. László designed all the furniture, per his usual custom, creating a visual splash with red cushy chairs and an overstuffed moss green sofa gathered around a large oval-shaped coffee table. A terra cotta brick fireplace spanned the length of one wall, forming a grand arch, flanked by massive bookshelves on each side. The mantel was topped by two wrought-iron candelabra with coordinated green tapers. Joan's bedroom contained a special closet called a "'turnabout' dressing room," reflective French vanity doors that moved on a track, opening up into a closet or closing together to form one full-length mirror.

Floor-to-ceiling windows predominated in almost every room, creating a spacious, airy feel and adding an optical flow; it was possible to see from one room to another, and even across the garden from one wing to another. The window-walls were rolled aside during the day, making for easy access to the courtyard. The clean, orderly lines accentuated this seamlessness between indoors and outdoors. Add to this interiors filled with green landscaping (such as potted plants embedded in tables and wall units) and, according to the *New York Times*, the house "look[ed] like an extensive private park." László, an "architect to the stars" (including Cary Grant and Barbara Stanwyck), later pronounced that of all his designs, his two favorites were his own home and Harrison's.

This showroom home served as proof that her career was on the rise; she was "a woman looking forward, not back," according to an architectural piece in the *Atlanta Constitution*. It was an opportunity to promote her personality, which is why she happily hosted tours for the journalists and photographers who trotted in from all corners. She held court "as if she were a congresswoman," according to the *Winnipeg Tribune*. In one publicity photo, she lounges in her courtyard mulling over script notes with writer Keith Winter as she smokes a cigarette and leisurely dangles one leg over her chair's arm rest. And in another, she pores over a screenplay while reclining in bed, wearing a sexy silk nightgown and robe, cozying up to some of her favorite accessories—her books and telephone.

Joan's new abode was ideal for hosting parties, at a time when the fad on the West Coast (at least per the *New York Times*) was "entertaining at home." She was known not for throwing large, lavish affairs but for regaling a few close friends. She fit the bill as "a disarming hostess [who] romps around her spacious home like a puppy." On a more solemn note, she opened her home up to soldiers on Sunday afternoons, serving up soup and receiving news from the British front.

The place also reflected the value Joan placed on privacy. Far removed from the bustle of cars and commerce down below, the hilltop roost offered seclusion and quiet. It diminished the chances of unwanted visitors or prying eyes and left its inhabitant free to fully preside over her romantic life. Her bedroom featured a concealed back entrance that led out to the courtyard and down the rear yard stepping stones.

It also meant she could spot anyone who approached, from almost any direction and from several blocks away. No question, Joan liked to be in control. She was also, perhaps subconsciously, revisiting a distant memory. The Grove in Guildford had rested on top of a hill above the village, granting a privileged view of bourgeois life.

Joan's investment in the Birchwood house was a gutsy decision. Separated from her family by the war, she was on her own and, at the time of the initial property purchase in late 1941, confronting one of the most precarious points of her career. (She received an inheritance after her father's death in 1942, but the money was funneled directly into an offshore account to protect it from the British government during the war.) But Joan wanted what she wanted: a house of her own. She wasn't the type to let self-doubt get in her way, let alone political upheaval or professional downfalls.

She was already facing career challenges. For all the fanfare surrounding Joan's Universal contract, she had only a one-picture deal. Despite her good work on *Phantom Lady*, Nathan Blumberg and Cliff Work declined to extend her contract before the film even released. "The front office attitude resented a woman in authority," she later recalled, adding, "I felt grateful to Universal for they had gambled on me. Naturally, I was hurt that they didn't think enough of me. I was like the young Hollywood starlets, an option orphan."

She decided to venture outside the studio system when she received a call from Hunt Stromberg. The man behind the Thin Man series and the Jeanette MacDonald / Nelson Eddy operettas—and one of the highest-paid executives in the United States—had resigned from MGM in a bold decision to form the independent Hunt Stromberg Productions. In fall 1943 he asked Joan to consider producing an adaptation of the play *Guest in the House*. Based on a story by Katharine Albert, it had enjoyed a successful New York run the year prior. United Artists would distribute.

Joan determined that *Guest in the House* made for a perfect follow up to *Phantom Lady*, and joining forces with Stromberg was an alluring prospect. She also was aware of the control afforded independent producers, who had just begun to consolidate their industry power, announcing the establishment of the Society of Independent Motion Picture Producers (SIMPP) in January 1942.

The organization had been formed by a small group of pioneer independents that included Charlie Chaplin, Douglas Fairbanks, Mary Pickford, and Samuel Goldwyn, precipitated by the need for moderately budgeted films to feed the expanding wartime movie market. Stromberg was the first person added to SIMMP after its formation.

Whereas at Universal Joan had had to adhere to a tight schedule, with Stromberg she had newfound freedom. "We have a forty-day schedule, but if we run a few days over, no one is going to have a fit," she explained. "This is a perfect set up."

The story line of the play *Guest in the House* offered promising material: A happily married couple, Ann and Douglas Procter, invite an emotionally troubled woman to stay at their home as a favor to Douglas's younger brother, Dan. As the beautiful patient Evelyn Heath settles in, she writes mad passages in her diary and begins to believe she's falling in love with Douglas, who is a commercial artist. Increasingly jealous of Douglas's live-in model, Miriam Blake, Evelyn poisons the household with false rumors about an affair between the husband and his muse. She continues on a path of domestic destruction, turning everyone against each other. Upon finding out she is going to be sent away, she cranks up the pressure, bringing scandal upon the family and provoking revenge.

In the planning phase, *Guest in the House* seemed to incorporate many of Joan's favorite ingredients: a gothic genre located in a Maine coastal setting, violence and sexual tensions lurking beneath the facade of an apparently happy home life, and a powerful female force at the heart of the narrative action. True, the character of Evelyn Heath as originally written left a lot to be desired, but in the film adaptation she needn't be a typical femme fatale. There was room to explore why she felt so alienated from the social fabric—especially once the filmmakers decided to use her diary and voice-over narration to explore her inner thoughts. Joan was set to coproduce and cowrite. Her collaborator on the script would be Elliot Paul, who had one credit—*A Woman's Face* (1941).

Anne Baxter was cast in the role of Evelyn, though Stromberg had initially wanted Barbara Bel Geddes. Joseph Cotten was tested for the lead, but the less intense Ralph Bellamy ended up playing Douglas Proctor, with Ruth Warrick supporting as Ann. The role of brother Dan (now a psychoanalyst rather than a nutritionist) went to Scott McKay. The model who becomes Evelyn's imagined rival would be played by Marie McDonald, whose nickname "the Body" suggested her suitability for the role.

Joan's friend Lewis Milestone would direct. He and Stromberg had plans for a one-picture-per-year deal, as "Milly" too sought to carve out his own territory. The director was coming off two powerful war movies, *Edge of Darkness* (which, like *First Comes Courage*, romanticized the Norwegian resistance) and *The North Star* (a highly regarded, controversial portrait of the Russian wartime experience), so *Guest in the House* represented lighter fare. Joan, Elliot Paul, and Milly worked on developing the material through November and December 1943. Though parts of the original story were going to be hammy regardless of what the filmmakers did to them—the frantic diary scribbling, the incessant sketching sessions meant to heal Evelyn's mind, the shrieks that pierce the house when the Proctors' young daughter shows her a pet bird (Evelyn is hysterically afraid of birds)—their creative inclinations tilted away from contrivances and clichés.

By late January 1944, however, Joan and Hunt Stromberg weren't seeing eye to eye. He wasn't taking her ideas seriously. Might she have proposed complicating the femme fatale angle, as her previous work had done? Perhaps she fought for a less sinister conclusion than having Evelyn flee the house in a fury and plunge off a cliff to her death (which is what happens in the final version). Ultimately, the partnership that had begun with so much promise ended. The *Hollywood Reporter* stated that Joan was quitting "over a misunderstanding" with the producer. The *Los Angeles Times* announced that she was leaving "the Hunt Stromberg set up" and "going to achieve independency more or less immediately."

That same week, the trades announced that she had purchased "The Blue House on Wagram," a magazine story by Greta Czinch, and was bidding on two other properties. She was feeling out distribution deals with both RKO and United Artists. Hedda Hopper stated that Harrison and Joan Fontaine were considering the prospect of forging their own independent company, pending Fontaine's intended suit against David O. Selznick. Taken together, these developments suggest that the real reason for Joan's departure may have been simply that she wanted to *be* the next Hunt Stromberg, not work for him.

As for the fate of *Guest in the House*, Stromberg reassigned the script to Ketti Frings (whose novel *Hold Back the Dawn* had been adapted into a 1941 Charles Boyer / Olivia de Havilland vehicle). Filming began in April at the

Providencia Ranch in Hollywood Hills (a location once used by D. W. Griffith and Cecil B. DeMille). As production ratcheted up in May, Milestone was struck with appendicitis and collapsed on the set. The emerging director Andre de Toth took over. Sporting a signature black patch over one eye (he had lost his sight to a childhood injury), de Toth had come up through the Hungarian theater before apprenticing with the mighty Alexander Korda. After two weeks on *Guest in the House*, other commitments, unfortunately, kept him from continuing. Finally, John Brahm, who had developed a reputation in melodrama—and for "filling in"—finished the picture. Milestone's hopes for an ongoing relationship with Stromberg came to an abrupt end.

For all of the speculation in the press, Joan's actual choice to follow up *Phantom Lady* turned out to be the gothic Louisiana mystery *Dark Waters*. Though on its face not so different from *Guest in the House*—it was an independent production with a UA distribution deal—*Dark Waters* would prove worlds apart both in tone and in its thoughtful treatment of the female protagonist. Originally published as a serial in the *Saturday Evening Post* in spring 1944, the story came from the husband-and-wife team of Francis and Marian Cockrell, who, having met at Tulane University a few years earlier, had been inspired by their Louisiana surroundings.

Dark Waters involves a traumatized woman's rescue. She has spent two weeks on a lifeboat after the ship she and her wealthy parents had taken from Batavia (now Jakarta, Indonesia) was torpedoed. Having lost her memory, with no known relatives—her parents died in the attack—she receives a letter from a long-lost aunt and uncle inviting her to recover at their estate. Once on her family's plantation and under a young psychiatrist's care, she worries that she suffers from insanity, telling her doctor that she hears ghostly voices and notices strange occurrences in the house. After a workman turns up dead, she frantically calls the doctor to the house. A deadly chase through the swamp ensues before the woman and the doctor manage to overpower the real culprits: the people posing as her "aunt" and "uncle," who in fact have murdered her true kin. They sought to kill her off so that they could have the plantation and her inheritance all to themselves.

Dark Waters would be a vehicle for *First Comes Courage* star Merle Oberon. Susan Hayward had owned the part for about a minute, but Oberon put her husband, Alexander Korda, on the job as her lobbyist—even though they were in the process of divorcing—and he worked the necessary angles with existing producers and potential directors, many of whom saw that he still carried a torch for his estranged wife. Ever elusive with her raven hair and almond-shaped, hazel eyes, Oberon was moving into a "haunted, romantic" phase, no longer the "eager, passionate girl who invaded London" as a café hostess in the 1930s. The role of Leslie Calvin, the character who would endure a dramatic journey from wearied castaway to heroine, offered her a chance to visually transform on-screen, while demonstrating the kind of emotional depth that had won her praise in *Wuthering Heights* (1939).

The executive producers were the Orsatti brothers, Frank, Ernie, and Victor, who anticipated the Corleone family in Francis Ford Coppola's *The Godfather* as they played the part of Hollywood power brokers. This is how they were viewed retrospectively by Andre de Toth, who found himself being seduced for the role of director by "full-time playboy, full-time agent, full-time pilot" Victor Orsatti. Unconvinced this was a real deal, a few days later de Toth was sitting in front of his former mentor Korda, lunching over the script and discussing an immediate start date. "'*We*' have to save [Merle] from a disaster . . . the dreadful script," Korda pleaded, according to de Toth. "It was 'our duty' to save her . . . and he almost cried and I almost cried. I said yes and felt noble about it." De Toth pried the details from Korda. What was the budget? Between $500,000 and $600,000, which set it well above B-level. Where would the picture be filmed? At General Services Studio, space provided by participating producer Benedict Bogeaus. They were looking at a genuine independent production.

It was May 1944 and Joan had already signed on, for which de Toth was more than grateful. The script, adapted by Marian Cockrell, may not have been as bad as de Toth claimed (he called it "the biggest piece of shit" he had ever read), but it did indeed need a lot of work. This was Cockrell's first attempt at a screenplay, and she was writing it solo, with her husband and writing partner called to serve in the US Marines. (She did have one consolation: they had negotiated a near-record-setting deal with Bogeaus, which totaled $100,000 when factoring in profit participation.) Though Joan was given cowriter status, she did not actually collaborate with Marian on the original script; the title was essentially given in lieu of producing credit. Rather, she would provide writing support at the next stage.

In addition to Joan, there were seven producers. All were male (of course) and not particularly receptive to having Harrison crash their club. De Toth remembered his initial dinner at the Bogeaus home in Beverly Hills, during which the former junkyard dealer turned producer (he had remade himself a couple times over) declared, "We have a woman 'producer.' I hope it will not offend you."

"What's wrong with women producers?" his wife, heiress Mimi Forsythe, asked, beating de Toth to the punch. Bogeaus walked the length of their formal dining room table and gave her ten condescending kisses, one for each bejeweled finger, before responding, "Nothing, dear, as long as they are producing children."

In truth, it was the film's male producers (Bogeaus, Arthur Landau, Carley Harriman, and James Nasser and his brothers, of the San Francisco theater chain) who were well out of their depth. Among their lapses was the fact that the studio space was only available for certain dates, and they were going into production with the new script barely begun. "Separately they were house-broken, together, they became a seven-headed dragon in panic," according to de Toth. "Joan, the only pro in the unholy co-op, was outvoted but hung in there, standing firm against a bunch of male chauvinists." The director made it clear that he would only speak to Harrison. She was the conduit back to the money men, even though de Toth was sure "she despised them more than I did."

Harrison had entered her deal with Bogeaus under the assumption they were equal partners. She gave enthusiastic interviews early in *Dark Waters'* production period expressing excitement about her prospects as an associate producer at United Artists: "Bogeaus handles the money and I take care of all the artistic angles. I pass on every detail. Fabrics for costuming and the completed garments, sets, lighting, casting." She thought she'd found her niche. Not too long after, she realized he didn't see her as an equal.

Joan summoned reinforcements, suggesting her friend Franchot Tone for the part of Dr. George Grover, the country doctor who becomes the primary love interest. Some of her colleagues pushed back on the choice, arguing that he was wrong for the part. But Joan liked the role for him because it was simple and earnest. Ever loyal, Tone was happy to help a friend in need, welcoming the opportunity to step outside the majors. (He ended up with a dose of mild regret; he didn't get along particularly well with Oberon.)

Joan's greatest contribution to *Dark Waters*, however, came in the form of a tall, craggy-faced Irish writer-director fresh from the European warfront (where he had filmed the documentary *The Battle of San Pietro*). His name was John Huston. He certainly knew his way around both the macabre (*The Maltese Falcon*, 1941) and the woman's film (*In This Our Life*, 1942). And he was spending a lot of time in Joan's company as his marriage to Lesley Black fell apart. Huston had only one true love, though: the racetrack. Joan knew that and used his weakness to her advantage. Desperate for money, he agreed to perform an uncredited rewrite on the long-awaited script.

Perhaps against their better judgment, Harrison and de Toth signed off on an unconventional arrangement brokered by wartime cameraman and John's close friend Jules Buck: Huston would be paid by the page. That way, beyond a required minimum, he could count on getting money every day, provided he churned out whatever scenes were needed for the next setup. Assuming they were approved by the director, of course.

The unusual arrangement appeared to be delivering dividends, as Huston spent his nights churning out pages and his days at the track. One particular morning, however, Joan saw the other producers file onto the soundstage. Jim Nasser, Landau, and Bogeaus, in particular, had questions for Harrison and de Toth. *The characters' names have been changed. Why? Where did all these new scenes come from? Does this require new sets, add more days to the schedule, inflate the budget?* The men were terrified that their budget was going up in smoke. Harrison remained calm and waited for their steam to run out. She and de Toth took a look at the day's script. Huston had turned in twenty-eight pages, but twenty-one of those had been recycled from *The Maltese Falcon*. Apparently, it was a big racing day at Hollywood Park and Huston wanted to go prepared. Harrison and de Toth concluded that there was enough original material to shoot for a few days, and Huston always came through. She had kept her cool, and the seven-headed dragon was kept at bay.

The Louisiana setting lent a special air to *Dark Waters*: the backwater bayous, sugarcane fields, and Spanish moss made for a peculiar gothic atmosphere. Though the Nasser brothers pushed for production to take place on location, in the end, most shooting occurred on the soundstage. An advance team of researchers and second-unit photographers, led by de Toth, traveled for two weeks to Three Rivers Plantation in Covington to gather art-design material before continuing on to rural Teche Country (north of New Orleans), where they filmed long shots of the stars' body doubles. Joan was not needed on that trip. Her place was back at the studio, where the crew attended to such tasks as making quicksand from mashed potatoes, cornmeal, coffee beans, and dampened corn flakes.

Joan took it upon herself to make sure that Oberon, who could exasperate even her closest friends, wouldn't balk at such challenges as wading through artificial quicksand. The actress was known for vacillating between stoic perfectionism and neurotic neediness. The final script called for Oberon to begin the story as a "blank" woman, completely drained of any memory of her life. Gradually, as the character begins to solve the mystery that the aunt and uncle are frauds, she regains her sense of self. True to the cinematic gothic, her psychological journey unfolds in tandem with her physical encounters with the family estate. The architectural spaces and soundscapes of the home function metaphorically as her psychic and mental landscape. *Dark Waters* returned Harrison to the themes of *Rebecca* and *Suspicion*, while also invoking *Jamaica Inn* (a woman stranded in unfamiliar territory with relatives she doesn't trust).

While this was comfortable terrain for Harrison, it was distressing for Oberon. She had welcomed—even fought for—the opportunity to show an unrefined side, yet she dreaded the prospect of letting her guard down. Her anxiety heightened as shooting approached (even as she made sure there was a space on set for her lover, Lucien Ballard, the cinematographer who had invented the "Obie," a light specially designed to "polish" Oberon's face).

Making things more challenging, the actress almost always wore an emotional mask, one that concealed a complicated family history. The official line was that she had been born to a British Army officer father and an English-Dutch-French mother as the couple traveled through Tasmania. The truth was that her mother, Constance Selby, was only twelve years old when she gave birth to Merle in Bombay. Her grandmother, Charlotte, raised her and her mother as sisters. Merle, whose maternal lineage descended from Sri Lanka and the Māori, spent her adult life passing as a white Western European, maintaining the charade that Charlotte was her mother and relegating her "sister" Constance to life's dim recesses. The actress kept a portrait of her "mother," in actuality a painting of an anonymous white woman, in the foyer of her Bel Air home.

But shepherding her lead actress through difficult emotional terrain was part of the job that Joan particularly embraced. Actors, she explained, are "all creative people, and creative people are not the easiest people in the world to handle. You have to be a diplomat and bring out the best in everyone." And given that this was Harrison's second project with Oberon, she was accustomed to the actress's vicissitudes.

The actress made it through *Dark Waters* to good reviews. Upon its November 1944 release, *New York Times* reviewer Bosley Crowther described the "killer-diller of a thriller" as "neatly produced and directed—and well-played by an excellent cast." Oberon's "fear-ridden, flexible female," he said, was "properly distraught."

Clearly, Joan had successfully managed a difficult performer. In fact, she'd probably enjoyed the challenge. Oberon's baroque personality must have fascinated her. She couldn't resist working with people whose surface lives disguised an inner emotional world that was constantly churning. Her next film would grant her one of her greatest opportunities to do just that.

14 | BEDEVILING ENDINGS

THE STAGE PLAY *UNCLE HARRY* offered an intriguing glimpse into the unusual undercurrents of a "family romance" in a quaint New Hampshire town. Penned by Thomas Job and produced by Clifford Hayman, the play had enjoyed a yearlong run in London and played four hundred performances on Broadway. To produce the film adaptation, Joan would return to Universal. Her reunion with the studio was announced in December 1944, one month after the premiere of *Dark Waters*.

Plans for the launch of *Uncle Harry* made headlines on February 13, 1945. This time, all signs indicated Joan had maximum support from Universal, which paid an impressive price for the script rights—over $150,000. The specifics of Joan's contract gave her further reason to smile. Universal was giving her full-fledged producer status, retiring the "associate" title, with a three-picture commitment. She would receive a lump sum payment of $30,000, plus $1,000 per week, and would soon be the second-highest-paid producer at the studio, behind Joseph Sistrom.

She was also fortunate to be working with power agent turned producer Charles Feldman, who would partly own and distribute the film. Feldman, who had helped package *Phantom Lady*, was bringing in his client Ella Raines to headline. But he wasn't interested in the details; he put production in Joan's hands. She signed a like-minded writer to perform the adaptation: Keith Winter, who had written British stage plays such as *The Rats of Norway* (1933) and *The Shining Hour* (1934) and participated in the war-effort collaboration *Forever and a Day* (1943). (Stephen Longstreet would later arrive to make substantial revisions.) And she secured Robert Siodmak to direct. Siodmak had just made the Ella Raines / Charles Laughton vehicle *The Suspect*, a Universal noir that struck many of Harrison's chords. Though she'd had good reason to go out on her own with Stromberg, she must have been relieved to be back in known territory.

Uncle Harry follows Harry Melville Quincey, a mild-mannered man in his late thirties who lives a dull life as everyone's "Uncle" in the fictional town of Corinth, New Hampshire. From a moneyed family, he is destined to live out his days with his two older sisters, Lettie and Hester, until a marriage announcement by former paramour Lucy rouses him into action. Harry's decision to win back Lucy spurs domestic tension and, specifically, hostility from the overly possessive Lettie. In the end, he kills Lettie, frames Hester for her murder, and nearly gets away with sending her to the gallows until he discovers that Hester has a final card to play.

For the screen version, Harrison worked with Winter to alter both character and plot. Now a textile desiger, Harry meets his love interest for the first time when she breezes in from New York City to provide some consulting for the mill where he works. No longer a domesticated woman between marriages (the original Lucy is a widow whose "outstanding characteristic is her extreme normality"), Deborah Brown (as she has been renamed) works as a fashion expert. She spots Harry, and they fall in love. As in the play, the engagement pushes Lettie over the edge; her affection turns to obsession as she spends months manufacturing reasons to prevent them from finalizing their marriage. Though conflicted by his concern for his more caring sister, Hester, Harry finally decides to liberate himself and elope to New York with Deborah. At this very moment, Lettie pretends that she has fallen ill, which keeps Harry home. Several weeks later, when Harry hears that Deborah has married her boss in New York, he prepares poisoned hot cocoa to give to Lettie. To Harry's dismay, Hester is mistakenly given the drink and dies. Lettie is presumed to be the murderer and led to the gallows. Harry reckons with the moral weight of his actions, which prevents him happiness with Deborah.

The film adaptation was titled *The Strange Affair of Uncle Harry* during preproduction and on its later rerelease but was named *Uncle Harry* for its initial run. For the title role, Joan looked no further than Hitchcock's gallery, selecting George Sanders, who had portrayed Scott ffolliott in *Foreign*

Correspondent and Jack Favell in *Rebecca*. (The Russian-born actor had paid his dues as a copywriter in a London-based advertising firm around the same time as Joan, before perfecting his debonair, often cavalier persona on the British stage.) The challenging role of Lettie Quincey, who slides the scale between distant and chilly to grotesquely saccharine, went to the talented Irish actress Geraldine Fitzgerald. She had a reputation for independent-minded, even stubborn characters, a persona fueled by her various rebellions against studio heads for assigning her mundane characters. Moyna MacGill, another Irishwoman and Angela Lansbury's mother, was cast as older sister Hester. Joan had seen her on stage several years earlier and made a note to keep her in mind for a suitable role.

Joan relished the chance to reteam with Ella Raines, who had consolidated her star status over the past year. The role of the fashion designer Deborah Brown played to her strengths: a modern, urban, stylish woman with an impish, knowing attitude. Though Raines's character was no spiderwoman in *Uncle Harry*, she would display a sexual experience and assertiveness that was completely overwhelming to the repressed bachelor. (The character had been a divorcée until censors forced a script change.) Deborah Brown was an ideal fit for a star such as Raines, who knew her own mind and sought to embody complicated women—those more in line with her friendly yet feisty personality.

"Deborah Brown" fashions were conceived for the film by famed designer Travis Banton, whose name had been synonymous with Marlene Dietrich and Carole Lombard at Paramount in the 1930s. It was no accident that the "style preview" publicity stills for the movie looked so similar to Harrison's own photo spreads; Banton's designs matched Joan's Hollywood corporate style to a tee. Harrison and Raines shared a mutual admiration for the designer's day and evening wear, as well as an abiding friendship with Banton. He dressed them similarly, in chic women's suit separates, with superior cuts and playful touches. *Uncle Harry* would prove a cornerstone in defining each woman's style—the two were photographed "all dressed up" with Banton on the set—and would influence their taste for years to come.

Harrison worked with Banton to code the characters' moral and psychological perspectives through fashion. By means of simple light and dark contrasts, Hester and Lettie were repeatedly represented in opposition, with the fair-haired widow Hester wearing black dresses and brunette Lettie in white. More intriguingly, Harry's bride-to-be is dressed in grays, stripes, and plaids, complicating the monochromatic, oppositional scheme established by the sisters. And Deborah wears what Banton called "little boy" type clothing— suits, ties, and sport jackets—which starkly contrast with Lettie's softer, more draped, or more decorative dresses. Joan specifically wanted her to be dressed in "mannish sports clothes—to emphasize her direct and forthright manner" as compared to Lettie, who should have an "extremely feminine wardrobe, complete with negligee and frills."

These were thoughtful if somewhat obvious ways to use costume cues to dramatize character and motive. But there were more playful designs at work too. On closer inspection, one can see that Harrison was in cahoots with Banton and Raines, playfully experimenting with fashion codes of drag. The "mannish" versus "frilly" opposition offered yet another way to express the spectacle of repressed gender relations and homosexual and heterosexual desires. The movie's campiness helps underscore the point that its key figures really were having fun with fashion both on-screen and off.

Joan and Ella themselves had become good friends, despite Joan being thirteen years the actress's senior. They socialized through Charles Feldman's social circuit and went nightclubbing with Dietrich and Greer Garson. They were a study in contrasts: brunette Ella versus blonde Joan; Ella's long, soft locks offsetting Joan's tight, short do; Ella's light-colored, curvy trench coat opposite Joan's checkered suit and black top hat. Stylish cross-dressing wasn't all that scandalous; Dietrich and Greta Garbo had made it fashionable a decade prior. When Joan and Ella were seen after hours in Banton's mannish styles, however, it specifically extended the *Uncle Harry* screen space into an exotic "real world" of nightclubs, supper parties, and red carpets. Highly attuned movie fans and industry insiders may have spotted the way the women were making mischief with notions of butch and femme.

In the case of Joan and Ella, however, there was a complicating factor. During this time, Raines had been keeping her marriage to Captain Kenneth Trout under wraps. The long-held secret had meant that for years she had thwarted advances from many of Hollywood's most sought-after bachelors. Without an obvious beau, she gradually became the subject of the lavender rumor mill, with "whispers hinting at something far worse" than a husband hidden away somewhere. As the actress's sexuality began to be questioned, clouds of suspicion began to loosely form around the producer too. "Everybody wants pictures of them together," commented Hedda Hopper, describing an evening when Marlene Dietrich invited them over for some scrambled eggs. Looking to protect Raines's star image, Universal curbed the accent on her sensuality and underscored her sportiness. "She spends her evenings pitching baseball with the kids in the street," the studio remarked, as if the tomboy angle would squash speculation.

With Raines, drag fashion was frivolous flirtation for the cameras. But there was a more serious side to Joan's relationships with women, and occasionally strong romantic attachments. She was no prude; she kept an open mind. Joan led an expansive love life at the time, safeguarded by protective studios and favorably disposed columnists. Some of her strongest bonds were with women, though she kept most at bay, maintaining a cool distance if she didn't feel an instant affinity.

Evelyn Keyes was someone with whom Joan had immediate chemistry. The glowing blonde (who was sometimes brunette) was jovial and animated—a real straight shooter. Born in Port Arthur, Texas, to a wealthy oil man, Keyes had moved with her mother as a youngster to Atlanta after the premature death of her father. It had been a group effort on the part of her sisters and grandmother to raise her as a perfect "Georgia Peach," which led to disappointment when she set out in her late teens to fulfill a Hollywood dream. A personal contract with Cecil B. DeMille brought this within reach but also unveiled the mechanical nature of the studio system. Full of vim and vigor (and sharp intelligence), Keyes rarely conformed. For all of the studios' efforts to drill out her southern accent, everything about her remained deep belle. These roots, plus many hours of training in acting, voice, and stage presence, helped position her to win the part of Scarlett O'Hara's younger sister Suellen O'Hara in *Gone with the Wind*. The score was both a blessing (it gave her epic visibility) and a curse (it pegged her as "secondary" and led to B-roles).

It was on the shared ground of *Gone with the Wind* and *Rebecca*—which is to say, the lot at Selznick International Pictures—that Harrison met Keyes, who actually auditioned for Joan, Alma, and Hitchcock during the *Rebecca* screen tests. Joan was more than ten years older than Evelyn, and more world-wise. Still, she had an appreciation for the clear-eyed view that her new acquaintance could offer on an industry that—to her—was completely foreign. Though Keyes herself had not been in Hollywood long, she provided a firsthand case study of how the system put women through the wringer. During the making of *Gone with the Wind*, she endured a botched abortion to avoid ruffling the feathers of Selznick, DeMille, and her soon-to-be-husband, businessman Barton Bainbridge. Not long after, in 1940, while she was seeing then-married Charles Vidor and separated from Bainbridge, her husband committed suicide. Keyes later reflected that she spent most of her life "looking for my new daddy." But no wallflower was she. She continued her relationship with Vidor, and in 1944 they married. It didn't last.

Keyes's liaison with Vidor overlapped with the production of *First Comes Courage*, when Harrison and Arzner were replaced by Vidor and a new set of writers. Keyes was under contract at Columbia at that time, so the two women encountered each other regularly. From then on, they were thick as thieves, indulging in mutual interests, from tennis to French to literature. (Keyes was a natural-born writer.) Men would come and go, but Joan was thankful to have Evelyn as a true confidante. Some who knew Joan well have speculated that their relationship was romantic (or at least that Joan wished it was), while others are dubious.

In any event, Joan was less likely than her actress friends to get caught up in rumors about her sexuality. On the one hand, she was less visible, and on the other, when the press did cover her, it was usually linking her to a long roster of male suitors. In spring 1945, during production of *Uncle Harry*, her most visible suitor of the moment was director—and US Army colonel—Anatole Litvak. Tola, as his friends called him, had returned from wartime service working on the acclaimed propaganda film *The Battle of Russia* and other entries in the Why We Fight series with none other than Irwin Shaw. Now he was filming RKO's *The Long Night* (1947). The *Los Angeles Examiner* followed Joan and Tola's romance through the month of April ("It's getting to be a habit with Col. Anatole Litvak and Joan Harrison"), spotting them at the Hotel de Crillon.

The Russian-born director spoke five languages and boasted a bold crown of prematurely white hair. Hailing from the old world, he fit her mold in many ways. Tola was, according to Edward G. Robinson, "surely one of the most urbane, sophisticated, gourmet, haute monde, anti-Nazis I've ever known," alluding in this last point to the controversial *Confessions of a Nazi Spy* (1939), which Litvak made in concert with the Roosevelt administration and which resulted in his being placed on Adolf Hitler's enemies list. Yet, in other ways, Tola made an unlikely romantic partner for Joan. He liked to dominate women in life (his first wife, actress Miriam Hopkins, complained that he believed she should capitulate to him as "the man of the house") and on the screen (where he preferred victims or self-sacrificing damsels).

Joan wasn't so wrapped up with Tola that she was ignoring John Huston, with whom she now shared a deep friendship. She spent much of her time at Huston's San Fernando Valley ranch, just past Edgar Rice Burroughs's Tarzana estate. Surrounded by stables, paddocks, and fruit trees, the Wisconsin pine-wood house was giant in scale—custom made to accommodate Huston's lanky build as well as the assortment of exotic reptiles and animals that skirted through. Tola was also a regular there, as were Sam Spiegel, William Wyler and wife Margaret Tallichet ("Tallie" became a lifelong friend of Joan's), and Humphrey Bogart and his soon-to-be-bride Lauren Bacall.

One romance unfolded right before Joan's eyes that she deeply cherished, adopting the couple as a treasure not to be trifled with: Jules Buck, who had been a fan magazine photographer before meeting Huston while on war assignment, and his consort Joyce Getz. The twenty-year-old glittering green-eyed actress had arrived in Hollywood several years earlier with Bacall (then Betty Perske), and she fell for Jules because "he was the first decent man I met." Soon known as a unit, "Jules and Joyce" were treated like family by John and his father, actor Walter Huston. They stayed over at John's ranch (also called "Tarzana," in light of its proximity to Burroughs's estate) almost as often as he did, given his restlessness. When they wed on January 28, 1945, John stood as best man. Completing the foursome, in the role of maid of honor, was their next closest friend, Joan. Going against bridesmaid norms, she wore a masculine Regency-style riding habit and a black topper, decked by a black veil.

The Bucks and the Hustons (John and Walter, that is) gave Joan a sense of family, but one that was separate from Hitch and Alma. Tarzana offered an escape hatch from Bel Air, Beverly Hills, and even her own Westwood. These boon companions also gave her stability during unpredictable times. On April 12, 1945, the day FDR passed away, she went to dinner with John, Walter, Jules, and Joyce. It was in "talking about the President" and dwelling "only on the man's greatness" that some of their "sense of loss went away," she later recalled.

A sigh of relief came in April, when German forces surrendered. Victory in Europe was declared on May 8, followed the next day by victory in Russia. The war in Europe had ended, and Joan could rest easier knowing that her mother and sister were safe.

She still spent many an evening with the Hitchcocks, having never really left the fold. During the months that the family was in New York supporting Patricia in her stint in *Violet* on Broadway, Joan even took in one of the Hitchcocks' Sealyham terriers, Johnnie. And when they hosted a quiet dinner on Bellagio Road, she rounded out a party of four (sometimes five), always up for whatever followed, whether dancing, Scrabble, or a late-night walk across the Bel Air golf course behind the house. When Whitfield Cook, a Yale graduate who had written *Violet* (along with a slew of short stories), visited Hollywood for the first time in spring 1945, he made note of Joan's proximity to the Hitchcocks, writing in his diary, "Mother and I to Hitchcocks for dinner. Joan Harrison was there. I took her home. She lives in a László house."

Production for *Uncle Harry* ran from mid-April through mid-June. Having found their groove, Harrison and Siodmak worked easily together now. The director joked that he looked forward to their story discussions, when Joan would arrive "carrying a handbag large enough to raise guinea pigs in," and the way she matter-of-factly would work her hands up to her curled coif when it was time for her to drive off the lot. "Out pops a hair pin. Then another. Then another. By the tens. By the hundreds. The pins release the tight curls." Siodmak, who famously enjoyed a happy marriage, nevertheless loved to draw pictures of his producer's blonde waves as they tumbled down her shoulders, juxtaposed to countless hairpins fanned across her desk.

By challenging the bourgeois notion that criminals are other people, far away, *Uncle Harry* spoke to one of Joan's most intense preoccupations. The way she saw it, people tended to associate criminal activity with gangsters or "more emotional types" because those incidents were more widely reported in the news. "We are shocked when we learn of a killing in polite society," she explained. She was on a "one-woman campaign to convince theatergoers that the upper- and middle-classes are just as capable of murder as their fellow humans on the other side of the tracks." Both the play (located in turn-of-the-century Victorian England) and the movie (set in contemporary, "quaint" New England) rested on a similar body of repressed conventions.

The parlor-room murder is shocking because of what the orderly space covers up: the entanglement of resentment, hostility, and erotic tension living quietly within Harry's home.

While the notion that "everyone is a potential killer," as Harrison put it, was disturbing, the story's sexual undercurrents—the sister's possessive and lustful love for her brother—were really what gave the film its charge. Joan upped the ante by decreasing Lettie's age from her forties to her midthirties, which made her rivalry with Deborah seem more believable (and more sexualized). The crux of the story, for the producer, was the love triangle between Harry, Deborah, and Lettie, caused by Lettie's unhealthy attachment and enabled by the other family members. Only Raines's character, who evinces a no-nonsense, pragmatic view of the world, sees the Quincey home as a place of outdated tradition and decay from which her fiancé must either escape or die.

Uncle Harry explored the subconscious implications of psychosexual relationships within the domestic realm, which interested Harrison because they hinted at stormy, unsettled dramas playing out in even the most conventional households. In this case, Lettie's affection turns to hate, and Harry's inertia leads to rage and eventually murder. Even Hester serves as a mirror, revealing her sisterly devotion to be no less conflicted.

The incestuous implications of the film, even if they are mere feelings and not behaviors on Lettie's part (and even if not reciprocated by Harry), made *Uncle Harry* not only controversial but potentially scandalous. Anticipating this, Universal's publicity department advised exhibitors to handle promotion with care, stating that only "once every ten to fifteen years a picture is produced with a theme so delicate, so extremely potent." The studio cautioned against disguising the movie as a standard murder mystery or tender romance, indicating that "every effort should be made to sell this picture's unusual theme in a frank and straightforward manner."

For production, Harrison and Siodmak followed the wartime norm of shooting almost entirely in the studio. Since the small-town New England milieu had bearing on the story, a second-unit camera crew traveled to New Hampshire to capture backgrounds of an unspecified mill town and several railroad stations (for one of the set pieces).

As production for *Uncle Harry* drew to a close, its ending began to cause consternation for Universal executives. Given that the original source material was filled with moral and sexual tensions, the adaptation was bound to require creative strategizing. For instance, the PCA was bothered by a brief revelation in which Hester tells Lettie that she's known all along "how she's felt" about Harry. But to the surprise of Harrison and Siodmak, it wasn't the censors but the Universal front office that started to show last-minute jitters about how to dole out punishment to Harry.

Harrison and her team originally scripted an ending in which Harry is confined to a mental institution after a final good-bye to Deborah. In a final scene, Deborah and Harry's psychiatrist stand on the platform and watch his train roll away. Hester has still died from poisoning, in this scenario, and Lettie has been wrongfully put to death, but Harry has received the narrative punishment required by the production code. Both Universal and Joseph Breen at the PCA office had deemed this satisfactory upon the script's submission in mid-March—and Breen had preapproved it one year prior when RKO proposed it to his office in hopes of getting the project off the ground with Fritz Lang at the helm.

But Universal was concerned that younger audiences, a substantial target demographic, would balk at the finale's dreary tone, so the studio started proposing new possibilities. Desperate to maintain the film's all-important August release date, one of Joan's higher-ups, production manager Martin Murphy, called for Siodmak to produce a new ending in late July. When he refused, veteran Universal director Roy William Neill was brought in to carry out Murphy's instructions. Harrison and Fitzgerald would not participate in any reshoots. In all, five endings were cut together. The *New York Times* described the process of endless edits and test screenings, including a preview at one Los Angeles theater that included all five endings. Joan felt utterly powerless.

Within a week, Universal had settled on a dream sequence ending, imitating the recently lauded *The Woman in the Window* (1944). In this version, Harry is awakened by Deborah, relieved to discover that the poisoning was a nightmare. Deborah, deciding not to marry the boss, has returned to reconcile with him. As they prepare to elope, Hester wishes them well and a conciliatory farewell message arrives from a bedridden Lettie. The dream framework alleviated studio anxieties because the most shocking events were contained inside Harry's mind. Not only did this erase Harry's complicity in Hester's murder *and* Lettie's death, but it allowed him to walk off into a bright future with his bride. Such an ending had the added narrative benefit of obscuring or alleviating some of Lettie's more transgressive behaviors, while still ensuring an on-screen punishment for her inside the dream.

The "cheat" conclusion enraged Joan. Everyone had agreed to the original ending months ago; this was no time for second-guessing. She now admitted she had been skeptical of Universal's commitment to her "professional integrity" from the start: "I doubted the studio's courage to retain an honest ending in which the boy does not get the girl, and I made a point of the ending I wanted before I signed the contract."

She was also irritated that her bosses were letting the youth market drive the decision. She saw *Uncle Harry* as more mature, intellectual fare. The risk involved with making pictures for adults, she said, was "not that audiences won't like them, because I believe motion picture audiences are daily becoming more adult, but that the people at the top of the studios don't yet realize that people of *all* ages, not just bobby soxers, patronize the theaters of America." Joan was also upset with Universal for the way it went about test screenings. The customers had shown up to see a movie of their choosing, only to have a random picture thrust upon them. "They haven't been pre-sold by trailers or advance ballyhoo," she complained, which meant they weren't predisposed favorably to her product. She also felt that too much stock was put into comment cards, which were unscientific by design. Why trust fifty preview cards from an audience of two thousand? "That's not a fair percentage," she said.

She had walked off the Universal lot before the picture was locked, ceding the two remaining projects on her three-picture deal, including an already-prepared adaptation of *The Third Eye*, an Ethel Lina White novel she adored. In abandoning her contract, she left behind her weekly salary.

By now, what once might have seemed like isolated incidents to Joan were forming an obvious pattern. When Joan looked at the studio system, she saw a bastion of patriarchal tradition that had become ossified. She identified the problem as an "industry too set against experimenting these days" and an older generation who had already had its chances in the field. "There aren't enough individualistic producers these days," she observed. "They follow patterns." The producer was "tired of being told again and again, we just can't afford to experiment." This was especially true for women, she reiterated, chafing at a Hollywood that encouraged them to passively "glass-gaze" and fixate on their looks. Her charge was to "look less, think more."

Thoughtful filmmaking was what she'd attempted with *Uncle Harry, Dark Waters,* and even *Guest in the House.* These were ambitious, fresh takes on families, romances, and domestic spaces. They aspired to challenge cinematic codes and narrative conventions in ways that were perceptive, artful, and complicated even for the independent realm. Yet Joan had been continually thwarted. Lacking common ground with her producers, she had found little space to explore or expand her unique cinematic interests.

For anyone in Hollywood, male or female, quitting Universal so noisily could have spelled disaster. Luckily, she had learned to cultivate the press. When *Life* magazine selected *Uncle Harry* as "movie of the month" in September, it gave Harrison prominent placement, praising the film as "tautly paced and expertly acted" while sympathetically chronicling her walk-off. *Screenland* and the *New York Times* emphasized her good taste in storytelling. But what Joan prized most of all was the front-page feature Hedda Hopper wrote for the *Los Angeles Times* on October 14, titled "Wrath Made Joan Harrison a Producer." Hopper positioned herself clearly in Harrison's corner, proclaiming her a "golden-haired ball of fire with the temper of a tarantula, the purring persuasiveness of a female arch-angel, the capacity of work of a family of beavers, and the sex appeal of a number one glamour girl."

Joan may have found herself temporarily out in the cold in a professional sense. But she had only to look out from her treetop dreamhouse to know she had made a home for herself in Hollywood.

15 | CRIMES AND MISDEMEANORS

JOAN WROTE TO HEDDA HOPPER on October 15 to thank her for the previous day's profile in the *Los Angeles Times*. "I never knew I was such an interesting person!" she exclaimed. "Seriously, though," Joan continued, "encouragement from someone like yourself means a great deal, because you understand the problems that confront one, both as a woman and a producer, when one tries to make a picture."

She ended her note with good news: RKO was on the verge of signing her for a two-picture deal. Within a day, it was official. The *New York Times* announced that she would join RKO to produce a George Raft mystery titled *Nocturne*. This did take her down a notch in terms of salary, paying her $19,500 per project (in contrast to $30,000 with Universal) and gave her only one secretary instead of two, but it meant she got to stay in the game.

RKO president George Schaefer's focus on prestige pictures by ambitious filmmakers had paid off in some cases, as with Hitchcock's *Suspicion*, but not in others. His most notable failures included Orson Welles's *Citizen Kane* (1941) and *The Magnificent Ambersons* (1942), which overextended the company and spelled the end of Schaefer's regime.

Joan returned to the fold during the administration of Charles Koerner. Moving away from intellectual and highbrow fare in favor of playing toward audiences, Koerner was leading RKO into a more powerful and fertile period. In short order, he took the studio into the black with light comedies, topical melodramas, detective films, and Val Lewton low-budget horrors like *Cat People* (1942) and *I Walked with a Zombie* (1943). Harrison wasn't deterred by

Koerner's preference for productions aimed at the broadest audience, because by the time she landed there, he was making room for Lewton's special unit and thoughtful adaptations such as Edward Dmytryk's psychological thriller *Farewell, My Lovely* (1944), released in the US as *Murder, My Sweet.*

Besides, through its many ups and downs, one thing had remained constant at RKO: artists and mavericks were always welcome. Women, in particular, could trust they would be treated well, in part because RKO wanted them to help gauge the tastes of its ever-growing female audience. Joan voiced her confidence in Koerner as she joined his ranks, pointing to the fact that he also had imported movie columnist turned screenwriter Harriet Parsons. She said, "Koerner knows how to treat woman producers." Harrison might have been issuing a challenge to the imperious head of Columbia Pictures, Harry Cohn, who in a surprise move had recently promoted Virginia Van Upp to executive producer. She had high hopes for her cohort, who were riding a good wave.

For *Nocturne,* Joan would report to executive producer Jack J. Gross, recently poached from Universal to head one of three RKO units. Script development started in early January 1946, with production set to begin on May 1. Though Joan was going against one of her cardinal rules in making a whodunit, the story's "behind the scenes" setting in Hollywood appealed to her. *Nocturne* would usher audiences through Los Angeles, taking fans directly to the intersection of Hollywood and Vine and to the doorstep of the famed Hollywood Studio Club, a dorm-style residence for young women trying to break into the movies. Dominated by atmosphere and mood, the film would teeter on the edge of a nighttime dream world, perpetually haunted by a piece of music (the *Nocturne* theme song) that provides a vital clue to a murder.

Celebrity detective Barney Ruditsky, who had recently retired from the NYPD to open his own L.A. nightclub—and who purportedly had ties to the mob—was hired as technical adviser. Joan selected as her screenplay collaborator the pulp novelist Jonathan Latimer, who had recently adapted Dashiell Hammett's *The Glass Key* (1942), proving he could more than hold his own with the likes of Hammett and Raymond Chandler. The director would be Edwin L. Marin—who had paid his dues in B-level genre pictures before making a name for himself with *A Christmas Carol* (1938)—aided by master cinematographer Harry J. Wild.

Joan Harrison's maternal grandfather, Alexander Forsythe Asher, opening the new Town Bridge as mayor of Guildford, England, February 5, 1902. Asher is the bearded man without a hat in the center of the crowd.
Courtesy of Guildford Institute Library, Guildford, UK

Downtown Guildford, High Street, 1930s. *Courtesy of Surrey Advertiser*

LEFT: Alfred Hitchcock and Alma Reville on the set of *The Mountain Eagle* (1926).
Photofest
RIGHT: Harrison and Hitchcock, developing stories in the 1930s.
Peter Stackpole / The LIFE Picture Collection via Getty Images

Joan and the Hitchcocks enjoying dinner in a New York City restaurant,
August 1937. *Bettmann via Getty Images*

Leaving a New York
City restaurant,
August 1937.
*Bettmann via Getty
Images*

Arriving in
Hollywood,
April 5, 1939.
Photofest

"Joanie and
Hitchy" in a rare
candid moment,
circa 1939.
Photofest

Harrison and Hitchcock on the Selznick lot during the making of *Rebecca*, 1939.
Peter Stackpole / The LIFE Picture Collection via Getty Images

Joan Fontaine and Judith Anderson in a memorable scene from
Rebecca (1940). *United Artists / Photofest | © United Artists*

In the Hitchcock home, Reville and Harrison scripting *Suspicion* (1941). *From the collections of the Margaret Herrick Library, Academy of Motion Picture Arts and Sciences*

Joan Fontaine and Cary Grant running through a scene with Hitchcock on the set of *Suspicion*. *RKO Radio Pictures / Photofest | © RKO Radio Pictures*

Writer Irwin Shaw (right foreground, in profile) and director George Stevens
(center, without a helmet) were part of a film crew that covered D-day and
the liberation of Dachau, 1944. *From the collections of the Margaret Herrick Library,*
Academy of Motion Picture Arts and Sciences

Cinematographer Pinckney Ridgell, theatrical director Joshua Logan, film director
Anatole Litvak, and Irwin Shaw filming American propaganda in the Bavarian Alps
during World War II, July 1945. *From the Irwin Shaw Collection, Howard Gotlieb Archival*
Research Center at Boston University

Phantom Lady (1944). Harrison's narrative themes aligned with the visual expressionism of director Robert Siodmak. *Universal Pictures / Photofest | © Universal Pictures*

Joan standing in the bedroom doorway of her home on Birchwood Drive. *Walter Sanders / The LIFE Picture Collection via Getty Images*

A writing corner nestled in Joan's living room, with a view through the treetops in the background.

Actor Herbert Marshall (left) and Robert Siodmak at Joan's home, around the time when Siodmak was directing *Uncle Harry* (1945). *Walter Sanders / The LIFE Picture Collection via Getty Images*

Screenwriter Keith Winter and Harrison on her courtyard terrace. *Walter Sanders / The LIFE Picture Collection via Getty Images*

Joan's vanity had a trick mirror with fold-out panels and an insert painting. Family photos in the background provided a hint of home. *Walter Sanders / The LIFE Picture Collection via Getty Images*

Striking a power pose while standing on the roof of her courtyard. *Walter Sanders / The LIFE Picture Collection via Getty Images*

Flirting with drag style against the backdrop of her front door. *Walter Sanders / The LIFE Picture Collection via Getty Images*

Star Ella Raines, Harrison, and costume designer Travis Banton on the set of *Uncle Harry*.

Joan served as bridesmaid at the wedding of Ella Raines and Robin Olds, February 1947.

At work with actor-director Robert Montgomery on the set of *Ride the Pink Horse* (1947). *Universal Pictures / Photofest | © Universal Pictures*

As part of a government plot in the comedic *Once More, My Darling* (1949), Montgomery's Collier Laing woos Marita "Killer" Connell (Ann Blyth), to the displeasure of her overprotective father (Taylor Holmes).

Joan and Clark Gable in early 1949. The couple made frequent public appearances around this time.

Sandwiched between actor Bruce Cabot and her date, Gable, Harrison was a guest at Errol Flynn's infamous "coming out" party, February 13, 1949.

Joan in early 1950, with actor Gilbert Roland.
From the collections of the Margaret Herrick Library,
Academy of Motion Picture Arts and Sciences

This candid of Joan was taken at the Beverly Hills Tennis Club, when she was in the company of Gilbert Roland. *From the collections of the Margaret Herrick Library, Academy of Motion Picture Arts and Sciences*

Kirk Douglas, Joyce Buck, and Joan during an extended vacation in 1951. *Courtesy of Joan Juliet Buck*

On a visit with Joyce Buck in Cannes, 1953. *Jules Buck, courtesy of Joan Juliet Buck*

Ella Raines at the El Morocco nightclub in New York City (circa the early 1950s) with Gore Vidal, whom Harrison groomed for television writing when she and Raines collaborated on *Janet Dean, Registered Nurse*. *Photofest*

Joan with her groom, the writer Eric Ambler. The couple married in
San Francisco on October 11, 1958. *Courtesy of Norman Lloyd*

Joan Juliet Buck, Eric Ambler, and Joan,
August 1978. *Jules Buck; courtesy of Joan Juliet Buck*

George Raft had spent the 1930s earning a reputation as a tough gangster type, one he feared had become a cliché by the time he was offered the lead in *Nocturne*. But here was an opportunity to play straight-arrow police lieutenant Joe Warne, whose only fault is that he becomes so wrapped up in a homicide case that he keeps investigating even after his superiors tell him to drop it. To the rest of the police force, Warne may be a lone wolf, but it's clear that his underlying intentions are good, in the vein of Humphrey Bogart's detective characters.

Though the role of Joe Warne had already been guaranteed to George Raft, Joan was heavily involved in casting the remaining roles. Originally hoping to give Jane Greer the part of Frances, one of the crime suspects, she eventually went with Lynn Bari, whom RKO borrowed from Twentieth Century Fox. By then the "Queen of the B's," Bari had replaced Claire Trevor as Fox's specialist in "other woman" and "saucy dame" roles. Later pondering the effects of typecasting, she explained, "I made a career of leering at Linda Darnell, Betty Grable, and Alice Faye. Usually I'd corner my woman backstage and say to her in a very nasty tone, 'He's all mine, all mine, you see? I've got him and you'll never take him away from me!' Then I'd stalk away, leaving Linda or Betty or Alice to slowly begin to cry in gorgeous Technicolor, close up."

The part of Frances's sister Carol went to Virginia Huston, whom RKO sold as Hollywood's "first bobby sox star." She was straight out of Omaha, Nebraska, and had a "remarkable facial resemblance to Joan Fontaine." Myrna Dell, a bit player coming off a string of Westerns, beat out Marion Carr for the part of the murder victim's suspiciously sexy housemaid, Susan Flanders. The role of the lieutenant's mother, Mrs. Warne, went to the veteran stage actress Mabel Paige; known as the "Idol of the South," her career dated to the turn of the century. The multitalented Joseph Pevney, after a successful run in Paul Muni's local "Key Largo" theatrical production troupe and, before that, Broadway and musical revues, made his film debut as "Fingers." Walter Sande, a dyed-in-the-wool character actor from the *Boston Blackie* series and dozens of A-list films, won the role of lead investigator Halberson, winning out over William Frawley.

The forty-one-day schedule was typical for a studio production. But *Nocturne* was extremely location heavy. Crucial interactions were to be shot at the Gotham Delicatessen, Brown Derby, Sunset Plaza Apartments and Pool in West Hollywood, and the Pantages Theatre at the corner of Hollywood and

Vine. Harrison was committed to shooting these real-life Los Angeles exteriors, to serve the "behind the scenes" flavor of the film, but this would mean cutting it close when it came to the production schedule.

Additional locations included the tavern O'Blath's, which stood in for the "Club Nocturne," and a dance hall near the intersection of Vine and Sunset Boulevard. RKO's B Building was used to imply the facade of the Hollywood Studio Club. The fabled RKO Marathon Gate appears as Raft's character drives onto the lot and continues on to a soundstage where a movie titled *Sinbad* is filming so that he can interview an actress. Douglas Fairbanks Jr. would appear as himself on the set of *Sinbad*, during a respite from filming the actual Technicolor *Sinbad the Sailor* on the RKO lot. The scene anticipated Billy Wilder's playful use of Cecil B. DeMille and the Paramount lot in *Sunset Boulevard* four years later.

Nocturne's production brought surprises, necessitating more trick photography and process shots than Joan had planned for. Sure, it was a location-driven film, but to establish a mood and evoke a musical tone, *Nocturne* needed to veer away from realism. Joan realized during the development phase that a layer of special effects would be required to elevate the look of the film. Beyond the use of miniatures, models, and matte shots in an intricate opening sequence and a suspenseful pursuit inside a photographer's studio, further optical devices and mattes were needed to create transitions between exteriors and interiors such as theater lobbies. This raised the budget in ways she didn't anticipate, as did process shots for the fight scenes and car chases. Set decoration and production design ended up costing more than expected as well.

Joan had more than enough experience by now to manage such details. She wasn't going to get flustered on her first production at a new studio; at least she wasn't about to let it show. Priority number one was ensuring that the budget held firm, even if individual costs varied. By the end of the shoot, the special effects, process shots, and production design went $6,870 over budget, but by managing to save $22,000 on her location shoots (the film required only $12,000 of the original $34,000 set aside for that purpose) and shaving two production days off the schedule, she delivered the film for $677,081—more than $8,000 under the original $685,258 budget she had been given. These numbers were earning her notice as a time- and cost-saving producer.

Joan's bent toward optical effects and higher-end art design in *Nocturne* may have been influenced by first-time collaborator Robert Boyle. She had known him as *Saboteur*'s associate art director and called him when she realized he was on hiatus waiting for a Hitchcock–Cary Grant project to come through (which never materialized, though a decade later Boyle would work on *North by Northwest*). Given the job of production designer on *Nocturne*, Boyle was brimming with ideas, spurred on by the supremely talented, Oscar-nominated art director Albert S. D'Agostino (*The Magnificent Ambersons*) and visual effects master Linwood Dunn.

The film's trickiest maneuver was its introductory tracking shot, which showcases the skills of all three: Boyle, D'Agostino, and Dunn. The opening title sequence reveals a nighttime Los Angeles cityscape in long shot from the perspective of the Hollywood Hills. The titles dissolve into a reverse aerial shot of the hills. After initially gliding slowly downward, through a combination matte shot and rear projection, the camera gradually tracks into the large glass window of a midcentury "California modern" house before sweeping into the home to show a man playing piano, narrowing in on his hands at the keys. This choreography was accomplished by carefully lining up the matte to match the size of the window and ensuring that the camera's aperture perfectly fit both. Like turning a key, this maneuver opens the action in one fell swoop.

In the film, Keith Vincent, a playboy songwriter, breaks it off with a woman he calls Dolores (seen only in the shadows as he dedicates his latest piano composition "Nocturne" to her), then a little while later is shot and killed. Chief of police Halberson determines Vincent's death to be suicide, but upon inspecting the crime scene, Lieutenant Warne is skeptical. He is pondering a gallery of glamour portraits of women on the man's wall when he notices an empty spot. Seeing the name "Dolores" written on the sheet music at Vincent's piano, he wonders if Dolores's picture was meant to hang there. After speaking with the butler and maid ("Once he even called *me* Dolores," the maid tells him), Warne decides to question as many women as possible, one by one. Frances Ransom, whom he tracks down at a swank swimming pool, proves to have a questionable alibi but a certain allure. Warne likes her salty, devil-may-care wit even if, and maybe because, it marks her as a guilty party. Growing increasingly worked up over the case and facing a possible suspension for disregarding orders, he decides to try to trap Frances. He invites her to the Keyboard Club and has pianist Ned "Fingers" Ford play "Nocturne." As he waits for Frances's reaction, he is surprised to see that it is actually her sister, Carol Page, a singer at the club, who grows alarmed at the song.

A surreptitious meeting with Carol sends Warne into an unpredictable, even surreal Hollywood underworld of movie sets and photographers' studios, steering him toward solving the mystery in an uncharacteristically comical moment: his elderly mother and her friend reenact the crime during a friendly conversation that ends with his mother accidentally firing a blank into her friend's temple. Eventually, returning to the Keyboard Club, Warne forces Fingers to confess to killing Vincent and trying to pin it on Frances. (Fingers was secretly married to Carol and murdered Vincent, who was his rival in both music and romance.) Now that Warne has vindicated Frances, the way is clear for their future. "I've got a mother that's anxious to meet you," he tells her.

The story line is a significant departure from *Nocturne*'s source material, an unpublished fifty-page story by Rowland Brown and Frank Fenton. In the original story, Carol's fiancé is the culprit, but he is a veteran (not a musician) recently returned from Saipan and cruelly manipulated by Vincent to believe he has lost Carol's affection. In the end, Warne encourages the police chief to rule the death a suicide so that the couple will be free to wed. Working with Jonathan Latimer, Joan guided the adaptation, turning the wounded veteran story into an investigation of women's experiences and the underside of the Hollywood dream.

In an indirect way, the film mulls over the illusory and exploitative nature of the Hollywood "star discovery" narrative that feeds on female fantasies of success. The question of whether young women like those in *Nocturne* were sexy symbols of empowerment or victims was making local headlines at the very moment that Joan was working on the script, which may well have served as an inspiration. In the *Los Angeles Times*, Bess M. Wilson posited, "The Hollywood Studio Club has been thought by the unknowing to be a house filled with glamour girls constantly receiving boxes of long-stemmed roses. On the other hand, it has been classified as a rescue home for wayward girls. It is neither of these." Wilson concluded that the women's dormitory should be viewed on par with a men's rooming house, because (especially given wartime shifts for women) its residents had attained the same freedom.

A number of small touches in the script indicate just how sensitive Joan was to the issue of female characterization. In the original story, for example,

Frances Ransom and Carol Page were not acquainted. In the film version, they are sisters, whose relationship raises the dramatic stakes and grants their characters greater psychological complexity. Thanks to Latimer's hard-boiled dialogue, Lynn Bari rivals and often outshines Raft in her delivery of Frances's colorful lines. When Raft offers to take her out on the town courtesy of "the city," she replies, "I can think of nothing less exciting. Imagine having your hand held by a city."

In the source material, Frances was a powerful star—a "famed actress of the stage and screen," according to the treatment—whom the lieutenant first spots at Schwab's Pharmacy, signing autographs for fans. To discuss the case, she invites him to her house, which is "a beautiful home, not quite as large as a country club, but with facilities as adequate." The decision to change Frances to a struggling bit player meant that power relations between women and men, as well as other women, were amplified. This was also a nod to Bari's own feelings of marginalization and to the fact that she was unable to shed her B-movie status. The star gratefully recognized that Harrison seemed particularly attuned to the female performers on the set, always tending to little details. Talking about wardrobe, Bari observed that Harrison "had great taste. She was with me for every pin they put in my suits. A man says, 'Oh you know, put her in something gray. Many of them don't give a damn.'"

One of the most female-centric (and quirky) elements of all is that the mystery in the film is solved by two older women quietly discussing murder and mayhem over coffee. That a hard-boiled lieutenant would live with his mother was unconventional enough at the time. But Mrs. Warne and her neighbor Mrs. O'Rourke's reenactment of the crime constitutes a truly subversive moment. It's as if the noir universe of *Nocturne* is momentarily interrupted while these ladies make a movie of their own. Playing opposite the iconic Mabel Paige in the part of Mrs. O'Rourke was Virginia Edwards, a lesser-known drama coach and stage actress who had recently opened a female-run theater company in New York City. She joined Harrison's growing list of inspired casting choices.

The two women play the scene pitch-perfectly, performing a highly ritualized set of conventions ("Sugar?" "Yes, three lumps." "Coffee cake?" "No, thank you.") while poring over the case in the parlor. The initial joke is that two elderly women would know so much about forensics and crime, and that they would go into such unpleasant details against the backdrop of this domestic setting.

As Mrs. O'Rourke asks about nitrate tests and the positioning of the pistol, Mrs. Warne corrects her, "*Revolver*, Mrs. O'Rourke. A pistol is an automatic weapon." The final punch line is delivered when Joe stumbles in and misreads the situation, but, assisted by an accidental and dramatic misfire of the prop weapon, he realizes the killer must have used blanks to stage Vincent's suicide—firing them from the murder weapon after it was placed in the dead Vincent's hand to leave a misleading evidence trail. Neither this twist nor, for that matter, the character of Joe's mother existed in the original source material. Joan was not only playing with generic conventions but also cutting against the grain of similar work being produced contemporaneously, such as *Murder, My Sweet* (1944), *Laura* (1944), and *The Big Sleep* (1946).

Nocturne did well when it opened in limited release in October 1946 and was subsequently put into wide release on January 2, 1947. The film's total gross of $568,000 counted toward RKO's 1947 box office numbers, ranking it as one of the studio's highest-performing pictures of that year. Harrison had played a large part in RKO's banner "rebound" year, which saw huge critical and commercial rewards with A-pictures like *Notorious* and *The Best Years of Our Lives*, as well as the B-level *The Spiral Staircase*, *Cornered*, and *Badman's Territory*.

Charles Koerner's formula had paid off. Unfortunately, he wasn't there to enjoy the fruits of his labor. He succumbed to a fast-progressing form of leukemia on February 2, 1946, only weeks after Joan's arrival. The corporate president, N. Peter Rathvon, who stepped in until a suitable replacement could be found, resolved to maintain RKO's momentum. The change in leadership must have given Joan pause. Would the studio continue to support her projects? The answer would come with her next endeavor, a star-laden production and her biggest-budget project yet: the $1.1 million *They Won't Believe Me*.

Joan prepped *They Won't Believe Me* in spring 1946 and had the budget in place by June, taking the same $19,500 base salary as with *Nocturne*. Joining the project as director was the witty Irving Pichel, a former member of the Algonquin Roundtable whose forte was anti-Nazi, pro-British material (*The Man I Married*, *The Moon Is Down*, *O.S.S.*). Harry J. Wild was back on board as cinematographer and would guarantee that the film adhered to RKO's increasingly popular "house of noir" style. Jonathan Latimer returned to write the screenplay, which was based on an unpublished 127-page novelette by Gordon McDonell, another native of Surrey who had recently made trade headlines when he sold Hitchcock the original story for *Shadow of a Doubt*.

Joan cast Robert Young as Lawrence Ballentine, a philandering stockbroker accused of murdering one of his girlfriends. She had made his acquaintance during his stint as the spy in *Secret Agent*; now she hoped to play him against the debonair "nice guy" type he had built at Fox, MGM, and RKO. Ballentine's secretary, Verna Carlson, who starts off as the object of his affection and winds up dead, would be played by Susan Hayward (borrowed from Walter Wanger). In supporting roles, Rita Johnson would take on the role of Ballentine's wealthy, affectionate wife, Greta. Joan cast Jane Greer as Janice Bell, the magazine writer who has Ballentine for "ten Saturdays" when the film opens. Actor salaries neared $200,000, with Young earning $100,000, Hayward $75,000, Johnson $12,000, and Greer $6,000.

Greer's role in *They Won't Believe Me* would propel her to stardom, giving her a break she directly attributed to the producer and her grooming during the casting process. Joan had told her, "I want to test you. But I want to test you as Jane Greer, not as Gale Sondergaard [the Spiderwoman in Universal's *Sherlock Holmes* series]." At the time, Greer sported brunette hair, dyed even darker to look like Hedy Lamarr. To tone down her austerity, Joan proposed she lighten her hair with a soap cap, rather than go all the way blonde. As both women reveled in the transformation, Joan concluded, "The difference is astounding. Now you look like a human being, like a beautiful young woman, you've got the part." She also worked up a new wardrobe, ensuring that Greer's Janice sported a customized suit. Without her new look, according to the actress, she would have never been selected for her next role, the one-of-a-kind Kathie Moffat in *Out of the Past*. Such efforts would soon earn Joan a reputation as a star maker.

Gordon McDonell's original story told Lawrence "Larry" Ballentine's story from his cell in San Quentin on the eve of his execution. "They have sent a prison stenographer in to me and there isn't much time," Larry explains. "I've just got to get down the facts as fast as I can." For the screen adaptation, Harrison worked with Latimer to transpose Larry's first-person narration to a courtroom setting. This change gave audiences the opportunity to serve as jury in Ballentine's trial, judging his transgressions as they witness—through flashback—his downward spiral. Putting her many years of trial watching to work, Joan drew out the powerful drama that lay inside the minute details and the customs and rituals of such proceedings. Hitchcock had mentioned in 1937 that if he were free to make any movie without thinking box office, he might like to film "a verbatim of a celebrated trial." Now Joan seemed to be coming close to that.

While the court scenes function primarily as a framing device, in which Larry takes the stand in his own defense, a certain tension arises by having the prosecutor introduce several characters from the story (and from the protagonist's life) at the outset. An impending sense of doom looms heavier over Larry's tale the deeper he goes, as it becomes clear that he cannot free himself—or those he most cares about—from his own perilous choices.

The defense begins by having Larry go back to the beginning of his twisted tale, which starts with a series of dates with Janice, a professional writer who knows his wife through the women's club. Tired of sneaking around, Janice announces as they leave their favorite New York City saloon that she is bound for Montreal. Caught up in the moment, Larry promises to meet her at the train station, but by that evening he has been corralled by his moneyed wife, Greta, into taking another train, this one a cross-country train to a fresh start for the couple in Los Angeles. After the well-connected Greta has set him up as a partner in a brokerage firm, Larry falls into his old habits and starts seeing his secretary, Verna, who does not conceal her gold-digging ways or the fact that she sees his partner, Trenton, on the side. Even when Greta ferries Larry farther away, to an isolated mountain ranch, he cannot shake his attraction to Verna.

Greta enjoys her daily trip to a hidden waterfall with her beloved horse, but Larry feels increasingly stifled. He writes Verna a check for $25,000, drawn on the joint bank account he keeps with Greta—it's her money—and instructs her to cash the check and then meet him at the general store near the ranch so they can run away together to Reno. There, he promises her, he will divorce his wife and marry her. But on the way to Reno, and just moments after Larry puts a dime-store ring on Verna's finger as a symbol of what is to come, the couple's car collides with an out-of-control truck. Larry is ejected from the car and suffers only minor injuries. Verna, trapped in the vehicle, is killed in the crash, and her body charred beyond recognition by the ensuing fire. When the police recover the ring from the accident, they assume that it's Larry's wife—that is, Greta—who has died. Larry decides to use the mix-up to his advantage, figuring he is now free to murder Greta and secure not only his freedom but an inheritance. Upon arriving home, he learns that the good-bye note he left for her prompted her to commit suicide, hurling herself down the embankment of her cherished waterfall.

Heading for an emotional breakdown, Larry travels to Latin America and lands in Jamaica, where he encounters Janice, whom he has not seen since he stood her up at the train station. After they rekindle their romance and return to Los Angeles, Larry discovers that Janice has actually been recruited by Trenton, his former partner, to glean information on Verna's whereabouts. Trenton's detective work prods the police to open an investigation that eventually leads to the discovery of Greta's corpse (still in the ravine). Larry is charged with her murder.

As Larry concludes his narration from the witness stand, he worries that the jury "won't believe" him.

The film, as constructed, simultaneously inhabits and subverts the tropes of the noir genre. It's not simply the lingering question of the crime—there are two corpses, but has there been a murder? It's also that the killing Larry sets out to commit, returning home to shoot Greta, arrives almost like an afterthought, after most of the dramatic action has occurred. The subsequent discovery that Larry knows more than he's letting on about Verna's whereabouts is likewise not the product of some police investigation or insurance inquiry—as in so many noirs—but rather initiated by Larry's business partner, Trenton. (Tom Powers brings the baggage of *Double Indemnity*'s expendable Mr. Dietrichson to the role.) Curious about the timing of Verna's disappearance—he notes that it coincided with Greta's death—Trenton somehow enlists Janice (whom we have no reason to believe he has ever met) to track down Larry. If the crime at the heart of the mystery was an accident, the "investigation" appears to be no less so. The film's flouting of generic conventions suggests that Harrison was much more interested in using the space of the film to explore her deeper interests in character, story, and subjectivity, specifically the relationship between narration and narrator.

The figure of the unreliable narrator is a common feature in classic noir, which meditated on the subjective nature of reality by calling into question the protagonist's explanation of events, often told in first person and in flashback. Because Larry takes the stand in his own defense at the start of his story, *They Won't Believe Me* takes the notion of the unreliable narrator and incorporates it directly into the plot. Larry has nothing to lose by lying, and has everything—his very life, in fact—to gain by mischaracterizing events in a way that exonerates him.

Within the world of the film, Larry is not only unreliable; he is indeterminate as a character. And yet the audience is solely at the mercy of his narration when it comes to ascertaining whether his self-portrayal is genuine. Indeed, whether to "believe" him is the film's governing question. But it is not the film's most pressing preoccupation. While *They Won't Believe Me* begins with a trial, it leaves uncertain the question of what crime has been committed, how and why it was carried out, and who the victim or victims were. While these unknown details hover over the story, creating tension, the real subject of the film appears to be the psychosexual relationships among the main characters, and how they uphold or fail to uphold institutional structures and marital norms.

One of the prevailing themes across Harrison's films is that marriage is best understood as a conspiracy between two people—a set of agreed-upon terms that are not always as pure and well intentioned as the church or law would have us believe. What happens when one member of the couple stops agreeing to the terms? These marital themes are most clearly seen in the manner by which Greta binds Larry to her (financially, as well as emotionally and psychologically). Yet for all his philandering, the great irony is that Larry doesn't appear to want out of his marriage at all. Verna senses this on the way to Reno, when Larry appears cavalier about getting to their destination.

In *They Won't Believe Me*, female characters are unusually three-dimensional and sympathetic, which is especially surprising given that their stories are narrated through Larry's narrow male point of view. All three actresses give exceptional performances, encouraged by the "actor's director" Irving Pichel to expand and experiment in their roles. The result is that, read as a feminist film, *They Won't Believe Me* is highly provocative, allowing for the possibility, proposed by critic Eddie Muller, that Larry assumes the typical femme fatale role, becoming the first "homme fatal" in noir.

They Won't Believe Me, then, was destined to come into conflict with the censors. Joseph Breen had a knee-jerk reaction to the synopsis that Joan submitted through RKO in mid-April 1946. In a letter to RKO executive William Gordon, Breen responded that the proposed production was "almost completely devoid of anything that suggests reasonable respect—or even recognition—of the common amenities of life, to say nothing of the seriousness, the dignity, or the importance of marriage." It was going to take a lot of wrangling—and rewriting—to produce a script that would gain Breen's approval. The initial synopsis, which indeed suffered from a too-trite treatment of both marriage and adultery, went through adjustments in the development phase so that all three characters showed (at least some) cognizance of their actions and the resulting consequences by the first script version. Upon reading this, Breen's office, however, still worried that the film did not uphold the sanctity of marriage and failed to present other voices that might offer "compensating moral values."

RKO's head of production, William Dozier, hosted a meeting between Joan's team and Breen. Dozier, by now a friend and mentor to Harrison, helped the parties reach an agreement for redressing the most flagrant code violations. They agreed that the writers would add gravity to the characters' actions and attitudes, shape Janice into a moral voice, look to eliminate places where Verna and Larry "pretend" to have an engagement or marriage (which would de-eroticize their adultery), and delete lines that suggested Greta condones Larry's affair. Joan also agreed to work with Latimer to grant Greta more dimension, so that she would serve as "more than a prop in the story."

A week later, as the shake-ups in the leadership of RKO continued, William Dozier was fired. Harrison's concerns over her standing with the studio must have grown.

Rewrites continued through the beginning of June, as Harrison and Latimer made the agreed-upon changes while addressing a host of more minor concerns. Sequences with promiscuity, scantily clad characters, and "writing dirty words" on the wall as a form of flirtation were seen as problems and promptly eliminated. Also, Verna was not allowed to ask Larry whether he "even [had] enough strength to come to work" after one of their romantic evenings, because of the line's potential (and no doubt intended) double meaning. Breen continually reminded Harrison's team that neither Janice nor Verna (in other words, the women committing adultery) should express more than the bare minimum of romantic or sexual desire. Many of the kisses between Larry and Verna were deleted. There was to be no "lustful, or passionate, or open-mouth kissing," according to Breen. In reference to Verna and Larry's first kiss, he made it clear that Verna "must not respond to Larry's kiss. It is agreeable to indicate that he is forcing himself upon her."

It must have been hugely frustrating for Joan—who had high aspirations for examining the big picture of romance and marriage—to get bogged down fighting for small details, especially for a woman's permission to "respond" while kissing. The production code's patriarchal standards were abundantly clear. Only those female characters who adhered to conventional roles were allowed sexual (or romantic) agency. Women who assumed more freedom deserved any punishment that came their way.

Joan pushed back against these standards at every turn. In the majority of cases, she ignored Breen's recommendations and plowed ahead, intent on producing the film as it was scripted. For every five changes Breen suggested, she would concede one. By July she had arrived at a shooting script with which she could live and which his office approved. She was still irked by the bar scene in which Larry tries to convince Janice that he's in love with her before she leaves for Montreal. The script called for two kisses. The first was to be Larry's passionate show of affection (in response to Janice's invitation to prove his true commitment to her—"You might kiss me") and the second would be a more delicate, tender gesture. Joan filmed a test reel two weeks before production began to show the PCA a sample scene. The response was negative. She was told by Breen's office that she could include the first kiss (for the purposes of a "story point") but the second kiss must "be eliminated entirely." Thus, Larry and Janice's most romantic moment was pared down to one kiss—though in the finished film, Young manages to sneak in a light peck on Greer's ear. Even the tiniest battles in the war for creative freedom were hard fought and rarely won.

Robert Boyle, working for the second time as Harrison's production designer, noticed that she took a perverse pleasure in these tiny battles. Unlike some executives, who were "closet-directors," harboring fantasies of photographing or designing a picture, she had no such inclinations. It was "the maneuvering and the politics of producing" that she loved most, Boyle said.

They Won't Believe Me is most memorable for its jaw-dropping ending: as the jury members file in to deliver their verdict, Larry suddenly bolts toward the courthouse window, setting in motion one of the most stunning conclusions of any studio-era film. The question of the final scene was actually up in the air until weeks into production. The original story by McDonell had concluded with Larry stating, "So I'm writing this. I'm writing this as a last chance, here in San Quentin. Perhaps they will believe this. Perhaps this will save me." His confession is meant to redeem him. Or is it? Playing with the poetic power of language and narration, Larry tells readers that if his manuscript has been published, then his words have saved him, and he has lived. If, however, readers see these pages in unpublished form, it is too late; he has been put to death.

This literary approach left Joan and her team with a challenge for the screen adaptation. As early as the synopsis stage in April 1946, she had decided to go with a finale in which Larry attempts to jump out of the courthouse window, which was (conveniently) on the first floor, suggesting that his only goal is escape. By August, in the busiest production period, she and Latimer moved the courthouse to a higher floor, thus shifting Larry's intent from escape to suicide—at the urging of Breen, who touted the need to punish the character for his morally offensive actions. But the particulars still needed working out. How would the film make it clear that Larry intends to kill himself? In one script version, Larry begins to contemplate suicide after the police lieutenant visits Larry's cell on the eve of the verdict. He tells Larry he's there to inspect for razor blades, mentioning that the previous defendant killed himself that way. However, further script revisions replaced this scene with an eleventh-hour jailhouse visit from Janice, granting the couple a final redeeming moment. The result was that the "motivating" mention of suicide was erased, making Larry's ultimate leap from a high window appear to come out of the blue.

Yet even after seven total script revisions and five weeks of production, Joan remained dissatisfied with the ending. In early October, in a last-ditch attempt at a highly unconventional resolution, she submitted to Breen an alternative ending in which Larry either escaped or was set free. His office balked. How could Larry, under the production code, be permitted a happy ending when he was "directly responsible for the death of his wife, and indirectly at least responsible for the death of Verna?" asked Breen. Joan got the message: Larry would have to die.

Working within this mandate, Harrison, Pichel, and Latimer made brave, bold choices. As the scene opens, Larry, from his place at the defendant's table, watches the jury file in to the courtroom. The camera cuts between close-ups of his face and medium shots of the jury members as they take their places in the box. As Larry slumps into his seat, he cannot hide his disappointment; he has read their faces and determined that they judge him to be guilty. An extreme long shot shows the bailiff handing off the folded-up verdict page to the judge, who passes it to the clerk. As the clerk begins to read the verdict aloud, there's a series of close-ups: Larry glances around nervously; Janice looks at Larry lovingly; a prosecution witness glares at Larry. Suddenly, in close-up, one of the female onlookers stands up and shrieks. Another close-up shows Janice rising to her feet and screaming, before the camera cuts back to the first woman. These frenzied static shots stand in for the central off-screen action. Next, we see Larry's body extending out from the window and over the ledge, high above city traffic. In an instant, a bullet from a policeman's gun hits him. As Larry dies, his body falls back into the room.

As order returns to the court, the clerk proceeds to read the verdict that pronounces him "not guilty." Hence, Larry's story closes with a profound lack of resolution. Beyond this, in terms of film form, there is a shocking reversal of audience expectation, in which character identification (to the extent that identification with the protagonist is achievable) is manipulated at the very last minute in ways that have not been foreshadowed. The film's cinematic and narrative approaches suggest that Harrison created space for her team to take risks. In terms of story, structure, and character, she was working at the height of her craft, immersed in the ideas that intrigued her most and operating at her biggest scale yet.

The "distinctly surprising and explosive climax" was appreciated upon its July 1947 release by *New York Times* critic Thomas M. Pryor, who found *They Won't Believe Me* engrossing entertainment. In *Time* magazine, James Agee asserted that "producer Joan Harrison and associates have brought the story to the screen with considerable skill." It didn't play so well in more conservative regions such as Rivesville, West Virginia; an exhibitor there wrote to *Motion Picture Herald* that "RKO Radio won't believe me when I tell them that this type of feature just doesn't go, and it is not worth half the price they want for it." When box office receipts were totaled, the film underperformed, though RKO assigned most of the blame to the against-type casting of Robert Young in the lead.

While a personal triumph, *They Won't Believe Me* had put Joan's resolve to the test. Not only had she mounted a cinematic challenge to traditional notions of romance and marriage, but she had done so as Hollywood—and America—were becoming dramatically more conservative. With World War II over, women who had found employment in wartime industries had been encouraged to return to traditional roles and forfeit the gains they had made in the workforce and beyond. As veterans returned from overseas, they were met by a wave of government and corporate propaganda idealizing a civilian life in which women served as mothers and homemakers. The political momentum that had grown out of women's participation in labor activities and the public sphere began to be quashed. The Equal Rights Amendment, proposed to Congress every year since 1923, was finally brought to the floor of the US Senate for a vote in 1946. It was defeated 38–35.

Was there still room in Hollywood for a "golden-haired ball of fire with the temper of a tarantula" like Joan?

Joan saw the shift toward marriage and domesticity reflected in her own orbit. Having divorced her high school sweetheart, Ella Raines had fallen in love with ace fighter pilot Robin Olds, whom she'd met in Palm Springs the year before. She asked Joan to serve as maid of honor at her wedding. On February 6, 1947, Raines and Olds tied the knot at the Westwood Methodist Community Church and celebrated with a reception at the Beverly Hills Hotel. It wasn't long before Ella was telling the press that "marriage is the best thing that can happen to a girl" and not much longer before she had assumed the role of a typical military wife, announcing a temporary retirement from her career to follow Olds to his new post in England.

For Joan, marriage had never been a goal. For her, it had always been career first. "Never had time for it," she once told the *Los Angeles Times*, referring vaguely to anything that would qualify her as "attached." But the press would become increasingly ambivalent in its representation of working women, vacillating between messages that celebrated and repudiated independence. In one instance, the *Hollywood Citizen News* reported she was just as "worried about butter" for her dinner party as her next script. She was even contemplating having a baby, according to some reports. This is highly unlikely, as Joan had never been maternal. In her later years, she would tell her caretaker, "If I'd had a child, someone like you would have had to look after it."

It was at this time, as the gender climate grew more conservative, that Joan met a fledgling contract writer at Columbia, Sarett Tobias. Tobias was a genuine Renaissance woman who had been learning the romantic comedy and musical ropes on *She Wouldn't Say Yes* (1945) and *Tars and Spars* (1946) as a protégée of Virginia Van Upp. By all accounts, Sarett entered people's lives with cyclonic force. At five feet, three inches, she was petite and gorgeous. Even in Hollywood, she turned heads when she walked into a room. As part of her chameleon image, she changed her hair color often, but not as frequently as she altered the hue of streaky highlights that framed her face. (Her beautifully sculpted nose was the result of a plastic surgery in her twenties.)

Sarett was in her early thirties when Joan first encountered her. At the time, she was looking to exit a Beverly Hills marriage to Dr. Milton Tobias, who was sixteen years her senior and the father of three young children (one of the daughters remembers calling their stepmother "Miss Princess"). Apparently, a studio contract offered the ticket out. This wasn't her first go-round. At the age of twenty, Sarett had wed Bob Hirsch, the owner of a chain of L.A. department stores. He had been stunned when she divorced him just a few years later in favor of Tobias.

Sarett had always been on the move. She was born in 1915 in Colorado Springs, Colorado, to Isador Rude, an Austrian immigrant who began life working in sweatshops, started a tailoring business, and built it into a large-scale department store. (Sarett, wanting to give the impression that she was to the manor born, pronounced her last name with a French accent, "Rudé," and frowned on those who didn't abide.) Isador made a success of himself in Dallas, fell in love with his secretary, and asked Sarett's mother, Ida, for a divorce. She promptly left the country for France, taking their infant daughter with her. She returned a few years later when she could be certain he'd gotten the message.

By her early teens, Sarett had mastered cosmopolitan travel alongside Ida, who imported fabrics for her husband's business. In the early 1930s, the Rudes retired to Los Angeles, and Sarett followed. Noted for her advanced intellect, she graduated from the University of Southern California at the age of fifteen.

Joan may not have foreseen that this fellow writer who flouted convention would eventually become an indispensable professional asset. But by all indications, Sarett was the most complicated character Joan ever knew, in real life or in fiction.

As the mood in Hollywood changed and pressure to conform heightened, a chief factor was the House Un-American Activities Committee (HUAC), an investigative body of the US House of Representatives. Organized to root out subversive activity, HUAC set its sights on Hollywood and the supposed Communist infiltration of the movie colony. Wartime films such as *Mission* to *Moscow* (1943), *The North Star* (1943), and *Song of Russia* (1944), which presented Stalinist or pro-Soviet themes at the urging of the Roosevelt administration (who depended on the Russians' support in fighting the Nazis), were now cited to label the participating filmmakers as "un-American." Many of the antifascist and prodemocracy activities that had energized the European émigré community in the early 1940s, such as the European Film Fund, were recast as politically threatening and potentially Communist.

Joan held her breath, for it was becoming clear that no one was immune. She didn't like to sit idly by as coworkers turned on each other and friends sold each other out. In the coming months, under the guiding hand of socially conscious RKO executive Dore Schary, who had replaced Bill Dozier, two of the studio's most successful talents, director Edward Dmytryk and producer Adrian Scott, would fall prey to the Red Scare.

As far as Joan was concerned, the worst was yet to come for RKO. In what was deemed the "biggest motion picture transaction since Twentieth Century took over Fox Films," Texas magnate, aviator, and filmmaker Howard Hughes bought nearly a hundred thousand shares of RKO stock for $8.8 million. Politically conservative and seeing the studio as an ideal propaganda machine, Hughes was preparing to embark on a series of Red Scare movies. He also announced he would require everyone on the RKO lot to sign loyalty oaths, and issued a memo that placed all story and cast approvals (and a host of other contractual considerations) under his personal control. Within months, one-third of RKO's workforce had either walked out or been fired. Joan had read the writing on the wall before many of her associates. After all, she had seen this script before, management changeover that translated to broken promises.

The final straw came in the form of yet another memo from the top. It was an ultimatum addressed to all RKO contract producers, but in Joan's mind it may as well have been addressed directly to her. All pictures were to be about one of two things, Hughes announced: "fighting and fornication." Before the eccentric tycoon had time to expound on this notion, Joan had left the building.

16 | LET IT RIDE

IN THE LATE 1940S, Joan had no trouble filling her proverbial dance card. At Ciro's, she dined with Tony Martin, the singer turned actor who was then appearing in Universal's *Casbah*. (She dated Martin just months before he married Cyd Charisse.) On the weekends, she would rendezvous with director Edmund Goulding in Palm Springs. And over cocktails at the Mocambo, she traded sweet nothings with Otto Preminger, who always seemed to be walking in and out of the picture.

But few people knew that Joan was entertaining an affaire de coeur in private. He was a tall, lean, elegant figure, boasting brilliant blue eyes and an earnest intelligence. She'd known him since she was a young woman, newly hired into Hitchcock's fold. She had worked closely with him on and off ever since, spurred on, as Hitchcock was, by the man's passionate work against anti-Semitism and Nazism, as well as his propaganda on behalf of the Allies during the war. The secret object of Joan's affection was Sidney Bernstein.

A powerful British businessman and head of the Granada movie palace chain, Bernstein had relocated to Hollywood late in the summer of 1947 to begin producing films with Hitchcock. Their newly formed Transatlantic Pictures was meant to provide independence for the director, with the innovative "single-take" film *Rope* set as the initial production. Sidney had moved his wife and home base to Beverly Hills' Palm Drive, as a show of his serious commitment as an investor and to overcome lingering doubts on the part of banks and partnering studios. Sidney and Hitch had big plans, with a vision to contract multiple directors and numerous stars. But Sidney had little actual producing experience, so this was a risky long-term career move.

Bernstein's change of address afforded him the chance to rekindle long-standing friendships, including with John Huston, Charlie Chaplin, and Joan. Yet Beverly Hills did not sit well with him. In a letter to his friend Ernestine Evans, a journalist and agent, he complained that "the fruit grows large but has no taste, the flowers no smell . . . the people flit from home to home, from job to job. Everything, so to speak, flows but nothing seems to get anywhere."

For this reason, Sidney tended to spend his evenings at Hitch and Alma's, savoring intimate conversation with a hand-selected guest list: Alida Valli and her husband, Oscar de Mejo; Ingrid Bergman and her husband, Dr. Petter Lindström; José Ferrer and his wife, Uta Hagen; Whitfield Cook and his writing partner, Anne Chapin; Celeste Holm and her husband, Schuyler Dunning; or Joseph Cotten and his wife, Lenore Kipp. After a time, Sidney's wife, Zoe Farmer, a stylish journalist fourteen years his junior, returned to England. Their marriage grew rockier as his stay in California lengthened, and would soon dissolve. But if he was surrounded by couples during these dinner parties, he rarely felt like a fifth wheel. Joan was often there by his side.

Sidney's inordinate affluence and stature elevated him, in Joan's mind, closer to her social level, above most Hollywood men. Beyond this, he was an intellectual wizard, having funneled his business acumen toward both creative interests (as an early film curator and distributor) and moral good (chronicling Nazi atrocities). Though he could be impetuous and quick to anger, part of his attractiveness was his inner quiet. He could play the impresario almost better than anyone but was by nature an introvert, inclined to sit back and listen rather than talk.

Joan gave herself points for keeping up with his erudite, well-versed ways. There's no overestimating how deep their emotional and intellectual relationship ran, though the physical dimension is left to rumor and speculation. His importance in her life at this time—and hers in his—serves as evidence that Joan was an active participant in the conversations around *Rope* and *Under Capricorn*. Joan did not disappear from Hitch and Alma's circle when she was producing solo projects. Quite the opposite, she remained deeply embedded in their lives and in those of their friends and colleagues.

If it occurred to Joan to go in with Bernstein and Hitchcock on their Transatlantic Pictures venture, she didn't entertain the thought for very long. Instead, in March 1947 she joined professional forces with the distinguished star Robert Montgomery as he made a dramatic new arrival on the Universal lot. Joan would produce; Montgomery, whom she had met when he starred in Hitchcock's romantic comedy *Mr. and Mrs. Smith*, would direct and act. He was in the process of signing a profit-sharing deal with the studio, including story control and the establishment of his own company, Neptune Productions. As his producing partner, Joan would be in a position to manage an independent unit under the umbrella of a major studio. Montgomery was not just open to her bringing him material—he required it; he had neither the time nor the inclination to go fishing for story ideas.

Joan could fill in a lot of other missing pieces for Montgomery. He had little experience managing budgets, call sheets, or the internal demands of upper management. As Joan assumed responsibility over day-to-day operations, she would free him up to play out his artistic ambitions. It had been five years since Joan had teamed up with anyone, but the timing seemed right.

She was partnering with Montgomery at an extraordinary turning point in his career. Montgomery had been with MGM since his arrival in Hollywood eighteen years earlier, at the start of the talkie revolution. One of the many imports from the New York stage, the actor had put his boyish good looks and elegant speaking voice to excellent advantage, hastening the displacement of silent stars who couldn't master the new medium. To his dismay, he soon found himself stifled as a glib playboy whose main function was to support the studio's leading ladies. How many ways were there to utter, "Tennis, anyone?"

After convincing L. B. Mayer to take a chance on him as a psychopathic killer in the 1937 *Night Must Fall* (and earning an Oscar nomination in the process), he found himself again relegated to undistinguished roles. It wasn't until his rousing performance as saxophone-playing boxer Joe Pendleton in the fantasy film *Here Comes Mr. Jordan* (1941) that audiences came to appreciate his full acting range.

By the mid-1940s Montgomery had returned from two years of active duty as a naval officer, having seen combat and been promoted to full commander. (He was awarded the Bronze Star for his efforts during the D-day invasion.) And he had made an unexpected directorial debut. While still on active duty and starring in the war movie *They Were Expendable*, he had been called on to take over the director's duties by John Ford, who had suffered a fractured leg on set. Montgomery proved he could direct and act in the same picture, all while meeting the demanding standards of Ford, no less. Facing a depleted roster of male talent (with Gable, Jimmy Stewart, and others still serving in the armed forces), MGM enticed Montgomery to remain in L.A. with the promise that he could direct a film of his choosing.

Montgomery seized the opportunity to fulfill a long-held ambition: a mystery told from the first-person perspective, in which the "camera-eye" is limited to the main character's subjective point of view. Raymond Chandler's novel *The Lady in the Lake* (1943) would serve as the vehicle for this experiment, with Montgomery playing detective Philip Marlowe, who is hired by publishing house editor in chief Adrienne Fromsett (Audrey Totter) to investigate the disappearance of her boss's wife so that the publisher can begin divorce proceedings and marry Adrienne. The first-time director confronted a series of challenges with subjective storytelling, such as the limitation on showing his face (which was possible only when, say, Marlowe looked in a mirror). The approach required other nontraditional conventions, including having the star directly addressing the audience (as Marlowe) to introduce and end the movie. ("You'll see it just as I saw it. You'll meet the people.") It also necessitated complicated camera rigs and extravagant set ups, so the budget kept climbing. Meanwhile, Montgomery faced pushback from studio heads, who realized (too late, apparently) that its A-list star would enjoy barely any screen time.

Upon its release in January 1947, *Lady in the Lake* impressed critics as a bold feat. *Newsweek* hailed it as "a brilliant tour de force," and *Cue* declared it a "revolution in movies." *Time* magazine noted, "Most of the formidable technical problems were ingeniously solved." Even those reviews that expressed skepticism, such as the *New York Times* ("The novelty begins to wear thin") congratulated Montgomery for attempting a new direction and "afford[ing] one a fresh and interesting perspective on a murder mystery."

Buoyed by *Lady in the Lake*'s success, the director saw a natural segue out of his MGM contract. The glossy studio had little interest in his pilot projects; one Montgomery "revolution" was about all executives could stomach. It was then that he made the decision to go to Universal—newly renamed Universal-International after a recent merger—and make Joan his collaborator. Montgomery's move to U-I represented a rejection of what he saw as MGM's lavish paint-by-numbers system. He reasoned, "The studios have got to realize that mere bigness doesn't count. Piling four or five A-list stars into one picture doesn't guarantee its success."

In many ways, Joan found in Bob a kindred spirit who yearned for smaller character-driven films that took risks. He was articulate and athletic and had a strong work ethic. His screen persona of the dapper socialite extended into his everyday life (supported by his well-off wife, Elizabeth Bryan Allen, whom he met on Broadway). And he displayed a remarkable respect for everything British, signaled by his signature Homburg hat and boutonniere. All these attributes endeared him to Joan, not to mention the fact that they were neighbors in Holmby Hills. (When Montgomery downsized from his seven-bedroom Tudor revival–style mansion toward the end of the war, he sold to none other than Franchot Tone.)

And yet Harrison and Montgomery were strange bedfellows. He had made a hard-right political turn earlier in the decade, after spending the 1930s lobbying on behalf of labor. He had in fact been one of the most active union organizers in the industry, founding the Screen Actors Guild (SAG) and serving as its president twice and spurring on the final vote for the Screen Writers Guild when it looked like a studio-backed union might hold it back. But he'd turned on the labor movement in 1940, apparently as a result of the looming prospect of war, Republican Wendell Willkie's presidential campaign against FDR, and his own friendship with fellow MGM actor (and future Republican US senator) George Murphy. What's more, Louis B. Mayer's studio was a "training ground for GOP activists," according to historian Steven J. Ross, and Montgomery was a quick study.

As HUAC ramped up the pressure in 1947, directors, writers, actors, and others in the industry were called before the committee to testify that they had not engaged in any "subversive" activity (or if they had, to confess and clear the record). Studios did little to protect their employees. Many of those called to testify before HUAC were forced to choose between being "friendly witnesses," which usually meant naming names—essentially, implicating colleagues in subversive activity—or refusing to testify, thus becoming "unfriendly witnesses" and risking court action.

As fears of the Red menace escalated, Montgomery worked with SAG leaders to draft testimony to assert to HUAC that the guild was not susceptible to the influence of Communists or the "lunatic fringe." He also exerted pressure as a leader of the conservative Motion Picture Alliance for the Preservation of American Ideals. The MPA-PAI was an industry group that, along with SAG, espoused antisubversive rhetoric and included the likes of John Ford, Clark Gable, Walt Disney, and Barbara Stanwyck and was led by George Murphy, by then also a former president of SAG, and current SAG president Ronald Reagan.

Beneath his carefully cultivated image and aloof personality, Montgomery kept an anguished past at bay. MGM publicity releases trumpeted that he had been born to an executive of a rubber company "in a large house on the banks of the Hudson River" in picturesque Fishkill Landing, New York. But there was a lot more to the story. Montgomery's parents were immigrants—his father was Irish, his mother Scottish—and the family had not always had it so easy. As a teenager, he achieved placement at the prestigious Pawling School for Boys, only to be called home when his father, Henry, committed suicide by leaping to his death on the Brooklyn Bridge in 1922. The tragedy made national headlines and created both scandal and confusion, since reports differed as to whether the victim had thrown himself into the river or onto the bridge's train tracks. Henry Montgomery's death left the family destitute, forcing sixteen-year-old Robert to leave school and seek out such arduous jobs as railway mechanic and oil tanker deckhand. Yet somehow a deep-seated love of writing led to small acting roles, eventually landing him on Broadway.

Bob, as he was known to friends, was someone who had overcome a complicated past, one not devoid of physical toil and economic hardship. Such people had always appealed to Joan. Beyond this, they shared a love of writing and a fierce independent streak. As a young man, Montgomery had taken up residence in a Greenwich Village apartment, where he knocked out short stories on a typewriter and submitted them, unsuccessfully, to magazines. At one point, his father's relatives proposed to pay his way through Princeton University on the condition that he study law or business. Refusing to stray from writing, he told them the only subject he would be interested in studying was journalism. (Joan, who had harbored her own journalistic ambitions, must have appreciated that element of the story in particular.) The offer was revoked.

So, while their politics may have been quite different, they had much more in common. Bob possessed an unblinking drive that Joan instantly recognized, and it bound them.

By outward measures, Joan had achieved the strongest position in her solo career. She had partnered with an A-list star and a top salary earner. (In 1947 the *New York Times* listed Montgomery's income as $250,000, just below that of Universal president William Goetz.) In a top position in his independent company at Universal, she was well positioned, at a time when box office returns were surging. (The industry was enjoying a huge rebound, with soldiers returning home and the economy stabilizing.) She could also be assured some shelter from the rising tide of the Red Scare, given Montgomery's political conservatism and his HUAC status as a "friendly witness." Her hope was that this studio—the site of so many of her hellos and good-byes—would finally allow her to do her best work.

She couldn't pretend, however, that Universal-International wasn't a mixed blessing for someone like her, coming in fresh. The studio was only now beginning to steady itself after its recent restructuring, which played out while Joan was at RKO. It began with an attempted megamerger in 1945 drawn up by British film magnate J. Arthur Rank, who had notions of forming an American block-booking system and forcing exhibitors to take his British product but quickly outfoxed himself. He ended up backing out, though he remained financially invested enough to oversee the merger of Universal with the young International Pictures, founded by Chicago attorney (and former president of RKO) Leo Spitz and William Goetz, son-in-law of Louis B. Mayer.

On July 30, 1946, the studio's reorganization into Universal-International was announced. In assuming the reins of the parent company, Spitz and Goetz wanted to explicitly brand U-I as a prestige house, finding the Abbott and Costello films, serials, and monster movies distasteful. Goetz spent more time on the ground—assisted by William Dozier, who was now U-I's associate head of production. Goetz quickly determined that, no matter how galling the prospect, the studio could not shed its B-grade bread-and-butter productions. But, at the same time, the company would put new resources toward literary adaptations, British imports, and star showcases. With this stated goal, Goetz issued the order to "fire anyone not qualified to work on high end productions." Hiring Montgomery was another part of this larger bid for prestige.

Joan saw the urgent need to avoid being pigeonholed as a B-level producer. Her strategy was to put forward new, bestselling novels by respected authors as material for superior Montgomery vehicles. *Lights Out* was the first to be announced, on March 12, 1947. This was realist fiction written by Baynard

Kendrick, known for his progressive politics and the popular series featuring "sightless detective" Captain Duncan Maclain.

Lights Out tells the story of Sergeant Larry Nevins, a white southerner blinded by sniper fire in World War II. He strikes up a friendship with another blinded GI, Joe Morgan, in the rehabilitation unit, though he doesn't realize until several months later, upon making a racist comment, that his new best friend is African American. Their bond seemingly severed, Nevins's story shifts to his return home to his fiancée in Florida, where he himself faces an onslaught of discrimination because of his disability. With his awareness raised, he sets off to find his own way, which includes renewing his friendship with Joe and falling in love with an idealistic liberal woman.

Lights Out qualified as adult fare, the kind of serious filmmaking Harrison was aiming for. It lent itself to the self-conscious, experimental approaches Montgomery was staking out, with the subjective perspectives of the blind characters offering up possibilities for the camera's eye. Montgomery and Harrison were determined to bring the project to the screen, convincing Universal-International to place it in their hands. U-I paid MGM $50,000 for the property, which was five times what MGM had paid for it a year earlier, and assigned it directly to Joan.

Joan and Bob, however, apparently found the book's critique of racial bias too controversial to address head-on. She told the *New York Times* that she would instead focus the script on the home front section, when Larry returns to his fiancée in Florida and takes a job in her father's business. She explained, "The color problem will not loom as large on the screen as it did in the novel . . . since the love story will be the primary subject in the screen treatment." It was perhaps expected that she would be drawn to the troubled domestic relationships awaiting the returning veteran, who was blind both physically and emotionally. But she insisted that the film would still confront racial issues, saying that the filmmakers would not be ruled by prejudice (what she termed "sectional prejudice in the United States") or "box office dictates."

Then, as quickly as it was announced, *Lights Out* was put on hold, replaced on the Montgomery-Harrison project roster by an adaptation of Dorothy Hughes's *Ride the Pink Horse*, a novel heralded by reviewers as quality fiction with "real characterization." Universal-International reported the reason for the switch was that the screenplay for *Ride the Pink Horse* was further along, noting that writers Ben Hecht and Charles Lederer had in fact completed it. Harrison and Montgomery would hold on to the *Lights Out* project for many more months—and keep it close to their hearts—but they eventually let it go.

It's true the script for *Ride the Pink Horse* was finished, but the driving force was Joan's eagerness to translate the book for the screen. She considered it a "little novel" trading in big ideas, with penetrating characters and settings. As soon as it was published in fall 1946, she had begun angling to secure its rights, seemingly willing all the pieces into place: first the studio, and then the star.

Hecht and Lederer each possessed a biting wit and keen intelligence, having written for Ernst Lubitsch, Howard Hawks, King Vidor, Rouben Mamoulian, and Hitchcock. It's possible that they began adapting Hughes's novel before Harrison and Montgomery were attached (an early notice mentioned Universal had Dan Duryea in mind for the lead), but once the team was firm, Joan revisited the script by the two master scribes. She saw the story a certain way.

Casting for *Ride the Pink Horse* began the first week of April 1947. Foremost on everyone's mind was who would play the female lead, a local Mexican Indian waif who rescues the film's embittered con man (Montgomery) in the end. Audrey Totter was given first consideration. The self-assured blonde was enjoying a winning streak being cast as a tough dame, and she had held her own as *Lady in the Lake*'s Adrienne Fromsett. For reasons unknown, the part went instead to an unlikely choice: eighteen-year-old Wanda Hendrix. At five foot two and ninety-five pounds, the diminutive actress, originally from Jacksonville, Florida, had been plucked from local theater as a teenager, offered a contract with Warners, and given a debut role alongside Charles Boyer in *Confidential Agent* (1945). By the time of *Ride the Pink Horse*, which was her fifth feature, she was at Paramount. Hendrix had neither Mexican nor Native American roots. (She was of Irish descent.) However, she had a special fondness for dialects and accents. In fact, one publication was so taken in that it declared that, without shedding her "native" accent and speaking better English, she wouldn't go far as an actress.

Having played Inspector Burgess to perfection in *Phantom Lady*, Thomas Gomez would now be cast as Pancho, a gregarious, often-drunk carousel operator (the "ride" referenced in the film's title) who befriends Montgomery's Lucky Gagin, refusing to be put off by his callous exterior and insisting that they relate to each other on level terms. In supporting roles, Art Smith was cast as the particularly sympathetic FBI agent Bill Retz, Fred Clark (in only his second film performance, after years of formal training with the American Academy of Dramatic Arts), would take a turn as deaf gangster Frank Hugo, and Andrea King would play Hugo's gold-digging girlfriend, who double-crosses Gagin.

A key distinction of *Ride the Pink Horse* was to be its locale in New Mexico, where author Dorothy Hughes made her home. So as not to rankle the citizens of Santa Fe, the studio relocated the film to the fictional town of "San Pablo," a composite of Santa Fe, Albuquerque, and Taos. Very few, if any, films in the noir cycle had capitalized on the desert milieu for psychological effect. The burnt-orange mesas, colorful markets and plazas, old cemeteries, and ancient rituals featured in the novel would translate well to the screen.

For production design, Joan again tapped Robert Boyle, who by now fully espoused her predilection for story and character over action. He was "getting more and more interested in relating the environment people found themselves in" to who they were. He believed that a film like *Ride the Pink Horse* could take you inside characters "so you saw their depth, you saw things you would never know . . . but you sensed something underneath the surface."

Art direction would fall to Bernard Herzbrun, who had worked often with Boyle and was a natural match for *Ride the Pink Horse*, as his aesthetic sensibility veered toward realism and location shooting. Director of photography Russell Metty, having come up with Gregg Toland and Orson Welles at RKO, was a practitioner of the long take and deep focus. Fully capable of burnishing a shine, he was a "rough and ready . . . no frills cameraman" who would stretch every dollar of this modest budget. Though designated an A-film, the biggest dollars were allocated to salaries for Montgomery, Hecht, and Lederer, requiring economical choices elsewhere.

On April 1, 1947, Harrison had accompanied Montgomery, Boyle, Universal business manager Edward Dobbs, and photographer Edward Jones on a scouting trip to Albuquerque. They deplaned a TWA flight to great local fanfare and were greeted by chamber of commerce director Norville Sharpe. Joan spent five days operating out of their base at the Hilton Hotel, getting a lay of the land, and trying to predict how many days of location shooting would ultimately be necessary. She quickly determined they would need to shoot only four or five locations there. The remainder could be reproduced in the studio. The better part of Joan's energy was spent generating goodwill among local business leaders and townspeople. The last thing she wanted to do was to alienate residents. They held solid marketing potential down the road.

Almost three weeks later, on April 20, she returned with the cast and forty crew members in tow to pick up those few select exteriors. Everyone settled in together several miles north of Santa Fe, at the landmark Bishop's Lodge, nestled deep among cloaked foothills that led to a centuries-old chapel. For the next few days, Joan made sure to capture all they would need to re-create the interiors of the famous Hotel La Fonda, run by the esteemed Fred Harvey. She also oversaw the filming of the age-old ceremony known as the "burning of Zozobra" (the god of bad luck), which would be incorporated into the script.

One of Joan's coups came during a brief visit to Taos, where she convinced the Lions Club to entrust its antique carousel, Tío Vivo (Uncle Lively), to Universal for several months. She persuaded the group to allow her to break down the equipment (which dated back to 1882), ship it to Los Angeles, rebuild it on the set, and then return it. All the Taos Lions Club asked in return was $2,000 compensation (which would be donated to children in need of eyeglasses), and a guarantee that Tío Vivo would never leave the care of their chosen chaperone, a Lions Club member by the name of Jiménez Martínez.

In the film version of *Ride the Pink Horse*, Lucky Gagin (in the book, named simply "Sailor") is an out-of-joint veteran who arrives in the border town of San Pablo with the intention of blackmailing a former war profiteer, Frank Hugo. The gangster Hugo (who requires an absurdly large hearing aid) has already killed Gagin's best friend to halt the blackmailing effort. Gagin wants revenge and raises the stakes by trying to extort the killer with a canceled check he's hidden in a local bus terminal locker (the check is proof that Hugo bribed a government official). On his way to Hugo's hotel room, a young Mexican American girl from outside the village, Pila, intercedes and ominously insists that Gagin accept a good luck charm. At the hotel, he misses a chance to meet up with Hugo, but he does have a run-in with the man's secretary, Jonathan.

As Gagin takes his leave, he realizes that government agent Bill Retz is hot on his trail and wise to his plan. Retz warns Gagin to leave town. Instead, he seeks out a hotel room, only to discover that there are no vacancies in town because of an upcoming fiesta. He sidles over to the local cantina, where he drinks the night away with jolly Pancho, the carousel operator who "houses" him for the night in his makeshift outdoor domicile. After being lured into a trap by Hugo and his girlfriend, Marjorie, Gagin is attacked by two of Hugo's henchmen. He kills one but is stabbed by the other, managing to escape into the bushes. Pila finds him and delivers him back to the safety of the merry-go-round, where she and Pancho nurse his wounds. When more of Hugo's men arrive, Pila conceals Gagin's hiding place by fanning her skirt over it, as Pancho creates a diversion by striking up the ride and inviting local children to hop on. But the impromptu plan takes a bad turn when the gangsters heartlessly pummel Pancho for information about Gagin's whereabouts as the children (and Pila) helplessly watch.

Afterward, Pila drags Gagin to an outward-bound bus, in hopes that he will be conveyed to safety. But while she's buying his ticket, he wanders back into danger, winding up in Hugo's room, with Pila by his side. He and Pila are both beaten violently by Hugo's men, and are rescued only by the appearance of Detective Retz. That's when Hugo puts Gagin to a final test, offering him $300,000 in exchange for the check. Gagin refuses the money and instead turns over the incriminating check to Retz.

A few days later, Gagin and Retz are having breakfast and discussing Pila. Gagin, suspecting Pila's feelings for him, worries about having to let her down easy. Retz urges Gagin to give in to his romantic impulses. When the three finally meet up in the town plaza, Pila surprises both men by initiating a good-bye before moving on cheerfully to rejoin her friends and neighbors and regale them with a retelling of the adventure of the past few days.

Ride the Pink Horse thwarts many noir conventions. The filming of the protagonist sidling into a Mexican border town is approached in a self-conscious way using a three-minute unbroken take. The sequences that introduce the character separate him from the typical antihero; the camerawork and scripting indicate his self-awareness—he understands that he is no less a thug than the high-class gangster Hugo, he's simply operating on a lower rung. Yet Gagin still has more to discover. Atypically, Gagin's narrative journey is defined by encounters with characters such as Pila and Pancho—native residents who appear at first marginal and who in the eyes of Anglo-American tourists are trivial and exotic—and he begins to see the possibility of a different life beyond his own limited horizon. He finds moral redemption, rendered clearly toward the end of the film when he hands over the check to Retz in Hugo's hotel room.

In contrast to other films with similar themes, the Mexican American characters do not function as mere vehicles for the main character's transformation.

Their role as his "supporters" and his "outsider" status are constructed in unusual ways, such as when Gagin's point of view of the locals is rendered askew when he enters the cantina, or when supposedly background characters (San Pabloans) are given perspective shots. Notably, Pila and Pancho speak Spanish for almost entire scenes, and the film does not bother with an English translation for Gagin or the audience. It could be argued that the Mexican American characters are rich, complex characters even while they embody stereotypes. As R. Emmet Sweeney puts it, Pila is both the exotic, ethereal unknown, and the "preternaturally, self-assured girl." In subtle and thoughtful ways, *Ride the Pink Horse* deconstructs racial and ethnic categories even as it participates in their making.

One of the most striking features of *Ride the Pink Horse* is that a petite Mexican Indian character from the hills takes over the action for the last third of the film. Pila's role as a powerful narrative agent is a notable departure from Hughes's novel and signals Joan's greatest contribution to the earliest draft of the screenplay. Reminiscent of her *Phantom Lady* adaptation, she transforms a literary female character who functions mainly as an inscrutable object for the male protagonist into someone indispensable. The book *Ride the Pink Horse* presents Pila as being fourteen years old, thereby making her an even less likely love interest for Sailor (Gagin) and more "unreal, alien" (and an immediate reminder that *he* is the true "alien"—or other—in this land). In the film, however, she functions as a guide from the start, directing Gagin to the hotel and forcing on him the protective good luck charm.

As the film progresses, Pila continues to secretly watch over him, which the camera shows by surreptitiously revealing her existence on the sidelines or background of his scenes. And by the time she takes over the last section of the film, she literally carries him from place to place (because he is too weak from his knife wound). As her tiny body holds up the weight of his tall, wounded frame, she creates an indelible image of female physical strength. His delirium requires her to be his eyes and ears—to make all the right moves. Her resolve becomes increasingly palpable in two harrowing scenes: as she makes the determination to save Gagin, which means she is forced to sit idly by while Hugo's thugs strike at Pancho (while she and the children on the merry-go-round anxiously watch, or try not to); and when the same men beat her up in the hotel room while Gagin lies on the floor, powerless to stop them.

The conclusion of *Ride the Pink Horse* subverts the convention of the fatalistic outcome that had by that time become associated with noir. That's because Harrison's films tended to have something in common: a reversal of expectation. The final sequence would set up audience anticipation to flow in one direction and then abruptly reverse course. In this case, she significantly revised the last passages of Hughes's book, which left the protagonist in circumstances that were ambiguous at best and most likely doomed. When the novel's Sailor realizes he's about to be caught by the federal agent and hauled away to prison, he shoots the man dead and begins to run from the town plaza toward Mexico. He's not quite sure whether the lawman is dead, but he knows he can never go back. Tears run down his face as he cries for the man he just shot, who didn't even carry a gun. Painting a stark picture of her damned protagonist, Hughes writes, "He ran on, into open country this quickly, plunging into the wastes of endless land and sky, stretching forever, for eternity, to the far-off barrier of the mountain." She cinches the novel on an economical, open-ended note: "Blindly, he stumbled on."

The film's ending, in contrast, plays out in brilliant relief, more like a romantic comedy than a mystery. It's the morning after the nightmarish events with the gangsters. Gagin and Retz have breakfast, with only the loose end of Gagin's relationship with Pila left to tie up. As the two men dine at the hotel, Gagin prepares to leave town and wonders how he will bid farewell to Pila. The stage is set for rom-com resolution, as Retz implicitly encourages Gagin to give in to a happy ending. The law man acts as a chorus for the audience, in a way, reflecting the narrative expectations that have been planted (even as these romantic insinuations defy logic, given that this is an interethnic relationship at a time when those were not permitted on-screen).

As the two men walk toward the plaza, the film cues viewers to identify with Retz, assuming (as he does) that the path will lead to a kiss and fade out. This heightens the surprise when, after a moment of suspended tension, Pila gives Gagin a peck on the cheek and sends him on his way. The big twist is that Pila has the presence of mind and strength of character to say good-bye. Even more remarkably, the film ends with her telling her story, narrating the events that have just transpired in the film, in Spanish, to her community, as we end on her gaze. In an added touch of camp, the two men, and not the heterosexual couple, walk off together into the sunset. The cut back to Pila as the final shot may well have been Montgomery's decision as a director. And the final banter between characters was likely written by Hecht and Lederer. The overall architecture of *Ride the Pink Horse*, however, bears the indelible stamp of Harrison. The final twist, the attention to a female gaze, and an unlikely heroine driving the action—these are Harrison's hallmarks.

As *Ride the Pink Horse* rolled out into theaters through the fall of 1947, most reviewers recognized its ambitiousness and craft. The *Boston Globe*'s Marjory Adams deemed the film "clever, taut, superbly told" and "richly told as to characterization, chock-a-block full of situations which keep that audience thrilled and excited." In the *New York Times*, Bosley Crowther congratulated Montgomery for "artfully fashioning a fascinating film within the genre" while making it "look shockingly literal and keep[ing] it moving at an unrelenting pace." The *Austin American Statesman*'s Eulamae Moore rejoiced that *Ride the Pink Horse* might finally signal Hollywood's embrace of a recent trend in foreign movies, hailing it as "a bold experiment in unorthodox endings."

In the *Baltimore Sun*, Montgomery spoke directly to the risk involved with the inconclusive finale, commenting, "I've gambled that the average age of a movie audience is a great deal older than twelve years. I've tossed out every cliché ending and left the ending to be formed in the minds of the audience." His comment put a fine point on one of Joan's ongoing pursuits—trying to reach a savvy, mature-minded audience. With *Ride the Pink Horse*, she had succeeded.

The film's critical success represented more than a skillfully made crime picture (though it certainly was that); it reflected very carefully calculated publicity strategies that ended up working in its favor. Joan helped sell the women's angle, going on a string of coast-to-coast radio interviews. She played up the centrality of the young teenage girl and raved about Wanda Hendrix's standout performance.

Initially, Universal had not thought to highlight these aspects of *Ride the Pink Horse*. The publicity firm hired by the studio, Monroe Greenthal Co., considered a host of angles, from Montgomery's star status (which they ultimately shied away from because, though he was a critics' darling, his box office performance was unpredictable), to action and menace (they thought better of this upon realizing how "unusual" the depiction of violence was, and removed most weapons from promotional art), to Andrea King's sex appeal (though they didn't want to oversell the importance of King's romantic story line). At a certain point, they found themselves at a loss; all they knew was that this was not "a normal type mystery." Upon viewing the final cut, the publicity agents arrived at the idea "that Wanda Hendrix's wonderful portrayal of the girl, Pila, would probably be one of the most talked about features of the picture." It was only natural that Harrison, who had been instrumental in embellishing this character, would now take an active role in promotion. After Montgomery and Hendrix, Harrison was next in line in the national advertising plan, a vital part of the movie's "star" package.

For many who were involved, the impact of *Ride the Pink Horse* was almost impossible to measure. The film poised Hendrix to stake a legitimate claim to stardom, and had she not tumbled into a harrowing, abusive marriage with World War II hero turned actor Audie Murphy, she might have graduated to bona fide stardom. (As it was, she remembered Pila as her favorite performance.) For his role as Pancho, Thomas Gomez was nominated for an Academy Award (for Best Supporting Actor), making history as the first Hispanic American to attain such an honor. (He lost to *Miracle on 34th Street*'s Kris Kringle, Edmund Gwenn.) And in July 1949, just eighteen months after its release, the film achieved perhaps its greatest distinction when it was selected by Jean Cocteau and his jury for the legendary Festival du Film Maudit in Biarritz, France, assuming its place as a criminally overlooked or "cursed film," among other now revered titles like Jean Vigo's *L'Atalante* (1934), John Ford's *The Long Voyage Home* (1940), and Robert Bresson's *Les Dames du Bois de Bologne* (*Ladies of the Park*, 1945).

It was in esteemed company, even if Joan might have preferred a hit instead.

17 | FULL CIRCLE, BY DEGREES

AS IT HAPPENED, THE release of *Ride the Pink Horse* coincided with Communist Red-baiting reaching a fever pitch. Battle lines were being drawn in Hollywood and across the country. Paranoia about the infiltration of "pinkos" was so rampant that the studio seriously considered changing the film's title to remove any potential association. Two weeks after the film's October 9 premiere in New York City, Robert Montgomery went to Washington, DC, to give "friendly" testimony before the House Un-American Activities Committee. Among the thirty-nine witnesses assembled in the crowded caucus room of the Old House Office Building, Montgomery was one of the more famous faces, bringing gravitas and an emphatic anti-Communist message from SAG.

These episodes placed Joan and the director further apart on the political divide. She was becoming increasingly agitated by the smear tactics being used against colleagues like Irving Pichel, Edward Dmytryk, and Herbert Biberman (Gale Sondergaard's husband), and worse, dear friend Lewis Milestone (one of the Hollywood's "Unfriendly Nineteen" who had been outcast by studios). She bore witness as people from her cherished inner circle—including John Huston, Jules Buck, Evelyn Keyes, Paul Henreid, Billy Wilder, John Houseman, and Anatole Litvak—flew cross-country as part of a twenty-five-person delegation they named the Committee for the First Amendment, on a self-proclaimed mission to protect the right of free speech. They intended to voice their opposition to the hearings, but once in Washington, they realized they were outgunned by the political machinery and attendant press. They hightailed it back to L.A. in early November, many of them ashamed at their own naïveté.

Ten members of the Hollywood community invoked their First Amendment rights and refused on principle to answer the committee's questions. "The Hollywood Ten," as the group came to be known, included not only Edward Dmytryk but also such notable screenwriters as Ring Lardner Jr. and Dalton Trumbo. On November 25, the House of Representatives cited the Hollywood Ten for contempt of Congress for refusing to say on the record whether they were members of the Communist Party. They were convicted and ordered to serve jail time.

That same week, the Motion Picture Association of America, the Association of Motion Picture Producers, the Society of Independent Motion Picture Producers, and eight studio heads held closed-door meetings to determine how best to proclaim the industry's patriotism and move past the disruption. Later that day, leaders issued a press release, known as the Waldorf Statement, "deploring" the actions of the Hollywood Ten and pledging not only to suspend them without compensation but to never employ them again unless they could clear themselves of the charges. After two years of petitions and a denied hearing at the Supreme Court level, the men would begin serving their prison sentences in spring 1950.

The threat of similar repercussions immediately threatened Houseman, Huston, and Henreid. Houseman was informally exiled, or "graylisted," while the latter two were officially added to the blacklist, though it took a year for them to piece it together. Henreid had just completed his Warner Bros. contract and therefore had no institutional backing. Dore Schary, then at MGM, eventually told him, "The studios will look after their own, Paul. You've got no one to protect you." The witch hunt would escalate to such a fervor that Irwin Shaw and Anatole Litvak would find it necessary to live out their remaining years in Europe.

Joan shared her anxiety with those who knew her best, Hitch and Alma. They too were deeply affected by the savage tactics used in the hearings. All three worried over who in their set might be targeted, and they spent many an evening through the summer and fall of 1947 focused on the topic with increasing dread. Sidney Bernstein, now like a member of the extended family, vehemently opposed the crackdown and donated to a defense fund. Whitfield Cook, gearing up to write *Stage Fright*, was so disgusted that he would soon turn away from Hollywood.

A pall tended to hang over the regular dinners that included Bernstein, Cook, Arthur Laurents, and Hume Cronyn (who were then collaborating on *Rope*), as well as favorite guests like Joseph Cotten and his wife, Lenore Kipp, and José Ferrer, as concerns festered over where this might lead. It was an era of studio-enforced loyalty oaths and surprise subpoenas, in which it wasn't uncommon to wake up to find that a long-time colleague was facing jail time, or see that a new slate of talent had been attached to the morning call sheet and have no idea whether they were "friendly" or "unfriendly" colleagues. Most in the room had contributed to the kinds of antifascist and refugee causes that were now being labeled subversive, and Laurents, Cronyn, Cotten, and Ferrer would all be blacklisted in 1951.

It would have been easy for Joan to use her producer status as cover until the storm blew over. Producers were aligned with management, after all, and that was the side of the industry that controlled the public narrative. Her partnership with Montgomery, who was seen as one of Hollywood's most committed anti-Communists, also promised to shield her from intense scrutiny. Yet for Joan this would have been a betrayal of her beliefs and her friends. While others began to abandon those who had formed the Committee for the First Amendment, and many on its DC trip chose to save face by disavowing the episode (Bogart's "I'm no Communist" article in *Photoplay* was one example), she continued to be visibly outspoken and attend public fundraisers. She was a faithful friend privately as well; Houseman remembered her as one of the few who continued to communicate with him at that time.

Harrison made no secret of her political affiliations at the time. Though she wouldn't acquire American citizenship for another decade, as the 1948 election season heated up, she contributed to third-party Progressive presidential candidate Henry Wallace's campaign, attending a dinner at Ciro's in which he blasted HUAC and the movie industry's compromising of its standards. The press took notice. An inflammatory article titled "Wallace Blasts at Film Firms" noted the presence in the audience of Harrison, Huston, Keyes, Sondergaard, and more than a dozen names of writers or actors who would soon be blacklisted.

Meanwhile, leading the charge for New York governor Thomas Dewey was Montgomery, vice president of the Hollywood Republican Committee. Though Joan and Bob each made their homes in opposing parties, they continued to mingle socially, taking in polo on the weekends and making the rounds at hosted dinners in the evenings. And she didn't let his politics stop her from anteing up in the fall of 1948 for his next directorial venture, the Universal-International romantic comedy *Once More, My Darling*.

The obvious question is why Joan would join forces with one of Hollywood's most conservative voices, and why stay the course with him for what would stretch out into four years. "We—my friends and I—we never understood that," said Norman Lloyd, who spent a lot of time in Joan's social circles and would ultimately work with her more closely than almost anyone.

One explanation could be that Joan compartmentalized Bob's politics because she found the work exciting, not to mention steady. From almost any perspective, the producing arrangement with U-I provided an exceptional platform. In terms of operations and creative power, she held tremendous sway, shored up by the formalization of Neptune Productions, Montgomery's independent company within the studio. Her access to literary material, writers, and crew was in some ways unprecedented. At a time when the industry was in crisis and friends' jobs were in jeopardy, she had found a good niche.

It may also be that Montgomery's politics were not so cut and dried. It appears that he was never so dogmatic that he let ideology dictate his choices in casting, crew, or professional associations.

Most pertinent to their collaboration at this time is this: Joan had landed well, but so had Bob. With Harrison on board as his producer, Montgomery's independent company within Universal showed unusual scope and vision. Through a November 1948 deal with the national Theatre Guild that gave Neptune rights to all of the guild's past and future stage plays, his unit achieved what Louella Parsons called "the movie coup of the year." He and Harrison were simultaneously plotting an early foray into television, signing him up to host and serve as the regular lead in the new CBS television series *Suspense* (as it prepared for a January 1949 move from radio), though he would instead launch the *Robert Montgomery Presents* series in January 1950.

As film production was shrinking, Joan was on the front lines with him, exploring how other outlets might strengthen Neptune (and applying many strategies from Hitchcock's playbook). As his creative producer, Joan was crucial—in fact, more central than she had been to Hitchcock. Montgomery had neither the expertise to run the business side nor the time. Directing while acting took concentration. "Robert Montgomery needed her much more than she needed him," film historian Eddie Muller has observed, pointing to the range of her contributions and suggesting that she was loyal to him, perhaps to a fault. She was often treated by the press, though, as little more than a functionary—someone who managed the day-to-day details that supported his vision, rather than the person at the helm.

Montgomery's personality made their ongoing working relationship and friendship all the more complex. Robert Boyle explained, "He was pretty hard to chum around with. . . . He was a very aloof man." Evelyn Keyes, when recalling the making of *Here Comes Mr. Jordan*, said, "We hardly spoke, he didn't have any sense of humor." Keyes described a publicity shoot after production was complete when they spent the day posing for still photographs, recounting, "So there we were, hugging, smiling and kissing in front of the camera, and he didn't say one single word to me."

Montgomery does not appear to have changed his stripes with Harrison. The screenwriter Oscar Saul, who would collaborate with both of them, described Montgomery as "a very cold, cruel man." He remembered Joan as "a very nice lady" but said the director "treated her like dirt." Saul continued, "Montgomery was drawn to very rich and 'aristocratic' people. He'd invite Harrison to his house if he'd give a party and then sort of ignore her or treat her like the help." She apparently excused his more disagreeable attributes. In the parlance, she gave him a bye, as was her custom when dealing with Hitchcock's antics.

Joan's relationship with Bob might have crossed over into romance, but no one has ever corroborated that beyond offering a curious anecdote: Though Joan didn't tend to be sentimental, she did keep a pair of china dogs on her shelf, well into old age. She had named each pup, as part of a long-standing inside family joke. One dog was named Clark, and the other was named Bob.

On December 2, 1948, Universal-International announced that Harrison and Montgomery would try their hands at romantic comedy, adapting Robert Carson's short story "Come Be My Love." Retitled *Once More, My Darling* for the screen, the production was originally budgeted at $780,000 and projected to take forty-four days. Before production began, the figure was whittled down to $750,000 and production time to thirty-three days. Anomalously, Joan received no producer's pay, a provision that was explicitly laid out (though not explained) in the budget sheet. Though it wouldn't have been out of the ordinary for Harrison and Montgomery to take a cut in salary in support of the picture, for her to go entirely uncompensated went against industry standards.

Universal-International, like most studios, was feeling the pinch. In stark contrast to two years earlier, when audience attendance was at a record high, the industry was in crisis mode, taking multiple hits from declining box office, the emergence of television, the HUAC hearings, and a growing trend of talent breaking away from long-term contracts in favor of independence. Executives were also reeling from the Paramount Decrees, the 1948 Supreme Court ruling that was going to force studio restructuring. U-I was bent on keeping production costs down, and general manager Eddie Muhl, informally referred to as the hatchet man, made it his personal mission to slash every budget, justified or not.

Robert Carson was hired to adapt his own *Saturday Evening Post* story. Earning $50,000 for the property rights and a weekly writer's salary, he was more than up to the task, having won an Academy Award for cowriting the original *A Star Is Born* in 1937. But it soon became clear that the team wanted free rein to rewrite scenes on the set, and Oscar Saul came on board as a dialogue writer and stayed to the end of production. Scripter of *Strange Affair* (1944) and *Road House* (1948), Saul had put on the 1937 children's play *Revolt of the Beavers* (along with Louis Lantz) as part of the Federal Theatre Project, coming under the scrutiny of the Dies Committee (an informal name for HUAC before it became a standing committee).

Michael Gordon, another lefty, was selected as director. Having managed the Group Theatre in the 1930s, Gordon had helped stage some of Clifford Odets's most stirring work. (In 1951, he too would be blacklisted.) Gordon made for an odd selection, as he was coming off a succession of mystery and crime films, including *The Web*, with Ella Raines and Edmond O'Brien. In fact, there had been a fleeting moment when another Universal contract director, Frederick De Cordova, who displayed a knack for romantic comedy, was assigned, but his time was consumed by *The Gal Who Took the West*. Filling out the more technical lines were cinematographer Franz Planer (a frequent collaborator with Max Ophüls) and art directors Robert Clatworthy and Bernard Herzbrun (the latter returning from *Ride the Pink Horse*). As a special touch, Elizabeth Firestone was commissioned to write the score. The twenty-five-year-old heiress to the tire fortune, according to publicity at the time, was the first woman to compose a Hollywood film.

Montgomery was set to play the lead role of Collier Laing, who has been discharged from the army and now aspires toward an acting career, contrary to his mother's hopes for him to return to his law practice. The biggest question was who would play the young, naive debutante Marita, whose unwitting trouble with a jewel thief forces Laing to be abruptly recalled to active duty—on an undercover mission to win her affection. Montgomery hoped for a reunion with one of his favorite costars, MGM's Audrey Totter (*The Lady in the Lake*, *The Saxon Charm*), and the trades began to sizzle with advance buzz in late January 1949 as preproduction began.

The role of Marita instead went to U-I's Ann Blyth, whose stunning performance as *Mildred Pierce*'s wicked teenaged daughter had earned her an Academy Award nomination, only to be followed by run-of-the-mill assignments. Splitting the difference between tomboy and glamour girl, perky Marita "Killer" Connell (so nicknamed for her lethal tennis shots) would offer Blyth a chance to show her funny, sexy side. Though she may not have been Montgomery's first choice, the actress recalled, "Working with Bob was a real treat. He certainly believed in me." From Joan, she did not receive the hands-on attention experienced by some previous rising female stars; however, as she put it, "If Ms. Harrison had not liked me, I certainly would have known about it." Joan had a way of letting people know where they stood.

Acclaimed stage actress Jane Cowl was selected to play Laing's overinvolved mother. As another example of a novel choice in mature female casting, this was a sound-film debut for Cowl, who had played in two silents in the late 1910s (except for an uncredited appearance in 1943's *Stage Door Canteen*). The part of the Laing housekeeper, Mamie, was conceived to be less stereotypical than most. Lillian Randolph, whose career spanned film (*The Bachelor and the Bobby Soxer*, *It's a Wonderful Life*), radio (*The Great Gildersleeve*, *Amos 'n' Andy*), and the stage, would bring added dimension to the character in a way that would disrupt the hierarchy of the Laing family. By the same token, given an unusually prominent place in the story, the role of Marita's chauffer Herman Schmelz went to the gravelly voiced, hard-nosed character actor Charles McGraw.

The film's plot revolves around the US Army's effort to regain stolen jewels from shady former GI Peter Vellon, who obtained them during the war.

Military investigators come across the first lead in years when the heiress Marita (a recent girlfriend of Vellon's) wears one of the large pendants carelessly yet conspicuously above her cleavage in a magazine advertisement for "Passionelle: A Perfume of Passion." An army colonel (Roland Winters) commissions Laing to go on a secret mission to woo her, in the hopes that Vellon will become so jealous that he comes out of hiding. Laing embraces the undercover job as the next best thing to a starring role, having just spent the day struggling as a bit-part lover boy trying to deliver romantic lines (e.g., "Once more, my darling, if say good-bye we must, once more, let me look at you," which inspired the title) first on an empty soundstage and then to a disinterested stagehand turned body double.

What Laing doesn't count on is how quickly he will fall for the over-protected, unreserved, verbose Marita. She confounds all his expectations, to the point that, though he has carefully inspected her picture, when he first meets her he doesn't recognize her at all, since she's wearing dark sunglasses, her hair piled under a sports cap, and a juvenile-looking white tennis outfit with large black letters spelling out KILLER across her bosom (replacing the pendant). Conceiving of herself as the kind of heroine she reads about in Victorian romance novels and ladies' magazine literary supplements, Marita doesn't realize that nearly all her utterances come out as sexual double entendre.

In order to further acquaint herself with Laing, whom she now refers to in the familiar as "Collie," she sneaks out of her father's villa at the Bel Air Hotel late at night wearing pajamas, covered by a mink coat (so as not to raise Mr. Connell's suspicions). Consequently, she spends the remainder of the evening scantily clad in loose-hanging sleepwear, eliciting shock from onlookers and continual attempts from Collie to cover her up with the fur. She remains obtuse toward their reactions and oblivious to their distress as they shield themselves from the overwhelming fragrance of Passionelle ("They gave me crates of it. . . . I practically swim in the stuff").

Collie hits his limit when she suggests announcing their courtship while still on their first date, insisting they impose upon Mrs. Laing and her dinner guests. The stuffy prigs gawk at his new pajama-wearing "Killer" girlfriend as she explains why their romance is moving so quickly: "Our meeting was like a Passionelle advertisement. . . . There was the awakening, the enchantment, the feeling of the world reborn, and the abandonment the company warns you to be careful of." By the time Collie and Killer take their leave, his mother has reasonably drawn the conclusion that the young woman is expecting his child. Only Mamie sees the true meaning of her words and likes Marita for who she is, whispering to Collie as he walks out the door, "You've never had a woman like that before," and closing the door (and the scene) with a dreamy smile.

In a gender-role reversal, Marita proposes marriage to Collie at a nightclub later that evening, to which he agrees for the sake of the mission (though it is increasingly obvious that he is susceptible to her charms). Just before they depart for a quickie Las Vegas wedding, the club photographer takes their picture, which the army colonel strategically places in the newspaper. The announcement of the elopement lures not only the jewel thief but also Marita's chauffer and Collie's mother to Las Vegas. For his part, the groom-to-be takes his time getting Marita to their destination, ensuring the bride's wrath when she realizes they'll be forced to spend the night in an auto camp until they can get a marriage license. Once Vellon has been caught and Marita grasps the full reality of the rushed romance (and the army's hand in it), she rejects Collie, saying she wants nothing to do with him ever again.

Racked with lingering feelings for Marita and a well-earned sense of honor, Collie spends the morning wandering through the Las Vegas hotel lobby seeking permission from relevant male authorities (her father, the chauffer, the army officials) to ask Marita for her hand in marriage. To his dismay, one at a time, they let him off the hook by telling him he owes her nothing. When he suddenly stumbles upon Marita pumping coins into a slot machine, she refuses to reconcile, though in her agitation, she orders him to get on his knees and apologize.

In yet another unconventional ending, the slot machine falls on his head, and when he comes to, he is being held affectionately by Marita. Looking around, he realizes he finally has the "audience" he has always hoped for (composed of their family members, military officials, and onlookers). He overcomes his loss for words by reverting to the lines from his earlier performance as a bit player ("Once more, my darling, if say good-bye we must, once more, let me look at you"), which, it is immediately apparent, will more than satisfy Marita's fantasy of a proper marriage proposal. This was not the conclusion in the short story or treatment; it was a last-minute surprise ending that Joan cooked up with the writers. (In the source material, the couple go walking in the hotel garden after the colonel gives Laing praise for a job well done. As the hero fumbles for a way to express his feelings, Marita springs a wedding proposal on him. Bold as ever, she's been keeping a marriage license at the ready in her purse.)

Long before they worked out the ending, Joan faced, at the onset of production, a gigantic hurdle that threatened to thwart the entire enterprise. As soon as principal photography began in mid-March 1949, Montgomery began having doubts about the director. Gordon was averaging only seven setups a day and wrapping each day around 7:00 PM. To Montgomery, who typically completed ten to thirteen setups per day and aimed for a 4:00 PM end time, Gordon was running through Neptune's valuable film and, by extension, the budget.

Under different circumstances, Joan might have exerted her considerable skill to smooth over the rising tensions, which caused prolonged rehearsals on set and aggravated the already-frayed nerves of Jane Cowl, who kept flubbing her lines. But as it was, Montgomery was quick to imagine himself at the helm and gave Gordon little room to self-correct. Eight days in, Harrison and Montgomery finally convinced the front office that the only solution was for Montgomery himself to replace Gordon as director—with the stipulation that the actor would forfeit 50 percent of the director's salary. In an official release, the studio announced the change was a "mutual agreement" based on "creative differences."

It turned out to be a move in the right direction. Gordon's footage, which included the dinner party and scenes between Collie and his mother in the Laing home, was quickly reshot, and the pace of production accelerated. Principal photography wrapped on April 21.

If in many of Joan's ventures she added depth to female characters, in this case one of her chief contributions was to maintain the unusually forceful and naive power that Marita displays in the original short story. The translation of the character from page to screen is nearly exact, including entire sections of dialogue. Between this and Blyth's pitch-perfect performance, Marita's rhetorical, emotional, and erotic energy structures the film. She is the figurative engine that drives the plot, underscored by the fact that she spends long spans of the film directing Collie to drive her here and there. When she asks him out for a date, proposes marriage, and pushes him to elope to Las Vegas, she exerts narrative agency and reverses gender roles, while Montgomery plays up Collie's part as the reluctant "blushing bride" for laughs.

But Harrison and her team again faced opposition from the Production Code Administration. Joseph Breen and his representatives, Milton Holdenfield and Jack Vizzard, thought it best to exercise caution when it came to both the transgressive nature of Marita's character and the unyielding double entendres. They focused on the fact that Marita would spend much of the film wearing only silk pajamas, specified in the script as loose-hanging and drawing attention to the area of her bosom. Breen expressed "concern that women's nudity is highlighted through costuming, especially the highlighting of her breasts in the pajamas." He suggested remedying the problem by keeping the character bundled in her fur coat at all times. Joan ignored the note and kept the character costumed as written.

The larger issue, for the PCA, was simply the premise of the film—at least its most salacious interpretation. The week that production began, Harrison and director Gordon had a standoff with Holdenfield and Vizzard. It was a protracted meeting in which the censors objected to the fact that "the whole story stems from suspicion of illicit sex and pregnancy" and ended in "a tug of war." Joan did not surrender and, while her team agreed to alter some dialogue here and there, she pushed ahead. She made the case that careful direction would ensure that any hints of promiscuity, illicit sexuality, and pregnancy were handled subtly rather than explicitly.

Joan championed both fidelity to the story and the integrity of the dynamic female character and, in turn, rendered a refreshing contrast to the spider-women, happy homemakers, and bobby soxers of the late 1940s. As with so many of Joan's films, one key way that *Once More, My Darling* conveyed Marita's special traits—and her various transformations—was through changes in costume, which was why she was reluctant to eliminate the risqué clothes prescribed by the script. In fact, of all the films Joan produced solo, *Once More, My Darling* paid the most attention to fashion, accessories, and fragrance as narrative devices. The story incorporated themes of female consumerism and women as powerful, self-conscious subjects in the world of style. Her own well-known love of women's fashion not only had obvious advantages when it came to the film's production, by then it was a part of the Joan Harrison stamp.

Her fashion savvy also came in handy when working with Universal's publicity department to generate promotions aimed at teenage girls. While they didn't manage to launch a perfume line called "Passionelle" or cinch an agreement with the Norman D. Waters ad agency for a proposed "Killer" sweatshirt tie-up, they did score deals with Strutwear hosiery and RC Cola for Blyth, including ad placement in dozens of women's magazines.

Joan had won many allies with these publications over the years, and curried favor with Hollywood columnists and fan magazines. Her efforts appeared to have paid off with *Once More, My Darling*, which received rave reviews in *Screenland, Modern Screen, Charm,* and *Seventeen,* and was selected as *Redbook*'s "Picture of the Month." The wide swath of coverage mitigated the tepid response from the general press, which tended to criticize the film for being slow, rambling, or outmoded. The *New York Herald Tribune* saw it as "a mixture of long, static conversational scenes and brief episodes of character humor," while the *New York Daily Tribune* repined that it "gives you the feeling that you are riding for miles on a flat tire." The *Daily Compass* surmised, "There were Mr. Montgomery and his little film, doing business on a corner the world passed by long ago.

In hindsight, it was an unfortunate miscalculation to think that a screwball romantic comedy would fare well at a moment when gritty noirs and high-minded literary adaptations were ruling the box office. At the time, however, Universal-International was just as surprised as Harrison that *Once More, My Darling* failed to get traction with the public. Publicist Hank Linet wrote to the studio, "I must admit that this picture has me baffled. Everybody seems to like it and, by and large, I think all the ads developed on it so far have been excellent in their approach. But for some reason we are not getting the openings," referring to test markets such as New Haven, Buffalo, and St. Louis. The age difference between Montgomery and Blyth didn't help matters; neither Collie's leading-man looks nor Marita's ardent, whimsical nature could explain why she would abruptly fall for a man more than twice her age.

Montgomery's three-picture deal with U-I was up—he had taken a star turn with Susan Hayward in *The Saxon Charm*—and Joan knew that it was time to plan her exit. She was setting her sights five thousand miles away in London. The UK held new opportunities, now that legal changes in the British quota system had made room for American coproductions. It was a perfect time to form a new company with David E. Rose, the American former head of Paramount's British branch, who was looking to make low-budget pictures. They formed the independent, London-based Coronado Productions, making an arrangement with the J. Arthur Rank–owned American company Eagle-Lion to distribute its films in the United States.

Joan already had a script in her hip pocket. *Eye Witness*, or *Your Witness*, as it was titled in Britain, had been scripted by two Columbia contract writers, Hugo Butler and Ian McLellan Hunter. Butler and Hunter were best friends and part of a "close quadrumvirate" with Dalton Trumbo and Ring Lardner Jr. The men were known for "working together, playing together, drinking together, and spending their evenings philosophizing, arm wrestling, and trying to top each other's jokes." That is, before Trumbo and Lardner were named as two of the Hollywood Ten and turned all their energy to appealing their prison sentences. By 1949 Butler and Hunter were also under fire as prominent "radicals" who had joined the Communist Party during the war—when "the Russians were our gallant allies, suffering terrible casualties but stopping the Germans at Stalingrad," according to Butler's wife, writer Jean Rouverol. Living with the knowledge that they had barely escaped the most recent round of investigations and under the vise grip of daily FBI surveillance and the dread that subpoenas were just around the corner, Butler and Hunter were looking to furnish surplus screenplays to whoever was in the market.

Joan, like many, was sympathetic to their situation and their need to build a defense fund. She saw the purchase of the property as going to a good cause, with the added benefit that the story had many selling points: it was a postwar crime plot involving an American pursuing a "fish out of water" investigation in England, allowing ample room for comic comparisons between the two cultures. And the starring role fit her former partner Montgomery like a glove, and the film lent itself to his direction.

Harrison brought the details of the deal to Montgomery, who had no film prospects for the first time in decades—and had never intended to stay in Hollywood this long anyway. He signed up to direct and star. The decision was probably an easy one; not only did *Eye Witness* appeal to the Anglophile in him, but many of the nautical locations also beckoned to him, bringing resounding memories of his naval days. He did so despite being fully aware of Harrison's progressive political sympathies and left-leaning financial backers, and of the fact that the script had been written by two suspected Communists facing the threat of the blacklist. If Montgomery was an extreme conservative, he also appeared able to put politics aside in his personal and professional relationships.

These joint projects had not applied the brakes to Harrison's love life. Perhaps prodded by her venture into romantic comedy, this was one of the few times in Joan's life that the seemingly hard-edged professional, who avoided Hollywood fairy tales, allowed herself to be swept off her feet. Clark Gable came calling, and Joan welcomed the king of Hollywood with open arms.

In the beginning, she primarily embraced the *idea* of Gable, as the man himself was much more complicated than the screen heroes he portrayed. She knew his reputation for womanizing and covering it up, and he was publicly linked to other women, including Virginia Grey and Paulette Goddard. And, even seven years later, he was still grieving Lombard's untimely death.

But he liked women who could make him laugh, and Joan fit the bill. It dawned on her gradually that his affections for her had begun to run deeper, and hers for him. What had won her over was how faithful he was, at least for a spell. She had caught on that three months was his usual run—for that time, he would sink his heart into an affair until an internal timer sent him on his way. But, with Joan, he kept coming back, like a pet pawing at the back door (or at that covert back entrance to her bedroom).

Though usually discreet, Joan liked to flaunt Clark, describing their courtship as "a meeting of the minds, and a meeting of other things as well." After nights of unbridled passion at Clark's ranch, as he escorted her out to her car, he would pause in his garden to pluck a single red rose for her. Doing his best Rhett Butler impression, he would place the rose in her hand and ask to see her again.

As their time together increased, gossip columnists and fan magazines took notice. Spotting them out to dinner, Hedda Hopper observed that Joan was holding the star's hand "practically during the whole meal." Pictures of the couple were splashed across a glamorous *Screenland* spread documenting Errol Flynn's infamous "coming out" party, meant to usher the moping Flynn back onto the market following a demoralizing divorce from Nora Eddington. (Staged around the aging swashbuckler's pool and catered by Mike Romanoff, the black-tie event took place on Valentine's Day eve, replete with mice races, a rumba band, Russian singers, a female impersonator, and a 350-person guest list that included everyone from Mary Pickford to Ava Gardner.)

Temporarily relocating to England meant that she would be away from Gable, who kept his little black book close at hand. It didn't occur to her to set work aside for Hollywood's king. She was tough enough to bear to see other women's names linked with Clark in the papers. Besides, her attention was always focused on the next project.

Joan's decision to produce *Eye Witness* was announced in May 1949, as *Once More, My Darling* was closing out. She had two more weeks to go at Universal-International, overseeing the film's editing. Robert Montgomery left for England to launch preproduction on *Eye Witness* in late May. On June 13, she joined him, stepping off the plane at London Airport smiling at photographers, dressed to perfection in a high-collared button-down suit dress and a brocade half hat and toting several books under her arm. She had made certain to arrive in time to celebrate her birthday with her mother, Faith, her husband, John, and two young nieces, Katharine and Muriel. From then on, whenever possible, she would aim for a June sojourn home.

In *Eye Witness*, Robert Montgomery would play Adam Heyward, an accomplished New York City attorney who feels obligated to go to England when a British comrade who once saved his life, Colonel Roger Summerfield (Leslie Banks), is accused of murder. Heyward arrives in Summerfield's provincial hometown and, upon seeing how unprofessional the investigation into the crime has been and realizing that a silent witness might have exonerating evidence, decides to defend his friend at trial. It becomes increasingly clear that the killer is a woman who, in a moment of self-defense, shot the victim in question (a stable hand who liked to lure ladies to his quarters by promising romantic readings and book exchanges). Though Heyward begins to suspect Alex Summerfield (Patricia Cutts), the attractive war widow who was married to Roger's brother, it is finally revealed that it was Roger's daughter, the susceptible teenager Sandy (Ann Stephens), who committed the act while attempting to escape the stable hand's sexual advances. Roger's freedom hinges on Adam's ability to convince young Sandy to overcome her reticence, tell her story in a public forum, and find a way to move forward with resilience and assuredness. By the film's third act, the legal mystery has become a female rite-of-passage story.

At the end of October, as *Eye Witness* came to completion, Joan's romantic involvement with Clark Gable revved up again. She was all smiles when he met her at the airport on her return from England. The couple fit in as many dinner dates as they could, many of them clandestine, before she scooted to New York to finish editing with Montgomery.

Joan and Clark were planning a trip to Hawaii for early December. At least it was rumored so by Walter Winchell, who reported that Gable was looking at "his most serious romance since Lombard." The papers had her pegged as "the next Mrs. Gable" as she cruised into the Christmas season, during which time they frequented the racetrack together, dined at Romanoff's, and attended a premiere of Gable's *Key to the City.*

This is why it was shocking when Joan awoke on December 21 to headlines that blazed, GABLE AND DOUG FAIRBANKS' WIDOW RACE AWAY TO SECRET WEDDING. Clark had spontaneously proposed to actress, model, and socialite Lady Sylvia Ashley, who said that she "answered 'Yes,' as fast as I possibly could." (Shortly before this, Anita Colby had been stunned while on a date with Gable when he asked her to marry him. She politely declined and, seeing he was overly anxious to start a family, warned him, "Please don't get married right now. . . . You might make a mistake.")

The papers were quick to paint Joan as the jilted lover. Clarence Brown, the director on Gable's next picture, expressed his surprise to the International News Service: "I saw him with Joan Harrison just the other night. He said nothing whatever about any marriage plans." Some who knew the actor had speculated that he would never wed again after losing Carole—it was common knowledge that he'd preserved her bedroom just as she'd left it—while others theorized that he yearned for children. Whatever the reason for his split-second decision, Joan looked as though she'd been left at an altar. No matter that she'd never aspired to it.

Clark's sudden nuptials may or may not have been a shot to the heart, but they were most definitely an attack on her pride. She was left to fend for herself as the press lumped her into a series of bypassed proposals. It was hard to tell what was worse, finding her name tossed in with a sea of Gable's purported dalliances (including Anita Colby, Virginia Grey, Paulette Goddard, Millicent Rogers, Dolly O'Brien), or being cast as the "other woman" in a drama that seemed destined to carry well into the next decade. One MGM press agent reportedly called Harrison's secretary at the studio probing for proof that she wasn't Gable's real bride. Was she sure "Sylvia Stanley isn't Joan's real name?" he asked, in a disingenuous effort to keep the story alive.

Not the type to toy around, and rarely inclined to play the victim, Joan answered the press with her usual aplomb. To one reporter, she "coolly denied she'd been 'left waiting at the church.'" She insisted, "We were just good friends. . . . There was nothing very romantic about it." When gossip columnists couldn't rouse a response from her, they tried another tack and made her lack of reaction part of the story. The *Los Angeles Examiner* related that Joan was "fed to the teeth over talk that she 'broke up' over Clark Gable's marriage to Sylvia." She kept her composure, and it would pay off in the long run. Gable's marriage to Lady Ashley would end within eighteen months, while Joan and Clark's involvement was by no means over.

The tumult in her personal life came at the same time she decided to make a professional split from Montgomery. As postproduction wrapped up on *Eye Witness*, his sights had shifted to returning to New York and its many opportunities in television and theater. As he saw the *Robert Montgomery Presents* TV series coming together at NBC (it premiered January 1950), Bob attached his previous producing partner Elliot Nugent to help with initial episodes, which were adaptations of successful Hollywood films. Joan, on the other hand, would do whatever necessary to continue producing motion pictures, whether it meant financing them through European low-budget or New York independent companies. She viewed television as a healthy option too, but not as a replacement for movies.

With *Eye Witness* due to hit London theaters just after New Year's Day, Joan hoped for an auspicious opening—something she could parlay into the next job. Having returned indefinitely to the States, she rang in the season at a party hosted by pal Ella Raines in her Coldwater Canyon home, surrounded by close friends. With Robert Siodmak there, it almost felt like earlier times.

It was an occasion to appreciate old acquaintances. But in the midst of such upheaval, she was fortunate to have new allies arriving on the scene. A make-shift family was beginning to form around her, and though she would have had no way of knowing it, these women would provide sanctuary for years to come. It had all started with a stay in London while shooting *Eye Witness*. During a visit with Norwegian Greta Gynt, who lived in a mews near Notting Hill Gate, Joan noticed that the glamorous star had two remarkable housekeepers from the East End. She was struck by the women's professionalism and attention to detail. She took a shine to one of them in particular, a cook named Nellie Williams, to whom she whispered in an aside, "If you ever decide that you want to come to America, call me. Simply reverse the charges. I will pay your way to come to Los Angeles and you can work for me."

Soon after her return to L.A., Joan's phone duly rang. It was Nellie with a special request. Gynt's two housekeepers were sisters, and Nellie didn't want to leave Rose behind. Joan proposed that Nellie come first, for a trial period, and if all went well, Joan would finance Rose's trip within two years. When Nellie agreed, Gynt was, predictably, peeved.

Soon, Joan came to more fully acquaint herself with Nellie, who lived in a modest maid's quarters—a small bedroom and bathroom tucked between Joan's kitchen and garage. Joan was not any more enlightened than other professional women in Hollywood; in fact, she could be more snobbish than most and was always better at writing maid characters than understanding them in real life. But she cared deeply for Nellie.

Joan learned from Nellie that she had been engaged to a sailor who was killed in action during the war. Around the same time, in 1942, Nellie and Rose's sister gave birth out of wedlock to a child named Margaret Georgina. Her middle name honored her father, who was black (though Margaret grew up believing she was white, only coming to know the truth in her midthirties). Within a few years, the sister abandoned the little girl to some strangers, leaving her essentially orphaned. When Nellie and Rose finally tracked the toddler down, they saw that she was unkempt and maltreated. They were able to 'lure her out of the house through a window by tempting her with a box of Black Magic chocolates. Once her aunts had her in their arms, they had no intention of letting go.

Nellie explained to Joan that help had come from an unlikely corner, the powerful British producer-director George King, for whom Rose had worked. When he learned the story, King wasted no time. "We'll take care of it," he assured Rose, and procured a private attorney to obtain what was generally unheard of in those days, a legal adoption for a single, poor woman from the East End. From the age of seven, the girl, now called Georgina, would be raised by the women she called Rose and Aunt Nellie. "Nellie was the brains, Rosie was the brawn," Georgina would later recall.

To Joan, Nellie spelled things out plain and simple. If she was going to stay in Los Angeles long term, she would need to provide not only for Rose but for Georgina as well. This would require Joan to pay their passage from England and assure their housing. But these arrangements would take some time.

By early 1950, Nellie had helped Joan to forge a happy home. Joan had also moved on from dogsitting the Hitchcocks' terrier Johnnie and now had her own Scottish terrier named James. And she soon resumed dating, taking up with Gilbert Roland, the Mexican-born actor who had recently made a comeback in Huston's *We Were Strangers* (1949). The dashing Roland won her respect on the tennis court—spending leisurely afternoons at the Beverly Hills Tennis Club—while treating her to late evenings on the town.

On January 26, 1950, one day after *Eye Witness*'s London release, Joan inked a long-term contract with Columbia Pictures. Joan Harrison to Do Series of Who-Dun-Its, announced Louella Parsons, who trumpeted her as the new high-end mystery producer on the lot. What remained unsaid was that Joan was coming in to fill the huge vacuum left when Virginia Van Upp recently resigned. Van Upp had become executive producer and right-hand woman to Columbia head Harry Cohn through hard work and unflagging loyalty. No one was quite sure why she had walked out on a seven-year contract, only two years into her renewal (though it became clear later that it was due to her desire to go independent), but it was a good guess that Cohn saw in Harrison his next Van Upp. For her launch, Joan would try to commission Cornell Woolrich to write a new original story, but she hedged her bets, conferring on possible scripts and meeting with writers over the next two months.

The trades reported her every move, perceiving any step as a possible hint toward her next project or package, such as when she had lunch in the commissary with friend Evelyn Keyes. Keyes was on strike from Columbia at the time, so she and Joan might have been talking shop instead. Or their attention could have been focused on affairs of the heart: four weeks prior, Keyes had divorced John Huston, who on that same day married a pregnant Enrica Soma in Mexico. Where Joan and Evelyn were concerned, the conversation never stopped at one subject.

Then, just as quickly as Joan had arrived at Columbia, she departed. On March 27 she resigned, announcing her intention to travel to England to make independent films. She'd barely had time to move into her office. Some columnists second-guessed whether she'd actually signed with Columbia at all. Her abrupt departure is one of the biggest question marks in her career. The easiest explanation is that she butted heads with Cohn, notoriously tyrannical, unprincipled, and foul-mouthed, who flagrantly sexually harassed the women at his studio (and everywhere else he went). Joan's patience for his usual antics would have been thin. Yet Cohn had established a reputation as a forceful advocate for Van Upp and actually had "the best record in Hollywood for promoting women's careers at all levels of production," according to historian J. E. Smyth. Women who gave as good as they got won his immediate respect, according to screenwriter Mary C. McCall Jr.

Perhaps a better explanation is that in the spring of 1950, something related to the HUAC hearings convinced Joan it was time to leave Hollywood. Spring 1950 was a high-water mark for the Red Scare. On January 25, former US State Department official Alger Hiss was convicted of perjury for allegedly participating in a spy ring, a case that brought former HUAC member Richard M. Nixon to national prominence. Three weeks later, in Wheeling, West Virginia, Senator Joseph McCarthy made a speech declaring there were 205 card-carrying Communists in the state department. It was no secret, according to Columbia writer Jean Rouverol, that a second wave of subpoenas loomed just over the horizon. The climate would continue to degenerate: the Hollywood Ten lost their Supreme Court appeals in late April, and the Red Channels list, naming 151 Hollywood industry figures accused of Communist connections, was published by the right-wing newsletter *Counterattack* on June 22. Five days later, President Truman's June 27 speech responding to North Korea's invasion of South Korea made it clear—the Cold War was turning hot and growing deadly.

If Joan had had cause to worry, Cohn may have even given her a heads-up. Despite the fact that he had signed the Waldorf Statement and wasn't above smear tactics, he had come to detest the loyalty oaths and had shown his willingness to stand up for seemingly "subversive" projects if he believed in them. Most tellingly, his inner sanctum included an attorney who advised him any time a Columbia employee was on the FBI's radar. Cohn had a protocol for tipping off his own people to let them know they were in the crosshairs, giving them an opportunity to plot an exit strategy. Might Joan's new boss have warned her that if she continued on at Columbia she was bound to end up on the blacklist?

As she prepared to leave Los Angeles indefinitely, her production plans kept wavering. First, she indicated that she had an option to produce an adaptation of Fan Nichols's *Possess Me Not*, a juicy pulp novel about two women ("Mary was hard" and "Michelle was soft") pining after a man who wants neither of them. This was followed by a report that Ella Raines was attached to star and coproduce the film version, set to begin production soon in London and Paris. All at once, the project was replaced with a collaboration with Curt Siodmak, an extremely low-budget ($200,000) film titled *Fire Island*, intended to be shot at New York's Saks Fifth Avenue, the Pavilion Restaurant, and Fire Island (already a gay enclave). According to *Variety*, production was set to start in August.

Joan had had enough. She would return to London to produce another Coronado coproduction financed by David E. Rose. *White Heather*, based on an original story by Philip MacDonald (with whom she had collaborated on *Rebecca*), would start filming in September. Nellie would hold down the fort at 874 Birchwood Drive, which would become standard practice.

Arriving in London in July 1950, Joan appeared to have come full circle—the Guildford girl who had done well for herself and was now coming home. Sporting the latest Manhattan fashion, a blue shantung suit with white lapels and cuffs, capped by a red-and-white Mandarin hat with mesh delphinium-blue veil, she sat for an interview with London's the *Star*. Smiling at the reporter and hitting all the right notes, she appeared to be relishing the attention. In point of fact, she was lying low.

18 | A NEW PROPOSAL

WHITE HEATHER, eventually retitled *Circle of Danger*, would tell the story of an American who comes to England after the war to uncover the truth behind his brother's mysterious death during a commando operation in occupied France. Pursuing each of the survivors of the raid one by one, he finally confronts the man who shot his brother and is forced to reckon with war's moral complexities.

Philip MacDonald adapted his story for the screen, and the highly skilled master of the macabre Jacques Tourneur directed. Assuming the leads were Welsh American actor Ray Milland (*The Lost Weekend*, *The Big Clock*) and British actress Patricia Roc, who had recently starred in Tourneur's *Canyon Passage*.

The script for *Circle of Danger* was completed in summer 1950, with Joseph Breen sending final comments on July 6. (Since RKO was partially financing with US dollars, the Production Code Administration was involved; there were minimal notes, mostly referencing liquor.) In August, as production began, the first order of business was to shoot the opening sequence on board a 115-ton schooner anchored in Plymouth Sound. A reporter described being present as the crew waited with bated breath for Milland to surface in his deep sea gear, lift up his helmet, and utter his first line to the camera. A collective exhale was heard as the actor carried it off with a smiling face. It was confmed that the complex set of earphones, mouthpieces, microphones, air tanks, and cameras had worked. For the next two months, Joan oversaw filming, mainly in the

241

area of Devon. Production also spanned London's Covent Garden market, the Welsh coal mines, and the Scottish Highlands.

Tourneur was an expert in directing highly stylized films on a shoestring budget, having completed such RKO horrors as *Cat People* and *I Walked with a Zombie*. His sensibility fit well with the material, which takes the protagonist Clay Douglas full circle to the beginning of his search only to learn that his brother is not the hero that he thought—that the men in his unit had no choice but to shoot him to protect the mission. As Chris Fujiwara puts it, "The typical Tourneur narrative is full of confusion and ambiguity, signs that point in no clear direction, and messages that circle back on the sender." Cinematographer Oswald "Ossie" Morris underscored these elements by diffusing the light and isolating human figures against a vast landscape. (A well-liked risk-taker who was rapidly earning a reputation as one of Britain's finest, Morris would go on to photograph eight of John Huston's films.)

Circle of Danger opened in April 1951 in the US (and one month later in the UK) to mixed reviews. "The camera certainly does move around a lot," the *Evening Standard* commented, complaining of the protagonist's rambling search and a script that was "a bit untidy." The critic did find that "the suspense is well-maintained." Many more reviewers criticized the lack of pacing and tension. Though Milland's acting held up, according to the *New York Times*, the film was "still an unexciting and largely placid adventure." Some noted that Patricia Roc's performance was wanting; her character's most discernible trait was a hay fever allergy, overused for comedic effect.

By spring 1951 Joan was back in Los Angeles. But not for long. Her good friend Joyce Buck (who went all the way back to John Huston's Tarzana days) was ready for a European vacation. She was tiring of running a high-end decor shop; sensing that a new wave of witch hunts was brewing, she found the atmosphere too stressful to remain. When Joyce painted a picture of antiquing, hotel hopping, and shopping for couture in Paris, Rome, and Venice, Joan didn't hesitate. The two women boarded a plane, along with Joyce's mother, Esta, leaving behind Joyce's husband, Jules, to care for three-year-old daughter Joan (Joan's namesake and goddaughter).

The ladies were in Antibes on their way to Rome when the *Los Angeles Examiner* reported that, upon her arrival at the hotel, Joan was met by a cable informing her that her Westwood home had been burgled. The casualties included an expensive Swiss gold watch given to her by Gable, along with thousands of dollars in furs, clothing, and jewels. The theft was less a source of irritation to Joan than the link, yet again, to Gable in the headlines. After all, she was having a dazzling time. Upon returning several months later, Joyce purred to her husband, "There's a wonderful world out there. We don't have to stay in Los Angeles one minute longer." They packed the family off to Europe.

Like Joyce, Joan had seen the light. For the next two years, she would toggle between London, Paris, and the South of France, sometimes in the company of Hitch and Alma, whose films suddenly created more opportunity for travel. She knew she always had a home in the enclave of Paris's Champs-Élysées, which—now that Franchot Tone, Tola Litvak, Irwin Shaw, Lewis Milestone, John Huston, Joseph Cotten, and others were taking extended jobs or vacations there—looked like "Hollywood's Sunset Boulevard," according to the *Daily Republican*. What the newspaper failed to comment on was the reason for the exodus of left-leaning Hollywood types.

Evelyn Keyes was part of the European scene. She flew to London to promote the independent thriller *The Prowler*, at the behest of producer Sam Spiegel, and found herself taking over his Grosvenor Square flat. (She preferred the dreary gray to the nightmarish "Technicolor spectaculars" of HUAC.) As Joan and Evelyn crossed paths, they competed for attention from a young, virile, and mostly shirtless Kirk Douglas, who was dividing vacation time between London and Rome. The *Los Angeles Examiner* made an item out of Harrison and Douglas. Then again, various reports surfaced that she was seeing "a lot of former flame" Gable in Paris and being escorted up and down the city's boulevards "in his biscuit-upholstered Jaguar."

She flirted with the possibility of returning permanently to Hollywood to take another stab at independent producing, even flying there in late 1952 to pitch a project that would star Gene Tierney. At the same time, she began to give a serious look at television. She signed a contract with Hal Roach Studios to associate-produce *Sunday Nights*, a thirty-minute dramatic series affiliated with the Screen Directors Guild.

She faced a stark reality: no work, no leads, no clear path forward. "She had a troubled look about her when I ran into her in New York," recounted Norman Lloyd. "That happened to be a fallow period. She was at sixes and sevens." It had always been work that kept her going; she felt its absence acutely.

In early 1953 she received an unexpected invitation. Ella Raines, now living in Cornwall-on-Hudson, New York, was launching a television series to be titled *Janet Dean, Registered Nurse*. She was anxious for Joan to produce the show. The thirty-minute, filmed dramatic series would be the first show to feature a nurse as the main character. It had lofty goals: to promote the profession, show women as problem solvers, and enlighten the public as to the psychological underpinnings of many of the day's physical and social ailments.

Ella Raines would star in the show and serve as president of the controlling Cornwall Productions, alongside Joan's longtime associate William Dozier, who was vice president. Dozier, who had conceived the basic idea, was in the meantime keeping his current post as a producer at CBS. Raines had spent some time developing the show, motivated to keep a hand in acting while tending to her toddler and infant. Behind the scenes, Laurance Rockefeller helped get the show off the ground by financing its production. As a third-generation member of the Rockefeller family and an aviation enthusiast, Laurance had become fast friends with Ella's husband, Robin Olds, appreciating his many exploits as an ace combat pilot. The series appealed to Rockefeller's philanthropic concern for medical and social welfare and offered a concrete forum through which he could express his adoration for the Olds family.

For Joan, the solo producing position on *Janet Dean* presented an opportunity not only to collaborate with two trusted friends but also to learn the medium of television, a new frontier filled with possibility. (In 1949 one household out of every ten had a television set. By the time *Janet Dean* aired, it was five out of every ten.) Moving to New York, where the industry was centered, she began hunting for a Manhattan flat.

It was announced on October 31, 1953, that Joan, "former right hand of Hitchcock," would debut as a television producer. According to *Billboard*, she crowned the list of "top film talent" joining the series, including mutual friend Travis Banton (in costuming) and directors Robert Aldrich, Jack Gage, and Peter Godfrey. (Godfrey was a British clown, conjurer, and dialogue director—coaching actors on their lines—with roots in the expressionist theater of the 1920s.) *Janet Dean* would be distributed through Motion Pictures for Television (MPTV), as part of head Matty Fox's larger strategy to expand into "network like" competition with ABC, NBC, CBS, and DuMont by combining MPTV's feature film library with new syndicated series. The goal was to secure an advance commitment from stations to air his independent product in early-evening slots. Having signed with Bromo-Seltzer manufacturer Emerson Drug Company to sponsor the series, he had guaranteed *Janet Dean*'s airing in class-A time in twenty-six major markets. It was slated for an early 1954 debut.

By the end of November 1953, thirteen of the season's thirty-nine scheduled episodes had been produced at the Marion Parsonnet Studios in Long Island. As developed by Harrison and Raines, Janet Dean's character was broadly outlined so that she could have a powerful impact on the lives of people across the social spectrum. As a private-duty nurse, her character was freed from the traditional confines of a hospital and frequently found herself confronting sobering challenges such as juvenile delinquency, racial discrimination, gang violence, and the stigma of polio.

Part of the premise was that Janet Dean was a member of the US Air Force Nurse Corps reserve, which meant she might be called into active duty—and pulled to any location around the world—at any moment. Episodes painted Raines's character as quick thinking, progressive minded, and action oriented—a role model for girls and women, one who always took the righteous path, such as when she convinced a scared eyewitness to a crime to testify or risked her safety to rescue people trapped in an elevator. MPTV's advertisements portrayed the series as a "suspenseful, unusual TV film show based on a nurse's exciting adventures among the rich and poor . . . in big cities and small towns . . . in peace and war . . . at home and abroad!"

Janet Dean, Registered Nurse was also a distinctive addition to the television roster because of its semidocumentary style. The series preferred realistic sets and actual locations (a result of budgetary constraints as much as aesthetic considerations), and according to MPTV, every episode was based on an actual case. Though such a social realist approach ran the danger of being perceived as too gritty for people's living rooms (especially with a woman at the center), Harrison and the "highly professional staff" were congratulated by *TV Guide* for their "well-done" production values. *Weekly Variety* saw potential for the series to "boost the merits of [television] production in the East" in general.

One of Joan's crucial tasks in her new role as television producer was working closely with writers to turn out thirty-five-page scripts in a limited time. In many cases, this involved offering guidance to someone who had achieved some stardom in fiction, film, or theater and was now looking to excel in TV. Gore Vidal, already a celebrated novelist, happened to be related to Raines by marriage. Seeing him continually thwarted by a competitive writers' market, Ella suggested he try his hand at a script for her series. "So I worked with Joan," recalled Vidal, who referred to her as "the producer of my first TV play."

In the episode Vidal wrote, "The Jinx Nurse Case," Janet helps a young nurse overcome doubts about herself when several fighter pilots, one after the other, end up killed in action. Though Vidal's work went uncredited (written under the pen name Cameron Kay), "The Jinx Nurse" led to his writing of "Dark Possession," a 1954 episode for the anthology series *Studio One* and ultimately landed Vidal representation at William Morris.

Given the show's relentless pace, which might mean shooting two episodes in one week at a rate of two to three days per show, Joan required strong reinforcements. She called on her friend Sarett Tobias, now named Sarett Rudley. She had graduated from screenplays at Columbia to writing for Broadway after marrying former Warner Bros. actor Herbert Rudley in the late 1940s. The couple had collaborated on the play *How Long Till Summer* in December 1949. A sobering look at racial discrimination, it was generally seen as sincere if "muddled and somewhat hysterical." Sarett had earned respect as fresh voice with a penchant for controversial subjects.

She had also gained a reputation for scandal. When she met her future husband, Herbert was married to actress Ann Loring, who did not take kindly to his moving in with Sarett six days after his son was born. Loring responded by filing a complaint against not her husband but Sarett. She sought $100,000 in damages on behalf of her infant son from Sarett for "maliciously" luring Herbert away from his home and into her own, "for the purpose of breaking the family" and "depriving the plaintiff" of paternal care. Loring lost the suit, and Sarett and Herbert wed in Carson City, Nevada, in August 1948. With *How Long Till Summer*, the Rudleys proved to be a productive creative duo, but their marriage soon dissolved.

When Sarett joined the *Janet Dean* team, she was on her fifth marriage, this time to a New York City lawyer named Daniel Glass. It was obvious that she took a liberal view toward nuptials. Altogether she would write five episodes for the series. As with Vidal, Joan gave her a unique opportunity to cut her teeth in this new medium.

To Joan's dismay, *Janet Dean* was not renewed following its initial thirty-nine episodes. In fact, the producing team had to approach Chase National Bank for a loan to finish out the final third of the season.

As spring 1954 approached, Joan could hardly have known that an entirely new chapter—what would approximate a second career—was in the making. She was on the mind of the no-holds-barred president of super-agency MCA, Lew Wasserman, who was fervently seeking out ways to expand television production. Wasserman had a big-picture vision for MCA, originally a booking agency for musical acts known as the Music Corporation of America that now boasted an ever-increasing array of business interests. Wasserman's plan was to edge out the competition by creating original content that employed his clients—actors, writers, and directors. He was in the process of convincing one client in particular to host a suspense series on CBS: Alfred Hitchcock. The thirty-minute filmed anthology series would create a perfect tie-in to the new *Alfred Hitchcock Mystery Magazine* (which Hitchcock himself had almost nothing to do with) and would launch Hitchcock as the first director of his stature to make a long-term commitment to the small screen. The "Master of Suspense" was not particularly enthusiastic about being associated with what he regarded as an extremely low art form. Yet he was willing to take a gamble on Wasserman's pitch, which, if it paid off, could bring him more recognition than any of his movies.

In most tellings, it was Hitchcock who initially proposed that his former protégée produce *Alfred Hitchcock Presents*. In actuality, it was Wasserman who did the convincing, pointing out that Harrison had the requisite skills: budgeting, casting, scripting, and the capacity to oversee the entire process from story selection to promotion. Hitchcock's role would be supervisory, limited to signing off on scripts and the final cut, appearing during short segments for each episode, and directing a limited number of episodes. He was going to remain hands-off, in order to keep his primary focus on his films. If the circumstances called for a point person to run the show—a showrunner, before such a term existed—Joan was the ideal candidate, Wasserman advised. Hitchcock responded, "Joanie? Are you sure?" How many times in the intervening years might the director have thought to hire her, and how often had something held him back? Only he knew. But deep down Hitch knew that his agent and friend had it right. It was time to call Joan.

First stop: the South of France. Joan joined Hitch and Alma at the Carlton Hotel in Cannes during the filming of *To Catch a Thief.* There, they began developing the series. She would later remember this as an idyllic respite, and a chance to visit Nice and the nearby countryside locations of *To Catch a Thief.* It was also a chance to go around with Cary Grant, who now felt like family.

With time to spare, Joan spent several months at a house Joyce Buck had rented in the hills above Cannes. Daughter Joan Buck remembers it clearly, because it was a crisis point in her parents' marriage, during which Jules remained away. At five years old, she experienced hushed voices and secretive conversations between Joyce and Joan. Later, she realized Joyce was having an affair with another man. "My mother was deciding whether or not to leave the marriage," explains Joan Buck. "I suspect, knowing that Joan was kind of naughty, that she may have encouraged her to follow her passion." In the end, Joyce chose to keep her family intact. Joan Harrison left Cannes for California.

In summer 1955 Joan took up residence as associate producer for *Alfred Hitchcock Presents* at Revue Productions, MCA's television subsidiary. Revue was located on the Republic Pictures lot, at 4024 N. Radford Avenue in North Hollywood (now Studio City). Hitchcock named the company that was to produce the show Shamley Productions. It was an homage to his and Alma's weekend retreat in Guildford, and a reminder to Joan of home.

She and Hitchcock had arrived at the formula they envisioned for the show; it would follow ordinary people caught up in extraordinary circumstance, with touches of British gallows humor, a macabre tone, a certain degree of suspense, and, most crucial of all, a twist almost "to the point of shock" that arrives in the last scene or even the last line. Joan's immediate task was to amass material that could be translated into scripts for quick production turnaround. Short on time to develop original ideas, she would glean source material published by well-established authors or filtered through popular periodicals. This was an important function of the *Alfred Hitchcock Mystery Magazine*, which now offered a means of finding—or growing—new talent.

Joan's purview extended well beyond finding stories, cultivating writers, and developing scripts. There was little, in fact, for which she wasn't ultimately responsible. "The way Joan Harrison kind of held the show together, everything went through her," observed John Lloyd, a primary art director for the series. Because she oversaw casting, she was in constant contact with MCA's

West Coast and East Coast talent offices. She chose directors and primary crew such as set decorators and costumers, managing any crises or personality issues during production. She kept a watch over on-set production, though she refrained from visiting the soundstage, remaining in her office from 9:00 AM until 6:00 PM unless called. The technical staff and rotating directors appreciated her hands-off style. In addition, she determined location shoots, some of which required extra planning when they took the crew to New York for East Coast–based episodes. "The show was beautifully run," recalled Norman Lloyd. "It was a dream, which is why it was seen as an honor to work for her."

Aside from these more creative aspects, a good deal of her time was taken up with more rote tasks, such as discerning whether story rights were available or if an agent had the authority to represent a writer. She and Hitch were in constant fear of falling into legal entanglements, and it was her job to ward off disaster.

Joan also made sure that Shamley stayed in good standing with the all-important commercial sponsors. Al Tenneyson, the representative from Lincoln-Mercury, appreciated that there was "never a knockdown, drag-out fight of any kind." In meetings, Tenneyson recalled, "Miss Harrison would act as hostess, and it was she who served the tea." This was part of a well-practiced performance. Lloyd explains, "She treated her profession as an operation aimed at all these men. They only thought about the bottom line, the dollar. Meanwhile, with her clothes, her manner, they would melt."

Underneath the facade, she was battling the pressure of constant deadlines. "It takes all the running you can do to stay in one place," she wrote as a guest columnist in the *Los Angeles Times*, self-consciously quoting *Alice in Wonderland*'s White Queen. She noted "the uncomfortable feeling that, should we fail to meet the air date, our audience might be treated to thirty minutes of silence and a blank screen."

In the early seasons of the series, the first year or two in particular, Joan and Hitchcock were intensely involved, perfecting the show's tone, look, structure, and workflow. They worked well together, sliding back with ease into familiar roles as "work wife" and "husband." According to their business memos, they were "Joanie" and "Hitchy" once again. Joan addressed her intraoffice correspondence "Dear Hitchy." On a cover page attached to a set of story notes, Hitchcock wrote, "Dear Joan, Just a few silly little comments. Love, Hitch." Their roles in day-to-day operations were clearly defined. Joan came to him for approval at three stages: the initial pitch, final script, and rough cut. In the story selection phase, she could expect him to be very rigorous. There were three categories: yes, no, and the "reserves" file. "His mind is like a threshing machine, chomping out ideas, ideas as we walk, ideas at meals, ideas every minute," Joan noted. It wasn't easy for a synopsis to get the green light.

Once a script was finished, Hitchcock limited his input to one- or two-sentence prompts, such as "Couldn't we have a sharper twist at the end?" or "We must be sure that Mrs. Bowlby [in Ann Bridge's "The Buick Saloon"] is psychic, so that only she, and no one else, can hear the voice in the saloon." Joan would assist writers with revising or fine-tuning to varying degrees, and when she needed to exert appreciable influence, she evoked the host's authority. ("I can't be certain Hitch will like this scene.")

In the final approval stage, Hitchcock was presented with the rough cut of the episode; he might suggest, for instance, the addition of a close-up shot. He almost never, if ever, rejected an episode once it had been shot. He either responded, "Very good" or "Good," which meant he liked it, or "Thank you," in which case he preferred to keep negative remarks to himself. After this sign-off, Joan had the green light to proceed with the final edit, scoring, and dubbing. It was a fast-paced process. Once a script was in place, there was one week allotted for preproduction (selecting director and cast, and technical preparation), three days for shooting (including one day for rehearsal, generous in early television), one week to reach the first cut, one week to edit the final cut, and an additional two weeks to finish.

Each episode began memorably with an opening title sequence that featured the director entering the screen in shadow to the tune of nineteenth-century French composer Charles Gounod's "The Funeral March of a Marionette," before stepping into a drawn outline of his portly figure. The title sequence then gave way to Hitchcock welcoming viewers with a droll "Good evening," before setting up the evening's story. One of Joan's responsibilities was to oversee the production of these "nod and a wink" prologues and wraparounds, in which Hitchcock framed the plot. She coordinated the handing off of scripts to James Allardice, the talented comedy writer ("a genius," according to Lloyd), who penned every one of the series' 359 wraparounds.

It was Joan's job to arrange the backgrounds and acquire the props called for by Allardice's scripts. She helped produce the segments, ensuring that they kept an even flow with—or at least some tacitly dark humorous relationship to—the stories they framed. Most crucially, as someone who had helped Hitchcock build the bridge between his persona and his work from a very early stage, Joan was an authority like almost no other on how to produce "Hitchcock." If he wasn't going to be intimately involved with the show, Joan could be trusted to certify the brand and see to it that the series was an extension of his persona.

While Joan guaranteed the show's "Hitchcock" quotient, she also provided a Harrison touch, playing a crucial historical role in importing film noir into television. According to noir historian Eddie Muller, the genre did not simply disappear in the 1950s, as is often perceived to be the case. In his view, "Noir actually shifted from the big screen to the small screen." Muller explained, "It ran its course in movie theaters, it moved to television, where a lot of the stories and actors and directors just moved, because that's where the new B-film was." This makes particular sense when one views noir as a writer's genre, rooted in 1930s and '40s detective fiction. Harrison, a writer at heart, was in her element inside a cynical, fatalistic universe of wronged men, fallen women, double-crosses, existentialist dilemmas, unexpected femme fatales, and convoluted plots and reversals.

In short, the films Joan had made in the 1940s were a perfect precursor to the "television noir" of *Alfred Hitchcock Presents.* Her preferred style had always been intimate and had valued character-based studies over action. And for her, story ruled. "She knew script very well. She knew story very well. And she knew actors," Lloyd remembers. Her strengths lent themselves superbly to the new medium. "There are examples of writers, directors of photography, and editors who made that transition from film noir to television," remarks Muller, "but Harrison made the transition better than anybody, more completely, and more happily. Arguably, there is not a single other person who worked in Hollywood noir who had a more successful career in television."

During her time in Europe and then while trying to get *Janet Dean, Registered Nurse* off the ground, she had moved her belongings out of 874 Birchwood and rented out the house. In the meantime, she had taken a one-bedroom apartment at 10500 Wilshire Boulevard, just one building away from the Wilshire Palm, where she and the Hitchcocks had first lived. The Spanish mission–style, garden-apartment building was owned by Loretta Young's mother, Gladys Belzer (who was landlady to more than one piece of real estate, and had an impeccable eye for interior decorating, filling her places with antiques and fine paintings) and could have itself been the subject of a teleplay or two. Next door to Joan lived Frank Sinatra, who was trying to hide the emotional wounds doled out to him by Ava Gardner. (The shrine he kept to Ava in his place didn't help, as he had "pictures of her everywhere, in the bathrooms, in the closets, on the refrigerator.") Sinatra's pal, the agent Irving "Swifty" Lazar, lived one door down. Television star Mary Sinclair and the singing group the Crosby Brothers also resided there at the time.

To look after the Wilshire Boulevard apartment, Joan relied on Rose, who by this point had joined her sister Nellie in Los Angeles, bringing along their niece Georgina. Joan would make good on her promise to provide for the family, ultimately arranging for Georgina to attend the private, Catholic Immaculate Heart High School in L.A.'s Los Feliz neighborhood, and keeping tabs on her long after she had grown into an adult. Since there wasn't room for everyone to board with her, she arranged for the three to live in a two-bedroom suite above the garage of a home at 323 South Spalding Drive in Beverly Hills. Rose also worked for the family who lived there. The sisters eventually purchased a cottage on South Spaulding Avenue in the L.A.'s less posh West Side neighborhood, but Nellie always worked as live-in staff for Joan if space allowed.

For now, however, Georgina and her two aunts were still getting settled. Once Hitchcock and Alma became acquainted with them, they asked Rose to join them for a special dinner party, which she thought was a work opportunity. Upon arriving, however, she realized the Hitchcocks had hosted the evening especially for Rose and their cook Chrystal. She and Chrystal delighted in gourmet food, fine china, and silver place settings. Upon hearing the account of the evening, Georgina asked, "Well, Auntie, did you do the dishes?" Rose replied, "Of course not."

One thing had remained constant through Joan's travels: her wardrobe. She let go of very little inventory and adhered to a strict organizational system. Georgina once surreptitiously took a peek into Joan's Wilshire apartment closet. She was taken aback at how neatly the shoes were lined up ("rows and rows of flats, for such narrow, small feet") and the way her clothes were meticulously arranged according to color. "All of her clothes were pressed to the nth degree," noted Georgina. "She was one crispy critter."

Still setting fashion trends, the sartorial line Joan walked between feminine looker and tough businesswoman was thinner than usual in the mid-1950s, when females, on-screen and off, were pressed into the more traditional roles of wives and mothers. The highly respected MCA talent agent Eleanor Kilgallen (who, from New York, funneled actors to Joan) was impressed by her chicness and saw her as a beacon for women entering the entertainment industry. Sister to Dorothy Kilgallen (the entertainment columnist and *What's My Line?* panelist), the agent was known for her trademark "proper" white gloves and was every bit as elegant as her clients, who included Grace Kelly and Robert Redford. "In early days of television," Kilgallen remarked, "there was a lot of prejudice against women in any position of authority. Even in the years of *Alfred Hitchcock Presents*, from my New York point of view, Joan was so far above the other ladies I knew. She was impeccably groomed, very chic. Other women were eager to become her, at least the ones that I knew."

For an entirely new generation, Joan modeled a recalibrated version of the working woman. Actress Carol Lynley, who first met her when she was cast in the 1957 episode "The Young One" at the age of sixteen, recalled, "Looking back, I realize what a precedent she set for me and particularly other girls, who only saw women as homemakers, or teachers, or nurses, or wallflowers. She made an impression on me as a powerful career woman."

Paul Henreid's daughter Monika delighted in the fact that Joan's self-assured manner agitated her father, an old-world gentleman to his core. As Joan's goddaughter, a teenaged Monika would watch Joan glide in for Saturday lunch wearing a simple outfit: a button-down white shirt, jeans, a designer watch, and no makeup but nails perfectly polished. Paul adored Joan, but after she left, he couldn't stop complaining about her casual attire. "'Women only look all right wearing slacks if they're riding a horse,' he would grumble. Women with strong personalities would drive my father crazy," Monika observes. "But Joan's strength was precisely what drew him in." Though there were other dominant women who dropped into the Henreid home—Hedy Lamarr made a self-mocking habit of bringing by her laundry on weekends, and Bette Davis frequented the household—the Henreids held hard to a custom that kept Hedy's, Bette's, and Joan's visits from coinciding. Paul felt that too much concentration of female power ran the risk of producing fireworks.

19 | BACK ON TOP

IN SPRING 1957, at the end of the second season of *Alfred Hitchcock Presents*, Joan was made full producer—a mere title change, but long overdue, especially now that Hitchcock had scaled back his involvement. The series had achieved undeniable eminence, with multiple Emmy wins and a Writers Guild Award nomination. Based on CBS's success with the show, NBC developed a mystery anthology series titled *Suspicion*. Shamley was contracted to produce ten *Suspicion* episodes, adding to Joan's workload. At this busy time, MCA purchased Universal Pictures, which had the effect of relocating Wasserman's Revue Productions—and the Shamley team—to the Universal-International lot.

The small set of bungalows assigned to Shamley were modest and gray, decorated in utilitarian style by the studio. Hitchcock's immediate reaction upon seeing Joan's office, and knowing her as he did, was, "No, no, she cannot work in that kind of office. We'll have to bring in our own designer." He dispatched several assistants to a Highland Avenue store in Beverly Hills that specialized in authentic Louis XV furniture. By the time her bungalow was finished, it looked like a movie set. "The actors loved it," Eleanor Kilgallen recalled. They appreciated that "they would do readings in such a lush place." Adding to the glamorous feel was the fact that Cary Grant's bungalow was directly across the way.

Dominating Joan's office was a large V-shaped desk, opposite two chairs designated for visitors. Cigarette in hand, she would slowly sip her coffee while fielding pitches or giving notes. Facing her, a giant gilded mirror hung on the wall. Given that Joan was predisposed to primping, especially in the presence of a man, a riveting ritual often ensued: A male fledgling writer, aiming to please, would compliment her on her taste in clothes or hairstyle. The more effusive the compliment, the more she would dote on herself—nodding, touching up her hair, checking herself in the mirror. "Oh, Joan, don't you think it would be a lovely scene if we could add this line?" the writer would propose, seizing the opportunity. "Oh yes, oh yes," she would reply. This might have been her version of the power play she had witnessed from male producers in so many back offices, designed to disarm the person sitting opposite her. Despite perceptions, she was the star of her own show and almost always in control.

To Joan, though, series television wasn't only a stage; it was a pipeline, a way to bring blacklisted talent back to work. Scores of writers, actors, and directors were still exiled from film and television—unemployed and deemed unemployable or, in the case of writers, working under pseudonyms. Kim Hunter recalled the cascading effect of television blacklisting: she was blocked from working at CBS, then ABC, then NBC after her name appeared on the Red Channels list and she refused to name names. Countless others suffered from not knowing where they stood in relation to Hollywood, and whether their "blacklist status" had changed. Television in the 1950s was subject to strict oversight by the Federal Communications Commission. Moreover, executives were beholden to sponsors and fearful of stirring up controversy. Someone in Joan's position attempting to break the blacklist—or even just bend it a bit—was taking a bold risk.

But with additional reinforcements needed for the third season of *Alfred Hitchcock Presents*, Joan looked to a particular name on the blacklist—Norman Lloyd. He not only was a good friend of the Hitchcocks but also brought to bear considerable assets in directing and acting. Supporting himself by doing theater in New York, he was by no means an easy sell—not even to Hitch, who greatly admired him. And even if Hitchcock agreed, there was still the question of Wasserman's approval.

Joan had been plotting her move far longer than either of her bosses knew. In league with Eleanor Kilgallen, she had been building her campaign for Lloyd gradually over time. To start with, she cast him as supporting character Lieutenant Orsatti in the second-season episode "Nightmare in 4-D." Even this small victory took the women several weeks, and a whirlwind of correspondence, to achieve.

On August 3, 1956, Harrison had written to Kilgallen about the episode, explaining that Lloyd was a personal friend and that there was "no one we'd rather use, both as an actor or a director." She described submitting his name to the agency, only to be turned down "for reasons of which I know you are very well aware." Lobbying her friend, she went on, "However, I believe things have eased up in that direction, so I will try submitting his name again." Over the next two weeks, the two women conspired across coasts, even engaging Kilgallen's hard-edged partner, Monique James, to step in when Kilgallen left for vacation. By September 18, Lloyd had the part. "Dear Eleanor," Joan wrote, "Finally, we seem to have won the battle!"

Joan and Eleanor would continue to mount their "frontline" work on Lloyd's behalf over the following year. When it was time to hire an assistant, Joan felt confident his path had been sufficiently cleared. She told Hitch so, and nudged him to make a firm request to Wasserman, which he did. But things didn't go as smoothly as they'd hoped. Wasserman called Hitchcock into his office. The president of Revue, Alan Miller, had advised against the hire. "There seems to be a problem about Norman Lloyd," Wasserman cautioned. Hitchcock replied tersely, "I want him." These three words were all that were needed. Wasserman acquiesced.

Lloyd may be the most visible example of how the *Alfred Hitchcock Presents* series resuscitated the career of someone who had effectively been exiled in response to HUAC and Hollywood's reaction to the Red Scare. But the list of blacklisted or "gray listed" talent hired by Joan for the Hitchcock series or for *Suspicion* is long, including Paul Henreid (director of forty-eight episodes), Robert Lees (writer of the *Alfred Hitchcock Presents* episode "Total Loss," under pseudonym J. E. Selby), John Ireland (actor on both *Suspicion* and *Alfred Hitchcock Presents*), Sam Jaffe (actor in two *Alfred Hitchcock Presents* episodes), and Louis Pollock (cowriter of the *Alfred Hitchcock Presents* episode "Breakdown"). By hiring Lewis Milestone to direct *Suspicion*'s "The Bull Skinner" (1958), Joan helped usher him out of exile—just as, four years prior, she had cast Kim Hunter in a special episode of *Janet Dean* ("The Putnam Case") as the main character's temporary replacement Nurse Sylvia Peters. Like many, Milestone and Hunter were able to reemerge one episode at a time.

As *Alfred Hitchcock Presents* continued through the late 1950s, the Shamley office garnered a reputation as one of the most creative, intellectual, and professional spaces in the television industry, with Joan and Norman working at optimum capacity, soon ably assisted by story editor Gordon Hessler (an aspiring director, bred in the world of documentaries) and Gordon's wife, Yvonne, as secretary. Newcomer Robert Bloch, whose episode "The Cure" would debut around the same time as Hitchcock's film adaptation of his novel *Psycho*, recalled just what "a pleasurable experience" it was to meet with them. "They were knowledgeable, literate, and witty. They didn't play games to impress lowly writers with their own superiority."

Joan had, in many ways, replicated the intimate Hitchcock roundtable she recalled from mid-1930s London. She led her own triumvirate now; Harrison, Lloyd, and Gordon Hessler formed a team that sounded out ideas, tested methods and bons mots, and delivered product on time. Henry Slesar, one of the most prolific writers on the series, noted the can-do atmosphere: "I remember that when I would get together with them at Shamley and the sky outside was overcast, they would all say, 'Isn't it a great day!'"

This structure, by which Joan ran the television side while Hitchcock presided over his films, brought out the best in both of them. Hitchcock, directing *Vertigo*, *North by Northwest*, *Psycho*, and *The Birds* in this period, was achieving new artistic and commercial heights. And *Alfred Hitchcock Presents*—and the creative energy around it—fueled him and nurtured his screen imagination. The two worked together in complementary ways. Hitchcock valued Joan's contributions to the film side, though they were understood to be informal and unsystematic.

Usually, this setup didn't cause hiccups, save for a notorious instance during the production of *Vertigo*, when Hitchcock's decision to follow Joan's instincts ended up causing his staff big headaches and costing Paramount a lot of money. The director had been consulting Harrison from the start; when Maxwell Anderson's first-draft screenplay didn't pan out, she was the one who recommended Alec Coppel as a replacement. The Australian-born writer's original stories inspired episodes of *Alfred Hitchcock Presents*, and he and his wife, Myra, struck up a lifelong friendship with Joan. And Hitchcock, in turn, had appreciated the 1953 film *Captain's Paradise*, cowritten by Coppel, enough to give him a chance at the *Vertigo* screenplay.

As *Vertigo* closed out postproduction, Hitchcock still harbored doubts about its narrative structure, specifically the way in which it revealed one character's role in the central mystery. The film versions that were being printed and shipped to theaters included the revelatory flashback two-thirds of the way through in which Judy (Kim Novak) writes a letter explaining her involvement in the death of the woman she had been hired to impersonate. Joan and Hitchcock had been turning this moment around from every angle, following months of discussion with *Vertigo*'s third screenwriter, Samuel A. Taylor. The two men were undecided, but she was convinced that the letter-writing scene disclosed crucial information too soon before the film's climax. If the audience had answers to the mystery well before Scottie (Jimmy Stewart) did, would *Vertigo* lose its suspense?

Per Joan's suggestion, the director had editor George Tomasini recut the film without this sequence. This was after the final version had been approved by Paramount president Barney Balaban and prints had been sent to exchanges nationwide. *Vertigo* associate producer Herbert Coleman recalled Hitchcock asking him to arrange for a last-minute private screening with several colleagues and cast members to assess the revised version on its own terms. Unaware that Joan had been weighing in, and not one of her fans (he liked having Hitchcock to himself), Coleman was annoyed when he arrived "to see her sitting right there beside Hitch." She wasn't focused on Coleman, however; her eyes were on the screen. When the lights came up, she stood up and declared, "Hitchy, how could anyone want your picture to be seen any different from this?" To Joan, there was no doubt; the answers to the mystery should come out at the end.

Hitchcock's reaction demonstrated that his trust in Joan's instincts had only strengthened over time. "Well, Herbie. That's it," Hitchcock said. "Release it just like that." The associate producer did not let this go without a fight. He ushered Hitchcock to a corner of the room, and the two entered into a yelling match in front of the group. This couldn't have been comfortable for Joan. According to Coleman, he went to the studio the next day and recalled five hundred prints from the exchanges. To remove Judy's letter-writing scene meant a polished reedit plus a new transition by composer Bernard Herrmann. Several weeks later, Paramount fielded further costs in order to reship the prints to distributors. The film was on the brink of distribution when Balaban, back in the home office in New York, caught wind of the change. He called the production office and spoke directly to Hitchcock. The result of his conversation was that Hitchcock told Coleman and the team to "put the picture back the way you had it."

If this episode caused tension between Joanie and Hitchy, or if either saw Balaban's intervention as an embarrassment, they put it behind them. It certainly did not stop the two from engaging creatively on his film projects. For example, she introduced him to *Psycho* novelist Robert Bloch. But she recognized that she didn't have the stomach to be intensely involved with that film—and in fact discouraged Hitchcock from making it. "This time, you're going too far," she told him. She also forwent the opportunity to participate in advance profit sharing in *Psycho*, requesting a raise instead.

The *Alfred Hitchcock Presents* series, not coincidentally, functioned as a reunion space for actors who had been featured prominently in Hitchcock's earlier films. In the first season alone, Joseph Cotten (*Shadow of a Doubt*), Claude Rains (*Notorious*), Thelma Ritter (*Rear Window*), and the Hitchcocks' daughter, Patricia (*Strangers on a Train*), had starring roles. With the exception of Ritter, all would return in future seasons, with Cotten eventually making three appearances in the series; Pat Hitchcock, four; and Rains, five (counting the next iteration of the series, *The Alfred Hitchcock Hour*). They would be joined by other actors closely associated with the director, including Theresa Wright (*Shadow of a Doubt*) in two episodes; Hume Cronyn (*Shadow of a Doubt*), two; Herbert Marshall (who had starred in the early British drama *Murder!*), two; and Joan Fontaine (*Rebecca, Suspicion*), one.

At the same time, the series served as a proving ground for actors Hitchcock had contracted or may have been considering for future film projects. Vera Miles, who starred in the series' very first episode, "Revenge," in October 1955, had by 1957 made her Hitchcock film debut in *The Wrong Man* (1956) and been cast as the lead in *Vertigo*. (After Miles became pregnant, she was replaced by Kim Novak; nevertheless, two years later, Hitchcock would cast Miles as Lila Crane, Marion Crane's sister, in *Psycho*. She would also star in two more episodes of the series.)

Likewise, Martin Balsam made his first *Alfred Hitchcock Presents* appearance in June 1958. The following year, he would secure the role of doomed detective Milton Arbogast in *Psycho*. Balsam would return for an encore in a 1961 *Alfred Hitchcock Presents* episode.

The case of Barbara Bel Geddes provides perhaps the most illustrative example of how actors would migrate between the small and big screens of the Hitchcock universe. Bel Geddes made her *Alfred Hitchcock Presents* debut in 1958, appearing in two episodes in rapid succession. "The Foghorn" aired on March 16, followed on April 13 by the classic "Lamb to the Slaughter," in which Bel Geddes's character disposes of the murder weapon she used to kill her husband—a frozen leg of lamb—by cooking it and serving it to the investigating officers. Less than a month after the second episode aired, Hitchcock's *Vertigo*, in which Bel Geddes plays main character Scottie Ferguson's best friend (and ex-fiancée), premiered. Bel Geddes would return to the series in successive seasons in 1959 and 1960.

One effect of this dynamic was to create the sense that Hitchcock's films and his television series—despite the fact that, in the series' ten-year run, he personally directed only 18 of 359 episodes—had an almost seamless relationship. Actors the audience remembered from earlier films would appear in the series; actors who might have first been associated with Hitchcock through the series would later turn up in his films.

As a brand name and a destination show, *Alfred Hitchcock Presents* became a competitive training ground for rising directors, writers, and actors. Directors Robert Altman, Stuart Rosenberg, and William Friedkin cut their teeth on it. Young actors featured included Carol Lynley, Gena Rowlands, John Cassavetes, Robert Redford, Steve McQueen, Bruce Dern, and Clint Eastwood (in an uncredited role). In addition to Bloch and Coppel, Joan cultivated such writers as Henry Slesar and the team of William Link and Richard Levinson. She was always bringing in seasoned pros like Garson Kanin, Ray Bradbury, John Cheever, Roald Dahl, and Ellery Queen.

British novelist Eric Ambler impressed Joan above all others. During winter 1958, she hired him to write "The Eye of Truth," an original teleplay for *Suspicion*. In the harrowing episode, a high-powered attorney (Joseph Cotten) goes to extreme measures to stop a young blackmailer (George Peppard) from disclosing the contents of his briefcase, which would reveal that the attorney's son has been responsible for a hit-and-run death.

Ambler's reputation preceded him. Born in London to music-hall marionette performers, he eventually dropped out of college and became an advertising copywriter. Writing some of his most celebrated works—*The Mask of Dimitrios*, *Epitaph for a Spy*, and *Journey into Fear*—before the age of thirty, Ambler was credited with revitalizing the British thriller, and has since been deemed the father of the modern spy novel. His work was committedly antifascist and proletariat; his characters are ordinary, everyday people who find themselves conscripted into "professional" espionage.

A star in literary circles, Ambler was meticulous in his appearance and had been endowed with the enviable gift of being able to produce the precise word at every turn. He also had a famous talent for mimicry and would wow people with his impressions of Charlton Heston and Stewart Granger.

While he was working on "The Eye of Truth," Ambler and Harrison began dating. Norman Lloyd surmised that Joan and Eric must have gone about their courtship "very carefully" because Lloyd—who was around on a daily basis—never caught on to it. "They were too clever," he says. "There they were, working away. He was writing the script. And then all of a sudden, Joan announced they were going to be married!" Ambler had long been married to American fashion correspondent Louise Crombie, whom he'd wed in 1939, on the eve of going into the service. Though he and Crombie had been separated for some time, the situation nevertheless required Joan to be discreet.

It's not as though Joan and Eric had only just met. He had made a tour through Hollywood in the mid-1940s, just after the war, which he had spent alongside John Huston and Jules Buck. She had known Eric at least that long. Now they were guarding their secret by finding ways to rendezvous between Los Angeles and London, usually by meeting in a New York hotel. Crombie and Ambler worked out a divorce settlement in May 1958.

On Saturday, October 11, 1958, Joan and Eric were married in San Francisco City Hall. They had spent the preceding week dodging gossip columnists, throwing them off the scent by sending two Universal Studios attorneys to a Bakersfield courthouse to obtain the license, with the requisite blood tests and Eric's divorce papers under their care. Hitchcock facilitated the weekend event by using his considerable clout to persuade superior court judge Gerald S. Levin to set aside his golf game and open up the chambers. As Alma watched, Hitch gave away the bride.

After a night of revelry with friends who had flown up from L.A., the newlyweds retired to their suite at the Mark Hopkins Hotel. The phone rang. It was three o'clock in the morning. When Ambler picked up, a reporter for London's *Daily Express* was on the other end. The reporter asked for confirmation that Eric and Joan had married, then posed a follow-up question: "Hadn't she been married to Clark Gable?" Eric assured the caller that he was her first husband, hung up, and went to sleep. A few days later, when the couple received a *Daily Express* clipping in the mail, they saw the headline announcing their wedding next to an enormous photo of Joan and Gable at an Academy Awards function. Joan couldn't help but be amused.

With no time to spare for a honeymoon, she didn't mind when Hitchcock hosted a black-tie banquet at Chasen's in honor of their wedding. One hundred guests poured in at three o'clock in the afternoon for the Edwardian-themed party. The French menu included caviar, sole fillets, tournedos Rossini, and roast partridge. Festivities didn't draw to a close until midnight.

Joan initially took up residence in Eric's rental home, in the 700 block of Camden Drive (Vincente Minnelli once lived there). In 1960 they purchased a New Regency–style house at the top of a steep road off Stone Canyon Road, one mile past the Bel Air Hotel. Tiered landscaping draped the front lawn of the two-story 1940 house, and a terraced canyon wall ran along the back. Joan and Eric shared a preference for its Georgian architecture (which recalled the Grove) over the Spanish mission homes and pueblo-style adobes then ascendant in Los Angeles. And while it lacked a pool, how highly pitched it stood on this vertically inclined, out-of-the-way cul-de-sac met Joan's central criteria of privacy. "The Amblers" were inspired by their new address, 10640 Taranto Way, to found a joint company named Tarantula Productions—a formality for now, with an eye toward future projects.

Two top-of-the-line television sets arrived promptly at Taranto Way, courtesy of Hitchcock (though paid for out the Shamley account). This was for the sake of business, according to the director, though his generosity could not be denied. Joan declined color TV sets, "knowing that Shamley had no money in reserves." She and Eric had little downtime anyway. Their favorite pastimes were shopping for antiques or hosting boon companions for champagne cocktails, which many friends thought they had invented. Eric now accompanied Joan on her usual rounds of afternoon coffees and evening soirees at the Milestones', Wylers', Coppels', or Henreids'.

On December 31, 1960, Joan and Eric rang in the new year, attending a black-tie party hosted by actor Francis Lederer and his wife, Marion, at their epic Simi Hills ranch. By then, the Amblers had settled into a workday rhythm. Joan left for her office at the Universal lot just after 8:00 AM, making the drive to the San Fernando Valley in her Chevrolet Bel Air hardtop coupe. Her husband would spend his writing days in the office on their home's first floor. Depending on the stage of his project, a typist would arrive in the morning to assist. Joan quipped that her best advice to career women was to "marry a writer," as she had, because they were quiet and had few domestic demands. The truth was that their routine was maintained with fine-tuned precision thanks to Nellie (who lived on Taranto Way with them) and Rose (who had an apartment nearby).

The routine would be dreadfully interrupted on the morning of November 5, 1961. The day began in customary fashion, with Joan leaving for the office at the usual time. Around 9:00 AM, word began to trickle in that a brush fire was sweeping over the valley. It had been an unusually dry fall season, now exacerbated by fifty-mile-per-hour Santa Ana winds blowing in from the desert. The local CBS radio station was reporting that the Los Angeles Fire Department was trying desperately to contain the blaze as it jumped from roof to roof. Upon hearing that an emergency had been declared, Joan put in a call to Eric. When the line gave her trouble, she paid little attention, figuring the wires were overloaded with calls well east of Bel Air.

When she received a call an hour later from Eric, she discerned right away that something was wrong. In a hoarse voice, he told her that the house had indeed sustained some damage and she should book the nearest available hotel. Not stopping to ask questions, she hung up and did just that. To reach him again, she dialed the number he had given her, a neighbor's phone. Picking up, he suggested she call their business manager, Bernie Skedron. The number, she responded, would be in one of their address books. And at this, there was a long pause. "Darling," he replied, "there are no address books anymore." The house was gone. All that was left was still ablaze in towering flames.

Joan swung into action, allowing no time to reflect. Her focus was on Eric and Nellie, who were for the moment stranded on Stone Canyon Road. (Eric's typist had left earlier when the winds picked up.) Nellie eventually made her way down, and Eric caught a ride with a neighbor. By then, Joan had supplied their Beverly Hills Hotel room with a new toothbrush, razor, and pair of underwear for Eric purchased from the hotel drugstore. She then teamed up with Nellie to equip him with a temporary set of slippers and silk pajamas (generously donated by Barbara Hutton's former butler) and enlisted a doctor to calm his nerves.

As for Joan's provisions, she had Nellie to thank for her quick thinking. When Nellie noticed that the roof appeared to be on fire, she seized Joan's fur coat and all the jewelry that she could. Next, she took one of Joan's nightdresses out of the washing machine. Joan so greatly appreciated the risk that Nellie had taken time for just a few material items that she was inspired to soldier on despite the fact that she had lost all of her other possessions—the letters, photographs, and paintings she had accrued over the past two decades. Two days later, as she and Norman Lloyd drove the winding, charred path up to Taranto Way to survey the ruins, a sweet smile overtook her. "She saved my mink coat," she announced to her companion with a mixture of relief and wonder. For Joan, there was no deeper show of devotion. Or perhaps it was just a potent reminder of how capricious and absurd life could be.

Eric found the fire much more difficult to bounce back from. "He was shell-shocked by it," Lloyd explains, recalling the ravaged, desolate look on Eric's face as he stared helplessly at the debris. And this from a man whom John Huston described as being "the coolest man I've ever seen under fire," having served alongside him in the army. "I'd look around when things started jumping and heaving under an artillery barrage," Huston recounted, "and Eric would be flicking dust off his boot." Lloyd understood Eric had seen combat in the war, "but this was something else, beyond his comprehension."

Part of Eric's unnerving had to do with how abruptly the blaze had announced itself that morning and how rapidly it spread beyond his control. The first sign that something was wrong had come when Nellie came to the office to tell him it appeared a fire had broken out on the roof. It was then that she raced around the house collecting what valuables she could, as he stood atop the second story, futilely attempting to put out the flames as the water pressure dropped. (Water was in short supply.) It was then that he regretted having no pool.

Within minutes, he and Nellie evacuated to the garage, which stood thirty feet below the house, out of the path of the blaze. They crouched together between two cars, braving smoke inhalation, as they watched the second story of the house crash down onto the first in a fiery burst. Soon after, they shared astonished looks as packs of wild animals—deer, rabbits, mountain lions—came racing out of the canyon, forced out by the driving winds. Help didn't arrive from the fire department for six hours. Although miraculously no lives were lost, the Bel Air / Brentwood fire was the most disastrous in Los Angeles history, with nearly five hundred homes lost and over sixteen thousand acres burned.

One of the casualties of the fire was the draft of the novel Eric had been writing, "The Light of Day." He had been storing the manuscript (and all his notes for future projects) in a fireproof safe, a fact that gave him comfort as he had men pry the safe open a few days after the conflagration. When the safe door swung ajar, however, all that remained was "a mass of grey ash that turned to powder when it was touched." When he finally went back to writing, he had to restart the novel from scratch. The empty page would present him with an unfamiliar challenge from that point forward: he found writer's block daunting.

Three weeks after the fire, Joan wrote to a British colleague, MCA agent John Findlay, "It really was an unbelievable experience, having to start life afresh just with the clothes you stand up in." She had to remain strong, if for no other reason than to hold up her husband. "I don't mind losing my possessions because clothing and furs and jewelry can be replaced," she stated at the time, though she admitted that her greatest loss was "family papers and photographs." She saw Eric as experiencing "the real tragedy."

As a temporary housing solution, she and Eric rented a house at 710 North Roxbury, several blocks off Beverly Hills' Rodeo Drive. Pinks and pastels dominated the interior decor, which Joan didn't mind but only added to Eric's growing depression. His office was particularly feminine, having been a teenage girl's bedroom. Nellie's efforts at levity, which consisted of teasing him about the dozens of dolls lined up in display cases, fell on deaf ears. Joan and Eric deliberated over whether to rebuild on Taranto Way, finally committing to reconstruct the house they'd had on the same plot. It would be resurrected within a year. The only difference was that this time there would be a pool.

Even as life returned to normal, Joan would pose a series of bewilderments to Eric, who often found himself playing "Nick" to her "Nora," à la *The Thin Man*. One day when they were making out their wills, he noticed a statement for £500,000. Asked by her husband where they should park the account, Joan gave a look of utter surprise and said, "Oh, this is the money Daddy gave me. I'd forgotten all about it." (The money had been passed down to her when her father died during the war, and her family put it in an offshore account to shield it from the government.) Eric's jaw dropped as he realized she had let roughly the equivalent of $1.4 million slip her mind. Sometime later, while they were visiting with her family, Joan's sister Faith referred to herself as the "younger sister." Turning to his wife, Eric inquired, "But I always thought *you* were the younger one! Joan, how old are you?" She had to confess that, indeed, she had shaved five years off her age. In actuality, Joan was two years and two days older than Eric.

She certainly had waited a long time to get married. In the 1950s, it was rare to be a bride at fifty-one years old. In another instance, the decision to marry later in life might have been chalked up to a shift in priorities—from career to personal life. But in Joan's case, considering the adamant views against the institution she had expressed for so many years, some had trouble accounting for the change. "All of a sudden a man appeared," Nellie's niece, Georgina, remembered.

While Eric knew that Joan's feelings for him were genuine, he wasn't under any illusion that he was her first love. Nor had she hidden the most private parts of her past. Many years into their marriage, he told their caregiver Jackie Makkink, "You know, the only person Joan ever really loved was a woman." Others in Joan's inner circle harbored suspicions that this was true, though they differed in their opinions as to the object of her affection, and no one discussed it at the time.

Of all the potential romantic partners, Sarett Rudley appears to be the most plausible. Not only did she maintain a central presence in Joan's life, but the producer also seemed to keep calling her back. At every professional opportunity, Joan summoned Sarett. Their work together on *Janet Dean, Registered Nurse* had gone well. Now, Sarett was a recurring writer on the *Alfred Hitchcock Presents* series. She first contributed "The Baby Sitter" (which aired in spring 1956), going on to write eight more episodes, in addition to "The Slayer and The Slain" for *Suspicion*.

By the mid-to-late 1950s, with her marriage to attorney Daniel Glass in the rearview mirror, Sarett had begun seeing British novelist Richard Mason. They began romancing near the release of his 1957 bestseller *The World of Suzie Wong*, a story about a love affair between a prostitute and a businessman turned artist set in Hong Kong. As reporters announced their impending nuptials, Sarett took the opportunity to break with heterosexual norms and declared that Mason's ex-wife, Felicity Cumming, a British actress who fancied herself a professional sexual adventuress, would be joining the couple on their honeymoon. "I never want to live anywhere without my Felicity," Sarett declared.

The strongest indication that Joan entertained romantic feelings for Sarett—whether reciprocated or not—is the timing of Joan's rather sudden courtship with Eric. She began making her pending nuptials with Eric known just as Sarett took up with Mason, and as the writer discontinued her involvement with the series.

Whatever the origins of her relationship with Eric, the marriage, for Joan, also contained professional possibilities. She hoped that she, Eric, and Hitch might form an independent film unit: a writer, producer, and director superteam. However, she didn't have to sit through too many dinners around the Hitchcocks' kitchen table to see that the chemistry wasn't going to work. Eric and Hitch would never get along. And there was the underlying thread that her former mentor still saw her as his own. "He considered *everyone* his personal property," Norman Lloyd says. "That was Hitch."

By some accounts, Hitchcock was becoming increasingly unpredictable as he entered his later years and his emotional and psychological insecurities worsened. According to Tippi Hedren, star of *The Birds* (1963) and *Marnie* (1964), the director's possessive behavior was frightening, even hellish, backed by the threat of career retaliation. Hedren recalled reaching out to others in Hitchcock's circle for support, but "nobody had any real answer to how I was going to solve the problem" of Hitchcock's power. Harrison had little involvement in Hedren's two films with Hitch, so it's unclear how much she knew about his treatment of the actress or how she might have responded if she did know. At the very least, Joan's track record indicates that she would have avoided enabling a toxic work environment, and she may have been growing increasingly disenchanted with the setup at Shamley.

By this point Joan was looking at a major professional transition. Network confidence in *Alfred Hitchcock Presents* seemed to be waning. The show had endured shifting time slots and even moved from CBS to NBC and back again. (It would eventually make one final move, returning to NBC.) In 1962 it had been rechristened *The Alfred Hitchcock Hour*, going from thirty to sixty minutes (primarily as a way to pick up more sponsorship dollars). Ready to scale back and skeptical about finding fresh material, Joan relinquished her position to Lloyd. She would now serve as producer on a limited number of shows each season but continue to play an essential role through the series' final install-ment in spring 1965. When the end came, NBC executives made no fanfare of the cancellation; they simply announced *The Alfred Hitchcock Hour* would not be renewed. It was becoming "a little too costly," according to the network.

A sober assessment—at this stage in her life, Joan was nothing if not clear-eyed—indicated that as a woman in her midfifties, staying in television without Hitchcock would be an uphill battle. She and Eric did try making Tarantula Productions a reality, developing the espionage series *Journey into Fear* (trad-ing on the title of Ambler's 1943 novel but based on an original concept by the author). Friend Bill Dozier signed on to executive-produce through his company Greenway Productions, in association with Twentieth Century Fox, but in fall 1966, when the pilot (which Joan produced) was shelved, Joan determined it was time for a break.

One thing she wouldn't have to worry about was money. Her work on *Alfred Hitchcock Presents* and *The Alfred Hitchcock Hour* had earned her a cache of MCA shares. Because of lenient tax laws, Switzerland held out the best hope for her and Eric to protect her windfall, not to mention Eric's continuing royalties. He proposed a move to Salagnon Island in Lake Geneva, near the large estate occupied by their friend Charlie Chaplin in Corsier-sur-Vevey. Having visited the Swiss Riviera town and its scenic surroundings, she saw his wisdom. The Amblers were bound for the Alps.

20 | INTO THE UNKNOWN

JOAN TOOK UP RESIDENCE with Eric at Chemin de l'Île de Salagnon 1 in Clarens in early 1968. The spacious apartment was nestled in a chalet-style building near the harbor on Lake Geneva. The balconies at both ends presented spectacular views of the glass-blue water and the snowcapped mountains. Joan loved that she could sun herself in the warmer months, surrounded by rugged foothills and spring flowers. Always more at home when surrounded by pastels, Joan went with pale green striped upholstery and cool interiors. The couple imported their furniture from California along with the paintings they had collected since the fire, ranging from Thomas Rowlandson to John Piper to Hugh Frazer. Eric's small office was lined with books, perhaps to spur his own productivity.

Joan set about to "arranging dull things like laundries and cleaners and where to buy the best meat." She looked to her new Italian housekeeper Nicoletta as a lifeline. "She doesn't speak much French and I don't speak any Italian! But we manage to communicate," she wrote to Paul and Lisl Henreid. No one could replace Nellie and Rose, who stayed behind in Los Angeles and sought out new employment. They remained in close touch. And when Eric wrote his memoir *Here Lies*, he dedicated the book to Nellie. He never forgot the lengths she went to during the Bel Air fire to save their things.

Joan and Eric developed close ties to neighbors such as James Mason and screwball writer-director Norman Krasna and his wife, Erle. Joan renewed her friendship with Charlie and Oona Chaplin and delighted when chums like the Premingers came through.

Despite the seeming pleasantness of her life, Joan soon came to a determination that, as she put it, "all the lovely scenery [in Clarens] can't make up for these dull Swiss." She shopped a concept for a supernatural series to Hammer Film Productions in London. By summer 1968 she was back in the producing game with *Journey to the Unknown*, a joint production from Hammer, Twentieth Century Fox, and ABC. The anthology series united British talent with past contributors to *Alfred Hitchcock Presents*. Partnered with Hammer producer Anthony Hinds, Norman Lloyd and Joan alternated producing duties. American stars such as Joseph Cotten, Vera Miles, and Barbara Bel Geddes headlined; veteran *Alfred Hitchcock Presents* series director Robert Stevens helmed the pilot. In the vein of *The Twilight Zone*, the show featured "every conceivable permutation of mystery, imagination, terror, and fantasy," with everyday people trapped in unusual or supernatural situations.

Setting the tone for *Journey to the Unknown*, the first episode, "Eve," focused on a lonely, shy sales clerk (Dennis Waterman) who falls in love with a beautiful mannequin in his shop window and slips into a fantasy, then a nightmare, when she comes to life (or so he believes). For the part of Eve, the mannequin, Harrison cast another familiar face, Carol Lynley, who gave a consummate performance that telegraphed the series' avant-garde, psychedelic hue. Subsequent episodes signaled a daring experimentation with gender and genre expectations that promised to be more radical than anything in the *Alfred Hitchcock* series. In "Miss Belle," based on a short story by Charles Beaumont of *Twilight Zone* fame, a pool cleaner (George Maharis) comes to the realization that he is working for a spinster (Barbara Jefford) so embittered against men that she has conditioned her young nephew Robert to believe he is a girl named Roberta. A kitchen showdown between the child and aunt ends in spilled milk and murder, and the episode concludes with "Robert" and the pool cleaner constituting a new family. To adapt this gender-bending gothic tale, Joan brought in Sarett Rudley.

Though prerelease fanfare set up *Journey to the Unknown* for success, and the team rolled out the series on ABC in the United States before its airing in the UK on ITV, the show ended after just one season. Joan chalked it up to unexpected challenges: poor weather conditions that led to limited filming time, a smaller pool of experienced technical talent in the UK, and fewer professional writers on hand.

Fortunately, that spring of 1970 Aaron Spelling was executive-producing a new crime show, *Zig Zag*, to be aired on ABC. The show's tagline was "Murder is the most deadly game. These three criminologists play it." Morton Fine (*Maverick*, *The Virginian*) and David Friedkin (*Frontier*, *I Spy*) created the series as a vehicle for Swedish actress Inger Stevens, whose career had been in decline. Stevens's character, Vanessa Smith, was an analytical, college-educated woman whose approach to detection differed dramatically from that of Jonathan Croft (George Maharis), who drew on his military training. Ralph Bellamy, playing Ethan Arcane, would lead the team. Spelling offered Harrison the role of producer on the show. An ensemble procedural represented a major departure for her, and because this deal brought her into Spelling's hip universe (which also included *The Mod Squad*, the ABC show about new-generation cops just then beginning to find its audience), she was opening up her work to a new generation.

Unfortunately, *Zig Zag* lived up to its name when, days after completing the pilot, Inger Stevens died of an overdose of barbiturates. Rather than pull the plug on the show, Joan and the other producers decided to recast the role. With Yvette Mimieux now in the lead, they reshot the episode and retitled the show *The Most Deadly Game*. It premiered in ABC's Saturday 9:30 PM slot on October 10, 1970. The whole thing, Spelling later recalled, just felt "dead on arrival. . . . The show just had a feeling like it was damned. We couldn't recover from the negative publicity." *The Most Deadly Game* lasted twelve episodes.

Joan was not altogether dissatisfied with the experience. It led to another offer from Spelling to produce an ABC Movie of the Week, which at that juncture was not too dissimilar from a full-scale feature film project. She pitched an original by Eric, a stalker story called *Love Hate Love*. To her delight, she and Eric were at last collaborators. Eric would write the script and George McCowan would direct. (McCowan had lensed the final *The Most Deadly Game* episode, as well as installments of *The FBI*, *The Invaders*, *The Mod Squad*, and *Run for Your Life*.) The real score was casting Ryan O'Neal, riding the success of *Love Story*, as the sensible engineer who finds himself going toe-to-toe with the unhinged man (Peter Haskell) who is pursuing his fashion model girlfriend (played by Lesley Ann Warren).

The production of *Love Hate Love* went smoothly. From her temporary home at the Beverly Wilshire Hotel, Joan wrote to Eric in Clarens that, apart from needing to adjust locations, "the scenes, dialogue, etc. remain intact with no violation from the network who have been surprisingly co-operative." When *Love Hate Love* aired on February 9, 1971, it was ABC's most popular offering that week, finishing seventh in the ratings.

During production, Joan had battled feelings of guilt over her prolonged absence from Eric. A trip he made to spend several weeks by her side proved equally problematic, as she blamed herself for hauling him across the globe and interrupting his writing. The strain on the marriage was palpable. Looking to placate him (and perhaps abate her insecurities), she pointed to their common purpose. "I know you won't feel, my darling, that I am dragging you back to California," she wrote, "because it is only temporary and it is our joint product."

Joan felt strongly about the importance of work in her life. "I'm just an old warhorse, who should retire but won't," she wrote to the Henreids, adding, "(I should say, warmare!)." She feared a future of being stuck at home as little more than helpmate to her novelist husband. "I refuse to be tied to domesticity," she asserted to Evelyn Keyes.

Yet she also loved Eric, even if she couldn't always resolve her complicated feelings, or express them. In a letter to her husband, she explained, "After I talked to you on the phone today, I realized that I really hadn't said what I meant to say—that I miss you more than I could have believed possible and would want you to be here tomorrow, if you could." Eric assured her that he too struggled with loneliness, writing, "Without you, my love, I cannot be tranquil under any circumstances." Still, Joan worried about the volatility in their relationship and its long-term consequences. "We have been going through such a difficult time," she wrote to him, "that it is easy to forget (temporarily) all that we mean to each other." Adding to these concerns was the fact that, after a prolonged period back in Los Angeles, Switzerland was even less alluring to Joan.

The compromise eventually came in the form of a London flat. At Joan's urging, the couple rented a spacious apartment with high ceilings, immense fireplaces, and an old kitchen (but they wouldn't be spending time there, so who cared?) in the prestigious neighborhood of Belgravia. Spending six months out of the year in London would give her entrée to friends, movies, and the theater. In February 1972 Joan took up residence at 33 Chesham Place.

The building's impressive white stucco Victorian exteriors belied the fact that the three-bedroom, four-story unit needed some work, so Joan oversaw repairs and decoration plans. Eric soon followed.

As enchanting as the prospect of dividing her time between Belgravia and Lake Geneva was, Joan still found herself pining for Los Angeles. She continued to travel there for several weeks, even several months, at a time. Staying at the Beverly Wilshire, she called on old friends: Paul and Lisl Henreid, Kendall and Lewis Milestone, and Evelyn Keyes. She began to dream about trading London for Beverly Hills and making *that* her home six months out of the year, about resuming her regular brunches with Evelyn and Academy screenings at the Marquis Theatre. She even thought about hitting the tennis courts, though she confessed that playing tennis was a stretch of the imagination: "I've given that up. Or it gave me up!"

But Joan knew the only justification for a California return was the possibility of long-term film or television work. A deal for another ABC Movie of the Week appeared then fell through. Likewise, a couple of British film projects, including an MGM-UK feature starring Peter Finch, cropped up but went nowhere. Joan had always known the downside of film and television, that it was a collaborative medium, one based on relationships. When the calls stopped coming, the curtain would close. She disclosed her frustration to Paul and Lisl: "I envy a talent that can work on its own—people like actors, directors, and producers can't!"

The realization must have been a chilling one. She had made her last film.

Over the next few years, she seemed adrift, in every sense. A compulsive letter writer, she was perpetually appending a forwarding address. To Evelyn, she disclosed, "I haven't said this to anyone else, but I wonder if I should have come on stronger with Eric and said that I wanted a place in California rather than here," adding that she would "give it a good whirl." Her husband intuited Joan's struggle. He gifted her a pair of hummingbird earrings that he had specially designed for her, inspired by the birds in their garden on Taranto Way.

She eventually told herself she wasn't going to miss being in an industry that was no longer, in her mind, taking risks or showing ambition. "I was always glad I was there," she affirmed to the Henreids, "when it was really exciting and companies were prepared to venture all kinds of different films." If it was a rationalization, it was not one without merit. Joan never developed a taste for compromise.

One interesting line was cast her way. The British publisher Heinemann invited her to pen her memoir. She wrote to Evelyn that she was preparing to lunch with an editor to discuss the prospect, quipping "Why not?" But the meeting bore no fruit.

Though no longer active in the industry, Joan kept up with cutting-edge cinema. She raved about Costa-Gavras's *Z* and looked forward to the opening of *A Clockwork Orange*—"for which I'm sure I will need a strong drink or a tranquilizer or both," she avowed to the Henreids. In 1974 she decried the fact that Ingmar Bergman's *Cries and Whispers* didn't win the Oscar for Best Picture, reproaching Academy voters who "probably thought about it as a foreign film." She was also deeply engaged with American politics, expressing disgust at Watergate (which she followed avidly), hope for a Democratic win in 1976 (though she wished Jimmy Carter's smile wasn't so wide and she bemoaned the sight of his mother wearing a campaign sweatshirt), and disdain for Ronald Reagan.

To her nieces and her friends' children, she was a source of wisdom. Joan's niece Kate Adamson appreciated that she was "always very tuned in to my sister Alexandria and me." It wasn't until the 1970s, when her aunt's work slowed, that she got to know her well. Partial to bestowing advice, Joan told Kate, "Be careful that you're not only focused on work. Make sure you make room for other things."

"She behaved like the perfect godmother, oh my God," marvels Joan Buck. "She showered me with letters, jewelry, and lunches out." The daughter of Joyce and Jules Buck treasured the classic necklace Joan gave her, which contained three small pearls "with room to grow." She comprehended in retrospect that Harrison was "such a conscientious godmother because she was raised that way. She was brought up to build a society—the way she built her films. She approached everything in a very constructed way." Joan Buck adds irreverently, "Just because she wore those tight suits, pastel colors, and the crimped hair style, she was still a free woman. She was my very own fairy godmother who subtly gave me the sense that I could do whatever I wanted to do."

Meanwhile, Joan worked to maintain the appearance that she was not too old to make one last splash. Writing to Kendall Milestone, who had been at the top of the Hollywood hostess list in the 1940s, she congratulated her dear pal on the fact she was still gracing the Beverly Hills scene. In a postscript,

Joan added, "We must try to enjoy life while we can and I, for one, intend to. I still have some wild oats to sow. Or maybe one wild oat."

Through it all, Joan kept up with Hitchcock, whose production had slowed since the end of their television series. *Torn Curtain* (1966), *Topaz* (1969), *Frenzy* (1972), and *Family Plot* (1976) received mixed critical reception upon their releases and were generally seen as evidence of his artistic decline. The director whose very name had come to be synonymous with box office success was now seen as out of step with the cultural and cinematic trends of the moment, with New American Cinema and big-budget disaster movies predominating, even though he no doubt had influenced them. A new generation would discover and come to admire Hitchcock through the rise of film societies and retrospectives, but au courant he was not.

Joan stayed in touch with Hitch mostly by phone, so as not to intrude on what was a difficult time for her old friend. Alma had suffered a second stroke in 1976 (after a paralyzing one in 1972), and her health was becoming increasingly frail, so much so that Hitchcock turned his attention toward her care, cooking meals and curtailing his hours at his office on the Universal lot. Now in his late seventies, he too soon began to show signs of decline, contending with hypertension, a heart condition, and the various discomforts of old age. Another reason Joan kept visits to Bellagio Road to a minimum was the tension between Hitch and Eric. "Come on, now, Joan, change the subject," her husband would say whenever the director came up in casual conversation.

There was very little getting away from Hitchcock, however. Though he no longer held sway over the box office, a slew of lifetime honors had been steadily coming his way. The British Academy of Film and Television Arts (BAFTA) Academy Fellowship in 1971. The Golden Globe Cecil B. DeMille Award in 1972. A Film Society of Lincoln Center Tribute in 1974. The culmination was the American Film Institute's Lifetime Achievement Award, presented to Hitchcock on March 9, 1979. Intended to single out an individual whose work has stood the test of time, this was seen by most as a necessary corrective to his never having won an Oscar for directing. Held at the Beverly Hilton, the award ceremony fielded an impressive guest list, including Ingrid Bergman, Cary Grant, Jimmy Stewart, Janet Leigh, Sean Connery, John Houseman, and Sidney Bernstein.

Joan would have been there too, of course, but her own health was flagging. And although CBS broadcast the event in the States a few days later, the ceremony didn't make it to British airwaves. So Joan wasn't privy to Hitchcock's speech, in which he expressed gratitude to the "thousands of actors, writers, editors, cameramen, musicians, technicians, bankers, exhibitors, and a variety of other criminals" with whom he had collaborated. He reserved special praise for Alma, who, sitting next to him at the guest-of-honor table, held back tears.

Joan was surely happy for Hitch. He was getting his due; indeed, if anything, his reputation was becoming even more burnished, with "genius" and "master" now routinely attached to his name. Yet it could not have been lost on her that, after all the years of working with Hitchcock, and less than a decade after her last film, the name Joan Harrison was already all but forgotten.

Harrison's rapid fade into the background, even as Hitchcock ascended in the public imagination with apparent ease, offers pointed lessons in the way that cultural institutions, cinematic movements, and trends in film criticism worked against her. In the 1970s, Hitchcock benefited from a surge of interest in his earlier work, but retrospectives and repertory cinemas, the enthusiastic writings of *auteur* theorists, and a full-blown *cult of the director* inflated his role at the expense of his collaborators' contributions. Hitchcock himself was happy to play along; to a filmmaker who had always spun his tales of production in his favor, often taking more than his fair share of credit, it was another opportunity to write himself into history. And while second-wave feminism was also on the rise, those seeking new heroines and her-stories sadly did not take note of Harrison's neglected body of work.

If the lack of recognition bothered Joan, she never showed it. "My aunt was very self-conscious," remarked her niece Kate Adamson. "She did not want to be fawned over. She simply wanted the recognition she deserved." In other words, she wasn't after pomp and circumstance; she just wanted her work to be remembered.

On April 29, 1980, a little more than a year after receiving the AFI Lifetime Achievement Award, Hitchcock passed away in his sleep. Alma's death followed two years later, on July 6, 1982. The two people with whom Joan had sailed on that glorious adventure so many years before were gone.

Joan was confronting her own mortality. A decline in motor skills and memory led her to visit a Los Angeles specialist recommended to her by Billy Wilder. Additional consultations in London followed, and the tests revealed some deterioration in the brain. Joan feared a tumor, but that was ruled out.

In a chilling development, Creutzfeldt-Jakob disease, more commonly known as mad cow disease, was considered, but that too turned out to be a false lead. Doctors eventually determined that the likeliest diagnosis was dementia due to "causes unknown." Simply referring to Joan's "disease" in vague terms, Eric didn't pretend to fully understand her decline. In his 1993 autobiography *Waiting for Orders: Memories and Other Fictions*, he reckoned, "The care has been professional, the courage has been Joan's."

Some of those closest to Joan were skeptical of the diagnosis of dementia, and worried that doctors, in a rush to judgment, had contributed to her medical ills. In the early stages, they prescribed barbiturates in heavy doses, which caused her mood to vacillate between lethargy and belligerence. When weaned off the medication, her health appeared to stabilize. It was not dementia but overmedication, they believed, that undermined her mental health. Patricia Gaynor, hired into the Ambler household as a personal assistant in the early 1980s, saw no signs of Alzheimer's or other forms of dementia at all: "Mrs. Ambler was so sharp, she could talk about anything." To Gaynor, the diagnosis became a self-fulfilling prophecy. "Because [Joan] had been told she was ill," she speculated years later, "she kind of acted ill; she didn't want to go out for appointments, she wouldn't give interviews. But there was nothing wrong with her."

As her world became increasingly narrow, Joan enjoyed watching tennis on television, even more so than reruns of classic films. Her favorite activity, reading, was no longer possible because of cataracts, though Joan being Joan, she would try to disguise this fact. She would often be found alone sitting with a book or newspaper in her lap, holding it upside down. One of her most attentive friends, Myra Coppel, widowed since Alec's death in 1972, looked in on her more than most. Myra was based in Spain, however, which meant that visits were limited.

Joan's attachment to Eric grew deeper during this period. In 1983, on the occasion of their twenty-fifth wedding anniversary, she gave him a card inscribed, "My dearest—With all my love which grows deeper every year. October 11, 1958 . . . almost twenty-five years ago so I love you twenty-five times as much. —Your wife." Samuel Goldwyn Jr. and his wife, Peggy, who visited London to help the couple celebrate, returned to Los Angeles with news of Joan's condition. Goldwyn communicated a diagnosis of Alzheimer's disease to the *Hollywood Reporter*, encouraging "everyone who's known Joan to drop her a note."

Jackie Makkink remembers that by the time she was hired on in late 1985 to work as the Amblers' housekeeper, "Mrs. Ambler looked like a very, very old lady." (She was seventy-eight then.) Her life was increasingly confined to a tightly circumscribed domestic space in ways that were not not so far from the gothic film worlds she had so consummately helped to construct some forty years prior.

Makkink recalls cloak-and-dagger intrigue being part of the fabric of the household, which included a personal assistant, a doorman, a housekeeper, a cook, and two nurses. A careless word or gesture could cause infighting among the staff that might result in a swift firing by Eric. A well-timed compliment might change the course of destiny, or so some employees believed, as they competed to win the Amblers' favor and hoped to be named in the will. This was a sphere of influence with which Joan had intimate familiarity, at least in books and movies. By now, a tinge of *Who's Afraid of Virginia Woolf?* tainted the Amblers' old Nick and Nora rapport. Sometimes this effect was augmented by company. The night Richard Burton and Elizabeth Taylor came for dinner, Dick and Liz gave their best George and Martha imitation, growing increasingly inebriated and hurling insults at each other across the table.

When they downsized in 1990, this quasi-gothic atmosphere carried over to Joan and Eric's next residence, on Bryanston Square. When Joan felt she wasn't receiving enough attention from Eric, she would dust her face with white powder so that she looked particularly pale and pretend to be "not well." She would sulk on the sofa, especially if he was preparing for a writing trip, complaining that the nurse and doctors would neglect her. To get him really riled up, she would begin telling stories of her romance with Clark Gable. Mentioning Hitchcock would also do the trick. One evening, as a fair-haired Patricia Gaynor enjoyed an informal dinner with the couple, Joan said to her, "Oh, Hitch would have loved you." When Gaynor inquired further, she replied, "Yeah, he really liked cool blondes, you know." At this, Eric squirmed noticeably. In moments like this one, she harked back to her producing days. She still had a knack for casting and had not forgotten how to stage a scene.

By summer 1994, Joan's mental and physical deterioration had accelerated. It was on Friday, August 12, that Jackie Makkink suspected she was becoming morbidly ill. "She began asking delirious questions," recalls Makkink, who split her time between housekeeping and caregiving. "Then on Sunday evening, she had a coughing attack. She always ate quickly, and she began to choke." The staff called on Eric, who sent for Joan's doctor. He came, settled her down, and left. When the coughing started up again, Joan lay in her double bed, with Jackie and a night nurse by her bedside. The doctor was en route back but wouldn't make it in time. Jackie, anticipating that the end was near, got into the bed with Joan. "I'm not an emotional person," she explains, "but I wanted to say good-bye to her. Then suddenly, she looked at me, gave me a lovely smile, and she closed her eyes." Joan was pronounced dead in the middle of the night on August 14, at the age of eighty-seven. The official cause would be listed as old age.

Eric reacted as though he'd been possessed. Spending time in Joan's room before the removal of her body, he came tearing out. Overcome with grief, he fell to the floor. "He passed out," remembers Jackie. "It took two of us to pick him up. If he'd fallen a few inches to the side, he would have hit his head on a four-inch marble slab." A shot of whiskey brought him to and calmed his nerves.

Faith's daughters, Alexandra Murray and Kate Adamson, were present, along with the house staff, when Joan's body was cremated at the Finchley Cemetery. No formal memorial was held. In obvious distress, Eric dealt with the unfortunate fact that Joan had left no final wishes regarding her remains by instructing Patricia Gaynor "to have her ashes scattered on the crematorium grounds." The Finchley staff honored the request, though they admitted to Gaynor that they found it a bit bizarre. She agreed.

Eric carried on for four more years. "He took his time dying. It's as though he wanted to get everything right, just as he did in life," observes Jackie, who stayed on after Joan's death. On October 22, 1998, sensing the end was near, she made a point of playing the song "Nearer My God to Thee," from the soundtrack of the recent *Titanic* movie, which had been gifted to Eric. (Forty years earlier, Eric had written the script for another *Titanic* retelling, *A Night to Remember*.)

Eric had grown fond of listening to the song in the yard at Bryanston Square. "He passed away as 'Nearer My God to Thee' played quietly in the background," Jackie describes. "Then as I sat alone waiting for the night nurse, a sudden stillness came over me. I was held there by a divine scent, a powerful floral aroma. I didn't want to move." Makkink envisioned the couple's spirits reunited in that moment. The woman who had known Joan so well in her final years could envision nothing less than a movie ending.

From the start, Joan Harrison had sought risk, adventure, and the daily grind of hard work. As a woman born into wealth and privilege, there was little that terrified her more than the easy road. To escape an idle life of coddling and docility, she had chosen a path with a great question mark at the end. She had blazed new trails for women in the Golden Age of Hollywood. She wrote or cowrote eight screenplays, earning two Academy Award nominations. Beyond this, she produced eight feature films, writing uncredited on many of them. She championed women's stories and alternative narrative methods. When she saw openings for expanding the roles of women in the industry, she joined forces with female writers, story editors, studio representatives, agents, and actresses, and teamed with Dorothy Arzner, the only woman director in the studio system at the time.

But it could be said that in television, and specifically with the *Alfred Hitchcock* series and *Suspicion*, Joan truly found her métier. Harrison helped pioneer the new medium. She produced 291 episodes for *Alfred Hitchcock Presents* and *The Alfred Hitchcock Hour*. Under her supervision, the series netted fourteen Emmy nominations and three wins, a Golden Globe, and accolades from the Directors Guild and the Writers Guild. In the additional five series she developed and produced, she took unusual risks with story and repeatedly departed from convention.

Within the demanding timetables and rigors of production, she carved out a way to translate one of her favorite forms—the short story—to a medium for which it was an ideal fit. She proved to be one of the most efficient and well-read executives in the industry—and one of the best at cultivating talent, bringing along a generation of maverick writers and directors.

Even as her career waned, she was prescient about the direction film and television would soon take, anticipating a robust market for the female detective genre. Joan was attuned to the feminist movement she saw forming in the mid-1960s. She was also vocal in her support of women's demands for equality. "Facts are facts," she told an interviewer, "and equal rights are one of them. It's inevitable. . . . Just remember, too, that women wouldn't have won if they hadn't been militant. I myself would prefer to win the battle by other than militant ways, but if it is not possible to do this—I say you better get militant!" It's a call that resonates to this day.

ACKNOWLEDGMENTS

THIS BOOK BEGAN WITH A TIP, which I suspect Joan Harrison would have appreciated. More specifically, it started with a practical lead offered to me years ago by Thomas Schatz, who pointed me to Harrison's missing place in film history. I was taking his graduate course on Alfred Hitchcock at the University of Texas at Austin, where some of Harrison's writing files are housed at the Harry Ransom Center. And so began my quest.

I didn't know then—a couple of decades ago—that I would one day write a book about Joan Harrison. It would take a lot of detours and many projects along the way before I arrived at this destination. But fortune smiled on me, bringing me into contact with an author whose work I'd read and admired for years. Scott Eyman became an instant booster, mentor, and, above all, friend. I am grateful to Scott and his wife, Lynn Kalber, for their encouragement. Molly Haskell has been a remarkable supporter too, most crucially helping me to gain my footing early on.

Indeed, numerous mentors and teachers helped form my approach to this subject. I am especially indebted to Sabrina Barton, Mary Desjardins, Judith Mayne, Terry Moore, Laura Mulvey, and Janet Staiger. I appreciate the ongoing support and collaboration of Vicki Callahan, Michael DeAngelis, Suzanne Leonard, Susan Murray, Diane Negra, Nicole Richter, William Rothman, and Shelley Stamp.

My research has inspired engaging and invaluable conversations with Tom Kemper, Patrick McGilligan, and Eddie Muller. I also thank Jeremy Arnold, Charles Barr, John Kern, Rochelle Miller, Mark Ruff, and Tim Snelson for helpful exchanges of ideas and information.

Norman Lloyd has been an incredible resource and inspiration. "Anything for Joan" is his resounding refrain. Measured by his admiration, she surely must have been someone to behold. It was also a pleasure to become acquainted with Joan Juliet Buck, who had a flair for evoking the Joan she had known in decades past. Monika Henreid offered rich insight into Harrison, becoming a terrific friend in the process.

I am grateful to Dr. Kate Adamson, Joan Harrison's niece, for providing details that no one else could, and to Andrew Asher, Joan's cousin, whose love of family history and genealogy was an enormous help. And given that there is no official collection

283

of Harrison's papers, I am particularly moved by three women's generous willingness to share their memories. Patricia Gaynor gave fond insights with great care. Jackie Makkink has been a friendly resource, a fount of knowledge, and a pleasure to know. Georgina Williams, who has made every conversation feel like a new adventure, is a gem.

Thanks to Inna Kurtich for generously opening up her home, and to the following people for providing interviews or background research: Ann Blyth, Edie Chanock, Amanda Cockrell, Chris Coppel, Susan Kohner, Peter Lewi, Patricia Hitchcock O'Connell, Christina Olds, and Pat Tone and his son Franchot Tone. A special thanks to the marvelous Allan Glaser, who wasn't obligated to send me materials that substantially improved this book, but did so anyway. I'm also indebted to those who gave me interviews before they passed away: Jay Presson Allen, Eleanor Kilgallen, Carol Lynley, and Joseph Stefano.

I'd like to single out Mary Troath, an ace researcher whom Pat McGilligan was kind enough to point me to. What can I say? Mary is no less than Sherlock Holmes *and* Dr. Watson, Nancy Drew, and *Law & Order: SVU*'s Olivia Benson all rolled into one.

David Rose, writer and Surrey historian, came through on many occasions with stories and materials. He is a treasure. I envy Guildford.

This book would not exist without the assistance of many first-rate archivists and librarians, including: Ned Comstock at the Cinematic Arts Library at the University of Southern California; Barbara Hall, Kristine Krueger, Jenny Romero, and Faye Thompson at the Margaret Herrick Library, Academy of Motion Picture Arts and Sciences; Nathalie Morris and Jo Botting at the British Film Institute; Steve Wilson at the Harry Ransom Center, University of Texas at Austin; Emily Wittenberg at the Louis B. Mayer Library, American Film Institute; the Charles E. Young Library special collections staff at UCLA; Martin Koerber at the Deutsche Kinemathek—Museum für Film und Fernsehen; Sarah Pratt at the Howard Gotlieb Archival Research Center, Boston University; Hilary Swett at the Writers Guild of America; Amanda Stow at the American Heritage Center, University of Wyoming; David Gleason at American Radio History; Ani Boyadjian at the Los Angeles Public Library; Gail Stein in the Historical Collection at the Beverly Hills Public Library; Amanda Ingram in the archive at St. Hugh's College, University of Oxford; Louise Miles, Guildford High School; and Lindsay Silver, Tudor Hall School, now in Oxfordshire.

I appreciate remote research assistance from Margi Tenney, Sarah Kess, Harlan Landry, Skye Cranney, Christina Villamor, and Alyssa Blanco.

I thank Jonathan Briehl, Karli Evans, the Biscayne Park Village crew who carried me through, and the Brockway Memorial Library staff in Miami Shores, who welcomed me with a smile into their quiet room on those afternoons that I managed to make it.

I'm grateful to Stephanie McNulty and Mary Colvin for their enduring friendship, to Kay Carsto-Trotsek for helping me put all the pieces together, and to those who never failed to ask how the book was going, among them: Grace Barnes, Margaret Cardillo, Nat Chediak, Ana Francois, Mitchell Kaplan, Konstantia Kontaxis, Steven Krams, John Lantigua, Duba Leibell, Tom Musca, Dennis Scholl, Ed Talavera, Rechna Varma, and Jim Virga.

This book was supported by a short-term residency in the Writers Room at the Betsy. Thanks to Deborah Briggs and the attentive staff at the Betsy.

Funding support was provided through a University of Miami Provost's Research Award and a UM School of Communication Creative Activity and Research Award through the Center for Communication, Culture, and Change. I would like to personally acknowledge the abiding moral support and enthusiasm of Greg Shepherd, dean of the School of Communication while the majority of this book was written. I'm glad for the guidance of Karin Wilkins, who is the current dean of the SoC.

I'm grateful to Susan Morgan, associate provost for research development at UM, for fostering this project. I extend my gratitude to my tremendous colleagues in the Department of Cinema and Interactive Media and staff members Carolyn Lopez (a.k.a. Wonder Woman) and Joselyn Garcia (a.k.a. Captain Marvel). I've also had the opportunity to work with outstanding students at the University of Miami, and their shrewd insights have contributed to this book. I thank the following students for various forms of research assistance: Katlyn Aviles, Sheeva Yamuna Dubey, Tatiana Faria, Annissa Omran, and Ramon Enrique Febus (a wiz at compiling and aggregating data). I owe a special debt to Kerli Kirch Schneider, who hung in there the longest, beginning with a Guildford Lewis Carroll tour and ending with date-checking for the filmography.

Thanks to my agent, the peerless Eric Myers, who took a chance on this project. By some miracle, Yuval Taylor, while at Chicago Review Press, was as sparked by the possibilities of *Phantom Lady* as I was. A warm thanks to my editor Devon Freeny, Kara Rota, and everyone else at Chicago Review Press. Devon and Kara are a dream to work with, and so is Chicago Review Press.

Some of us are blessed with people in our lives who spot qualities in us that we don't quite (yet) see in ourselves. They tend to us with special care. I think my aunt Barbara Jowaisas intuited that I was passionate about film and women well before I did. She nurtured this along, and for good reason—perhaps for her own reasons as well. Aunt Barbara has passed on, but I cherish all the gifts she gave me, whether in little packages, or from the heart, or in spirit. May she live on in this book.

I thank my father, Ken Lane, who imparts wisdom, openness and a Zen philosophy on everyone he encounters and whom I have the luxury of knowing close up. Thanks to the rest of the Lane family—Deborah, Kevin, and Kate—for their encouragement.

To my mother, Gretchen Gaines, I owe deep gratitude for her infinite patience. She buoyed me through this very long process. My fervent desire to untangle Joan Harrison's life must have seeds in a conversation my mother and I began long ago, reaching back generations to the half-hidden tales of the women in our family. Thanks also go to the inimitable Saul Weiner, Valri Gaines Hamilton, Lisa Balkanli, and everyone in the Gaines set, and to my in-laws, Hilda González and Gaspar González Sr., who provide unqualified support in all things.

Finally, I am grateful to my son, Sebastián, who shines his light on my every day. And to my husband, Gaspar González, a consummate storyteller, my champion, and my love. When the contours of *Phantom Lady* first took shape, he instantly took to the idea, and he cheered me on to the end. And, wonder of all wonders, he never tired of hearing about Joan. I couldn't have done it without you, G.

FILMOGRAPHY

Film

1937

November 1937

Young and Innocent (alternative US title: *The Girl Was Young*)

As development assistant. Producer: Edward "Ted" Black. Director: Alfred Hitchcock. Screenplay by: Charles Bennett, Edwin Greenwood, and Anthony Armstrong, based on the novel *A Shilling for Candles* by Josephine Tey (pen name of Elizabeth MacKintosh). Continuity: Alma Reville. Dialogue: Gerald Savory. Photography: Bernard Knowles. Art Director: Alfred Junge. Editor: Charles Frend. Assistant Director: Pen Tennyson. Costumes: Marianne. Musical Director: Louis Levy.

Cast: Nova Pilbeam (Erica Burgoyne), Derrick de Marney (Robert Tisdall), Percy Marmont (Colonel Burgoyne), Edward Rigby (Old Will), Mary Clare (Aunt Mary), John Longden (Detective Inspector Kent), George Curzon (Guy), Basil Radford (Uncle Basil), Pamela Carme (Christine Clay).

B&W, Gaumont-British, 84 mins.

1938

November 1, 1938

The Lady Vanishes

As development assistant. Producer: Edward "Ted" Black. Director: Alfred Hitchcock. Screenplay by: Sidney Gilliat and Frank Launder, based on the novel *The Wheel Spins* by Ethel Lina White. Continuity: Alma Reville. Photography: John J. Cox. Art Director: Alex Vetchinsky. Editor: R. E. Dearing. Assistant Director: Tom D. Connochie. Musical Director: Louis Levy.

Cast: Margaret Lockwood (Iris Henderson), Michael Redgrave (Gilbert), Paul Lukas (Dr. Hartz), Dame May Whitty (Miss Froy), Cecil Parker (Mr. Todhunter), Linden

Travers (Mrs. Todhunter), Naunton Wayne (Caldicott), Basil Radford (Charters), Mary Clare (Baroness).
B&W, Gainsborough Pictures / Gaumont-British, 97 mins.

1939

October 13, 1939
Jamaica Inn
As cowriter. Producer: Erich Pommer and Charles Laughton (uncredited). Director: Alfred Hitchcock. Screenplay by: Sidney Gilliat and Joan Harrison, based on the novel by Daphne du Maurier. Dialogue: Sidney Gilliat. Additional Dialogue: J. B. Priestley. Photography: Bernard Knowles and Harry Stradling Sr. Art Director: Tom Morahan. Editor: Robert Hamer. Assistant Director: Roy Goddard. Costumes: Molly McArthur. Music: Eric Fenby. Special Effects: Harry Watt.
Cast: Charles Laughton (Sir Humphrey Pengallan), Horace Hodges (Chadwick), Maureen O'Hara (Mary Yellan), Hay Petrie (Sam), Frederick Piper (Davis), Emlyn Williams (Harry the Peddler), Herbert Lomas (Dowland), Clare Greet (Granny Tremarney).
B&W, Mayflower Pictures / Paramount Pictures, 98 mins.

1940

April 12, 1940
Rebecca
As cowriter. Producer: David O. Selznick. Director: Alfred Hitchcock. Screenplay by: Robert E. Sherwood and Joan Harrison, based on the novel by Daphne du Maurier. Adaptation by: Philip MacDonald and Michael Hogan. Photography: George Barnes. Art Director: Lyle R. Wheeler. Editor: Hal C. Kern. Assistant Director: Edmond F. Bernoudy. Music: Franz Waxman. Special Effects: Jack Cosgrove.
Cast: Laurence Olivier (Maxim DeWinter), Joan Fontaine (the Second Mrs. DeWinter), George Sanders (Jack Favell), Judith Anderson (Mrs. Danvers), Nigel Bruce (Major Giles Lacy), Reginald Denny (Frank Crawley), C. Aubrey Smith (Colonel Julyan), Gladys Cooper (Beatrice Lacy).
B&W, Selznick International Pictures / United Artists, 130 mins.

August 16, 1940
Foreign Correspondent
As cowriter. Producer: Walter Wanger. Director: Alfred Hitchcock. Screenplay by: Charles Bennett and Joan Harrison. Dialogue: James Hilton and Robert Benchley. Photography: Rudolph Maté. Art Director: Alexander Golitzen. Editor: Dorothy Spencer.

Assistant Director: Edmond F. Bernoudy. Costumes: I. Magnin & Co. Music: Alfred Newman. Special Effects: Paul Eagler.

Cast: Joel McCrea (Johnny Jones, a.k.a. Huntley Haverstock), Laraine Day (Carol Fisher), Herbert Marshall (Stephen Fisher), George Sanders (Scott ffolliott), Albert Bassermann (Van Meer), Robert Benchley (Stebbins), Edmund Gwenn (Rowley), Eduardo Ciannelli (Mr. Krug).

B&W, Walter Wanger Productions / United Artists, 120 mins.

1941

November 14, 1941

Suspicion

As cowriter. Producer: Harry E. Edington. Director: Alfred Hitchcock. Screenplay by: Samson Raphaelson, Joan Harrison, and Alma Reville, based on the novel *Before the Fact* by Francis Iles (pen name of Anthony Berkeley Cox). Photography: Harry Stradling Sr. Art Director: Van Nest Polglase. Editor: William Hamilton. Assistant Director: Dewey Starkey. Costumes: Edward Stevenson. Music: Franz Waxman. Special Effects: Vernon L. Walker.

Cast: Cary Grant (Johnnie), Joan Fontaine (Lina), Cedric Hardwicke (General McLaidlaw), Nigel Bruce (Beaky), Dame May Whitty (Mrs. McLaidlaw), Isabel Jeans (Mrs. Newsham), Heather Angel (Ethel), Auriol Lee (Isobel Sedbusk).

B&W, RKO Radio Pictures, 99 mins.

1942

April 24, 1942

Saboteur

As cowriter. Producers: Frank Lloyd, Jack H. Skirball, and John Houseman (uncredited). Director: Alfred Hitchcock. Screenplay by: Peter Viertel, Joan Harrison, and Dorothy Parker. Photography: Joseph A. Valentine. Art Director: Jack Otterson. Editors: Otto Ludwig and Edward Curtiss (uncredited). Assistant Director: Fred Frank. Music: Frank Skinner. Special Effects: John Fulton.

Cast: Pricilla Lane (Patricia Martin), Robert Cummings (Barry Kane), Otto Kruger (Charles Tobin), Alan Baxter (Freeman), Clem Bevans (Nielson), Norman Lloyd (Frank Fry), Alma Kruger (Mrs. Henrietta Sutton), Vaughan Glaser (Philip Martin).

B&W, Frank Lloyd Productions / Universal Pictures, 108 mins.

1943

July 29, 1943

First Comes Courage

As cowriter. Producer: Harry Joe Brown. Directors: Dorothy Arzner and Charles Vidor (uncredited). Screenplay by: Joan Harrison (uncredited), Melvin Levy, and Lewis Meltzer, based on the novel *The Commandos* by Elliot Arnold. Adaptation by: George Sklar. Photography: Joseph Walker. Art Directors: Lionel Banks and Rudolph Sternad. Editor: Viola Lawrence. Assistant Director: William Mull. Music: Ernst Toch. Cast: Merle Oberon (Nicole Larsen), Brian Aherne (Captain Allan Lowell), Carl Esmond (Major Paul Dichter), Isobel Elsom (Rose Lindstrom), Fritz Leiber (Dr. Aanrud). *B&W, Columbia Pictures, 88 mins.*

1944

January 28, 1944

Phantom Lady

As producer and cowriter. Producer: Joan Harrison. Director: Robert Siodmak. Screenplay by: Bernard C. Schoenfeld and Joan Harrison (uncredited), based on the novel by William Irish (pen name of Cornell Woolrich). Photography: Elwood "Woody" Bredell. Art Directors: John B. Goodman and Robert Clatworthy. Editor: Arthur Hilton. Assistant Directors: Seward Webb and Will Sheldon (uncredited). Costumes: Vera West. Hat Designer: Kenneth Hopkins. Musical Director: Hans J. Salter. Cast: Franchot Tone (Jack Marlow), Ella Raines (Carol "Kansas" Richman), Alan Curtis (Scott Henderson), Aurora Miranda (Estela Monteiro), Tomas Gomez (Inspector Burgess), Fay Helm (Ann Terry), Elisha Cook Jr. (Cliff Milburn), Andrew Tombes (Bartender), Regis Toomey (Detective), Joseph Crehan (Detective). *B&W, Universal Pictures, 87 mins.*

July 24, 1944

The Seventh Cross

As cowriter. Producers: Pandro S. Berman and Edwin H. Knopf (uncredited). Director: Fred Zinnemann. Screenplay by: Helen Deutsch and Joan Harrison (uncredited), based on the novel by Anna Seghers. Photography: Karl Freund. Art Directors: Cedric Gibbons and Leonid Vasian. Editor: Thomas Richards. Assistant Director: Horace Hough. Costumes: Irene. Music: Roy Webb. Cast: Spencer Tracy (George Heisler), Signe Hasso (Toni), Hume Cronyn (Paul Roeder), Jessica Tandy (Liesel Roeder), Agnes Moorehead (Madame Marelli), Herbert Rudley (Franz Marnet), Felix Bressart (Poldi Schlamm), Ray Collins (Wallau). *B&W, MGM, 112 mins.*

November 21, 1944

Dark Waters

As producer and cowriter. Producers: Benedict Bogeaus, James Nasser, and Joan Harrison (uncredited). Director: Andre de Toth. Screenplay by: Marian B. Cockrell, Joan Harrison, and John Huston (uncredited), based on the novel by Francis M. Cockrell and Marian B. Cockrell. Additional Dialogue: Arthur T. Horman. Photography: Archie Stout and John J. Mescall. Art Director: Charles Odds. Editor: James Smith. Assistant Director: Joseph Depew. Costumes: Greta. Music: Miklós Rózsa. Special Effects: Harry Redmond Jr.

Cast: Merle Oberon (Leslie Calvin), Franchot Tone (Dr. George Grover), Thomas Mitchell (Mr. Sydney), Fay Bainter (Aunt Emily), Elisha Cook Jr. (Cleeve), John Qualen (Uncle Norbert), Rex Ingram (Pearson Jackson), Nina Mae McKinney (Florella).

B&W, Benedict Bogeaus / United Artists, 90 mins.

1945

August 17, 1945

The Strange Affair of Uncle Harry (alternative title: *Uncle Harry*)

As producer. Producers: Charles K. Feldman and Joan Harrison. Director: Robert Siodmak. Screenplay by: Stephen Longstreet, based on the play *Uncle Harry* by Thomas Job. Adaptation by: Keith Winter. Photography: Paul Ivano. Art Directors: John B. Goodman and Eugène Lourié. Editor: Arthur Hilton. Assistant Director: Melville Shyer. Costumes: Travis Banton. Musical Director: Hans J. Salter. Special Effects: John P. Fulton.

Cast: George Sanders (Harry Melville Quincey), Geraldine Fitzgerald (Lettie Quincey), Ella Raines (Deborah Brown), Sara Allgood (Nona), Moyna MacGill (Hester Quincey), Samuel S. Hinds (Dr. Adams).

B&W, Universal Pictures, 80 mins.

1946

November 11, 1946

Nocturne

As producer and cowriter. Executive Producer: Jack J. Gross. Producer: Joan Harrison. Director: Edwin L. Marin. Screenplay by: Jonathan Latimer and Joan Harrison (uncredited), based on a story by Frank Fenton and Rowland Brown. Photography: Harry J. Wild. Art Director: Albert S. D'Agostino. Production Designer: Robert F. Boyle. Editor: Elmo Williams. Assistant Director: James H. Anderson. Costumes: Renié. Music: Leigh Harline. Special Effects: Russell A. Cully and Linwood Dunn (uncredited). Montage: Harold Palmer. Technical Adviser: Barney Ruditsky.

Cast: George Raft (Joe Warne), Lynn Bari (Frances Ransom), Virginia Huston (Carol Page), Joseph Pevney (Ned "Fingers" Ford), Myrna Dell (Susan Flanders), Edward Ashley (Keith Vincent), Walter Sande (Halberson), Mabel Paige (Mrs. Warne), Queenie Smith (Queenie).
B&W, RKO Radio Pictures, 87 mins.

1947

July 16, 1947
They Won't Believe Me
As producer. Executive Producer: Jack J. Gross. Producer: Joan Harrison. Director: Irving Pichel. Screenplay by: Jonathan Latimer, based on a story by Gordon McDonell. Photography: Harry J. Wild. Art Directors: Albert S. D'Agostino and Robert F. Boyle. Editor: Elmo Williams. Assistant Director: Harry D'Arcy. Costumes: Edward Stevenson. Music: Roy Webb. Special Effects: Russell A. Cully.
Cast: Robert Young (Lawrence "Larry" Ballentine), Susan Hayward (Verna Carlson), Jane Greer (Janice Bell), Rita Johnson (Greta Ballentine), Tom Powers (Trenton), George Tyne (Lieutenant Carr), Don Beddoe (Thomason).
B&W, RKO Radio Pictures, 95 mins.

October 8, 1947
Ride the Pink Horse
As producer and cowriter. Producer: Joan Harrison. Director: Robert Montgomery. Screenplay by: Ben Hecht, Charles Lederer, and Joan Harrison (uncredited), based on the novel by Dorothy B. Hughes. Photography: Russell Metty and Maury Gertsman (uncredited). Art Directors: Robert F. Boyle and Bernard Herzbrun. Editor: Ralph Dawson. Assistant Director: John Sherwood. Costumes: Yvonne Wood. Music: Frank Skinner.
Cast: Robert Montgomery (Lucky Gagin), Wanda Hendrix (Pila), Andrea King (Marjorie Lundeen), Thomas Gomez (Pancho), Art Smith (Bill Retz), Rita Conde (Carla), Iris Flores (Maria), Grandon Rhodes (Mr. Edison), Fred Clark (Frank Hugo).
B&W, Universal-International, 101 mins.

1949

September 24, 1949
Once More, My Darling
As producer. Producer: Joan Harrison. Directors: Robert Montgomery and Michael Gordon (uncredited). Screenplay by: Robert Carson, based on his story "Come Be My

Love." Additional Dialogue: Oscar Saul. Photography: Franz Planer. Art Directors: Bernard Herzbrun and Robert Clatworthy. Editor: Ralph Dawson. Assistant Director: John Sherwood. Costumes: Orry-Kelly. Music: Elizabeth Firestone. Special Effects: David S. Horsely.

Cast: Robert Montgomery (Collier "Collie" Laing), Ann Blyth (Marita "Killer" Connell), Jane Cowl (Mrs. Laing), Charles McGraw (Herman Schmelz), Taylor Holmes (Jed Connell), Roland Winters (Colonel Head), Lillian Randolph (Mamie).

B&W, Neptune Productions / Universal-International, 92 mins.

1950

January 25, 1950 (UK); August 26, 1950 (US)

Eye Witness (alternative UK title: *Your Witness*)

As producer and cowriter. Executive Producer: David E. Rose. Producer: Joan Harrison. Director: Robert Montgomery. Screenplay by: Hugo Butler, Ian McLellan Hunter, and Joan Harrison (uncredited). Additional Dialogue: William Douglas-Home. Photography: Gerald Gibbs. Art Director: Ralph Brinton. Editor: Lito Carruthers. Assistant Director: Kenneth K. Rick. Costumes: Phyllis Dalton. Music: Malcolm Arnold.

Cast: Robert Montgomery (Adam Heyward), Leslie Banks (Colonel Roger Summerfield), Felix Aylmer (British Judge), Andrew Cruickshank (Sir Adrian Horth), Patricia Cutts (Alex Summerfield), Harcourt Williams (Richard Beamish), Ann Stephens (Sandy Summerfield).

B&W, Coronado Productions / Warner Bros. / Eagle-Lion, 100 mins.

1951

April 17, 1951

Circle of Danger

As producer. Executive Producer: David E. Rose. Producer: Joan Harrison. Director: Jacques Tourneur. Screenplay by: Philip MacDonald. Photography: Oswald Morris and Gilbert Taylor. Art Director: Duncan Sutherland. Editor: Alan Osbiston. Assistant Director: Kenneth K. Rick. Costumes: Phyllis Dalton. Music: Robert Farnon. Choreography: Betty Buchel and Philip Buchel.

Cast: Ray Milland (Clay Douglas), Patricia Roc (Elspeth Graham), Marius Goring (Sholto Lewis), Hugh Sinclair (Hamish McArran), Naunton Wayne (Reggie Sinclair), Edward Rigby (Idwal Llewellyn).

B&W, Coronado Productions / RKO Radio Pictures / Eagle-Lion, 86 mins.

Television

Schlitz Playhouse (1952, 1957)

Season 1

#46 "Double Exposure" (August 15, 1952)

As cowriter. Producer: Edward Lewis. Director: Robert Boyle. Writers: Joan Harrison and Philip MacDonald, based on the story by Ben Hecht. Photography: Paul Ivano. Art Director: Charles D. Hall.

Cast: John Beal, Amanda Blake, John Brown.

B&W, Meridian Productions for CBS, filmed at Revue Studios, 30 mins.

Season 6

#32 "The Traveling Corpse" (May 3, 1957)

As producer. Producer: Joan Harrison. Director: James Neilson. Writers: Joel Murcott, based on a story by Norman Matson. Photography: William A. Sickner. Art Director: John Meehan.

Cast: Robert Anderson, John Baragrey, Jane Buchanan.

B&W, Revue Studios for CBS, filmed at Revue Studios, 30 mins.

Janet Dean, Registered Nurse (1954–1955)*

Season 1 (39 scheduled episodes)

Premiered February 1, 1954 (Denver, CO); March 23, 1954 (New York City)

Retitled *The Ella Raines Show*, October 12, 1954

As producer. Producer: Joan Harrison. Photography: J. Burgi Contner. Art Directors: Hank Aldrich and Robert Gundlach. Editor: Lora Hays. Technical Adviser: Harriet Stambach.

Cast: Ella Raines (Janet Dean).

B&W, Cornwall Productions / WRCA Productions for first-run syndication, filmed at Marion Parsonnet Studios, distributed by Motion Pictures for Television (MPTV), sponsored by Emerson Drug Company, 30 mins.

---

* The information presented here is the most complete and accurate account of the credits for the series to date, aggregated from the Library of Congress, the *Ross Reports* Television Index, and the William Dozier Papers at the American Heritage Center. Many public sources offer either incorrect or conflicting details, which is not surprising given the inaccessibility of records and the show's limited availability. Four episodes of the series exist in archives; several more may be held by personal collectors. Most installments are presumed lost.

Known Episodes*:

#1 "The Kennedy Case"
Director: Jack Gage. Writer: Franz Spencer (pen name of Franz Schulz).
Cast: Stella Andrew, Curtis Cooksey, Charles Nolte, Dorothy Peterson.

#2 "The Goodale Case"
Director: Peter Godfrey. Writer: Victor Wolfson.
Cast: Margaret Wycherly, William Prince, Patty McCormack, Katherine Anderson, David Winters, Anne Ives.

#3 "The Kimball Case" (alternative title: "The Kittering Case")
Director: Unknown.† Writer: Unknown.
Cast: Louise Allbritton, Malcolm Brodrick.

#4 "The Bennett Case"
Director: Unknown. Writer: Unknown.
Cast: Darren McGavin, Cloris Leachman, Hildy Parks.

#5 "The Edwards Case"
Director: Robert Boyle. Writer: Sarett Rudley.
Cast: Murray Matheson, Melville Cooper, Marcel Hillaire, John McGovern, Alan Haines.

#6 "The Johnson Case"
Director: Robert Boyle. Writer: James P. Cavanagh.
Cast: Everett Sloan, Janet Wood, Phillip Pine, Leora Thatcher, Ann Sorg, Walter Kohler.

---

* Titles are available for thirty-six of the thirty-nine episodes originally scheduled to be produced. They are listed here in the order in which they aired, though exact air dates are not available; because the series aired in syndication rather than on a network, dates varied from market to market. There's no evidence that the final three episodes ever aired; it's possible that the episode order was cut and they were never even filmed.

† NOTE ON DIRECTORS: Following the pilot, which was helmed by Jack Gage, Peter Godfrey and Robert Boyle were contracted to direct twelve episodes (with Robert Aldrich's name mentioned in trade publications early on). Episodes did not necessarily air in the order they were produced. Godfrey was assigned the first eight, then stepped down. Boyle completed the remaining four. The second set of thirteen episodes were assigned to Robert Boyle and James Neilson. (According to Boyle, he and Neilson directed alternating episodes.) Little documentation exists concerning the direction of the final set of episodes, although Boyle had departed by then and some records indicate that Neilson covered those episodes.

#7 "The Erskine Case"
Director: Peter Godfrey. Writer: William Kendall Clarke.
Cast: Don Hanmer, Nellie Burt, Addison Richards, Gerald O'Loughlin, Truman Smith, Gloria Scott Backe, Logan Field, Dorothy Blackburn, Jim Nolan.

#8 "The Leslie Case"
Director: Unknown. Writer: Harry Junkin.
Cast: Cathleen Nesbitt, Shepperd Strudwick, Patty McCormack, Charles Nolte, Lisa Howard, Allen Tower.

#9 "The Garcia Case"
Director: James Neilson. Writer: Victor Wolfson.
Cast: Sal Mineo, Will Kuluva, Miriam Goldina, Adnia Rice, Pidge Jameson, Dehl Berti.

#10 "The Hutchins Case"
Director: Unknown. Writer: Harry Junkin.
Cast: Natalie Schafer, Ruth Warrick, Iggie Wolfington, Norma Crane, Philip Bourneuf, Tony Bickley, Alan Manson, Charles McClelland.

#11 "The Banks Case"
Director: Unknown. Writer: Max Wilk.
Cast: Katharine Bard, Henry Jones, John Marriott, Robert H. Harris, Robert Baines, Ann Dere, Robert Webber.

#12 "The Sloane Case"
Director: Unknown. Writers: Marie Baumer and Victor Wolfson.
Cast: Natalie Schafer, Carrie Bridewell, Addison Richards, June Hunt, Justice Watson, Donald Curtis, Charles Quinlivan, Rusty Lane, Maurice Shrog.

#13 "The Walsh Case" (alternative title: "The Waldo Case" or "The Wadelo Case")
Director: Unknown. Writer: Sarett Rudley.
Cast: Paul Langton, Georgann Johnson, Susan Hallaran, Eulabelle Moore, Gerald O'Loughlin, E. A. Krumschmidt, Leona Powers, Charles Dingle.

#14 "The Jinx Nurse Case"
Director: Peter Godfrey. Writer: Cameron Kay (pen name of Gore Vidal).
Cast: Anne Sargent, Lenore Lonergan, Ralph Stanley, Ralph Sumpter, Wayne Carson, Richard Davalos, John Hudson, Betsy Palmer, and Laurinda Barrett.

#15 "The Van Horn Case"
Director: James Neilson. Writer: Max Wilk.
Cast: Eva Marie Saint, Darren McGavin, Ginger McManus, Sara Floyd, Charles Thompson, Harrison Dowd, Leora Thatcher, Griff Evans, Lester Lonergan.

#16 "The Coleman Case"
Director: Unknown. Writer: Max Wilk.
Cast: Bethel Leslie, Sara Seegar, Frank Overton, Isobel Elsom, June Walker.

#17 "The Randall Case"
Director: Unknown. Writer: Lenore Coffee.
Cast: Geraldine Brooks, John Baragrey, Doris Dowling, Vinton Hayworth, Melissa Weston, Frank Milan, Spencer Davis.

#18 "The Talbot Case"
Director: Unknown. Writer: Max Wilk.
Cast: Meg Mundy, Lenore Lonergan, Russell Hardie, John McGovern.

#19 "The Martinez Case"
No credits available.

#20 "The Gillis Case"*
Director: Unknown. Writer: Sylvia Berger.
Cast: Mona Knox, Scott McKay, Jack Warden, June Martel, Russell Hardie, Alan Foster.

#21 "The Blake Case"
Director: Unknown. Writer: William Kendall Clarke.
Cast: Ed Begley Sr., Steve Holland, Jim McKay, John Archer, Frederick O'Neal, Cliff Hall, John O'Hare.

#22 "The Norton Case"
Director: Unknown. Writer: Harry Junkin.
Cast: Paul Langton, Hildy Parks, Alan Manson.

---

* To date, "The Gillis Case" has been missing in official listings such as IMDB, though some sources have cited the title as unknown and noted the synopsis (Nurse Dean convinces a model to make new changes after her face is burned in an explosion). "The Gillis Case" aired in August 1954.

#23 "The Lewis Case"
Director: Unknown. Writer: Irving Elman.
Cast: Philip Kenneally, Dan Morgan, Frank Biro, Raymond Bramley, Arthur Hanson, Manny Seamon, Howard Soligny, James Seamon.

#24 "The Bradshaw Case"
Director: Unknown. Writer: Irving Elman.
Cst: John Baragrey, Victor Rendina, Virginia Gilmore, Haila Kirkland, Michael Tolan, Joanne Tree, Douglas Rutherford, Dennis Bohan, Mary Barclay.

#25 "The Applegate Case"
Director: James Neilson. Writer: Irving Elman.
Cast: Cathleen Nesbitt, Cameron Prud'Homme.

#26 "The Winters Case"
Director: Unknown. Writer: Sarett Rudley.
Cast: Rex Thompson, Katharine Bard, Edward Binns, Darryl Richard, Carl Frank, Jonathan Harris, Sam Schwartz.

#27 "The Gage Case"
No credits available.

#28 "The Burlingame Case"
Director: James Neilson. Writer: Patricia Coleman.
Cast: John Kerr, Charles Dingle, Marjorie Barrett, Stefan Schnabel, Francis Compton, Ann Dere, Frances Meehan.

#29 "The Bellamy Case"
No credits available.

#30 "The Gomez Case"
Director: Peter Godfrey. Writer: Max Wilk.
Cast: Darren McGavin, Grace Valentine, Donald McClelland, Lewis Charles, Julian Noa, Philip Hepburn, Leonard Elliot, Lothar Rewalt.

#31 "The Benton Case"
Director: Unknown. Writer: Victor Wolfson.
Cast: Shepperd Strudwick, Gerald Price, Irma Sandrey, Frank Hobi, Miriam Goldina.

#32 "The Murch Case"*
Director: Unknown. Writer: Victor Wolfson.
Cast: Doro Merande, Martin Huston, Harry Bellaver, Frieda Altman, Donald McClelland, Pidgie Jamieson, Jim Nolan.

#33 "The Baker Case"
Director: Unknown. Writer: Sarett Rudley.
Cast: Olive Deering, Susan Hallaran, Patty McCormack, Lawrence Fletcher, Stephen Chase.

#34 "The Jennings Case"
Director: Unknown. Writer: Harry Junkin.
Cast: Lorne Greene, John Newland, Jeff Harris, Viola Roache.

#35 "The Barton Case"
Director: Unknown. Writer: Sarett Rudley.
Cast: Martin E. Brooks, Phyllis Hill, Harold Vermilyea, Mikhail Rasumny, Paul Zukofsky, Douglas Rutherford.

#36 "The Putnam Case"
Director: James Neilson. Writer: William Kendall Clarke.
Cast: Kim Hunter (Nurse Sylvia Peters), Leo Penn, Vinton Hayworth, Clarence Derwent.

Alfred Hitchcock Presents (1955–1962)

1955–1956
Season 1 (39 episodes)
Sundays, 9:30–10:00 PM on CBS
As associate producer. Associate Producer: Joan Harrison. Select Directors: Alfred Hitchcock, James Neilson, and Robert Stevens. Select Writers: Francis M. Cockrell, Marian B. Cockrell, Robert C. Dennis, Louis Pollock, Sarett Rudley, Harold Swanton, and Alexander Woollcott. Writer, Opening/Closing Monologues: James B. Allardice. Photography: Reggie Lanning, John L. Russell, and Lester Shorr. Art Directors: Martin Obzina and James Redd. Editorial Supervisor: Richard G. Wray. Editor: Edward W. Williams.

---

* "The Murch Case" has been missing from previous episode listings, though some sources have cited the title as unknown and referenced the synopsis (Janet Dean assists a neighborhood boy and his friends in the search for a rabid dog). "The Murch Case" aired in December 1954.

Assistant Directors: Richard Birnie, Jack Corrick, Jim Hogan, and Jack Voglin. Wardrobe Supervisor: Vincent Dee. Music Supervisor: Stanley Wilson. Host: Alfred Hitchcock. *B&W, Shamley Productions for CBS, filmed at Revue Studios, in association with MCA-TV, sponsored by Bristol-Myers, 30 mins.*

Harrison produced all 39 episodes of season 1. Notable episodes include:
#1 "Revenge" (October 2, 1955)
#2 "Premonition" (October 9, 1955)
#5 "Into Thin Air" (October 30, 1955)
#7 "Breakdown" (November 13, 1955)
#8 "Our Cook's a Treasure" (November 20, 1955)
#9 "The Long Shot" (November 27, 1955)
#10 "The Case of Mr. Pelham" (December 4, 1955)
#11" Guilty Witness" (December 11, 1955)
#16 "You Got to Have Luck" (January 15, 1956)
#23 "Back for Christmas" (March 4, 1956)
#25 "There Was an Old Woman" (March 18, 1956)
#26 "Whodunit" (March 25, 1956)
#27 "Help Wanted" (April 1, 1956)
#30 "Never Again" (April 22, 1956)
#32 "The Baby Sitter" (May 6, 1956)
#38 "The Creeper" (June 17, 1956)

1956–1957
Season 2 (39 episodes)
Sundays, 9:30–10:00 PM on CBS
As associate producer. Associate Producer: Joan Harrison. Select Directors: Jules Bricken, Herschel Daugherty, Alfred Hitchcock, and Robert Stevens. Select Writers: James P. Cavanagh, Francis M. Cockrell, Marian B. Cockrell, Ellery Queen, and Sarett Rudley. Writer, Opening/Closing Monologues: James B. Allardice. Photography: Reggie Lanning, Lionel Lindon, John L. Russell, Lester Shorr, Bud Thackery, and John F. Warren. Art Directors: John Lloyd and Martin Obzina. Editorial Supervisor: Richard G. Wray. Editor: Edward W. Williams. Assistant Directors: Richard Birnie, Jack Corrick, Hilton A. Green, Jim Hogan, and Ronald R. Rondell. Wardrobe Supervisor: Vincent Dee. Music Supervisor: Stanley Wilson. Host: Alfred Hitchcock.
B&W, Shamley Productions for CBS, filmed at Revue Studios, in association with MCA-TV, sponsored by Bristol-Myers, 30 mins.

Harrison produced all 39 episodes of season 2. Notable episodes include:

#1 "Wet Saturday" (September 30, 1956)

#2 "Fog Closing In" (October 7, 1956)

#8 "Conversation over a Corpse" (November 18, 1956)

#13 "Mr. Blanchard's Secret" (December 23, 1956)

#16 "Nightmare in 4-D" (January 13, 1957)

#17 "My Brother, Richard" (January 20, 1957)

#18 "The Manacled" (January 27, 1957)

#20 "Malice Domestic" (February 10, 1957)

#22 "The End of Indian Summer" (February 24, 1957)

#23 "One for the Road" (March 3, 1957)

#24 "The Cream of the Jest" (March 10, 1957)

#25 "I Killed the Count: Part 1" (March 17, 1957)

#26 "I Killed the Count: Part 2" (March 24, 1957)

#27 "I Killed the Count: Part 3" (March 31, 1957)

#28 "One More Mile to Go" (April 7, 1957)

1957–1958

Season 3 (39 episodes)

Sundays, 9:30–10:00 PM on CBS

As producer. Producer: Joan Harrison. Associate Producer: Norman Lloyd. Select Directors: Robert Altman, Paul Henreid, Arthur Hiller, Alfred Hitchcock, and Robert Stevens. Select Writers: Roald Dahl, Robert C. Dennis, Joel Murcott, Sarett Rudley, and Stirling Silliphant. Writer, Opening/Closing Monologues: James B. Allardice. Photography: Joseph F. Biroc, Reggie Lanning, Lionel Lindon, John L. Russell, and John F. Warren. Art Directors: John J. Lloyd and John Meehan. Editorial Supervisor: Richard G. Wray. Editors: Edward W. Williams and Marston Fay. Assistant Directors: Ben Bishop, James H. Brown, Jesse Corallo, Frank Fox, Hilton A. Green, Jim Hogan, George Lollier, Ronald R. Rondell, and Will Sheldon. Wardrobe Supervisor: Vincent Dee. Music Supervisor: Stanley Wilson. Host: Alfred Hitchcock.

B&W, Shamley Productions for CBS, filmed at Revue Studios, in association with MCA-TV, sponsored by Bristol-Myers, 30 mins.

Harrison produced all 39 episodes of season 3. Notable episodes include:

#1 "The Glass Eye" (October 6, 1957)

#3 "The Perfect Crime" (October 20, 1957)

#7 "Enough Rope for Two" (November 17, 1957)

#8 "Last Request" (November 24, 1957)

#9 "The Young One" (December 1, 1957)
#23 "The Right Kind of House" (March 9, 1958)
#26 "Bull in a China Shop" (March 30, 1958)
#28 "Lamb to the Slaughter" (April 13, 1958)
#33 "Post Mortem" (May 18, 1958)
#35 "Dip in the Pool" (June 1, 1958)

1958–1959
Season 4 (36 episodes)
Sundays, 9:30–10:00 PM on CBS
As producer. Producer: Joan Harrison. Associate Producer: Norman Lloyd. Select Directors: Paul Henreid, Arthur Hiller, Alfred Hitchcock, Norman Lloyd, and Robert Stevens. Select Writers: Francis M. Cockrell, Ray Bradbury, Garson Kanin, and Bernard C. Schoenfeld. Writer, Opening/Closing Monologues: James B. Allardice. Photography: Ernest Haller, Lionel Lindon, John L. Russell, and John F. Warren. Art Directors: John J. Lloyd and Arthur Lonergan. Editorial Supervisor: Richard G. Wray. Editor: Edward W. Williams. Assistant Directors: James H. Brown, Charles S. Gould, Hilton A. Green, Ronald R. Rondell, Will Sheldon, Abby Singer, and Dolph Zimmer. Wardrobe Supervisor: Vincent Dee. Music Supervisor: Frederick Herbert. Host: Alfred Hitchcock.
B&W, Shamley Productions for CBS, filmed at Revue Studios, in association with MCA-TV, sponsored by Bristol-Myers, 30 mins.

Harrison produced all 36 episodes of season 4. Notable episodes include:
#1 "Poison" (October 5, 1958)
#3 "The Jokester" (October 19, 1958)
#6 "Design for Loving" (November 9, 1958)
#16 "Out There—Darkness" (January 25, 1959)
#20 "The Diamond Necklace" (February 22, 1959)
#29 "Banquo's Chair" (May 3, 1959)
#32 "Human Interest Story" (May 24, 1959)
#34 "A True Account" (June 7, 1959)

1959–1960
Season 5 (38 episodes)
Sundays, 9:30–10:00 PM on CBS
As producer. Producer: Joan Harrison. Associate Producer: Norman Lloyd. Select Directors: Herschel Daugherty, Hilton A. Green, Arthur Hiller, Alfred Hitchcock, and

Stuart Rosenberg. Select Writers: Charlotte Armstrong, Robert Bloch, Ray Bradbury, and Stirling Silliphant. Writer, Opening/Closing Monologues: James B. Allardice. Photography: Neal Beckner, Lionel Lindon, John L. Russell, and John F. Warren. Art Directors: Raymond Beal, John J. Lloyd, Arthur Lonergan, Martin Obzina, and George Patrick. Editorial Supervisors: David J. O'Connell and Richard G. Wray. Editor: Edward W. Williams. Assistant Directors: Ben Bishop, James H. Brown, Jack Doran, Frank Fox, Hilton A. Green, Frank Losee, and Ronald R. Rondell. Wardrobe Supervisor: Vincent Dee. Music Supervisors: Frederick Herbert and Joseph E. Romero. Host: Alfred Hitchcock.

B&W, Shamley Productions for CBS, filmed at Revue Studios, in association with MCA-TV, sponsored by Clairol and Bristol-Myers, 30 mins.

Harrison produced all 38 episodes of season 5. Notable episodes include:
#1 "Arthur" (September 27, 1959)
#2 "The Crystal Trench" (October 4, 1959)
#10 "Special Delivery" (November 29, 1959)
#15 "Man from the South" (January 3, 1960)
#17 "The Cure" (January 24, 1960)
#20 "The Day of the Bullet" (February 14, 1960)
#22 "Across the Threshold" (February 28, 1960)
#33 "Party Line" (May 29, 1960)
#35 "The Schartz-Metterklume Method" (June 12, 1960)*
#37 "Escape to Sonoita" (June 26, 1960)

1960–1961
Season 6 (38 episodes)
Tuesdays, 8:30–9:00 PM on NBC
As producer. Producer: Joan Harrison. Associate Producer: Norman Lloyd. Select Directors: John Brahm, Paul Henreid, Alfred Hitchcock, Ida Lupino, Stuart Rosenberg, and Don Weis. Select Writers: Charlotte Armstrong, Robert Bloch, John Cheever, Henry Slesar, and Halsted Welles. Writer, Opening/Closing Monologues: James B. Allardice. Photography: Neal Beckner, John L. Russell, and John F. Warren. Art Directors: John J. Lloyd, John Meehan, and Martin Obzina. Editorial Supervisor: David J. O'Connell. Editor: Edward W. Williams. Assistant Directors: George Bisk,

---

* In this episode Patricia Hitchcock makes her final appearance in the series, playing Rose the maid. Chris Coppel, son of author and screenwriter Alec Coppel (*Vertigo, Alfred Hitchcock Presents*), performs an uncredited role as one of the children in the Wellington family.

John Clarke Bowman, James H. Brown, Jack Doran, Frank Fox, Charles S. Gould, Ronald R. Rondell, Will Sheldon, and Wallace Worsley Jr. Wardrobe Supervisor: Vincent Dee. Music Supervisors: Frederick Herbert and Joseph E. Romero. Host: Alfred Hitchcock.

B&W, Shamley Productions for NBC, filmed at Revue Studios, in association with MCA-TV, sponsored by Ford Motor Company and Revlon (alternating), 30 mins.

Harrison produced all 38 episodes of season 6. Notable episodes include:
#1 "Mrs. Bixby and the Colonel's Coat" (September 27, 1960)
#5 "The Five-Forty-Eight" (October 25, 1960)
#10 "Sybilla" (December 6, 1960)
#19 "The Landlady" (February 21, 1961)
#22 "The Horse Player" (March 14, 1961)
#23 "Incident in a Small Jail" (March 21, 1961)
#29 "The Pearl Necklace" (May 2, 1961)
#32 "Self Defense" (May 23, 1961)

1961–1962
Season 7 (39 episodes)
Tuesdays, 8:30–9:00 PM on NBC
As producer. Producer: Joan Harrison. Associate Producer: Norman Lloyd. Select Directors: Alan Crosland Jr., Robert Florey, Bernard Girard, and Alfred Hitchcock. Select Writers: Richard Levinson, William Link, Henry Slesar, and Harold Swanton. Writer, Opening/Closing Monologues: James B. Allardice. Photography: Neal Beckner, Dale Deverman, John L. Russell, and John F. Warren. Art Directors: John J. Lloyd and Martin Obzina. Editorial Department Head: David J. O'Connell. Editor: Edward W. Williams. Assistant Directors: Donald Baer, Lester Wm. Berke, George Bisk, James H. Brown, Edward K. Dodds, Frank Fox, Charles S. Gould, Frank Losee, Ronald R. Rondell, and Wallace Worsley Jr. Wardrobe Supervisor: Vincent Dee. Music Supervisor: Joseph E. Romero. Host: Alfred Hitchcock.

B&W, Shamley Productions for NBC, filmed at Revue Studios, in association with MCA-TV, sponsored by Ford Motor Company and Revlon (alternating), 30 mins.

Harrison produced all 39 episodes of season 7. Notable episodes include:
#2 "Bang! You're Dead" (October 17, 1961)
#10 "Services Rendered" (December 12, 1961)
#11 "The Right Kind of Medicine" (December 19, 1961)
#12 "A Jury of Her Peers" (December 26, 1961)

#29 "The Matched Pearl" (April 24, 1962)
#33 "The Opportunity" (May 22, 1962)
#38 "Where Beauty Lies" (June 26, 1962)
"The Sorcerer's Apprentice" (unnumbered, aired in syndication only)

Suspicion (1957–1958)

Season 1 (20 of 42 episodes)
Mondays, 10:00–11:00 PM on NBC
As associate producer. Executive Producers: Alfred Hitchcock and Alan Miller.* Associate Producer: Joan Harrison.† Photography: Ellsworth Fredericks, Reggie Lanning, John L. Russell, and John F. Warren. Art Directors: Frank Arrigo, John J. Lloyd, and Arthur Lonergan. Editorial Supervisor: Richard G. Wray. Editors: Marston Fay, Daniel A. Nathan, and Edward W. Williams. Wardrobe Supervisor: Vincent Dee. Music Supervisor: Stanley Wilson. Hosts: Dennis O'Keefe and Walter Abel.
B&W, Shamley Productions / Revue Productions / Revue Studios for NBC, filmed at Revue Studios, in association with MCA-TV, 60 mins.

#1 "Four O'Clock" (September 30, 1957)
Director: Alfred Hitchcock. Writer: Francis M. Cockrell, based on a story by Cornell Woolrich.
Cast: Nancy Kelly, E. G. Marshall, Richard Long, Tom Pittman, Harry Dean Stanton.
Shamley Productions / Revue Studios.

#3 "The Other Side of the Curtain" (October 14, 1957)
Director: James Neilson. Writer: James P. Cavanagh, based on the story by Helen McCloy (pen name of Helen Clarkson).
Cast: Donna Reed, Jeff Richards, Herbert Anderson.
Revue Productions / Revue Studios.

---

* *Suspicion* was produced by three different arms within Revue Studios. Shamley Productions was responsible for ten filmed episodes, with Hitchcock as executive producer. Revue Productions filmed ten more episodes, executive produced by Alan Miller. Executive producer S. Mark Smith was responsible for the series' twenty-two live shows, which were produced at NBC Studios in New York.
† Harrison's associate producer credit is misleading in this context. She was performing the responsibilities typical of a television producer for all filmed episodes, whether they were made by Shamley or Revue Productions. She was not involved in the twenty-two live shows, for which Mort Abrahams served as producer.

#5 "The Story of Marjorie Reardon" (October 28, 1957)
Director: John Brahm. Writer: John Kneubuhl, based on a story by Susan Seavy.
Cast: Margaret O'Brien, Rod Taylor, Henry Silva.
Revue Productions / Revue Studios.

#7 "Heartbeat" (November 11, 1957)
Director: Robert Stevens. Writer: Ernest Kinoy, based on a story by Terence John.
Cast: David Wayne, Pat Hingle, Barbara Turner, Warren Beatty, Frank Campanella.
Shamley Productions / Revue Studios.

#9 "The Flight" (November 25, 1957)
Director: James Neilson. Writer: Gene L. Coon and Halsted Welles.
Cast: Audie Murphy, Jack Warden, Everett Sloane, Susan Kohner.
Revue Productions / Revue Studios.

#10 "Rainy Day" (December 2, 1957)
Director: James Neilson. Writer: Michael Pertwee, based on a story by W. Somerset
Maugham.
Cast: Robert Flemyng, George Cole, John Williams, Tom Conway, Arthur Gould-Porter.
Shamley Productions / Revue Studios.

#12 "Doomsday" (December 16, 1957)
Director: Bernard Girard. Writer: Sy Bartlett.
Cast: Dan Duryea, Robert Middleton, Charles Bronson, Edward Binns, Robert Corn-
thwaite.
Revue Productions / Revue Studios.

#15 "Lord Arthur Savile's Crime" (January 13, 1958)
Director: Robert Stevens. Writer: Francis M. Cockrell, based on the story by Oscar Wilde.
Cast: Ronald Howard, Rosemary Harris, Gladys Cooper, Sebastian Cabot, Melville
Cooper.
Shamley Productions / Revue Studios.

#17 "Comfort for the Grave" (January 27, 1958)
Director: Jules Bricken. Writers: Halsey Melone and Virginia Spies, based on the story
by Richard Deming.
Cast: Paul Douglas, Jan Sterling, Anthony Caruso, Herbert Rudley, Lyle Talbot.
Revue Productions / Revue Studios.

#18 "Meeting in Paris" (February 10, 1958)
Director: James Neilson. Writers: Stirling Silliphant and Elliot West, based on a story by Elliot West.
Cast: Rory Calhoun, Jane Greer, Walter Abel, Maurice Marsac, Roger Til.
Shamley Productions / Revue Studios.

#19 "A Touch of Evil" (February 17, 1958)
Director: John Brahm. Writer: Halsted Welles, based on a story by E. J. Kahn Jr. (uncredited).
Cast: Harry Guardino, Audrey Totter, Bethel Leslie, John Carradine, Jacqueline Mayo, Luis Van Rooten.
Revue Productions / Revue Studios.

#23 "The Eye of Truth" (March 17, 1958)
Director: Robert Stevens. Writer: Eric Ambler.
Cast: Ken Clark, Elvera Corona, Joseph Cotten, Leora Dana, Thayer David, George Peppard.
Shamley Productions / Revue Studios.

#25 "The Bull Skinner" (April 7, 1958)
Director: Lewis Milestone. Writer: Ernest Kinoy.
Cast: Rod Steiger, John Beal, Sally Brophy, Harold J. Stone, Perry Lopez.
Shamley Productions / Revue Studios.

#27 "Fraction of a Second" (April 21, 1958)
Director: John Brahm. Writer: Kathleen Hite, based on the story "Split Second" by Daphne du Maurier.
Cast: Bette Davis, Barry Atwater, Marian Seldes, Judson Pratt, Linda Watkins, Whit Bissell, Dorothy Adams.
Revue Productions / Revue Studios.

#28 "The Way Up to Heaven" (April 28, 1958)
Director: Herschel Daugherty. Writer: Marian B. Cockrell, based on the story by Roald Dahl.
Cast: Marion Lorne, Sebastian Cabot, Patricia Smith, Kathryn Givney, Selmer Jackson.
Shamley Productions / Revue Studios.

#30 "Protégé" (May 12, 1958)
Director: Jules Bricken. Writer: Richard Berg.
Cast: Agnes Moorehead, Phyllis Love, William Shatner, Jack Klugman.
Revue Productions / Revue Studios.

#32 "Voice in the Night" (May 26, 1958)
Director: Arthur Hiller. Writer: Stirling Silliphant, based on the story by William Hope Hodgson.
Cast: Barbara Rush, James Donald, Patrick Macnee, James Coburn.
Shamley Productions / Revue Studios.

#33 "Death Watch" (June 2, 1958)
Director: Ray Milland. Writers: John Hawkins and Ward Hawkins.
Cast: Edmond O'Brien, Janice Rule, Horace McMahon, Florence Marly, Edward Binns.
Revue Productions / Revue Studios.

#35 "The Woman Turned to Salt" (June 16, 1958)
Director: Robert Stevens. Writer: Stirling Silliphant, based on the story by F. Tennyson Jesse.
Cast: Michael Rennie, Pamela Brown, Susan Oliver, Rafael Campos, Jane Rose.
Shamley Productions / Revue Studios.

#36 "Eye for Eye" (June 23, 1958)
Director: Jules Bricken. Writers: Jameson Brewer and John Kneubuhl, based on the novel *An Eye for an Eye* by Leigh Brackett.
Cast: Ray Milland, Macdonald Cary, Kathleen Crowley, Andrew Duggan, Dorothy Green.
Revue Productions / Revue Studios.

Startime (1960)

Season 1
#27 "Incident at a Corner" (April 5, 1960)
As producer. Producer: Joan Harrison. Associate Producer: Norman Lloyd. Director: Alfred Hitchcock. Writer: Charlotte Armstrong, based on her novel. Photography: John L. Russell. Art Director: John J. Lloyd. Editor: Edward W. Williams. Costumes: Vincent Dee. Music Supervisor: Frederick Herbert.
Cast: Vera Miles, George Peppard, Paul Hartman.
Color, Hubbell Robinson Productions / Shamley Productions for NBC, 60 mins.

Alcoa Premiere (1962)

Season 1

#13 "The Jail" (February 6, 1962)

As producer. Producer: Joan Harrison. Associate Producer: Norman Lloyd. Director: Norman Lloyd. Writer: Ray Bradbury. Photography: Ellsworth Fredericks. Art Director: John J. Lloyd. Editorial Department Head: David J. O'Connell. Editor: Edward W. Williams. Assistant Director: Edward K. Dodds. Costumes: Vincent Dee. Music Supervisor: Stanley Wilson.

Cast: Fred Astaire, John Gavin, James Barton.

B&W, Avasta Productions / Revue Studios for ABC, filmed at Revue Studios, 60 mins.

The Alfred Hitchcock Hour (1962–1965)

1962–1963

Season 1 (12 of 32 episodes)

Thursdays, 10:00–11:00 PM on CBS

As producer. Producers: Joan Harrison, Norman Lloyd. Associate Producer: Gordon Hessler. Select Directors: Alan Crosland Jr., Paul Henreid, Alfred Hitchcock, Alf Kjellin, and Jack Smight. Select Writers: Marc Brandel, Alec Coppel, William D. Gordon, Alfred Hayes, and Henry Slesar. Writer, Opening/Closing Monologues: James B. Allardice. Photography: Benjamin H. Kline, Lionel Lindon, William Margulies, John L. Russell, and John F. Warren. Art Directors: Frank Arrigo, Raymond Beal, Howard E. Johnson, Russell Kimball, John J. Lloyd, Alexander A. Mayer, Martin Obzina, and George Patrick. Editorial Department Head: David J. O'Connell. Editors: Lee Huntington, Tony Martinelli, Douglas Stewart, and Edward W. Williams. Assistant Directors: Donald Baer, Ben Bishop, James H. Brown, Carter DeHaven III, Edward K. Dodds, Frank Fox, Hilton A. Green, Frank Losee, Ronald R. Rondell, Ray Taylor Jr., and Wallace Worsley Jr. Wardrobe Supervisors: Vincent Dee and Burton Miller. Music Supervisor: Stanley Wilson. Host: Alfred Hitchcock.

B&W, Shamley Productions for CBS, filmed at Revue Studios, in association with MCA-TV, multiple sponsors, 60 mins.

Harrison produced the following episodes:

#3 "Night of the Owl" (October 4, 1962)

#4 "I Saw the Whole Thing" (October 11, 1962)

#7 "Annabel" (November 1, 1962)

#8 "House Guest" (November 8, 1962)

#10 "Day of Reckoning" (November 22, 1962)

#13 "Bonfire" (December 13, 1962)

#15 "The Thirty-First of February" (January 4, 1963)
#16 "What Really Happened" (January 11, 1963)
#20 "The Paragon" (February 20, 1963)
#23 "The Lonely Hours" (March 8, 1963)
#28 "Last Seen Wearing Blue Jeans" (April 19, 1963)
#29 "The Dark Pool" (May 3, 1963)

1963–1964
Season 2 (8 of 32 episodes)
Thursday, 10:00–11:00 PM on CBS

As producer/executive producer. Producers: Joan Harrison and Norman Lloyd. Associate Producer: Gordon Hessler. Select Directors: Bernard Girard, Alf Kjellin, Joseph Pevney, and Robert Stevens. Select Writers: John Collier, William Fay, Joel Murcott, Alvin Sargent, and Henry Slesar. Writer, Opening/Closing Monologues: James B. Allardice. Photography: Benjamin H. Kline, Lionel Lindon, William Margulies, Richard L. Rawlings, John L. Russell, Bud Thackery, Robert Tobey, and John F. Warren. Art Directors: Raymond Beal, Howard E. Johnson, Russell Kimball, John J. Lloyd, and Alexander A. Mayer. Editorial Department Head: David J. O'Connell. Editors: John C. Fuller, Danford B. Greene, John M. Haffen, Bud S. Isaacs, Tony Martinelli, Douglas Stewart, and Edward W. Williams. Assistant Directors: Donald Baer, Lester Wm. Berke, Ben Bishop, George Bisk, Ridgeway Callow, Chuck Colean, Edward K. Dodds, Jack Doran, Milton Feldman, Ray Taylor Jr., and Dolph Zimmer. Wardrobe Supervisors: Vincent Dee and Burton Miller. Music Supervisor: Stanley Wilson. Host: Alfred Hitchcock.
B&W, Shamley Productions for CBS, filmed at Revue Studios, in association with MCA-TV, multiple sponsors, 60 mins.

Harrison produced the following episodes:
#5 "Blood Bargain" (October 25, 1963)
#7 "Starring the Defense" (November 15, 1963)
#9 "The Dividing Wall" (December 6, 1963)
#10 "Good-Bye, George" (December 13, 1963)
#13 "The Magic Shop" (January 10, 1964)
#14 "Beyond the Sea of Death" (January 24, 1964)
#25 "The Ordeal of Mrs. Snow" (April 14, 1964)
#31 "Isabel" (June 5, 1964)*

---

* Harrison was credited as executive producer for this episode.

1964–1965
Season 3 (3 of 29 episodes)
Thursdays, 10:00–11:00 PM on NBC
As producer. Producer: Joan Harrison. Directors: Joseph Pevney and Robert Stevens. Writers: Harlan Ellison, Oscar Millard, John Wyndham, and James Yaffe. Writer, Opening/Closing Monologues: James B. Allardice. Photography: William Margulies and John F. Warren. Art Director: Alexander A. Mayer. Editorial Department Head: David J. O'Connell. Editor: Edward W. Williams. Assistant Directors: Edward K. Dodds, Frank Losee, and Ray Taylor Jr. Wardrobe Supervisor: Burton Miller. Music Supervisor: Stanley Wilson. Host: Alfred Hitchcock.
B&W, Shamley Productions for NBC, filmed at Revue Studios, in association with MCA-TV, multiple sponsors, 60 mins.

Harrison produced the following episodes:
#10 "Memo from Purgatory" (December 21, 1964)
#11 "Consider Her Ways" (December 28, 1964)
#16 "One of the Family" (February 8, 1965)

Journey to the Unknown (1968–1969)

Season 1 (17 episodes)
Thursdays, 9:30–10:30 PM on ABC (US)
As executive producer. Executive Producers: Joan Harrison and Norman Lloyd. Producer: Anthony Hinds. Photography: Martin Curtis, Ben Knoll, Arthur Lavis, David Muir, and Kenneth Talbot. Art Directors: William Kellner, Keith Norman, and Roy Stannard. Editors: Ronald J. Fagan, Brian Freemantle, and Inman Hunter. Wardrobe Supervisors: Dolly Hodges, Mary Gibson, and Klara Kerpin. Music Supervisor: Philip Martell. Stunts: Chris Webb.
Color, Hammer Films Productions, filmed at MGM British Studios, distributed by 20th Century Fox Television, 60 mins.

#1 "Eve" (September 26, 1968)
Director: Robert Stevens. Writers: Michael Ashe and Paul Wheeler, based on the story "Special Delivery" by John Collier.
Cast: Carol Lynley, Dennis Waterman, Michael Gough.

#2 "Jane Brown's Body" (October 3, 1968)
Director: Alan Gibson. Writer: Anthony Skene, based on the story by Cornell Woolrich.
Cast: Stefanie Powers, David Buck, Alan MacNaughtan.

#3 "The Indian Spirit Guide" (October 10, 1968)
Director: Roy Ward Baker. Writer: Robert Bloch.
Cast: Julie Harris, Tom Adams, Tracy Reed.

#4 "Miss Belle" (October 24, 1968)
Director: Robert Stevens. Writer: Sarett Rudley, based on the story "Miss Gentilbelle" by Charles Beaumont.
Cast: George Maharis, Barbara Jefford, Kim Burfield.

#5 "Paper Dolls" (November 7, 1968)
Director: James Hill. Writer: Oscar Millard, based on the novel by Leslie P. Davies.
Cast: Michael Tolan, Nanette Newman, Barnaby Shaw.

#6 "The New People" (November 14, 1968)
Director: Peter Sasdy. Writers: John Gould and Oscar Millard, based on the story by Charles Beaumont.
Cast: Robert Reed, Jennifer Hilary, Patrick Allen.

#7 "One on an Island" (November 21, 1968)
Director: Noël Howard. Writer: Oscar Millard, based on the story "One on a Desert Island" by Donald E. Westlake.
Cast: Brandon De Wilde, Suzanna Leigh, John Ronane.

#8 "Matakitas Is Coming" (November 28, 1968)
Director: Michael Lindsay-Hogg. Writer: Robert Heverly
Cast: Vera Miles, Leon Lissek, Gay Hamilton.

#9 "Girl of My Dreams" (December 5, 1968)
Director: Peter Sasdy. Writers: Michael J. Bird and Robert Bloch, based on the story by Richard Matheson.
Cast: Michael Callan, Zena Walker, Justine Lord.

#10 "Somewhere in a Crowd" (December 12, 1968)
Director: Alan Gibson. Writer: Michael J. Bird.
Cast: David Hedison, Ann Bell, Jane Asher.

#11 "Do Me a Favor and Kill Me" (December 19, 1968)
Director: Gerry O'Hara. Writer: Stanley Miller, based on a story by Frederick Rawlings.
Cast: Joseph Cotten, Judy Parfitt, Douglas Wilmer.

#12 "The Beckoning Fair One" (December 26, 1968)
Director: Don Chaffey. Writers: John Gould and William Woods, based on the story by Oliver Onions.
Cast: Robert Lansing, Gabrielle Drake, John Fraser.

#13 "The Last Visitor" (January 2, 1969)
Director: Don Chaffey. Writer: Alfred Shaughnessy.
Cast: Patty Duke, Kay Walsh, Geoffrey Bayldon.

#14 "Poor Butterfly" (January 9, 1969)
Director: Alan Gibson. Writer: Jeremy Paul, based on a story by William Abney.
Cast: Chad Everett, Bernard Lee, Fay Compton.

#15 "Stranger in the Family" (January 16, 1969)
Director: Peter Duffell. Writer: David Campton.
Cast: Janice Rule, Maurice Kaufmann, Anthony Higgins.

#16 "The Madison Equation" (January 23, 1969)
Director: Rex Firkin. Writer: Michael J. Bird.
Cast: Barbara Bel Geddes, Allan Cuthbertson, Sue Lloyd.

#17 "The Killing Bottle" (January 30, 1969)
Director: John Gibson. Writer: Julian Bond, based on the story by L. P. Hartley.
Cast: Roddy McDowall, Ingrid Boulting, Barry Evans.

The Most Deadly Game (1970–1971)

Season 1 (13 episodes)
Saturdays, 9:30 PM–10:30 PM on ABC
As producer. Executive Producers: Aaron Spelling, Morton S. Fine, and David Friedkin.
Producer: Joan Harrison. Created by: Morton S. Fine and David Friedkin.
Cast: George Maharis (Jonathan Croft), Ralph Bellamy (Ethan Arcane), and Yvette Mimieux (Vanessa Smith).
Color, Aaron Spelling Productions for ABC, filmed at Paramount Studios, 60 mins.

#0 "Zig Zag" (unaired)
Director: David Friedkin. Writers: Morton S. Fine and David Friedkin.
Cast: Inger Stevens (Vanessa Smith).

#1 "Little David" (October 10, 1970)
Director: Philip Leacock. Writer: Burton Wohl.
Cast: Cathleen Cordell, Roger Davis, Marj Dusay.

#2 "Witches' Sabbath" (October 17, 1970)
Director: Unknown. Writer: Unknown.
Cast: Herb Armstrong, Barry Atwater, Michael Baseleon.

#3 "Gabrielle" (October 24, 1970)
Director: Unknown. Writer: Unknown.
Cast: Diana Ewing, Roy Glenn, Vince Howard.

#4 "Breakdown" (October 31, 1970)
Director: Unknown. Writer: Unknown.
Cast: Joe Don Baker, Harry Basch, Tom Bosley.

#5 "Who Killed Kindness" (November 7, 1970)
Director: Unknown. Writer: Andy White.
Cast: Carol Lynley, Sheree North, Andrew Prine.

#6 "Photo Finish" (November 14, 1970)
Director: Unknown. Writer: Unknown.
Cast: Eileen Brennan, Ingeborg Kjeldsen, Craig Littler.

#7 "War Games" (November 28, 1970)
Director: Lee Madden. Writer: Jack Miller.
Cast: Peter Brown, Frank Farmer, Pat Harrington Jr.

#8 "Nightbirds" (December 12, 1970)
Director: Unknown. Writer: Unknown.
Cast: John Bakos, Jeff Bridges, Norman Lloyd.

#9 "Model for Murder" (December 19, 1970)
Director: Unknown. Writer: Unknown.
Cast: Frank Converse, Barbara Hale, Roland Bob Harris.

#10 "The Classic Burial Position" (January 2, 1971)
Director: Unknown. Writer: Shimon Wincelberg.
Cast: Skye Aubrey, Hugh Beaumont, Anjanette Comer.

#11 "The Lady from Praha" (January 9, 1971)
Director: Unknown. Writer: Unknown.
Cast: Brenda Benet, Hank Brandt, May Britt.

#12 "I, Said the Sparrow" (January 16, 1971)
Director: George McCowan. Writer: Marion Hargrove.
Cast: Dick Cavett, John Fiedler, Joan Huntington.

Love Hate Love (February 9, 1971)

Made-for-television movie of the week
Tuesday, 8:30–10:00 PM on ABC
As producer. Executive Producer: Aaron Spelling. Producer: Joan Harrison. Director: George McCowan. Writer: Eric Ambler, from a story by Robert Summerfield and Eric Ambler. Photography: Archie R. Dalzell. Art Director: Paul Sylos. Editor: George W. Brooks. Assistant Director: Wes Barry. Music: Lyn Murray. Costumes: Nolan Miller. Special Effects: Joe Lombardi.
Cast: Ryan O'Neal, Lesley Ann Warren, Peter Haskell, Henry Jones, Jeff Donnell.
Color, Aaron Spelling Productions for ABC, filmed at Paramount Studios, 74 mins.

NOTES

Prologue. Wanted: Young Lady, by Producer

"For your consideration": Hopper, "Wrath Made Joan Harrison a Producer."

Years earlier, her parents had: Hopper, "Wrath Made Joan Harrison a Producer."

"a town-and-country marriage": Hopper, "Wrath Made Joan Harrison a Producer."

the Advertiser's sole proprietor: "Honor for a Surrey Journalist," *Elgin Courant*, November 12, 1901.

"I expect you to give": Daggett, "It's a Woman's World Too," 22; Berch, "Hitchcock Alumna."

"Why don't you marry": Lewis, "Murder, She Says."

Joan found his male bias illuminating: Author's interview with Kate Adamson, May 14, 2013.

"Be sure to wear a hat": Taylor, *Hitch*, 133.

"She stalked up to the gentleman": Berch, "Hitchcock Alumna."

The "commissionaire" took her: Lewis, "'Murder,' She Says," 70.

"Do you speak German?": Lewis, 70.

"Well, you're hired anyway": "Cosmopolite of the Month: Joan Harrison," *Cosmopolitan*, 8.

The lunch conversation: Virginia Wright, untitled *Daily News* clipping, ca. 1944, Joan Harrison files, AMPAS.

"an absolute passion on the subject": Daggett, "It's a Woman's World Too," 22.

Knowing of her obsession: "Specialty: Murder," *TV Guide*.

"every grisly detail": "Specialty: Murder," *TV Guide*.

at a young age: Ackroyd, *Alfred Hitchcock: A Brief Life*, 10.

"superb masterpiece": Review of *Phantom Lady*, *Film Daily*, January 26, 1944.

as J. E. Smyth illuminates: Smyth, *Nobody's Girl Friday*, 24–37.

"she placed a recognizable mark": Obituary for Joan Harrison, *London Times*.

"From my New York": Author's interview with Eleanor Kilgallen, 2000.

"But for Joan": Author's interview with Carol Lynley, June 5, 2015.

"fighting and fornication": Ambler, *Story So Far*, 100.
"There's no mistaking": Author's interview with Eddie Muller, April 8, 2016.
"nursed his unarticulated longings": Spoto, *Dark Side of Genius*, 229.

1. At Home

"golden afternoon": Rose, *Guildford: Remembering 1914–1918*, 20.
"My friend, do as Abraham did": "The History of a Successful Enterprise," *Surrey Advertiser*, July 1964, *Surrey Advertiser* clippings file, GBM.
"guiding mission": Author's interview with David Rose, July 8, 2016.
"Advertising is to business": "History of a Successful Enterprise," *Surrey Advertiser*.
"by gentlemen, for gentlemen": "History of a Successful Enterprise," *Surrey Advertiser*.
On June 11, 1867: Eliza Mure, 1861 Census, Shropshire, Wellington, District 4; Andrew Asher's personal files, Shanklin, Isle of Wight.
After some deliberation: Collyer and Rose, *Images of Guildford: Surrey Advertiser*, 8.
Eliza died of heart failure: Asher's personal files; death certificate and burial records for Eliza Mure, Ancestry.com.
a romance had been blooming: Asher's personal files; author's interview with Andrew Asher, June 17, 2016.
Mayor Asher's greatest deed: "History of a Successful Enterprise," *Surrey Advertiser*; Newman, *Guildford Life: Past and Present*, 187–188.
Millie and Walter welcomed: Muriel Mary Harrison, Church of England Baptisms, 1813–1912, Surrey, England.
Jack Forsyth followed: Jack Forsythe Harrison, England and Wales Civil Birth Registration, 1837–1915; Jack Forsythe Harrison, Church of England Baptisms, 1813–1912, Surrey, England.
the Harrisons moved to the Craigmore: 1911 England Census, Guildford, Surrey; Surrey England Electoral Registers, 1832–1945, Walter Harrison, 1909–1930. Some records note the family living at 12 Wodeland Road, which was the same residence (sandwiched between Wodeland and Mareschal Roads).
Joan was born on June 20, 1907: Joan Mary Harrison birth certificate, dated June 20, 1907, Guildford, Surrey, General Register Office, BXCA 338456. In Harrison's passports (held in the Eric Ambler Collection, HGRC) and her school registration at the Sorbonne, her date of birth is likewise listed as June 20. Her civil birth registry, baptism record, and death certificate erroneously give her birthdate as June 26, 1907. Patricia Gaynor, Harrison's personal secretary in the 1980s and '90s, remembers Joan celebrating her birthday on June 20. She speculates that the confusion may have stemmed from the fact that, when written carelessly, a 0 can resemble a 6.

"no parochial bounds": Obituary for Walter Harrison, *Surrey Advertiser*, November 21, 1942.

many who knew her later: Author's interview with Kate Adamson, May 14, 2013; Patricia Gaynor e-mail correspondence to the author, September 19, 2017.

Jack, in fact, played the part: "Fun in Fairyland," *Surrey Advertiser*, January 1914.

Nearly every one of the town's: Rose and Parke, *Guildford History Tour*, 13.

She would be a royalist: Gaynor e-mail correspondence to the author, September 19, 2017.

"poems, stories, nature items": Zuma Palmer, "Capable Producer," *Hollywood Citizen News*, July 27, 1959, clipping, Joan Harrison files, AMPAS.

"a tuppence": Author's interview with Adamson, May 14, 2013.

GHS's stated mission: Howard Bailes, "The First One Hundred Years," *Guildford High School: One Hundred Twenty-Five Year Commemorative Book* (Guildford High School, 2013), 7.

Guildford High School emphasized: William Harvey, "The Modern Day School for Girls," *Town and Country News*, October 17, 1930.

"habitually committing adultery": Petition for Divorce, William Puxley Pearse vs. Anna Hairstens Robison Pearse and Lancelot Miller (January 20, 1908), England and Wales Divorce Records, 1858–1916.

Two months after the divorce: Obituary for Anna Hairstens Robison Pearse, *Hampshire Chronicle and General Advertiser*, March 14, 1908, 7.

"ordinary persons for characters": Millstein, "Harrison Horror Story."

"Women have written lots": "Hitchcock's Female Cohort," *Atlanta Constitution.*

2. Wartime

published the news item the next day: Oakley, *Guildford in the Great War*, 13–14.

As each report arrived: Rose, *Guildford: Remembering 1914–1918*, 27.

Loud cheers erupted: Oakley, *Guildford in the Great War*, 21.

Joan and her fellow pupils: Rose, *Guildford: Remembering 1914–1918*, 66.

Even before the war: Rose, 16–17.

British officials put heavy pressure: Rose, 38.

"plunged the town into inky": Oakley, *Guildford in the Great War*, 146.

"unmistakable shape": Rose, *Guildford: Remembering 1914–1918*, 105.

"causing the windows to rattle": Rose, 104.

"lots of loud, excited voices": Rose, 105.

"scare the hell out of people": Jordan Golson, "WWI Zeppelins: Not Too Deadly, but Scary as Hell," *Wired*, October 3, 2014, https://www.wired.com/2014/10/world-war-i-zeppelins/.

"terrifying": Kate Adamson, e-mail message to the author, March 14, 2017.
"The home front in Guildford": Rose, *Guildford: Remembering 1914–1918*, 17.
it was not easy ushering: "History of a Successful Enterprise," *Surrey Advertiser.*
Walter, in particular, seized: "History of a Successful Enterprise," *Surrey Advertiser.*
Joan moved away: Lieber, "Joan Harrison Biography."
Tudor Hall offered an elite: Charmian Snowden, *Tudor Hall: The First Hundred Years, 1850–1946* (Banbury, UK: Tudor Hall School, 2000), 20–42.
"after a term's trial": Guildford High School Yearbook, 1924–1925, 17.
In senior year: Guildford High School Yearbook, 1924–1925, 10.
"Before tea, we danced": "The Book Dance Given by Form IV," *Guildford High School Magazine*, 1921–1922, 17.
"so I could get the passes": "Specialty: Murder," *TV Guide.*
keeping her fascination hidden: Lieber, "Joan Harrison Biography."
"how criminal acts were committed": Daggett, "It's a Woman's World Too," 22.
When Joan announced her intention: Author's interview with Adamson, May 14, 2013; author's interview with Gaynor, August 31, 2017.

3. Beyond the Village

feasted on the wonders: Author's interview with Adamson, May 9, 2017.
The view was overturned: Offen, "The Second Sex," 280–281.
Upper-class and upper-middle-class: Offen, 277.
"adverse political and cultural climate": Offen, 283.
"personal project": Schwartz, *Serious Endeavor*, 18.
but most women had not: Schwartz, 53.
"in the back of the hall": Senior Member Reminiscences file (1920s), St. Hugh's College archive, Oxford.
"at boarding school": Schwartz, *Serious Endeavor*, 45.
"the place to be seen": Reminiscences file (1920s), St. Hugh's.
Students were expected to dress: Reminiscences file (1920s), St. Hugh's; West, "Reminiscences of Seven Decades," 94–103; Schwartz, *Serious Endeavor*, 46, 54–55.
"was a period of great fun": Reminiscences file (1920s), St. Hugh's.
who often broke curfew: Reminiscences file (1920s).
"We lost our hearts to him!": Reminiscences file; West, "Reminiscences of Seven Decades," 98–99, 119.
"My strongest memory of her": Rita Landale, personal e-mail to Mary Troath, ca. spring 2000, provided to the author.
"delightful little singing voice": Landale to Troath.

The "second-year" play: Reminiscences file (1920s), St. Hugh's; "The Second Year Play," *Imp*, 1928, 17.

Joan chose courses: Harrison tutorial reports, 1926–1929, St. Hugh's College, Oxford.

"airy, refined character sketches": "Specialty: Murder," *TV Guide*.

"By untiring efforts": J.H., "The Third Year vs. S.R.C.," *Imp*, March 2, 1928, 17.

"We certainly set the world": Reminiscences file (1920s), St. Hugh's.

"Joan led a gay life": Landale to Troath, ca. spring 2000.

She once told a story: Lewis, "Murder, She Says," 55.

"Feel[ing] like one of": Lewis, 55.

"very satisfactory": Harrison tutorial reports, 1926–1927, St. Hugh's College, Oxford.

"it was the most interesting": Harrison tutorial reports, 1927–1929, St. Hugh's College, Oxford.

"I could have done with more": Reminiscences file (1920s), St. Hugh's.

Joan could capitalize: By the time of her death, Harrison's academic reputation preceded her. An obituary in the *New York Times* stated that she had earned Oxford's highly coveted PPE (Politics, Philosophy, and Economics) degree, making assumptions based on the self-promotion Harrison had cultivated over the years surrounding her college education. "Joan Harrison, a Screenwriter and Producer, Is Dead at 83," *New York Times*.

"I want to be a newspaperwoman": Berch, "Hitchcock Alumna."

"You will never be a success": Author's interview with Adamson, May 9, 2017.

Meanwhile, older sister Muriel: Obituary for Muriel Mary Harrison, *Tablet: The International Catholic News Weekly*, July 23, 1938.

"When I came out of college": Gates, "Talented TV Producer."

"It was a great moment": Lesley Blanch, *On the Wilder Shores of Love: A Bohemian Life* (London: Virago, 2015), 160.

"I felt I had gone": Daggett, "It's a Woman's World Too," 22.

"At the end of the day": "Specialty: Murder," *TV Guide*.

One story has it: Lewis, "Murder, She Says," 55.

She had been there six months: Berch, "Hitchcock Alumna."

"I had a little talent": Murray Schumach, "Woman Produces a Mystery Series," *New York Times*, November 1, 1960.

"All I'm after": "Specialty: Murder," *TV Guide*.

"to learn about life": Florabel Muir, "Joan Harrison Worrying about Butter," *Hollywood Citizen News*, June 15, 1946, Harrison file, AMPAS.

"he had probably heard": "Old Bailey Keeper," *Hull Daily Mail*, September 28, 1940.

"He was one of those Uncles": "Specialty: Murder," *TV Guide*.

Joan spent other days: McCreadie, *Women Who Write*, 145; "Keeper of the Old Bailey," *Times*, May 28, 1941.

If she had paused to compare: Guildford High School Yearbook, 1929–1930, 1930–1931, and 1931–1932.

"A secretary can learn": "Specialty: Murder," *TV Guide*.

"the largest cinema": David Atwell, *Cathedrals of the Movies: A History of British Cinemas and Their Audiences* (London: London Architectural Press, 1981), 57–58.

4. Birth of a Master

didn't think formal education: Hitchcock, "Woman Who Knows Too Much."

"either unprofessional or lecherous": Muller, "Murder, She Made," 15.

Not only was Hitchcock's: McGilligan, *Darkness and Light*, 163.

Hitchcock promptly noted: McGilligan, 164.

"The motion picture industry": Daggett, "It's a Woman's World Too," 22; "Hers Is a Horrifying Business," *Hartford Courant*, May 7, 1944.

When he offered her: Daggett, "It's a Woman's World Too," 22.

Biographer Patrick McGilligan describes: McGilligan, *Darkness and Light*, 5, 13.

"movie mad": Joan Weston Edwards, "Making Good in the Film Trade," February 26, 1927, clipping, AMPAS; "Alma in Wonderland," *Picturegoer*, December 1925, 48.

"I regarded myself": Chandler, *It's Only a Movie*, 47.

"since it is unthinkable": Mrs. Alfred Hitchcock as told to Martin Abramson, "My Husband Alfred Hitchcock Hates Suspense," *Coronet*, August 1964, 12–17.

Alma negotiated a higher salary: Hitchcock, "Woman Who Knows Too Much."

"imaginations met": Chandler, *It's Only a Movie*, 12.

"she'd been working in films": Reville, "Cutting and Continuity," 10.

"Was that all right?": McBride, "Mr. and Mrs. Hitchcock," 225.

"the finest British production": "The Lodger," *Bioscope*, July 6, 1926, in Rachel Low, *The History of British Film 1918–1929* (London: Allen & Unwin, 1971), 168.

By the middle of 1927: Ryall, *Alfred Hitchcock*, 91.

BIP enabled Hitchcock: Ryall, 91.

Block booking and other: Ryall, 51.

In 1927, British companies: Wood, *British Films*, 115.

reception at the box office tended to be mixed: See review of *The Ring*, *Bioscope*, October 6, 1927; review of *The Ring*, *Times*, November 22, 1927; review of *Blackmail*, *Times*, June 24, 1929; "Juno and the Paycock: New British Talking Film," *Times*, January 1, 1930; "Juno and the Paycock: An Irish Talkie," *Manchester Guardian*, January 1, 1930.

He would feature only: Ryall, *Alfred Hitchcock*, 62.

"Hitchcock films": Ryall, 118.

"I think you'll find": McGilligan, *Darkness and Light*, 164; Truffaut, *Hitchcock*, 91–92.

"chaos world": Durgnat, *Strange Case*, 20.

"the thing the spies are after": David Boyd, *Perspectives on Alfred Hitchcock* (Boston: G. K. Hall, 1995), 31.

"Call me Hitch": Chandler, *It's Only a Movie*, 125.

"I had heard of him": Houseman, *Run-Through*, 479.

she was asked into the office: Spoto, *Dark Side of Genius*, 163.

"I knew Hitchcock liked": Chandler, *It's Only a Movie*, 159.

"lady pose": Buchanan, "Alfred Hitchcock Tells a Woman."

"Have you slept with anyone?": McGilligan, *Darkness and Light*, 163.

"Oh my gosh, I'm terribly": "Blackmail Test Take (1929): Alfred Hitchcock," BFI, published March 2, 2009, video, 0:42, https://www.youtube.com/watch?v=7Z8mSwzSQQk.

"Well, I'll not spoil": Hopper, "Wrath Made Joan Harrison a Producer." In this account, Harrison suggests the audition was for the lead role, though it was more likely a standard studio screen test.

5. True Crime Pays

"Everything was so large": "Money Comes Second," *Woman's Hour*.

"listened bewilderedly": Youngkin, *Lost One*, 92.

"I was too curious": Daggett, "It's a Woman's World Too," 22.

To his credit: "Joan Harrison, a Screenwriter and Producer, Is Dead at 83," *New York Times*.

"Mr. Hitchcock likes to have plots": Hopper, "Wrath Made Joan Harrison a Producer."

"He allowed me to see": Luther, "Work Seven Mondays a Week."

"No detail of the work": Gates, "Talented TV Producer."

"generous and diplomatic": Author's interview with Jay Presson Allen, October 7, 2000.

With Joan, Hitchcock was: "Girls, Don't Let Femininity Slip: Women Warned to Guard Sex Appeal," *Los Angeles Times*, July 5, 1957, Joan Harrison file, AMPAS.

"I was able to invade": Daggett, "It's a Woman's World Too," 22.

She shadowed him: Schiebe, "Screenwriting Last Entry."

"constructionist": McGilligan, "First-Class Constructionist," 35.

"but only touching": Bennett, "The Writer Speaks."

"We practically lived": Bennett.

"dialectic between the dominant": Barr, *English Hitchcock*, 15.

sometimes worked *"with"*: Barr, 15.

"never did a damned": McGilligan, "First-Class Constructionist," 27. Bennett claimed that Hitchcock came up with the idea of giving Alma continuity credits so as to line his pockets.

"Working with Hitchcock": Houseman, *Run-Through*, 480.

"was really an original idea": Montagu, "Interview with Ivor Montagu," 88.

"set the tone": McGilligan, *Darkness and Light*, 156.

becoming the *"third collaborator"*: Barr, *English Hitchcock*, 15.

Born July 7: O'Connell and Bouzereau, *Alma Hitchcock*, 98.

She had cowritten: Reville's screenplays include *Sally in Our Alley* (1931), *Nine Till Six* (1932), *The Water Gipsies* (1932), and *Forbidden Territory* (1934). She rarely if ever received solo writing credit.

"informal film society": Montagu, "Working with Hitchcock," 192.

"In this way": Montagu, "Interview with Ivor Montagu," 72.

"Do you have to go now?": Lewis, "Murder, She Says," 70.

"seared in her mind": McCrary and Falkenburg, "New York Close Up."

a description that has led: A 2013 Criterion Collection DVD edition of the film goes so far as to "point out" Joan—erroneously—during the audio commentary.

"The actress in the movie": McCrary and Falkenburg, "New York Close Up."

her fleeting moment: Harrison's appearance as a body double may have occurred in a longer version of the film, not currently in circulation. An eighty-minute print existed at one time, according to the American Film Institute catalog. See https://catalog.afi.com/Catalog/MovieDetails/8676, accessed February 27, 2017.

"glorious melodrama": Review of *The Man Who Knew Too Much*, *Kine Weekly*, January 4, 1935, 25.

"Hitchcock leaps once again": Balcon, *Lifetime in Films*, 62; Ryall, *Alfred Hitchcock*, 103.

the Harrisons likely only saw: Advertisement for *The Man Who Knew Too Much*, *Surrey Mirror*, February 15, 1935.

For Christmas 1934: McGilligan, *Darkness and Light*, 168.

The trip to the Palace Hotel: McGilligan, "First-Class Constructionist," 27; Bennett and Bennett, *Hitchcock's Partner in Suspense*, 68.

"I like to ski": Chandler, *It's Only a Movie*, 91.

It was a symbolic postscript: Hitchcock, "My Own Methods," 3; Truffaut, *Hitchcock*, 106–107.

6. Bigger Steps

churned out pages: Hitchcock, "My Screen Memories."

"I suppose the first blonde": Angell, "The Time of My Life."

"She was 'smart and sexy'": Leff, audio commentary, *The 39 Steps*.

To understand Carroll: Haskell, *From Reverence to Rape*, 349–353.

"suddenly became another person": Hopper, "Hitchcock: He Runs on Fear."

"cold, unfeeling, humorless": Hitchcock, "My Screen Memories."

"At the heart of the English": Angell, "The Time of My Life."

"You know why": Truffaut, *Hitchcock*, 91–92.

"Madeleine Carroll was my choice": Chandler, *It's Only a Movie*, 12.

"but not a bit of it": McGilligan, *Darkness and Light*, 179; Hellman, "Alfred Hitchcock," 38–39.

this also irked Bennett: Bennett recounted this story with various alterations, at times amused at Hitchcock's hijinks, other times irritated at Harrison's presence. He casts Joan's appearance as incidental in one interview, implying that it was perfectly natural for her to be there because, after all, "she was his secretary." See Bennett, "Import from England," 6.

"Joan had iron in her": Author's interview with Norman Lloyd, August 2000.

"There are only two women": Spoto, *Dark Side of Genius*, 229.

"chess figures": Chandler, *It's Only a Movie*, 126.

contending with wagging tongues: Wright, untitled *Daily News* clipping.

"silent, gray romantic gloom": Donald Spoto, "His Longings Hung Grayly over Family," *Atlanta Constitution*, April 12, 1983.

he was a "family man": McGilligan, *Darkness and Light*, 176.

"would have been a 'poof'": Taylor, "Was Alfred Hitchcock a Misogynist?," 9.

"suffered personal discomfort": Bennett and Bennett, *Hitchcock's Partner in Suspense*, 71.

"there are interesting gaps": McGilligan, *Darkness and Light*, 176.

"a woman of elegance": Hitchcock, "Elegance Above Sex."

Mr. Memory, the performer: Mr. Memory, based on early twentieth-century performer Datas the Memory Man, was an addition by Hitchcock's team. In Buchan's novel, the clue of the thirty-nine steps turns out to refer to an actual staircase. The climax is a physical struggle between Hannay and the conspirators as they attempt to board a yacht destined for a German ship.

part of a larger conversation: Rothman, *Hitchcock: The Murderous Gaze*, 137–138.

"couplet vignettes": Ryall, *Alfred Hitchcock*, 139.

"the most successful": Review of *The 39 Steps*, *Daily Mirror*, September 9, 1935.

"Hitchcock is a genius": Sidney Carroll, review of *The 39 Steps*, *Sunday Times*, June 9, 1935, clippings file, BFI.

"probably the best": "The 39 Steps," *Variety*, June 19, 1935.

"Time came to mean nothing": "Good Looking Enough to Be a Star," *Gloucester Citizen*.

On weekday evenings: Bennett and Bennett, *Hitchcock's Partner in Suspense*, 67.

They skied, boated, and read: Author's interview with Patricia Hitchcock O'Connell, July 24, 2000.

King's Road had been occupied: Décharné, *King's Road*, 10–23.

Jazz poured forth: Décharné, 27–28.

she would have been tracking: Décharné, 29.

"In the book": Hitchcock, "Life Among the Stars," 48.

Joan began to have major: Lieber, "Joan Harrison Biography"; Gates, "Talented TV Producer."

"an exquisite study": Press book for *The Girl Was Young / Young and Innocent*, 1938, 6, production files, AMPAS.

Harrison was looking: *Young and Innocent* lent itself toward numerous marketing opportunities specifically targeted toward young women and girls in their teens, as demonstrated by the Gaumont-British press book. Recommended campaigns included tie-ins with cosmetics, perfume, knitting, and clothes (such as Erica's central dress), not to mention suggestions to hold community discussion groups focused on "the problem of 'how much should parents influence their daughter's choice of boyfriends?'" See press book for *The Girl Was Young / Young and Innocent*, 1.

Joan accompanied Hitchcock: Bennett and Bennett, *Hitchcock's Partner in Suspense*, 84.

It became clear that: Bennett and Bennett, 84.

"went into a huddle": Hitchcock, "Life Among the Stars," 48–49.

direct genealogical line: As Maurice Yacowar points out, *Foreign Correspondent* is similar in that "the young man leads a girl to break with her father in a more dramatic situation." See Yacowar, *Hitchcock's British Films*, 251n4.

"designed as a deliberate symbol": Yacowar, 183.

"As her Uncle Basil": Yacowar, 178.

"normal everyday people": Review of *Young and Innocent*, *Monthly Film Bulletin*, November 1937.

"outstanding example": Review of *Young and Innocent*, *Cinema*, November 25, 1937.

"As you watch the story": Review of *Young and Innocent*, *Film Weekly*, February 5, 1938.

his personal favorite: Hutchinson and Paley, "Genius of Alfred Hitchcock."

"commit murder": Cinema: The New Pictures, *Time*, February 14, 1938.

"new Britain was in the": Ryall, *Alfred Hitchcock*, 35.

With reinforced concrete: Collyer and Rose, *Images of Guildford: Surrey Advertiser*, 57; "History of a Successful Enterprise," *Surrey Advertiser*.

They fully expected him: "History of a Successful Enterprise."

7. A Team of Three

"was not a good sailor": Author's interview with Patricia Hitchcock O'Connell, July 24, 2000.

watch it lie fallow: "Director Delivers Script," *Maryland Cumberland Times*, November 14, 1937.

Joan's whirlwind junket: "Falstaff in Manhattan, *New York Times* September 5, 1937; Marian Squire, "The Girl's View," *Variety*, September 8, 1937.

According to Launder: Brown, *Launder and Gilliat*, 89.

"all in the family": McGilligan, *Darkness and Light*, 207.

as Thomas Schatz suggests: Schatz, *Genius of the System*, 258, 260, 270.

"supervise a number": Kerzoncuf and Barr, *Hitchcock Lost and Found*, 108.

"what makes the Hitchcock": David O. Selznick, memo to Kay Brown, June 11, 1937, Hitchcock folders, David O. Selznick Collection, HRC.

"With the help of my wife": Hitchcock, "My Own Methods," 7.

"a traveling artist's sketchpad": *New York Herald Tribune*, July 14, 1940, cited in Leff, *Hitchcock and Selznick*, 60.

"Hitchcock says it is essential": Noll Gurney, memo to Ned Kaufman, June 23, 1938, Hitchcock folders, Myron Selznick Agency files, HRC.

"You see what happened": Montagu, "Interview with Ivor Montagu," 88.

but by this time: Schatz, *Genius of the System*, 272.

"rough attractiveness": Leff, *Hitchcock and Selznick*, 182.

special aptitude: Obituary for Muriel Mary Harrison, *Tablet*, 27.

"rescued": Author's interview with Jackie Makkink, August 15, 2017.

"only a teacher": Author's interview with Jackie Makkink, August 15, 2017.

died within a few hours: Obituary for Father Eric Burrows, SJ, *Tablet: The International Catholic News Weekly*, July 23, 1938, 26.

succumbing to related infections: Death certificate, Radcliffe Infirmary, Oxford, July 9, 1938; "Road Crash Deaths: Three Die in Two Accidents," *Western Morning News*, July 11, 1938, 7; obituary for Muriel Mary Harrison, *Tablet*, 27.

"Millie really didn't want": Author's interview with Kate Adamson, January 23, 2017.

"indispensable": Noll Gurney, memo to Ned Kaufman, June 23, 1938, Hitchcock folders, Myron Selznick Agency files, HRC.

proposed it to Hitchcock immediately: "Hers Is a Horrifying Business," *Hartford Courant*, May 7, 1944.

she'd learned that the adaptation: de Rosnay, *Manderley Forever*, 144.

"Joan Harrison is Hitchcock's mouthpiece": Jenia Reissar, memo to David O. Selznick, ca. June 1938, Hitchcock folders, David O. Selznick Collection, HRC.

"for a maximum of twenty": Contract between David O. Selznick and Hitchcock, 14, Hitchcock folders, Contracts section, Myron Selznick Agency files, HRC.

took in a Yankees game: McGilligan, "Hitchcock Dreams of America," 26.

the Selznick-Hitchcock deal: "Hollywood Signs Hitchcock," *Daily Herald*, July 8, 1938; "Anglo-American Film Agreement," *Times*, July 11, 1938; "Picture Grosses: Hitchcock to Direct 'Titanic' in Hollywood," *Variety*, July 13, 1938.

"The more I think": Val Lewton, memo to David O. Selznick, June 15, 1938, Hitchcock folders, David O. Selznick Collection, HRC. See also Schatz, *Genius of the System*, 269–270.

Reissar proposed to act as a straw buyer: Schatz, *Genius of the System*, 270.

treat du Maurier's novel: Schatz, 270.

Sidney Gilliat came on board: Brown, *Launder and Gilliat*, 94

After hearing this: Malone, *Maureen O'Hara*, 17.

"We evolved": Brown, *Launder and Gilliat*, 94.

Hitchcock found it troubing: Hitchcock, "Lecture at Columbia University," 274.

"It's very difficult": Bogdanovich, *Cinema of Alfred Hitchcock*, 20.

"truly discouraged": Truffaut, *Hitchcock*, 138–139.

"mercurial": Angell, "The Time of My Life."

She was riding high: Malone, *Maureen O'Hara*, 14–16.

she demanded her name be removed: "Jamaica Inn," *Monthly Film Bulletin*, May 31, 1939.

"fifty worst films of all time": Harry Medved and Randy Dreyfuss, *The Fifty Worst Films of All Time (and How They Got That Way)* (New York: Warner Books, 1978).

efforts to rehabilitate: "Daphne du Maurier Walk," *Woman's Hour*; the Coen Film Collection performed a 4K digital restoration, which premiered to great fanfare at the 2014 Cannes Film Festival.

"[Laughton's] dominance over": Yacowar, *Hitchcock's British Films*, 199.

Some, even Hitchcock: See, for example, McGilligan, *Darkness and Light*, 228.

$5,000 flat fee: Jock Whitney, memo to David O. Selznick, November 9, 1938, Hitchcock folders, David O. Selznick Collection, HRC.

She worried most: Author's interview with Kate Adamson, May 14, 2013.

seemed freeing for Joan: Author's interview with Kate Adamson, May 14, 2013.

"She didn't encourage the idea": Author's interview with Kate Adamson, January 23, 2017

8. Going Hollywood

they boarded a train: March 22, 1939, Florida Passenger Lists, for Joan Harrison, A3993, Arriving in Miami from Havana, Cuba, 1936–1948; March 22, 1939, Index to Alien Arrivals by Airplane to Miami, FL, 1930–1942.

the Hitchcocks resided on the top: Hellman, "Alfred Hitchcock," 41–43.

They preferred her space: Spoto, *Dark Side of Genius*, 215.

Billy Wilder would find himself there: Author's interview with Norman Lloyd, June 27, 2014; Hellman, "Alfred Hitchcock," 41–43: Spoto, *Dark Side of Genius*, 215; 1940

Census, Los Angeles, Los Angeles County, California, roll m-t0627-00407, page 2A, enumeration district 60-221B, Ancestry.com.

Pat Hitchcock fondly remembers: O'Connell and Bouzereau, *Alma Hitchcock*, 94.

John Rosselli had recently married: 1940 Census, Los Angeles, Los Angeles County, California, roll m-t0627-00407, page 2A, enumeration district 60-221B, Ancestry.com.

next door to the Chateau Colline: Tina Daunt, "Taking to Ramparts to Defend Chateau: Plan to Replace Building with Condo Sparks Bid to Win Landmark Status," *Los Angeles Times*, August 12, 2001; 10337 Wilshire Boulevard, "Designated Historic Cultural Monuments," Department of City Planning, City of Los Angeles, June 9, 2010, https://preservation.lacity.org/commission.

"When the Rodeo Land": Niven, *Bring on the Empty Horses*, 15.

also a chief supplier: Description of Shirley Temple equestrian costume (*Just Around the Corner*, 1938), *Theriaults: The Dollmasters* (catalog), accessed April 12, 2018, https://www.theriaults.com/catalog-search?keys=shop&page=7.

"the hub of the movie": Niven, *Bring on the Empty Horses*, 16; Hellman, "Alfred Hitchcock," 39.

came to try the famed cuisine: Betty Goodwin, *Chasen's: Where Hollywood Dined, Recipes and Memories* (Los Angeles: Angel City Press, 1996), 21.

"buffet-style supper-party circuit": McGilligan, *Darkness and Light*, 244.

Sales of the book: Leff, *Hitchcock and Selznick*, 38.

work on overall structure: Robey, "Alfred Hitchcock's Rebecca."

"rather grim": Forster, *Daphne du Maurier*, 138–139.

"an exquisite love story": Forster, 138.

The story stemmed from her own: Forster, 433n7.

"a marriage that had failed": Forster, 138.

"the most fascinating story": Kay Brown, memo to David O. Selznick, June 24, 1938, Hitchcock folders, David O. Selznick Collection, HRC.

"probably exemplifies the feeling": Val Lewton, memo to David O. Selznick, July 11, 1938, Hitchcock folders, David O. Selznick Collection, HRC.

"much less passive": Jock Whitney, memo to David O. Selznick, November 9, 1938, David O. Selznick Collection, HRC.

"a change in the Girl": Alfred Hitchcock, memo to David O. Selznick, November 18, 1938, David O. Selznick Collection, HRC. Hitchcock gave this memo to Kay Brown to hand-carry back to the US for delivery to Selznick. (All quotes contained in this paragraph.)

"this is how most": David O. Selznick, memo to Alfred Hitchcock, June 12, 1938, Alfred Hitchcock Collection, AMPAS.

"reactions of running": Selznick, memo to Hitchcock.

sensitivity to class distinctions: Harrison Writers files, *Rebecca*, David O. Selznick Collection, HRC.

"uncued and unjustified": David O. Selznick, memo to Alfred Hitchcock, July 12, 1939, Alfred Hitchcock files, HRC.

"I think we would become": David O. Selznick, memo to Jock Whitney, September 6, 1939, *Rebecca*, MPAA file, AMPAS.

"The whole story of Rebecca": Selznick, memo to Whitney.

claiming he was needed: Robey, "Alfred Hitchcock's Rebecca."

the last 10 percent: Spoto, *Dark Side of Genius*, 221; Leff, *Hitchcock and Selznick*, 52.

as the producer rode high: Schatz, *Genius of the System*, 280–281; Leff, *Hitchcock and Selznick*, 53.

"too shallow": Alfred Hitchcock, memo to David O. Selznick, August 19, 1938, Alfred Hitchcock Collection, AMPAS.

"she doesn't seem at all right": David O. Selznick, memo to Jock Whitney, August 18, 1939, Alfred Hitchcock files, David O. Selznick Collection, HRC.

"It was perhaps better for us": Chandler, *It's Only a Movie*, 127.

"Fontaine was just too coy": Alfred Hitchcock, memo to David O. Selznick, August 19, 1938, Alfred Hitchcock Collection, AMPAS. See also Alma Reville and Joan Harrison, notes on *Rebecca* screen tests, August 19, 1938, Alfred Hitchcock Collection, AMPAS.

"much more moving": Alfred Hitchcock, memo to David O. Selznick, August 19, 1938, Alfred Hitchcock Collection, AMPAS.

"too much Dresden china": Reville and Harrison, notes on *Rebecca* screen tests.

The camera would follow: Scenes September 16–October 16, 1939, Writers Materials, *Rebecca*, Alfred Hitchcock files, David O. Selznick Collection, HRC; Leff, *Hitchcock and Selznick*, 53.

"a wedding night not to remember": Fontaine, *No Bed of Roses*, 106.

"We realized during the war": Leff, audio interview with Joan Fontaine.

Nearly one hundred people were killed: "Has a Hurricane Ever Made Landfall in California," *KCET*, October 25, 2016, https://www.kcet.org/shows/lost-la/has-a-hurricane-ever-made-landfall-in-california; "Tropical Storm Kills 56 on California Coast," *Brownsville Herald*, September 25, 1939.

"crisis-prone rhythm": Leff, *Hitchcock and Selznick*, 75.

Joan closed out the year: McGilligan, *Darkness and Light*, 253; Spoto, *Dark Side of Genius*, 233.

The picture was redubbed: David O. Selznick to Alfred Hitchcock, January 24, 1940, Alfred Hitchcock files, HRC; Schatz, *Genius of the System*, 289–290.

"shedding quite a few tears": Daggett, "It's a Woman's World Too," 22.

The one-week interval: "Last Night's Rain Fails to Dampen Activities at Lincoln Film Premiere," *Miami Daily News*, March 22, 1940.

"an altogether brilliant film": Frank Nugent, "Rebecca," *New York Times*, March 29, 1940.

"more stirring than the novel": Josh Mosher, "Current Cinema: Rebecca," *New Yorker*, March 29, 1940, 71.

"mark of quality": "Rebecca," *Film Daily*, March 26, 1940.

named best movie: "'Rebecca' Wins Critics' Poll," *Film Daily*, January 14, 1941.

personally promoted it: West, "Reminiscences of Seven Decades," 121.

the one she was most proud of: Author's interview with Jackie Makkink, August 15, 2015; author's interview with Norman Lloyd, June 2015.

9. Oscar Calls

sum of $2,300: Though Reville goes uncredited, Wanger paid her over $2,300 for her contribution. See General (Financial) files, Alfred Hitchcock Collection, AMPAS, 1939–1940; agreement between Selznick International Pictures and Walter Wanger Productions Inc., September 26, 1939, Producer's Legal File, United Artists (UA).

"based on an original story": Foreign Correspondent treatment, November 20, 1939, Foreign Correspondent production files, Alfred Hitchcock Collection, AMPAS.

"When the producer Walter": Wilkonson, "He Makes the Movies Move."

"This is the story": Foreign Correspondent treatment, November 20, 1939.

"exceeding brilliance": Screenplay for *Foreign Correspondent*, November 20, 1939, Alfred Hitchcock Collection, AMPAS.

"becomes convinced": Screenplay for *Foreign Correspondent*, November 20, 1939.

Bennett worked with Joan: Screenplay for *Foreign Correspondent*, June 5, 1940, Alfred Hitchcock Collection, AMPAS. Spoto, *Dark Side of Genius*, 235; Bernstein, *Walter Wanger*, 417.

Robert Benchley was also conscripted: Bernstein, *Walter Wanger*, 161–162.

"Frankly, we don't know": Crowther, "Credit—Where Is It Due?"

"Rock of Gibraltar": McGilligan, *Darkness and Light*, 70.

"were a triumvirate": Leff, audio interview with Joan Fontaine.

"That woman is consumed": Taylor, *Hitch*, 15.

"I believe Hitch's married life": Bennett and Bennett, *Hitchcock's Partner in Suspense*, 71. According to the book's notes, the woman in question would have been born ca. 1907.

"Hitchcock responded": Taylor, "Was Alfred Hitchcock a Misogynist?"

"Alma was so petite": Chandler, *It's Only a Movie*, 125.

possessed a secret flair: O'Connell and Bouzereau, *Alma Hitchcock*, 84.

"Alma was very short": O'Connell and Bouzereau, 149. In a letter to Patricia, Whitfield Cook remembers her in the following way: "Alma was truly a filmmaker. Hitchcock always went back to her. And frankly so did I." See page 151.

"Alma was different": Chandler, *It's Only a Movie*, 50.

"If it ever appeared": Author's interview with Norman Lloyd, June 27, 2014.

His two films for RKO: Douglas W. Churchill, "Screen News Here and in Hollywood: Hitchcock to Direct for RKO," *New York Times*, June 29, 1940; Spoto, *Dark Side of Genius*, 242.

Joan and Hitchcock went to Ottawa: Taylor, *Hitch*, 145.

joined a small group: Glancy, *When Hollywood Loved Britain*, 170–178.

agitating against isolationism: McGilligan, *Darkness and Light*, 256; Glancy, *When Hollywood Loved Britain*, 169–170.

Hitchcock informed Bernstein: McGilligan, *Darkness and Light*, 271.

Joan visited the Grove: Author's interview with Kate Adamson, January 23, 2017; Spoto, *Dark Side of Genius*, 242.

expedite the evacuation: *New York Daily News*, August 26, 1940, cited in Glancy, *When Hollywood Loved Britain*, 169.

Jones, Carol, and ffolliott: Bernstein, *Walter Wanger*, 161.

the film of which he was proudest: Wanger said, "People won't notice until later when they've been thinking about the picture. At least, I think they won't, and I think it is there." See Eileen Creelman, "Picture Plays and Players," *New York Sun*, August 1940.

"easily one of the year's finest": Bernstein, *Walter Wanger*, 161–162.

"alien immigrants": Author's interview with Monika Henreid, October 24, 2015; Starr, *The Dream Endures*, 375.

"She gave the best parties": Author's interview with Norman Lloyd, April 2016.

"Viennese island": Author's interview with Monika Henreid, October 24, 2015.

The "diasporados": Gemünden, *Continental Strangers*, 13.

"I rarely spoke, I mainly listened": Author's interview with Norman Lloyd, April 2016.

"Joan would think": Author's interview with Chris Coppel, June 2017.

"he liked to win": Author's interview with Jackie Makkink, August 15, 2015; author's interview with Norman Lloyd, August 2000.

he was trying to steer Joan: *Los Angeles Examiner*, April 4, 1941, clipping, Joan Harrison files, AMPAS; Dan Winkler, letter to Hitchcock, October 18, 1939, Hitchcock folders, Myron Selznick files, HRC.

"Proximity brought forth romance": Author's interview with Norman Lloyd, June 2014.

"rumors of affairs with actresses": Zolotow, *Billy Wilder in Hollywood*, 101.

"straight down the line": Author's interview with Jackie Makkink, August 15, 2015.

"*He would have picked*": Author's interview with Pascale "Pat" Franchot Tone, June 21, 2018.

hoping for a long-term relationship: Joe Graham, memo to Myron Selznick, August 6, 1940, Hitchcock folders, Myron Selznick Agency files, HRC.

He noted that she would be paid: Joe Graham, memo to Myron Selznick, August 6, 1940, Hitchcock folders, Myron Selznick Agency files, HRC.

10. Building Suspense

"*through the eyes*": J. R. McDonough, memo to Harry Edington, RKO, June 3, 1940, quoted in Krohn, "Ambivalence (*Suspicion*)," 84.

robust $550,000 budget: Krohn, "Ambivalence (*Suspicion*)," 86.

"*world's largest dining*": "Palladium Will Open to Halloween Throngs," *Los Angeles Times*, October 27, 1940.

Joan and Alma spent their days: Author's interview with Patricia Hitchcock O'Connell, August 2000.

"*Arguments?*": Barnsley, "Women Authors Disagree."

"*I drank more*": McGilligan, *Darkness and Light*, 279–280.

"*That story broke more*": McGilligan, 279.

"*Some women give birth*": Iles, *Before the Fact*, 3.

"*It did seem a pity*": Iles, 233.

like a prolonged suicide note: Krohn, "Ambivalence (*Suspicion*)," 107.

"*Analyzing her subject*": Iles, *Before the Fact*, 221.

"*unwitting detective*": Faubert, "Role and Presence of Authorship in Suspicion," 44.

RKO's concerns: Krohn, "Ambivalence (*Suspicion*)," 112. Krohn performs an artful comparison of the numerous script drafts. See also Worland, "Before and After the Fact"; and Auiler, *Hitchcock's Notebooks*.

"*The only mistake*": Fontaine, *No Bed of Roses*, 134.

"*we know we cannot believe him*": Script files for *Suspicion*, March 6, 1941, and April 23, 1941, Alfred Hitchcock Collection, AMPAS.

the couple feeds the milk: *Suspicion* final script, with revised changes, December 28, 1940, *Suspicion* script folder, RKO Studio Collection, UCLA.

"*Fade out and fade in*": Truffaut, *Hitchcock*, 142.

he lured Grant to the project: Krohn, "Ambivalence (*Suspicion*)," 71–72. Krohn notes that Lina's nickname "letter-box" and the novel's numerous references to mail and postage must have caught Joan Harrison's eye, as they are threaded throughout various drafts of the script. Hitchcock then went out of his way to film such details, perhaps for metaphorical or literary reasons. See Krohn, 104–106.

Was this supposed to be a thriller: Worland, "Before and After the Fact," 14–15.

"Joanie and I have written": McGilligan, *Darkness and Light*, 289.

"You could not take": Krohn, "Ambivalence (*Suspicion*)," 97.

"the series of pictures": Iles, *Before the Fact*, 1.

"a far finer film": Reviews from the *New York Herald Telegram*, *New York Times*, and *PM* are quoted in an ad in *Variety*, November 26, 1941.

"The closing scenes": "Suspicion," *Harrington's Reports*, September 27, 1941, 154.

"This certainly seems suggestive": Joseph Breen, memo to Joseph J. Nolan, February 6, 1941, *Suspicion* folder, MPAA files, AMPAS.

"Isobel glances around": *Suspicion* final script, *Suspicion* script folder.

earned a wealth of experience: Though *Suspicion* occupied most of Joan's time, she was developing other Hitchcock vehicles through the summer and fall of 1941. One such project was an "erotic story" in the vein of *The 39 Steps* tentatively conceived for Ingrid Bergman. Based on a true account, it followed a "young wife of a military attaché [. . .] and a close male friend, [who] after being kidnapped, are chained together by Chinese brigands for six months" and must wind their way through Asia until they can set things right. Hitchcock told David O. Selznick that Harrison already had the treatment completely outlined, though he may have been bluffing on how far along she was. See David O. Selznick, memo to Val Lewton, April 2, 1941, David O. Selznick Collection, HRC.

11. Hitting Hurdles

"rushing into different rooms": "Hitch Tops, Flagg Sits," *Hollywood Citizen News*, November 6, 1941, clipping, Hitchcock files, AMPAS.

Hitchcock became irate: David O. Selznick to Alfred Hitchcock (drafted, unsent), September 22, 1941, David O. Selznick Collection, HRC.

Houseman exercised his fine skills: Houseman, *Run-Through*, 479.

"For some time, she was mine": Taylor, "Was Alfred Hitchcock a Mysogynist?"; author's interview with Norman Lloyd, June 27, 2014. Though Houseman disclosed his relationship with Joan to Hitchcock's biographer John Russell Taylor in the mid-1980s, one assumes he was guided by chivalric impulses when writing a rather terse description of her in his own memoir. He mentions her briefly as "an able, well-tailored English blonde who had been [Hitchcock's] assistant in London." See Houseman, *Unfinished Business*, 236. He offers no hint of romance, yet, their friendship never cooled, which his book also happens to mention ever so briefly. Later, when his career hit his lowest ebb as a result of the blacklist, Joan was one of the very few people who continued to write him. Houseman, *Run-Through*, 478–479.

Houseman was eager to confront: Houseman, *Unfinished Business*, 237.

"I would have to try": Daggett, "It's a Woman's World Too," 22.

Harrison and Viertel ran: Shnayerson, *Irwin Shaw*, 104.

Sunday, December 7: For one brief but illuminating account of December 7, 1941, see Brackett, *"It's the Pictures That Got Small,"* Kindle loc. 3216.

"an indefinite period": Joan Harrison agreement summary, December 8, 1941, Paramount Pictures contract files, AMPAS.

"tremendously enthusiastic": Othman, "New Motion Picture Producer Has Pretty Legs."

"Without her, this place changed": Swindell, *Screwball*, 14.

he never did fully recover: Ruth Waterbury, "How Clark Gable Is Conquering Loneliness," *Photoplay*, August 1942, 34.

No one can say for sure: Taylor, "Was Alfred Hitchcock a Mysogynist?"

recently catapulted him: Shnayerson, *Irwin Shaw*, 93.

"always seemed delighted": Shnayerson, 17.

"She wore a skirt": Author's interview with Norman Lloyd, June 27, 2014.

essentially separated: Shnayerson, *Irwin Shaw*, 110–115.

Joan had the kinds of qualities: Shnayerson, 153.

"It was not flirtatiousness": Author's interview with Norman Lloyd, August 2000.

"Irwin was the best lay": Shnayerson, *Irwin Shaw*, 132.

"'You look at them as if'": Irwin Shaw, "The Girls in Their Summer Dresses," *New Yorker*, February 4, 1939, 17–19.

the writer wasn't always so attuned: Shnayerson, *Irwin Shaw*, 88–92, 153.

"the thinking for both": Mayne, *Directed by Dorothy Arzner*, 110–111.

"We can't have this": Elliott Arnold, *The Commandos: A Novel* (New York: Duell, Sloan and Pearce, 1942), 236.

"At the end of every rehearsal": Margulies, "Tribute to Dorothy Arzner," 17.

she directed all location: Peary and Kay, "Interview with Dorothy Arzner," 10–14.

with a severe facial rash: Walker and Walker, *Light on Her Face*, 245.

she had trouble focusing: Higham and Moseley, *Merle*, 152.

precarious position: Walker and Walker, *Light on Her Face*, 245.

"Arzner's off the picture": Walker and Walker, 246. Vidor was initially brought in on February 15 to "complete the few remaining scenes," but then took a break (presumably for rewrites) and resumed more extensive production on April 28. See "Arzner III; Vidor Winds Columbia's 'Night,'" *Hollywood Reporter*, February 15, 1943; "Vidor Replaces Arzner, Columbia Resumes 'Attack,'" *Hollywood Reporter*, April 28, 1943.

"to finish it in fast order": Walker and Walker, *Light on Her Face*, 246. Oberon grew to dislike Vidor, whom she saw as volatile and high-strung. He would come to the set unprepared and attempt to cover it up with "fire and brimstone." See Higham and Moseley, *Merle*, 173.

"The studios didn't think": Hopper, "Hedda Hopper's Hollywood." Even with the change in directors, *First Comes Courage* was still marketed as an Arzner picture, with an eye toward female audiences. See press book for *First Comes Courage*, Columbia Pictures, 1943, BFI; review of *First Comes Courage*, *Motion Picture Herald Product Digest* (September 11, 1943): 1530.

"What came out": Othman, "New Motion Picture Producer Has Pretty Legs."

"wondering whether there was something wrong": "Money Comes Second," *Woman's Hour*, quoted in Ware, "British Girl."

"And I've just this minute": Hopper, "Hedda Hopper's Hollywood."

an original story titled "Jackpot": Joan Harrison and Helen Deutsch, synopsis of *Jackpot*, December 11, 1941, Ray Spencer Papers, Paramount Pictures, 1937–1944, UCLA.

"He is not only": Kronenberger, "Remembered After Darkness."

They experimented: *Seventh Cross* files, March 30, 1943, March 31, 1943, April 3, 1943, and April 6, 1943, MGM script files, AMPAS.

Cronyn and Tandy rehearsed: Neve, "Past Master of His Craft," 86.

"at a time": Neve, 147.

"The script was so unsuitably cast": "Money Comes Second," *Woman's Hour*, quoted in Ware, "British Girl."

She wondered if she had been spoiled: Ware, "British Girl."

"Everything I wrote": Hedda Hopper, "Producer Joan Harrison Wins Filmdom's Respect," *Baltimore Sun*, October 14, 1945; Ware, "British Girl."

she wanted some guarantee: Niemeyer, "Pretty Girl in a Big Job."

"I had no desire": Ware, "British Girl."

If you feel so strongly: Othman, "New Motion Picture Producer Has Pretty Legs"; Niemeyer, "Pretty Girl in a Big Job."

12. Phantom Lady

"first woman producer": Untitled article, *Los Angeles Examiner*, April 30, 1943, Harrison files, AMPAS.

"anywhere, with dimples": Berch, "Hitchcock Alumna."

"golden-haired ball of fire": Hopper, "Wrath Made Joan Harrison a Producer"; Jerry D. Lewis, *Collier's*, August 14, 1943, 55; Scheuer, "Producer's Spurs Won by Woman."

"tilt[ed] one blond eyebrow": Cinema: The New Pictures, *Time*, February 28, 1944.

"Well, want any leg art, boys?": *Phantom Lady* publicity photo (caption), Universal Pictures, 1943, Doheny Library, USC; Cinema: The New Pictures, *Time*, February 28, 1944.

"from the woman's angle": Lewis, "Murder, She Says," 55.

"a formula which has never": "Phantom Lady First Mystery for Lady Fans," press book for *Phantom Lady*, Universal Pictures, 4.

"Women need something": Berch, "Hitchcock Alumna."

Universal now aimed to distribute: Schatz, *Genius of the System*, 340–345.

Joan set up shop: Berch, "Hitchcock Alumna."

"shiny-faced American babe": "Ella Raines, Quick to Attain Cinema Stardom," press book for *Uncle Harry*, Universal Pictures, 2.

They were Carol in the flesh: Snelson, *Phantom Ladies*, 5–6.

"she turns out to be a nightmare": Smith, "Light in the Dark," 31.

Calling the situation "swell": Joan Harrison, quoted in Grams and Wikstrom, *Alfred Hitchcock Presents Companion*, 36.

"the familiarity": Schatz, *Genius of the System*, 250.

"only a sort of vague": Schatz, 250.

he had no experience in film: Canfield, "Boss Man Is a Lady," 79.

"but I believe a new writer": Niemeyer, "Pretty Girl in a Big Job," 3H, 61. Schoenfeld enjoyed a long career, mostly in television but also writing the films *The Dark Corner* (1946) and *Caged* (1950), which have been reappraised over time.

Joan had justification: Cinema: The New Pictures, *Time*, February 28, 1944, 94; "Just Can't Afford to Experiment," *Indianapolis Star*, May 28, 1944, 23; Smyth, *Nobody's Girl Friday*, 107. The union policies that forced Harrison to choose between belonging to the Producers Guild or the Writers Guild probably contributed to her marginalization in historical records. Her official writing credits are not formally listed in Writers Guild of America West directories.

"wrong man": Muller, "Murder, She Made," 18.

the director hand-carried a print: Deborah Lazaroff Alpi, *Robert Siodmak: A Biography, with Critical Analyses of His Film Noirs and a Filmography of All His Works* (Jefferson, NC: MacFarland, 1998), 105.

"would be fortunate to have": Joan Harrison, interview with Lutz Bacher, January 26, 1980, quoted in Lutz Bacher, *Max Ophuls in the Hollywood Studios* (New Brunswick, NJ: Rutgers University Press, 1996), 34–35. Siodmak would later help Ophüls land his first studio job. As Ophüls was on the verge of deciding to return to Europe, Siodmak advised him not to leave until doing at least one successful American picture. Siodmak convinced Universal to hire him for *The Exile*, which led to three more significant achievements and an esteemed career. See Greco, *File on Robert Siodmak*, 21–22.

They envisioned a film: "Phantom Lady, Ominous Thriller, Almost Silent," press book for *Phantom Lady*, Universal Pictures, 3.

He tutored him in the art: Cairns, "Dark Mirrors"; Greco, *File on Robert Siodmak*, 21.

"the largest in the studio's history": "Pre-war Canvas Shades 'Phantom,'" press book for *Phantom Lady*, Universal Pictures, 4.

shooting the backlot as an "open street": Niemeyer, "Pretty Girl in a Big Job."

"against the conventional": Taylor, *Hitch*, 51.

"always thought of him": Niemeyer, "Pretty Girl in a Big Job."

"Mentally": Author's interview with Pascal "Pat" Franchot Tone, June 21, 2018.

Joan would recall: Canfield, "Boss Man Is a Lady," 80–81.

"I stayed up all night": Wright, untitled *Daily News* clipping, 23.

an ideal match: Contract actress Louise Allbritton was under consideration, according to early press notices.

Feldman had stolen her: McCarthy, *Howard Hawks*, 347.

"I loved [Howard] and adored him": McCarthy, 348–349.

touted the headline: "Ella Raines: The Pretty Young Star Began Her Career by Being Incorporated for $1,000,000 by a Production Firm," *Life*, February 28, 1944, 22.

"a bit of inward groaning": Raines, "Role I Liked Best," 95.

"The usual studio designer": Niemeyer, "Pretty Girl in a Big Job."

"that her clothes would be ordinary": "Overnight Star in Finest Dramatic Role of Season," press book for *Phantom Lady*, Universal Pictures, 4.

"Chick-a Chick": Songwriters Eddie Cherkose and Jacques Press filed a $20,000 suit against Universal in July 1944 for neglecting to give them screen credit for the song. The outcome is unclear.

Production began in mid-September: "Pictures Now Shooting," *Hollywood Reporter*, September 17, 1943; October 22, 1943, 11.

"hat of horror": "Hat Causes Much Havoc in 'Phantom,'" press book for *Phantom Lady*, Universal Pictures, 3; "Exhibit the Hat of Horror in Lobby," press book for *Phantom Lady*, Universal Pictures, 6.

"it really was four characterizations": Raines, "Role I Liked Best," 95.

"The audience had to feel": Raines, 95.

as Michael Walker points out: Walker, "Robert Siodmak," 115.

"how far the sheltered Kansas": Smith, "Light in the Dark," 28.

"the relationship between Carol": Joseph Breen to Maurice Pivar, September 3, 1943, and screenplay for *Phantom Lady*, August 24, 1943, *Phantom Lady* file, MPAA files, AMPAS.

"jam session [is] used": James Agee, review of *Phantom Lady*.

she hovers outside: See, for example, Snelson, *Phantom Ladies*, 111.

fifty thousand Ouija boards: Gertrude Berger, "The Ouija Board Comes Back," *New York Times*, September 10, 1944.

"to engage with the emotional": See Snelson, *Phantom Ladies*, 91; W.K. "Anxiety and Spiritualism Related," *New York Times*, October 29, 1944.

"a womanly experiment": Heffernan, "Pretty, Blue-Eyed Blonde"; Monahan, "'Phantom Lady' at Fulton Lively."

marked a turning point: Nevins, "Translate and Transform," 137.

Joan was part of a new vision: Spicer, *Film Noir*, 113; Spicer, *Historical Dictionary of Film Noir*, 231–234; Biesen, *Blackout*, 128–136; Walker, "Robert Siodmak," 110–115; Telotte, *Voices in the Dark*, 30.

"a new horror cycle": Stanley, "Hollywood Shivers." See also Stanley's "Hollywood Flash."

"the only wartime product": Schatz, *Genius of the System*, 345.

making herself invaluable: "Virginia Van Upp," *Hollywood Reporter*, February 15, 1944.

"their heads together": See Smyth, *Nobody's Girl Friday*, 262n119.

13. New Associations

"an intellect, a lady": Marlene L. Laskey, interview by Paul László, November 7, 1984, Oral History Program, Architecture and Urban Planning Library, UCLA, 1986, https://archive.org/stream/designingwithspi00lasz/designingwithspi00lasz_djvu.txt.

"look[ed] like an extensive private park": Mary Roche, "Out of the West," *New York Times*, November 11, 1945.

"a woman looking forward": Eugenia Harty, "Hollywood's Woman Producer Is Most Glamourous Girl in Town," *Atlanta Constitution*, August 13, 1943.

"as if she were a congresswoman": Inga Arvad, "Rita Hayworth Barred by Studio," *Winnipeg Tribune*, January 22, 1944.

"entertaining at home": Roche, "Out of the West."

"a disarming hostess": Harty, "Hollywood's Woman Producer."

"The front office attitude": Joan Harrison, cited in Grams and Wikstrom, *Alfred Hitchcock Presents Companion*, 36.

she received a call from Hunt Stromberg: Hunt Stromberg biography (press release), ca. 1944, Stromberg files, AMPAS; "Stromberg Resignation Made Official," *Motion Picture Herald*, February 14, 1942.

Joan to consider producing: "Joan Harrison May Produce Stromberg Pix," *Hollywood Reporter*, December 28, 1944.

"We have a forty-day schedule": Joan Harrison, cited in Grams and Wikstrom, *Alfred Hitchcock Presents Companion*, 36.

filmmakers decided to use her diary: Sandy Flitterman-Lewis, "Guest in the House: Rupture and Reconstitution of the Bourgeois Nuclear Family," *Wide Angle* 4, no. 2 (1980): 24–26.

Stromberg had initially wanted: Production files for *Guest in the House*, Hunt Stromberg papers, AMPAS.

He and Stromberg had plans: "Stromberg, 'Milly' Tie For One Per Year," *Hollywood Reporter*, January 26, 1944.

"over a misunderstanding": "Harrison Exits," *Hollywood Reporter*, January 21, 1944.

"the Hunt Stromberg set up": Edwin Schallert, "Joan Harrison Buys Next Screen Subject," *Los Angeles Times*, January 27, 1944.

She was feeling out distribution deals: Schallert, "Joan Harrison Buys Next." She was bidding on "The Shallow Urn" by Gamond Percy.

Harrison and Joan Fontaine were considering: Hedda Hopper, In Hollywood, *Hartford Courant*, May 30, 1944.

After two weeks: Charles Higham, *Hollywood Cameraman* (New York: Garland, 1986), 48.

finished the picture: *Guest in the House* opened to mixed reviews in December 1944.

had been inspired: Author's interview with Amanda Cockrell, March 10, 2015.

he worked the necessary angles: Louella Parsons, "Susan Hayward Is Removed from Cast of Dark Waters, Merle Oberon Is Given Role," *Fresno Bee*, May 8, 1944.

"haunted, romantic": Higham and Moseley, *Merle*, 231.

"full-time playboy": Andre de Toth and Anthony Slide, *De Toth on de Toth: Putting the Drama in Front of the Camera* (London: Faber and Faber, 1996), 55. For his description of the Orsatti brothers as the Corleone family, see Andre de Toth, interview with Alain Silver, *Film Noir Reader 3: Interviews with Filmmakers of the Classic Noir Period*, edited by Alain Silver and James Ursini (New York: Limelight Editions, 2002), 11.

"the biggest piece of shit": De Toth, interview with Silver. 11.

a near-record-setting deal: De Toth, interview with Silver, 11; author's interview with Amanda Cockrell, March 10, 2015. Bogeaus competed with MGM and Fox before landing the *Dark Waters* purchase, reportedly conferring "one of the highest prices ever paid for a magazine serial. See Edwin Schallert, "Dark Waters' Purchase Registers High Price," *Los Angeles Times*, January 17, 1944.

"We have a woman 'producer'": Andre de Toth, *Fragments: Portraits from the Inside* (New York: Faber and Faber, 1994), 329.

"Separately they were housebroken": De Toth, *Fragments*, 329.

"she despised them more": De Toth and Slide, *De Toth on De Toth*, 55.

"Bogeaus handles the money": Joan Harrison, cited in Grams and Wikstrom, *Alfred Hitchcock Presents Companion*, 36.

Some of her colleagues pushed back: De Toth, *Fragments*, 333.

But Joan liked the role: "Dark Waters: A New Thrilling Arrival," press book for *Dark Waters*, United Artists, 1944, 12, AMPAS.

he didn't get along particularly well: Higham and Moseley, *Merle*, 167.

his marriage to Lesley Black fell apart: De Toth, interview with Silver, 11.

Huston always came through: De Toth, *Fragments*, 333; de Toth, interview with Silver, 11.

where they filmed long shots: "Dark Waters Staff Film Bayou Country," press book for *Dark Waters*, United Artists, 13.

making quicksand from mashed potatoes: Higham and Moseley, *Merle*, 167.

The actress was known for vacillating: Higham and Moseley, 231.

complicated family history: "Merle Oberon as George Sand," *Life*, February 5, 1945, 68.

a portrait of her "mother": Higham and Moseley, *Merle*, 91.

"all creative people": Canfield, "Boss Man Is a Lady," 81.

good reviews: "Dark Waters a Hit at Globe Theater," *Brooklyn Daily Eagle*, December 12, 1944; Jack O'Brian, "*Dark Waters* Is Admirable," *Beatrice (NE) Daily Sun / Associated Press*, December 24, 1944; "Notes on Things," *Gazette* (Ontario), July 28, 1944; "Screen News: Joan Harrison to Make *Third Eye* at Universal," *New York Times*, December 28, 1944; Edwin Schallert, "Harrison to Do *Knave*," *Los Angeles Times*, February 7, 1945.

"killer-diller of a thriller": Bosley Crowther, "The Screen: *Dark Waters*, a Thriller," *New York Times*, November 22, 1944.

14. Bedeviling Endings

Plans for the launch: "Screen News: Sanders, Misses Raines and Fitzgerald Teamed," *New York Times*, February 13, 1945.

The specifics of Joan's contract: Universal Studio Salaries Report, 1945–1947, Universal Studios, box 23370-78.

But he wasn't interested: Charles Feldman to Clifford Hayman, September 4, 1944, and to Emmett Ward, June 10, 1945, Charles K. Feldman papers, AFI.

"outstanding characteristic is her": Thomas Job, *Uncle Harry: A Play in Three Acts* (New York: Samuel French, 1942), 13.

The film adaptation was titled: The film was retitled *Uncle Harry* for its theatrical run and later distributed as *The Strange Affair of Uncle Harry* (adhering to the preproduction title). In 1957 a version was released under the title *Zero Murder Case* when Universal sold it to National Telefilm Association (neatly timed with the success of the *Alfred Hitchcock Presents* series). I reference it here as *Uncle Harry* for economy's sake.

friendly yet feisty personality: Author's interview with Christina Olds, June 21, 2017. See also Gertrude Shanklin, "It's No Life for a Sissy," *Screenland*, October 1946, 48, 70, 71.

"all dressed up": Caption, *Strange Affair of Uncle Harry* publicity photo, Universal Pictures files, USC.

"little boy": "Production Highlights," press book for *Uncle Harry*, Universal Pictures, 2.

"whispers hinting at something": James Robert Parish and Lennard DeCarl, *Hollywood Players: The Forties* (CreateSpace, 2015), 598.

"Everybody wants pictures": Hedda Hopper, On Hollywood, *New York Daily News*, October 12, 1943.

"She spends her evenings": Cited in Parish and DeCarl, *Hollywood Players*, 598.

drag fashion was frivolous: Author's interview with Norman Lloyd, August 2000, June 2013, and April 2016.

during the Rebecca screen tests: Reville and Harrison, notes on *Rebecca* screen tests.

"looking for my new daddy": Allan Earbietz, "Scarlett O'Hara's Younger Sister," *New York Times*, July 28, 1977.

Keyes was a natural-born writer: Author's interview with Allan Glaser, January 5, 2019.

Joan was thankful to have Evelyn: Joan Harrison to Evelyn Keyes, January 2, 1970, September 13, 1973, December 18, 1973, and July 17, 1976, in possession of the author.

Some who knew Joan: Author's interview with Georgina Williams, August 10, 2016; author's interview with Allan Glaser, January 5, 2019; author's interview with Joan Buck, April 16, 2019.

"It's getting to be a habit": Untitled clippings, *Los Angeles Examiner*, April 7, 1945, April 13, 1945, and April 30, 1945, Harrison files, AMPAS.

"surely one of the most": Michelangelo Capua, *Anatole Litvak: The Life and Films* (Jefferson, NC: McFarland, 2015), Kindle locs. 731, 758.

"the man of the house": Capua, Kindle locs. 731, 756.

"he was the first decent man": Joan Juliet Buck, *The Price of Illusion* (New York: Simon and Schuster, 2017), 25.

"talking about the President": Joan Harrison to John Huston, April 9, 1950, Walter Huston condolences, John Huston papers, f. 1118, AMPAS.

one of the Hitchcocks' Sealyham terriers: Alma Reville to Carol Stevens, November 10, 1944, Financial Account (Alma Reville Hitchcock), 1944, general files, Alfred Hitchcock Collection, AMPAS.

"Mother and I": Whitfield Cook, diary entry, May 1, 1945, Cook Diaries, 1935–1949, Whitfield G. Cook Collection, HGRC.

"carrying a handbag": Robert Siodmak, "A New Approach," *Los Angeles Daily News*, August 20, 1943.

"more emotional types": "'Everyone a Potential Killer,' Says Producer," press book for
    Uncle Harry, Universal Pictures, 1945, 2, USC.

"everyone is a potential killer": "'Everyone a Potential Killer,'" 2.

"once every ten to fifteen years": "'Everyone a Potential Killer,'" 1.

"how she's felt": Joseph Breen to Maurice Pivar, March 26, 1945, *Uncle Harry* PCA
    files, AMPAS.

Breen had preapproved it: Joseph Breen to Fritz Lang, May 27, 1943, and Joseph Breen
    to Lee Marcus (RKO Pathé), July 28, 1943, *Uncle Harry* PCA files, AMPAS.

Murphy's instructions: Joseph Breen to Maurice Pivar, July 25, 1945, *Uncle Harry* PCA
    files, AMPAS.

endless edits and test screenings: Hollywood Jottings, *New York Times*, August 19,
    1945; Irving Hoffman, "Critics Vent Wrath at Hays Code for Uncle Harry End,"
    Hollywood Reporter, August 27, 1945. See also Greco, *File on Robert Siodmak*, 62.

"professional integrity": Virginia Wright, untitled *Daily News* clipping, ca. 1944, Harrison
    files, AMPAS.

"not that audiences won't like them": Canfield, "Boss Man Is a Lady," 83.

already-prepared adaptation: Virginia Wright, untitled *Daily News* clipping, ca. 1944,
    Harrison files, AMPAS; "Joan Harrison to Make 'Third Eye' at Universal," *New
    York Times*, December 28, 1944. Harrison's third picture was slated to be an
    adaptation of Percy Marks' *The Knave of Diamonds* (1943). She had been willing
    to negotiate with Universal on a solution to the ending, and Saunders offered to
    donate time to retakes, but in the end the studio was unwilling to compromise.
    (See Wright, 23.)

"industry too set against": H. C. Norris, "Within the Velvet Glove," *Philadelphia Inquirer*,
    March 12, 1944.

"tired of being told": Heffernan, "Pretty, Blue-Eyed Blonde."

"glass-gaze": Norris, "Within the Velvet Glove."

"movie of the month": Roche, "Out of the West"; Canfield, "Boss Man Is a Lady," 79–83.

"golden-haired ball": Hopper, "Wrath Made Joan Harrison a Producer."

15. Crimes and Misdemeanors

"I never knew": Joan Harrison to Hedda Hopper, October 15, 1945, Hedda Hopper
    files, box F 1582, AMPAS.

it was official: "News of the Screen: Joan Harrison Signed by RKO," *New York Times*,
    October 16, 1945.

His most notable failures: Richard B. Jewell with Vernon Harbin, *The RKO Story* (New
    York: Arlington House, 1982), 10–12.

more powerful and fertile: Jewell with Harbin, 14;

"Koerner knows how": Muir, "Joan Harrison Worrying."

aided by master cinematographer: Ned Marin, Edwin's brother, was a vice president in Charles Feldman's agency. The assignment might have been a result of Harrison's close ties to the agency.

went with Lynn Bari: Screen test notes, April 16, 1946, *Nocturne* production files, RKO files, box 157, UCLA; Leo Verswijver, *"Movies Were Always Magical": Interviews with 19 Actors, Directors, and Producers from the Hollywood of the 1930s Through the 1950s* (New York: McFarland, 2003), 65.

"I made a career": Lynn Bari to Lee Mortimer, quoted in Ray Hagen, *Killer Tomatoes: Fifteen Tough Film Dames* (New York: McFarland, 2012), 27.

"first bobby sox star": Victor Gunson, "Hollywood Gets First Bobby-Sox Star: She Is Virginia Huston, a Find from Omaha," *Evening Independent* (Massillon, OH), March 28, 1946, 9.

"Club Nocturn": Call sheets, May 17, 1946, *Nocturne* production files, RKO files, box 157, UCLA.

she delivered the film: Budget detail, May 17, 1946, *Nocturne* production files, RKO files, box 157, UCLA.

This choreography was accomplished: Robert F. Boyle, interview by George E. Turner, 1998, 123–124, Oral History Program, AMPAS.

"The Hollywood Studio Club": Bess M. Wilson, "Studio Club's Twenty-Four Years of Service Impressive," *Los Angeles Times*, February 24, 1946.

"famed actress": Sweeney Among the Nightingales (*Nocturne*) treatment, May 29, 1945, 4–5, *Nocturne* story files, RKO files, box 1190, UCLA.

"had great taste": Jeff Gordon, *Foxy Lady: The Authorized Biography of Lynn Bari*, (Albany, GA: BearManor Media, 2018), 274.

female-run theater: "It's Fifty Times for a Laugh Time," *Brooklyn Daily Eagle*, October 9, 1943.

he sold Hitchcock the original story: Gordon McDonell's short story "Shadow of a Doubt" came to Hitchcock's attention when his wife, Mary McDonell, brought it to her boss David O. Selznick's attention. She was Selznick's West Coast story editor in the early 1940s.

her grooming: William Hare, *Hitchcock and the Methods of Suspense* (New York: McFarland, 2007), 272. Harrison had initially pushed for Greer to take Verna's role, but RKO insisted on their own Susan Hayward.

"I want to test you": Lee Server, *Robert Mitchum: Baby I Don't Care* (New York: Macmillan, 2002), 121.

"The difference is astounding": Server, 121.

a new wardrobe: Verswijver, *"Movies Were Always Magical,"* 65.

"They have sent a prison": Gordon McDonnell, "They Won't Believe Me" (unpublished novel), n.d., 1, RKO files, box 1199, UCLA.

"a verbatim of a celebrated trial": Hitchcock, "My Own Methods."

"homme fatal": Eddie Muller, Introduction to *They Won't Believe Me*, Noir Alley, Turner Classic Movies, October 8, 2017.

"almost completely devoid": Joseph Breen to William Gordon, April 26, 1946, 1, *They Won't Believe Me* PCA files, AMPAS.

"compensating moral values": Joseph Breen to William Gordon, April 25, 1946, 1, *They Won't Believe Me* PCA files, AMPAS.

helped the parties reach an agreement: Houseman, *Run-Through*, 275–285.

"more than a prop": Breen to Gordon, April 25, 1946, 1.

"writing dirty words": Breen to Gordon, April 26, 1946, 3.

"even [had] enough strength": Joseph Breen to William Gordon, May 28, 1946, 2, *They Won't Believe Me* PCA files, AMPAS.

"lustful, or passionate": Breen to Gordon, May 28, 1946, 2.

"be eliminated entirely": M. Holdenfield, memo to RKO, July 9, 1946, *They Won't Believe Me* PCA files, AMPAS.

"closet-directors": Boyle, interview by Turner, 126.

"So I'm writing this": McDonnell, "They Won't Believe Me," 124.

still needed working out: Production for *They Won't Believe Me* ran from June 6 through October 5, 1946, with a reshoot of the final courthouse scene on October 29.

In one script version: *They Won't Believe Me* story files, August 7, 1946, RKO files, box 1200, UCLA.

further script revisions: *They Won't Believe Me* story files, September 25, 1946, RKO files, box 1200, UCLA.

"directly responsible for the death": Joseph Breen, memo to Melniker, October 8, 1946, *They Won't Believe Me*, PCA files, AMPAS.

"distinctly suprising": Thomas M. Pryor, "They Won't Believe Me," *New York Times*, July 17, 1947.

"producer Joan Harrison": Cinema: The New Pictures, *Time*, June 23, 1947.

"RKO Radio won't believe me": Rivesville, WV, exhibitor to *Motion Picture Herald*, February 21, 1948, quoted in Mark A. Viera, *Into the Dark: The Hidden World of Film Noir, 1941–1950* (New York: Running Press Adult, 2016), Kindle loc. 2286.

"marriage is the best thing": John L. Scott, "Ella Raines Will Sail to Join Mate," *Los Angeles Times*, November 14, 1948.

"Never had time for it": Scheuer, "Producer's Spurs Won by Woman."

"worried about butter": Muir, "Joan Harrison Worrying."

contemplating having a baby: Hopper, "Wrath Made Joan Harrison a Producer."

"If I'd had a child": Author's interview with Jackie Makkink, August 4, 2015.

Her beautifully sculpted nose: Author's interview with Edith Tobias Chanock, May 2017.

"Miss Princess": Author's interview with Chanock.

Sarett, wanting to give the impression: Author's interview with Chanock.

Noted for her advanced intellect: Author's interview with Chanock.

"biggest motion picture transaction": Jewell with Harbin, *RKO Story*, 226.

everyone on the RKO lot: Melvin E. Matthews, Jr., *Duck and Cover: Civil Defense Images in Film and Television from the Cold War to 9/11* (Jefferson, NC: McFarland, 2011), 34.

placed all story and cast approvals: Richard B. Jewell, *Slow Fade to Black: The Decline of RKO Radio Pictures* (Berkeley: University of California Press, 2016), 85.

one-third of RKO's workforce: Donald L. Bartlett and James B. Steele, *Howard Hughes: His Life and Madness* (New York: W. W. Norton, 2011), 168.

"fighting and fornication": Ambler, *Story So Far*, 100.

16. Let It Ride

traded sweet nothings: Hedda Hopper, On Hollywood, *Los Angeles Times*, May 15, 1948; Harrison Carroll, "Behind the Scenes," *Lancaster Eagle-Gazette*, June 23, 1950; miscellaneous untitled clippings, January–December 1948, Harrison file, AMPAS.

"the fruit grows large": Caroline Moorehead, *Sidney Bernstein: A Biography* (London: Jonathan Cape, 1984), 101.

Joan was often there: Whitfield Cook, diary entries, May 1947–December 1948, Cook Diaries, 1935–1949, Whitfield G. Cook Collection, HGRC.

Sidney's inordinate affluence: Obituary for Sidney Bernstein, *Independent*, February 6, 1993, https://www.independent.co.uk/news/people/obituary-lord -bernstein-1471201.html; Moorehead, *Sidney Bernstein*, 32.

Joan would produce: Harrison's three-picture contract was technically with Universal. Montgomery's contract specified that he star in three Universal pictures. His producing agreement gave him the option to offer his acting services out to other studios. He had the authority to exercise choice over story, cast, and his producing partner. He never elected a producer other than Harrison while at Universal.

"a brilliant tour de force": "Camera-Eye Montgomery," *Newsweek*, February 3, 1947, 73.

"revolution in movies": Jesse Zunser, "Revolution in Movies," *Cue*, January 18, 1947, 12–13.

"Most of the formidable": Review of *Lady in the Lake*, *Time*, January 7, 1947.

"The novelty begins to wear thin": TMP, "The Screen in Review," *New York Times*, January 29, 1947.

"The studios have got to realize": Bob Thomas, "Robert Montgomery Foresees Vast Change in Movie-Making Industry," *Harrisburg Telegraph*, March 21, 1947.

studio-backed union: Miranda J. Banks, *The Writers: A History of American Screenwriters and Their Guild* (New Brunswick, NJ: Rutgers University Press, 2015), Kindle loc. 1286.

"training ground for GOP activists": Steven J. Ross, *Hollywood Left and Right: How Movie Stars Shaped American Politics* (Oxford: Oxford University Press, 2011), 47.

"lunatic fringe": Testimony of Robert Montgomery, Communism in the Motion Picture Industry, October 23, 1947, Hearings Before the Committee on Un-American Activities, *House of Representatives* (Washington, DC: Government Printing Office, 1947), 205. The 167-page FBI file on Montgomery that runs from January 21, 1954, to December 29, 1960, traces nearly ten instances in which he supported "Communist fronts," labor strikes or causes such as the Spanish Civil War, though these all appear to have occurred before World War II. He continued to maintain thick ties with friends and colleagues from his more left-leaning days, rarely letting politics get in the way. Close observers of Montgomery have suggested that he was not as staunch a conservative as most historians have assumed.

"in a large house": Robert Montgomery biography (press release), 1947, *Lady in the Lake* files, MGM Collection, USC.

The tragedy made national headlines: "Man Jumps to Death from Brooklyn Bridge: Hundreds See Death from Trolley to Rail," *Philadelphia Inquirer*, June 25, 1922; "Wealthy N.Y. Rubber Firm Head Drowns Himself in River," *Denver Post*, June 26, 1922.

landing him on Broadway: "Robert Montgomery," *Current Biography*, 1948, 457.

The offer was revoked: James Robert Parish and Don E. Stanke, *The Debonairs* (1975; repr. New York: Arlington House, 2015), Kindle locs. 8238–8239.

Montgomery's income: "Bogart's Pay Top for Film Players," *New York Times*, February 6, 1949.

He ended up backing out: Bacher, *Max Ophuls in the Hollywood Studios*, 65. See also "International Pictures," Hollywood Renegades Archive, 2005, https://www.cobbles.com/simpp_archive/international_universal.htm.

a prestige house: Nate Blumberg continued in his role as president; Cliff Work was pushed aside to a senior executive position.

"fire anyone": Bacher, *Max Ophuls in the Hollywood Studios*, 68.

"The color problem": Thomas F. Brady, "Hollywood Tackles the Facts of Life," *New York Times*, March 16, 1947.

"real characterization": Clip Boutell, "Late Books Have Many Good Points," *Daily Press* (Newport News, VA), October 6, 1946.

She considered it a "little novel": Boyle, interview by Turner, 127.

"native": Wanda Hendrix, "The Role I Liked Best," *Saturday Evening Post*, September 23, 1961, 65.

"getting more and more": Boyle, interview by Turner, 139.

"so you saw their depth": Boyle, 140.

"rough and ready": Boyle, 176.

great local fanfare: "Movie Actor Robert Montgomery Is Greeted," *Albuquerque Journal*, April 2, 1947.

Everyone settled in together: "To Make Movie in Santa Fe," *Clovis (NM) News Journal*, April 20, 1947.

re-create the interiors: "World Famous Hotel Shown in Melodrama Hit," press book for *Ride the Pink Horse*, Universal Pictures, 1947, 1, USC.

"burning of Zozobra": "Camera Shoots Ancient Ritual for the First Time," press book for *Ride the Pink Horse*, Universal Pictures, 1.

All the Taos Lions Club: Press book for *Ride the Pink Horse*, Universal Pictures, 1.

"preternaturally, self-assured girl": R. Emmet Sweeney, "Border Incidents: *Ride the Pink Horse* (1947) and *The Hanged Man* (1964)," *Streamline: The Filmstruck Blog*, March 10, 2015, http://streamline.filmstruck.com/2015/03/10/border-incidents -ride-the-pink-horse-1947-and-the-hanged-man-1964/.

deconstructs racial and ethnic categories: During production, Montgomery told an interviewer that he intentionally staged long scenes dominated by Spanish dialogue, and resisted the studio's inclination toward a large orchestral score in favor of a five-piece Mexican band because he subscribed to realist and experimental cinematic values. See Howard C. Heyn, "Fresh Screen-Telling Angle Tackled Again by Montgomery," *Cincinnati Enquirer*, July 29, 1947, 15.

"unreal, alien": Dorothy Hughes, *Ride the Pink Horse* (New York: Mysterious Press, 2013; orig. publ. 1947), Kindle loc. 389.

two harrowing scenes: The staging, camerawork, and cutting in these two scenes are worth noting for the way that they are meant to "work" on the viewer. This film brings viewers deep into its world, in order to comment on the relationship between spectatorship, violence, and power relations. Montgomery continues to go unappreciated for his directorial sophistication and his interest in pondering character relationships through long takes and the deep space of the frame (as seen in *The Lady in the Lake*). At the same time, Harrison's own interest in such techniques is worth exploring, especially considering that she was in constant conversation with Hitchcock and Sidney Bernstein during the making of *Rope* through 1947.

"He ran on": Hughes, *Ride the Pink Horse*, Kindle loc. 3336.

"clever, taut, superbly told": Marjory Adams, review of *Ride the Pink Horse*, *Boston Globe*, November 5, 1947.

"artfully fashioning a fascinating film": Bosley Crowther, review of *Ride the Pink Horse*, *New York Times*, October 9, 1947.

"a bold experiment": Eulamae Moore, review of *Ride the Pink Horse*, *Austin American Statesmen*, January 17, 1948.

"I've gambled": Donald Kirkley, Theater Notes, *Baltimore Sun*, November 16, 1947.

raved about Wanda: Press book for *Ride the Pink Horse*, Universal Pictures, 1.

"a normal type mystery": Press book for *Ride the Pink Horse*, 1.

17. Full Circle, by Degrees

"friendly" testimony: Bernard F. Dick, *Radical Innocence: A Critical Study of the Hollywood Ten* (Lexington: University Press of Kentucky, 2015), 2–4.

twenty-five-person delegation: The trip by the Committee for the First Amendment was supported by financial donations from unlikely places, such as Universal chairman William Goetz, who one month later signed his name to the Waldorf Statement. See Larry Ceplair and Steven Englund, *The Inquisition in Hollywood: Politics in the Film Community, 1930–1960* (Urbana: University of Illinois Press, 2003), 276.

"deploring": "Movies to Oust Ten Cited for Contempt of Congress: Major Companies Also Vote to Refuse Jobs to Communists," *New York Times*, November 26, 1946.

"The studios will look": Paul Henreid with Julius Fast, *Ladies Man: An Autobiography* (New York: St. Martin's, 1984), 193.

turn away from Hollywood: McGilligan, *Darkness and Light*, 414.

Houseman remembered her: John Houseman, *Front and Center* (New York: Simon and Schuster, 1979), 283.

An inflammatory article: "Wallace Blasts at Film Firms," *Des Moines Register*, October 2, 1948.

leading the charge: Bob Thomas, Hollywood Notes, *Asbury Park (NJ) Press*, October 20, 1948.

"We—my friends and I": Author's interview with Norman Lloyd, June 2015.

"the movie coup of the year": Louella Parsons, "All Guild Plays Go to Robert Montgomery," *Democrat and Chronicle* (Rochester, NY), November 21, 1948.

he would instead launch: John Caldwell, "Suspense Is Back with Spine Tingler at 8 P.M.," *Cincinnati Enquirer*, January 3, 1948.

"Robert Montgomery needed her": Author's interview with Eddie Muller, August 8, 2016.

"He was pretty hard": Boyle, interview by Turner, 128.

"We hardly spoke": Leo Verswijver, "Evelyn Keyes: The Atmosphere on the Set of *Gone with the Wind* Was Almost Party-Like," *Film Talk*, December 5, 2014, https://filmtalk.org/2014/12/05/evelyn-keyes-the-atmosphere-on-the-set-of-gone-with-the-wind-was-almost-partylike/.

"a very cold, cruel man": Davis, *Words into Images*, 165.

no producer's pay: Budget and costs for *Once More, My Darling*, Universal-International, box 271, folder 13, and daily minutes of committee meetings for *Once More, My Darling*, March 2–11, 1949, Universal-International files, box 758, folder 25309, USC.

slash every budget: Bacher, *Max Ophuls in the Hollywood Studios*, 115.

the first woman to compose: Press book for *Once More, My Darling*, Universal-International, 1949, 2, USC.

Montgomery hoped for a reunion: "Come Be My Love," *Hollywood Citizen News*, January 28, 1949.

"Working with Bob was a real treat": Author's interview with Ann Blyth, June 2, 2016.

Bel Air Hotel: These scenes were shot on location at the Bel Air Hotel. Originally, the plan was to film at a Santa Barbara hotel, which Montgomery and Harrison held out for well into production but finally relented for budgetary reasons, in part as a compromise to avoid friction after Montgomery insisted on replacing Gordon. Daily Minutes, committee meeting.

only seven setups a day: Daily minutes of committee meetings for *Once More, My Darling*, March 14–25, 1949, Universal-International files, box 758, folder 25309, USC.

"mutual agreement": Studio Roundup, *Showmen's Trade Review*, April 2, 1949.

"concern that women's nudity": Joseph Breen, memo to Joan Harrison and Michael Gordon, March 9, 1949, *Come Be My Love* PCA files, AMPAS.

"the whole story stems": Milton Holdenfield and Jack Vizzard, memo to Joan Harrison and Michael Gordon, March 16, 1949, *Come Be My Love* PCA files, AMPAS.

handled subtly: Joseph Breen, memo to Joan Harrison and Michael Gordon, March 24, 1949, *Come Be My Love* PCA files, AMPAS.

"a mixture of long, static": Reviews are cited in a memo from Phil Gerard to Lipton-Horwitz, September 26, 1949, Universal publicity files, box 525, folder 15556, USC.

"I must admit": Hank Linet, memo to David Lipton, September 13, 1949, Universal publicity files, box 525, folder 15556, USC.

Eagle-Lion to distribute: Oddly, though Rank was involved in the American distribution, it was Warner Bros. that released the film in the UK. See David Shipman, Joan Harrison Obituary, *Independent*, August 26, 1994, https://www.independent.co.uk/news/people/obituary-joan-harrison-1385798.html.

"close quadrumvirate": Jean Rouverol, *Refugees from Hollywood: A Journal of the Blacklist Years* (Albuquerque: University of New Mexico Press, 2000), 36.

"the Russians were our gallant allies": Rouverol, 23.

whoever was in the market: Butler narrowly escaped being served a subpoena by fleeing with his family to Mexico, where he lived for years as an ex-patriot. Hunter would eventually be blacklisted. At the same time that he was writing *Eye Witness*, Hunter agreed to front his name so that Dalton Trumbo could earn a salary for *Roman Holiday*, written in 1949 and produced in 1952. See Paul Buhle and David Wagner, *Radical Hollywood: The Untold Story Behind America's Favorite Movies* (New York: New Press, 2003), 86.

"a meeting of the minds": Author's interview with Jackie Makkink, October 2015.

"practically during the whole meal": Hopper, On Hollywood, *Tampa Tribune*, March 7, 1949.

Pictures of the couple: "Errol Flynn's Coming Out Party," *Screenland*, June 1949.

the black-tie event: Thomas McNulty, *Errol Flynn: The Life and Career* (New York: McFarland, 2011), 228.

She was all smiles: Louella Parsons, "Goldwyn Changes Scene, Rents Studio from Selznick," *San Francisco Examiner*, October 31, 1949.

before she scooted to New York: Hedda Hopper, Looking at Hollywood, *Chicago Tribune*, November 9, 1949; Sheilah Graham, "Money Troubles Hit New Film," *Tampa Times*, November 17, 1949.

"his most serious romance": Walter Winchell, "Walter Winchell's Broadway," *St. Louis Post-Dispatch*, December 8, 1949, 59.

"the next Mrs. Gable": Tex McCrary and Jinx Falkenberg, "Childhood in Courtroom Launched a Film Career," *Boston Daily Globe*, December 16, 1949; Sheilah Graham, "Gable's New Bride Is Chic and Gay, and She Can Cook Too," *Cleveland Plains Dealer*, January 11, 1950.

GABLE AND DOUG FAIRBANKS' WIDOW: Florabel Muir, "Gable and Doug Fairbanks' Widow Race Away to Secret Wedding," *Greensburg (IN) Daily News*, December 21, 1949.

"answered 'Yes'": Aline Mosby, "Ex-Girlfriends 'Flabbergasted,'" *Republican and Herald* (Pottsville, OH), December 21, 1949.

"Please don't get married": Lyn Tornabene, *Long Live the King: A Biography of Clark Gable* (New York: G. P. Putnam's Sons, 1975), 337.

"I saw him with Joan": Chuck Panama, "Marriage of Gable to Lady Ashley Drops Like Bombshell in Hollywood," *Greensburg (IN) Daily News*, December 21, 1949, 3.

"Sylvia Stanley isn't Joan's real name": Erskine Johnson, "Is Sylvia Joan's Real Name," *Independent Record* (Helene, MT), March 23, 1950.

"cooly denied": Mosby, "Ex-Girlfriends 'Flabbergasted.'"

"fed to the teeth": No title, *Los Angeles Examiner*, January 26, 1950, clipping, AMPAS.

it almost felt like earlier times: Hedda Hopper, "Mother of Champion, Next for Ida Lupino," *Los Angeles Times*, December 25, 1949.

"If you ever decide": Author's interview with Georgina Williams, August 10, 2016.

"We'll take care of it": Author's interview with Georgina Williams, August 10, 2016.

won her respect: Dorothy Kilgallen, "Voice of Broadway," *Shamokin (PA) News-Dispatch*, January 11, 1949.

JOAN HARRISON TO DO SERIES: Louella Parsons, "Joan Harrison to Do Series of Who-Dun-Its," *Philadelphia Inquirer*, January 26, 1950.

Joan would try to commission: "Joan Harrison Now Columbia Producer," *Morning Call* (Allentown, PA), March 5, 1950.

The trades reported her every move: Behind the Scenes in Hollywood, *Gaffney Ledger* (Cherokee, SC), March 18, 1949.

Keyes had divorced John Huston: "Mexican Divorce Ends Evelyn Keyes' Marriage," *Los Angeles Times*, February 11, 1950, 2.

Some columnists second-guessed: Edwin Schallert, "Schary Writes Episode," *Los Angeles Times*, March 27, 1950, 43.

"the best record": Smyth, *Nobody's Girl Friday*, 131.

won his immediate respect: Smyth, 131.

second wave of subpoenas: Rouverol, *Refugees from Hollywood*, 1–3, 22–25.

set to start in August: "Fire Island Begins Around Mid-August," *Variety*, June 1950.

18. A New Proposal

the Production Code Administration was involved: Joseph Breen to Joan Harrison, July 6, 1950, *Circle of Danger* file, MPAA files, AMPAS.

In August, as production began: "Salvage Operations" (press release), Coronado Productions, n.d., Joan Harrison files, BFI.

"The typical Tourneur narrative": Chris Fujiwara, *Jacques Tourneur: The Cinema of Nightfall* (Baltimore: Johns Hopkins University Press, 2001), 3.

"The camera certainly does move": Review of *Circle of Danger*, *London Evening Standard*, April 19, 1951, Joan Harrison clippings file, BFI.

"still an unexciting": "Ray Milland in Circle of Danger," *New York Times*, July 12, 1951.

Westwood home had been burgled: Louella Parsons, In Hollywood, *Los Angeles Examiner*, August 6, 1951, Harrison clippings file, AMPAS.

"There's a wonderful world": Buck, *Price of Illusion*, 30.

"Hollywood's Sunset Boulevard": "Champs Elysees Compared to Hollywood's Sunset," *Daily Republican* (Monongahela, PA), October 15, 1948.

"Technicolor spectaculars": Evelyn Keyes, *Scarlett O'Hara's Younger Sister: My Lively Life in and Out of Hollywood* (Secaucus, NJ: Lyle Stuart, 1977), 168.

item out of Harrison and Douglas: "Snapshots of Hollywood Collected at Random," *Los Angeles Examiner*, June 17, 1952, clipping, AMPAS.

"a lot of former flame": Louella Parsons, Hollywood Day by Day, *Boston Evening American*, December 17, 1952; Dorothy Kilgallen, "Voice of Broadway," *Courier-Journal* (Louisville, KY), September 14, 1952.

She flirted with the possibility: Louella Parsons, Hollywood Day by Day.

She signed a contract: "Film Report," *Broadcasting*, April 7, 1952, 96.

"She had a troubled look": Author's interview with Norman Lloyd, August 2000.

It had lofty goals: "Joan Harrison Signed for Cornwall Vidpix," *Variety*, October 22, 1953. Both the American Nurses' Association and the National League of Nursing endorsed the series. The show sparked a public conversation about "positive and negative images" of nurses in the media. See Larry Wolters, "Where to Dial Today," *Chicago Daily Tribune*, April 9, 1954, A4; John Crosby, "Ella Raines in Nurse Role on TV Is Not Very Medical," *Modesto Bee*, June 21, 1954, 9.

Ella Raines would star: Bob Foster, "Ella Raines Finds Gold Mine in TV," *San Mateo (CA) Times*, July 31, 1954.

fast friends with Ella's husband: Robin Olds with Christina Olds and Ed Rasimus, *Fighter Pilot: The Memoirs of Legendary Ace Robin Olds* (New York: St. Martin's Griffin, 2011), Kindle loc. 3767.

The series appealed: Author's interview with Christina Olds, June 21, 2017.

five out of every ten: Thomas Doherty, *Cold War, Cool Medium: Television, McCarthyism, and American Culture* (New York: Columbia University Press, 2005), 6; Albert Abramson, *The History of Television, 1942 to 2000* (Jefferson, NC: McFarland, 2003), 22–45.

"top film talent": "'Janet Dean' Gets Top Film Talent," *Billboard*, October 31, 1953.

Having signed with Bromo-Seltzer: "MPTV's 'Major Expansion' Move Would Strengthen Distribution," *Billboard*, October 2, 1954.

"suspenseful, unusual TV": Advertisement for *Janet Dean, Registered Nurse*, *Broadcasting/Telecasting*, November 30, 1953, 55.

every episode was based on an actual case: "Ella Raines to Star in Series About Nurse," *Chicago Daily Tribune*, April 4, 1954.

"highly professional staff": *Janet Dean, Registered Nurse* clippings and articles folder, 1953–1954, William Dozier Papers, box 5, AMC.

"boost the merits": "New Telepix Show," *Weekly Variety*, March 31, 1954.

"So I worked with Joan": Fred Kaplan, *Gore Vidal: A Biography* (New York: Open Road Media, 2013), 372.

Vidal's work went uncredited: Kaplan, 373.

"muddled and somewhat hysterical": Jack Gaver, "How Long Till Summer," *Louisville (KY) Courier Journal*, December 28, 1949.

"maliciously" luring Herbert away: Rudley v. Tobias, civ. no. 16102. 2nd dist., div. 1, March 19, 1948.

Wasserman who did the convincing: Author's interview with Norman Lloyd, April 2016; McGilligan, *Darkness and Light*, 515. "Lew brought Joan back," according to Lloyd.

"Joanie? Are you sure?": John McCarty and Brian Kelleher, *Alfred Hitchcock Presents: An Illustrated Guide to the Ten-Year Television Career of the Master of Suspense* (New York: St. Martin's, 1985), 16–17; author's interview with Norman Lloyd, June 2014.

chance to go around with Cary Grant: Author's interview with Jackie Makkink, August 2015.

"My mother was deciding whether": Author's interview with Joan Juliet Buck, April 16, 2019.

"to the point of shock": McCarty and Kelleher, *Alfred Hitchcock Presents*, 9–10; Alfred Hitchcock to Mary Elsom, February 24, 1955, Alfred Hitchcock Collection, folder 1274 (correspondence, 1955–1962), AMPAS.

"The way Joan Harrison kind of held": Grams and Wikstrom, *Alfred Hitchcock Presents Companion*, 38.

remaining in her office from 9:00 AM: Bob Thomas, Hollywood, *Austin American Statesman*, June 1, 1963, 18.

"The show was beautifully run": Author's interview with Norman Lloyd, June 2014.

fear of falling into legal entanglements: See various memos and letters, Alfred Hitchcock Collection, folder 1274 (correspondence, 1955–1962), AMPAS.

"never a knockdown, drag-out fight": McCarty and Kelleher, *Alfred Hitchcock Presents*, 34.

"She treated her profession as an operation": Author's interview with Norman Lloyd, June 2014.

"It takes all the running you can do": Joan Harrison, "The TV Scene: Deadlines Enemy of Show Makers," *Los Angeles Times*, October 31, 1958.

"His mind is like a threshing machine": "Alfred Hitchcock—Director, TV or Movies, Suspense Is Golden," *Newsweek*, June 11, 1956.

"Couldn't we have a sharper twist": "Hitchcock's Comments on Television Stories," November 13–14, 1957, Alfred Hitchcock Collection, folder 1274 (correspondence, 1955–1962), AMPAS.

"Very good" or "Good": Author's interview with Norman Lloyd, June 2014.

one week allotted for preproduction: Production schedules, *Alfred Hitchcock Presents* files, box 172835, USC.

James Allardice, the talented comedy writer: Allardice would wait until she had six to seven scripts in hand before doing his part, then Hitch would turn in his performances in a critical mass. Allardice once scored a record, churning out twelve in one weekend.

"Noir actually shifted from the big screen": Author's interview with Eddie Muller, April 8, 2016.

"It ran its course in movie theaters": David Bushman, "Interview with Eddie Muller: Czar of Noir," *Medium*, July 11, 2017, https://paleymatters.org/eddie-muller-czar -of-noir-a07298c4c621.

"She knew script very well": Author's interview with Norman Lloyd, June 2014.

"There are examples of writers": Author's interview with Eddie Muller, April 8, 2016.

"pictures of her everywhere": James Kaplan, *Frank: The Voice* (New York: Anchor, 2011), 652.

Lazar, lived one door down: E. J. Fleming, *Movieland Directory: Nearly 30,000 Addresses of Celebrity Homes, Film Locations, and Historical Sites in the Los Angeles Area, 1900–Present* (New York: McFarland, 2010), 439; author's interview with Georgina Williams, October 2016.

Rose also worked for: Author's interview with Georgina Williams, August 10, 2016.

"Well, Auntie, did you": Author's interview with Georgina Williams, October 2016.

"rows and rows of flats": Author's interview with Georgina Williams, October 2016.

"In early days of television": Author's interview with Eleanor Kilgallen, August 2000.

"Looking back, I realize what a precedent": Author's interview with Carol Lynley, June 5, 2015.

"'Women only look all right wearing slacks'": Author's interview with Monika Henreid, October 2015.

too much concentration of female power: Author's interview with Monika Henreid, October 2015.

19. Back on Top

"No, no, she cannot work": Author's interview with Norman Lloyd, June 2014.

"The actors loved it": Author's interview with Eleanor Kilgallen, August 2000.

"Oh, Joan, don't you think": Author's interview with Norman Lloyd, June 2014.

she was blocked from working: Jeff Kisseloff, "Another Award, Other Memories of McCarthyism," *New York Times*, May 30, 1999.

"no one we'd rather use": Harrison to Kilgallen, August 1956–May 1958, *Alfred Hitchcock Presents* files, box 172835, USC.

"There seems to be a problem": Author's interview with Norman Lloyd, April 2016.

Louis Pollock: Pollock's writing career was cut short when he was mistaken for someone with a similar name, Louis Pollack, who had appeared before HUAC. It took

Pollock years to clear the record, though writing the second episode of the series' first season offered a boost.

what "a pleasurable experience": McCarty and Kelleher, *Alfred Hitchcock Presents*, xi.

"I remember that when I would": McCarty and Kelleher, 17.

the one who recommended Alec Coppel: Author's interview with Chris Coppel, June 2017. Hitchcock brought in Samuel Taylor as a third writer after letting Coppel go. When Taylor was initially assigned sole writing credit, Coppel filed a dispute with the Writers Guild. On the guild's determination, both Coppel and Taylor received official credits; Maxwell Anderson, the first writer, did not.

Unaware that Joan had been weighing in: Herbert Coleman, *The Man Who Knew Hitchcock: A Hollywood Memoir* (Lanham, MD: Scarecrow Press, 2007), 263.

He ushered Hitchcock to a corner: Dan Auiler, *Vertigo: The Making of a Hitchcock Classic* (New York: St. Martin's, 1998), 160.

"put the picture back": Coleman, *The Man Who Knew Hitchcock*, 265.

"This time, you're going too far": Stephen Rebello, *Alfred Hitchcock and the Making of Psycho* (Newburyport, MA: Open Road Media, 2010), 67.

He also had a famous talent: Author's interview with Patricia Gaynor, July 2017.

"They were too clever": Author's interview with Norman Lloyd, June 2014.

Now they were guarding their secret: Author's interview with Patricia Gaynor, July 2017.

Hitchcock facilitated the weekend event: Eric Ambler, *Waiting for Orders: Memories and Other Fictions* (New York: Vintage, 2012), Kindle loc. 1615.

"Hadn't she been married": Ambler, Kindle loc. 1639.

One hundred guests poured in: Bob Thomas, Hollywood.

residence in Eric's rental home: Ambler, *Waiting for Orders*, Kindle loc. 1564.

a New Regency–style house: Ambler, Kindle locs. 1657–1662.

found a joint company named Tarantula Productions: Hollywood Roundup, *Television Digest*, March 1961, 5.

"knowing that Shamley had no money": Joan Harrison to Jerry Adler (production coordinator), August 24, 1959, *Alfred Hitchcock Presents* files, box 172835, USC.

making the drive to the San Fernando Valley: Ambler, *Waiting for Orders*, Kindle loc. 1678; "Specialty: Murder," *TV Guide*.

"marry a writer": Bob Hull, "Marry a Writer, Advises One Lady Producer: They're Quiet," *Hollywood Reporter*, April 5, 1968.

"Darling," he replied: Ambler, *Waiting for Orders*, Kindle loc. 1720.

enlisted a doctor to calm his nerves: Ambler, Kindle loc. 1700.

"She saved my mink coat": Author's interview with Norman Lloyd, June 2014.

"the coolest man": John Huston, *An Open Book* (New York: Alfred A. Knopf, 1980), 113.

"but this was something else": Author's interview with Norman Lloyd, June 2014.

Help didn't arrive from the fire department: Ambler, *Waiting for Orders*, Kindle loc. 1716–1745.

nearly five hundred homes lost: Frank Borden, "LAFD History: The Bel Air Fire, November 6, 1961, Revisited," *Firemen's Grapevine: Los Angeles Firemen's Relief Association*, October 31, 2015; Scott Harrison, "From the Archives: The 1961 Bel Air Fire of 1961," *Los Angeles Times*, May 17, 2017, https://www.latimes.com /visuals/photography/la-me-fw-archives-the-1961-bel-air-brush-fire-20170419 -story.html.

"a mass of grey ash": Ambler, *Waiting for Orders*, Kindle loc. 1789.

"It really was an unbelievable experience": Joan Harrison to John Findley, MCA agent (England), November 27, 1961, *Alfred Hitchcock Presents* files, box 172835, USC.

"I don't mind losing my possessions": Bob Thomas, Hollywood.

"the real tragedy": Bob Thomas, Hollywood; Harrison to Findley.

teasing him about the dozens of dolls: Ambler, *Waiting for Orders*, Kindle loc. 1799.

whether to rebuild on Taranto Way: Harrison to Findley.

"Oh, this is the money": Author's interview with Jackie Makkink, August 2016.

"But I always thought": Author's interview with Kate Adamson, May 14, 2013.

"All of a sudden a man appeared": Author's interview with Georgina Williams, October 2016.

"You know, the only person": Author's interview with Jackie Makkink, August 2016.

fancied herself a professional: Felicity Anne Cumming Mason penned two sexual memoirs chronicling two different phases of her love life, *The Love Habit* (1978) and *The Love Quest* (1991).

"I never want to live anywhere": "Not a Crowd," *Los Angeles Times*, September 29, 1961.

a writer, producer, and director superteam: Author's interview with Norman Lloyd, June 2014.

"He considered everyone his personal property": Author's interview with Norman Lloyd, April 2016.

"nobody had any real answer": Kelly McEvers, "Three Generations of Actresses Reflect on Hollywood, Harassment—and Hitchcock," *All Things Considered*, NPR, aired November 16, 2016.

"a little too costly": McCarty and Kelleher, *Alfred Hitchcock Presents*, 55.

20. Into the Unknown

she could sun herself: Joan Harrison to the Henreids, September 23, 1973, Paul Henreid Collection, AMPAS; Joan Harrison to Evelyn Keyes, March 18, 1973, in possession of the author.

Eric's small office was lined with books: Robert Emmett Ginna, "Outside His Window, Within His Heart, Eric Ambler Still Finds the Stuff of Great Spy Novels," *People*, June 6, 1977, 22.

"arranging dull things like laundries": Joan Harrison to the Henreids, August 23, 1968, Paul Henreid Collection, AMPAS.

He never forgot the lengths: Author's interview with Georgina Williams, October 2016. Georgina went on to become a jazz singer. "My aunt Nellie would have liked for me to become an opera singer," Georgina explains. "I loved her, but we always clashed. She was quite the lady. She was always pushing me to dress with the perfect clothes and shoes and act 'just so.' To be more like Miss Harrison, I guess. But that wasn't the kind of person I was."

renewed her friendship with Charlie and Oona: Joan Harrison to Henreids, December 21, 1970, and January 23, 1972, Paul Henreid Collection, AMPAS.

"all the lovely scenery": Joan Harrison to the Henreids, March 13, 1968, Paul Henreid Collection, AMPAS.

"every conceivable permutation": "Journeying to a Successful Series," press release for *Journey to the Unknown*, Hammer Film Productions, 1968, 1.

"dead on arrival": Aaron Spelling with Jefferson Graham, *A Prime-Time Life: An Auto-biography* (New York: St. Martin's, 1996), 81.

"the scenes, dialogue, etc. remain intact": Joan Harrison to Eric Ambler, April 2, 1970, in possession of the author.

"I know you won't feel": Joan Harrison to Eric Ambler, April 1, 1970, in possession of the author.

"I'm just an old warhorse": Joan Harrison to the Henreids, January 23, 1972, Paul Henreid Collection, AMPAS.

"I refuse to be tied to domesticity": Joan Harrison to Evelyn Keyes, September 13, 1973, in possession of the author.

"After I talked to you on the phone": Joan Harrison to Eric Ambler, April 1, 1970, in possession of the author.

"Without you, my love": Eric Ambler to Joan Harrison, June 8, 1972, in possession of the author.

"We have been going through": Joan Harrison to Eric Ambler, March 23, 1969, Eric Ambler Collection, HGRC.

"I've given that up": Joan Harrison to Eric Ambler, January 2, 1970, in possession of the author.

"I envy a talent": Joan Harrison to the Henreids, September 21, 1974, Paul Henreid Collection, AMPAS.

"I haven't said this to anyone else": Joan Harrison to Evelyn Keyes, September 13, 1973, in possession of the author.

a pair of hummingbird earrings: Eulogy for Eric Ambler given by Patricia Gaynor, Garrick Club, London, June 1999.

"I was always glad I was there": Joan Harrison to the Henreids, July 12, 1973, Paul Henreid Collection, AMPAS.

"Why not?": Joan Harrison to Evelyn Keyes, September 13, 1973, in possession of the author.

"for which I'm sure": Joan Harrison to the Henreids, January 11, 1970, and January 23, 1972, Paul Henreid Collection, AMPAS.

"probably thought about it as a foreign film": Joan Harrison to the Henreids, June 9, 1974, Paul Henreid Collection, AMPAS.

"always very tuned in": Author's interview with Kate Adamson, May 2013.

"She behaved like the perfect godmother": Author's interview with Joan Buck, April 16, 2019.

"We must try to enjoy life": Joan Harrison to Kendall Milestone, March 9, 1978, Lewis Milestone Collection, correspondence file, AMPAS.

Alma had suffered a second stroke: McGilligan, *Darkness and Light*, 731.

"Come on, now, Joan, change the subject": Author's interview with Patricia Gaynor, August 2017.

"My aunt was very self-conscious": Author's interview with Kate Adamson, May 2013.

"The care has been professional": Ambler, *Waiting for Orders*, Kindle loc. 2361.

"Mrs. Ambler was so sharp": Author's interview with Patricia Gaynor, August 2017.

One of her most attentive friends: Author's interview with Chris Coppel, June 2017.

"My dearest—With all my love": Joan Harrison, cards to Eric Ambler, October 11, 1983, Eric Ambler Collection, HGRC.

"everyone who's known Joan": George Christy, "The Great Life," *Hollywood Reporter*, December 29, 1983, Harrison files, AMPAS.

"Mrs. Ambler looked like": Author's interview with Jackie Makkink, August 2015.

A well-timed compliment: Christy, "Great Life."

Richard Burton and Elizabeth Taylor came for dinner: Author's interview with Jackie Makkink, August 2016.

pretend to be "not well": Author's interview with Jackie Makkink, August 2015.

To get him really riled up: Author's interview with Patricia Gaynor, August 2017.

"Oh, Hitch would have loved you": Author's interview with Patricia Gaynor, August 2017.

"She began asking": Author's interview with Jackie Makkink, August 2015.

"He passed out": Author's interview with Jackie Makkink, May 2016, August 2017.

"to have her ashes scattered": Patricia Gaynor, e-mail correspondence to the author, May 3, 2019.

"He took his time dying": Author's interview with Jackie Makkink, May 2016. Patricia Gaynor, who also stayed on the staff until Eric Ambler's death, took care to have his ashes scattered in the same area as Joan's, on the grounds of the Finchley crematorium. Patricia Gaynor, e-mail correspondence to the author, May 3, 2019.

"Facts are facts": Mert Guswiler, "People Are Surprised I Deal in Murder," *Los Angeles Examiner*, June 7, 1971; "Unusual Suit," *Jersey Journal*, February 1, 1947; Booton Herndon, "In the Case of Junior Versus the Other Woman," *Detroit Times*, May 25, 1947.

SELECTED
BIBLIOGRAPHY

Archives (Key)

AFI	Louis B. Mayer Library, American Film Institute
AMC	American Heritage Center, University of Wyoming
AMPAS	Margaret Herrick Library, Academy Motion Picture Arts and Sciences
BFI	British Film Institute
GBM	Guildford Borough Museum
GHSA	Guildford High School Archive
HGRC	Howard Gotlieb Archival Research Center, Boston University
HRC	Harry Ransom Center, University of Texas at Austin
UCLA	Charles E. Young Library, University of California, Los Angeles
USC	Cinematic Arts Library, Doheny Memorial Library, University of Southern California
UVSC	Universal Studios Collection

Published Sources

Abramson, Martin. "My Husband Alfred Hitchcock Hates Suspense." *Coronet*, August 1964, 12–17.

Ackroyd, Peter. *Alfred Hitchcock: A Brief Life*. New York: Penguin/Random House, 2015.

Agee, James. Review of *Phantom Lady*. *Nation*, February 26, 1944.

Allen, Richard. "Daphne du Maurier and Alfred Hitchcock." In *A Companion to Film and Literature*, edited by Robert Stam and Alessandra Raengo, 298–325. Malden, MA: Blackwell, 2004.

Ambler, Eric. "An Interview with Jay Presson Allen." In *Framing Hitchcock: Selected Essays from the Hitchcock Annual*, edited by Sidney Gottlieb and Christopher Brookhouse, 206–218. Detroit: Wayne State University Press, 2002.

———. *The Story So Far: Memories & Other Fictions*. London: Weidenfeld & Nicolson, 1993.

Angell, George. "The Time of My Life" (interview with Alfred Hitchcock). BBC Home Service, recorded July 30, 1966, aired August 28, 1966.

Atlanta Constitution. "Hitchcock's Female Cohort Is 'Blood-Thunder' Expert." October 10, 1960.

Auiler, Dan. *Hitchcock's Notebooks: An Authorized and Illustrated Look Inside the Creative Mind of Alfred Hitchcock*. New York: Spike, 1999.

Balcon, Michael. *A Lifetime in Films*. London: Hutchinson, 1969.

Barnsley, Mary. "Women Authors Disagree, So Hollywood Has Only One Feminine Writing Team." *Daily Boston Globe*, June 15, 1941.

Barr, Charles. *English Hitchcock*. Moffat, Scotland: Cameron & Hollis, 1999.

Bennett, Charles. "Charles Bennett: Import from England." Interview in *Words into Images: Screenwriters on the Studio System*, edited by Ronald L. Davis, 3–19. Jackson: University of Mississippi, 2007.

———. "The Writer Speaks: Oral Histories of Film and Television Writers." Interview with Janet Leigh. Writers Guild Foundation, recorded May 1, 2015. https://www.youtube.com/watch?v=KKRloFW177s.

Bennett, Charles, and John Charles Bennett. *Hitchcock's Partner in Suspense: The Life of Screenwriter Charles Bennett*. Lexington: University of Kentucky Press, 2014.

Berch, Barbara. "A Hitchcock Alumna: Introducing Joan Harrison, Hollywood's Only Full-Fledged Woman Producer." *New York Times*, June 27, 1943.

Bernstein, Matthew. *Walter Wanger: Hollywood Independent*. Minneapolis: University of Minnesota Press, 1994.

Biesen, Sheri Chenin. *Blackout: World War II and the Origins of Film Noir*. Baltimore: Johns Hopkins University Press, 2005.

Bogdanovich, Peter. *Cinema of Alfred Hitchcock*. New York: Museum of Modern Art, 1963.

Brackett, Charles. *"It's the Pictures That Got Small": Charles Brackett on Billy Wilder and Hollywood's Golden Age*. Edited by Anthony Slide. New York: Columbia University Press, 2015. Kindle.

Brown, Geoff. *Launder and Gilliat*. London: BFI, 1977.

Buchanan, Barbara J. "Alfred Hitchcock Tells a Woman That Women Are a Nuisance." *Film Weekly*, September 20, 1935.

Cairns, David. "Dark Mirrors: The Dual Cinema of Robert Siodmak." *Moving Image Source*. Museum of the Moving Image, June 3, 2010.

Canfield, Alyce. "Boss Man Is a Lady." *Screenland*, September 1945, 42–43, 79–83.

Carroll, Lewis. *Through the Looking Glass, and What Alice Found There*. Philadelphia: Henry Altemus, 1897.

Chandler, Charlotte. *It's Only a Movie: Alfred Hitchcock, A Personal Biography*. New York: Simon & Schuster, 2005.

Collyer, Graham, and David Rose. *Images of Guildford: Surrey Advertiser*. Derby: Breedon Books, 1998.

Columbia Pictures. Press book for *First Comes Courage*. 1943. BFI.

Cosmopolitan. "Cosmopolite of the Month: Joan Harrison." February 1947, 8.

Crowther, Bosley. "Credit—Where Is It Due?" *New York Times*, January 12, 1941.

Cypert, Rick. *The Virtue of Suspense: The Life and Works of Charlotte Armstrong*. Selinsgrove, PA: Susquehanna University Press, 2008.

Daggett, Ann. "It's a Woman's World Too." *Modern Screen*, February 1945, 20, 22.

Davis, Ronald L., ed. *Words into Images: Screenwriters on the Studio System*. Jackson: University of Mississippi, 2007.

de Rosnay, Tatiana. *Manderley Forever: A Biography of Daphne Du Maurier*. New York: St. Martin's, 2017.

Décharné, Max. *King's Road: The Rise and Fall of the Hippest Street in the World*. London: Weidenfeld & Nicholson, 2005.

Durgnat, Raymond. *The Strange Case of Alfred Hitchcock*. Cambridge, MA: MIT Press, 1974.

Faubert, Patrick. "The Role and Presence of Authorship in Suspicion." In *Hitchcock and Adaptation: On the Page and Screen*, edited by Mark Osteen, 41–57. Lanham, MD: Rowman & Littlefield, 2014.

Fontaine, Joan. *No Bed of Roses*. New York: Morrow, 1978.

Forster, Margaret. *Daphne du Maurier*. London: Arrow, 1993.

Gates, Dorothy E. "Talented TV Producer Wins Honor." *Christian Science Monitor*, December 1, 1960.

Gemünden, Gerd. *Continental Strangers: German Exile Cinema, 1933–1951*. New York: Columbia University Press, 2013.

Glancy, H. Mark. *When Hollywood Loved Britain: The Hollywood British Film, 1939–1945*. Manchester: Manchester University Press, 1999.

Gloucester Citizen. "Good Looking Enough to Be a Star." December 3, 1949.

Grams, Martin, Jr., and Patrik Wikstrom. *The Alfred Hitchcock Presents Companion*. Churchville, MD: OTR, 2001.

Greco, Joseph. *The File on Robert Siodmak in Hollywood: 1941–1951*. Dissertation .com, 1999.

Hanson, Helen. *Hollywood Heroines: Film Noir and the Female Gothic Film*. New York: I. B. Tauris, 2008.

Harper, Sue. *Women in British Cinema: Mad, Bad, and Dangerous to Know*. London: Continuum, 2000.

Hartford Courant. "Hers Is a Horrifying Business." May 7, 1944.

Haskell, Molly. *From Reverence to Rape: The Treatment of Women in the Movies*. 2nd ed. Chicago: University of Chicago Press, 2016.

Heffernan, Harold. "Pretty, Blue-Eyed Blonde Clicks as Movie-Producer." *Indianapolis Star*, May 26, 1944.

Hellman, Geoffrey T. "Alfred Hitchcock: England's Biggest and Best Director Goes to Hollywood." *Life*, November 20, 1939, 33–34, 36, 38–39, 40, 41–43.

Higham, Charles, and Roy Moseley. *Merle: A Biography of Merle Oberon*. London: New English Library, 1983.

Hitchcock, Alfred. "Elegance Above Sex." *Hollywood Reporter*, November 20, 1962.

———. "Lecture at Columbia University, March 30, 1939." In *Hitchcock on Hitchcock: Selected Writings and Interviews*, vol. 1, edited by Sidney Gottlieb, 267–274. Berkeley: University of California, 1995.

———. "Life Among the Stars." *News Chronicle*, March 5, 1937. Reprinted in *Hitchcock on Hitchcock: Selected Writings and Interviews*, vol. 1, edited by Sidney Gottlieb, 27–50. Berkeley: University of California Press, 1997.

———. "My Own Methods." *Sight & Sound*, June 1937. Reprinted as "Direction" in *Footnotes to the Film*, edited by Charles Davy, 3–15. London: Lovat Dickson, 1938.

———. "My Screen Memories." In collaboration with John K. Newnham. *Film Weekly*, May 2–30, 1936.

———. "The Woman Who Knows Too Much." *McCall's*, 1956.

Hollywood Citizen News. "Hitch Tops, Flagg Sits." November 6, 1941. Clipping, Alfred Hitchcock Collection, AMPAS.

Hopper, Hedda. "Hedda Hopper's Hollywood: Lady Comes Through." *Harrisburg Telegraph*, May 17, 1943.

———. "Hitchcock: He Runs on Fear." *Los Angeles Times*, August 17, 1958.

———. "Wrath Made Joan Harrison a Producer." *Los Angeles Times*, October 14, 1945.

Houseman, John. *Run-Through: A Memoir*. New York: Simon & Schuster, 1972.

———. *Unfinished Business: Memoirs, 1902–1988*. New York: Applause Books, 2000.

Hutchinson, Pamela, and Tony Paley. "The Genius of Alfred Hitchcock at the BFI: Ten of His Lesser-Known Gems." *Guardian*, July 4, 2012.

Iles, Francis. *Before the Fact: A Murder Story for Ladies*. New York: Doubleday, 1932.

Indianapolis Star. "Just Can't Afford to Experiment." May 28, 1944.

Kapsis, Robert. *Hitchcock: The Making of a Reputation*. Chicago: University of Chicago Press, 1990.

Kawin, Bruce F. "Authorship, Design, and Execution." In *How Movies Work*, edited by Bruce F. Kawin, 291–301. Berkeley: University of California Press, 1992.

Kerzoncuf, Alain, and Charles Barr. *Hitchcock Lost and Found: The Forgotten Films*. Lexington: University of Kentucky, 2015.

Krohn, Bill. "Ambivalence (*Suspicion*)." In *Hitchcock Annual, 2003–2004*, edited by Sidney Gottlieb and Richard Allen, 67–116. London: Wallflower, 2009.

Kronenberger, Louis. "Remembered After Darkness: The Greatest Horror Is That the Horror Is True." *New York Times Book Review*, September 27, 1942.

Lane, Christina. "Stepping Out from Behind the Grand Silhouette: Joan Harrison's Films of the 1940s." In *Authorship and Film*, edited by David A. Gerstner and Janet Staiger, 97–117. New York: Routledge, 2003.

Lane, Christina, and Josephine Botting. "What Did Alma Think: Continuity, Editing, Writing, and Adaptation." In *Hitchcock and Adaptation: On the Page and Screen*, edited by Mark Osteen, 221–236. Maryland: Rowman & Littlefield, 2014.

Leff, Leonard. Audio commentary. *The 39 Steps*. Criterion Collection, 2012. DVD.

———. Audio interview with Joan Fontaine. *Rebecca*. Criterion Collection, 2017. DVD.

———. *Hitchcock and Selznick: The Rich and Strange Collaboration of Alfred Hitchcock and David O. Selznick in Hollywood*. London: Weidenfeld & Nicolson, 1987.

Leitch, Thomas. "Hitchcock and His Writers: Authorship and Authority in Adaptation." In *Authorship in Film Adaptation*, edited by Jack Boozer, 63–84. Austin: University of Texas Press, 2008.

Lewis, Jerry D. "Murder, She Says." *Collier's*, August 14, 1943, 55, 70.

Lieber, Perry. "Joan Harrison Biography." RKO Studios, 1946.

Life. "Ella Raines: The Pretty Young Star Began Her Career by Being Incorporated for $1,000,000 by a Production Firm." February 28, 1944, 22.

London Times. Obituary for Joan Harrison. August 2, 1994.

Luther, Mary Lou. "Work Seven Mondays a Week." *Los Angeles Times*, May 11, 1960.

Malone, Audrey. *Maureen O'Hara: The Biography*. Lexington: University of Kentucky Press, 2013.

Margulies, Lee. "Tribute to Dorothy Arzner." *Action* 10, no. 2 (1975): 17.

Mayne, Judith. *Directed by Dorothy Arzner*. Bloomington: Indiana University Press, 1994.

McBride, Joseph. "Mr. and Mrs. Hitchcock." *Sight & Sound* 45, no. 4 (Autumn 1976): 224–225.

McCarthy, Todd. *Howard Hawks: The Grey Fox of Hollywood*. New York: Grove Press, 1997.

McCrary, Tex, and Jinx Falkenburg. "New York Close Up: The Next Mrs. Clark Gable." *New York Herald Tribune*, December 15, 1949.

McCreadie, Marsha. *The Women Who Write the Movies: From Frances Marion to Nora Ephron*. Secaucus, NJ: Carol Publishing Group, 1994.

McDougal, Dennis. *The Last Mogul: Lew Wasserman, MCA, and the Hidden History of Hollywood*. New York: Crown, 1998.

McGilligan, Patrick. *Alfred Hitchcock: A Life in Darkness and Light*. New York: Harper-Collins, 2004.

———. "First-Class Constructionist: Charles Bennett." In *Backstory 1: Interviews with Screenwriters of Hollywood's Golden Age*, edited by Patrick McGilligan, 17–48. Berkeley: University of California Press, 1986.

———. "Hitchcock Dreams of America." In *Hitchcock Annual, 2002–2003*, edited by Sidney Gottlieb and Richard Allen, 1–31. London: Wallflower, 2009.

Millstein, Gilbert. "Harrison Horror Story." *New York Times*, July 21, 1957.

Modleski, Tania. "Suspicion: Collusion and Resistance in the Work of Hitchcock's Female Collaborators." In *A Companion to Alfred Hitchcock*, edited by Thomas Leitch and Leland Poague, 162–180. Malden, MA: Wiley-Blackwell, 2011.

———. *The Women Who Knew Too Much: Hitchcock and Feminist Theory*. 2nd ed. New York: Methuen, 2005.

Monahan, Kaspar. "'Phantom Lady' at Fulton Lively 'Who Dun It.'" *Pittsburgh Press*, April 1, 1944.

Montagu, Ivor. "An Interview with Ivor Montagu." *Screen* 13, no. 3 (1972): 71–113.

———. "Working with Hitchcock." *Sight & Sound* 49, no. 3 (Summer 1980): 189–193.

Monthly Film Bulletin. "Jamaica Inn." May 31, 1939.

Morris, Nathalie. "The Early Career of Alma Reville." In *The Hitchcock Annual Anthology: Selected Essays from Volumes 10–15*, edited by Sidney Gottlieb and Richard Allen, 41–69. London: Wallflower, 2009.

Muller, Eddie. "Murder, She Made: The Exceptional Career of Joan Harrison." *Noir City: A Publication of the Film Noir Foundation* (Fall 2015): 14–24.

Neve, Brian. "A Past Master of His Craft: An Interview with Fred Zinnemann." Reprinted in *Fred Zinnemann: Interviews*, edited by Gabriel Miller, 145–156. Jackson: University of Mississippi Press, 2005.

Nevins, Frances M. "Translate and Transform: From Cornell Woolrich to Film Noir." In *Film Noir Reader 2*, edited by Alain Silver and James Ursini, 137–157. New York: Limelight Editions, 2003.

New York Times. "Joan Harrison, a Screenwriter and Producer, Is Dead at 83." August 25, 1994.

Newman, Stanley. *Guildford Life: Past and Present*. Derby: Breedon Books, 2008.

Niemeyer, Harry. "Pretty Girl in a Big Job." *St. Louis Post-Dispatch*, March 5, 1944.

Niven, David. *Bring on the Empty Horses*. New York: G. P. Putnam's Sons, 1975.

Oakley, William H. *Guildford in the Great War: The Record of a Surrey Town.* Guildford: Billings and Sons, 1934.

O'Connell, Patricia Hitchcock, and Laurent Bouzereau. *Alma Hitchcock: The Woman Behind the Man.* Berkley, CA: Berkley Trade, 2003.

Offen, Karen. "The Second Sex and the Baccalauréat in Republican France, 1880–1924." *French Historical Studies* 13, no. 2 (1983): 280–281, 277, 283.

Othman, Fred. "New Motion Picture Producer Has Pretty Legs, Lots of Glamour." *Louisville Courier-Journal*, September 27, 1943.

Palmer, R. Barton. *Hollywood's Dark Cinema: The American Film Noir.* New York: Twayne, 1994.

Peary, Gerald, and Karyn Kay. "An Interview with Dorothy Arzner." *Cinema* 34 (1974): 10–14.

Petro, Patrice. "Rematerializing the Vanishing 'Lady': Feminism, Hitchcock, and Interpretation." In *A Hitchcock Reader*, 2nd ed., edited by Marshall Deutelbaum and Leland Poague, 126–136. Malden, MA: Wiley-Blackwell, 2009.

Picturegoer. "Alma in Wonderland." December 1925, 48.

Raines, Ella. "The Role I Liked Best." *Saturday Evening Post*, January 17, 1948, 95.

Raubicheck, Walter, and Walter Srebnick. *Scripting Hitchcock: Psycho, the Birds, and Marnie.* Urbana: University of Illinois Press, 2011.

Reville, Alma. "Cutting and Continuity." *Motion Picture Studio*, January 13, 1923, 10.

Robey, Tim. "Alfred Hitchcock's Rebecca: Rows, Rivalries and a Movie Classic." *Daily Telegraph*, October 16, 2009.

Rose, David. *Guildford: Remembering 1914–1918.* Stroud, UK: History Press, 2015.

Rose, David, and Bernard Parke. *Guildford History Tour.* Gloucestershire: Amberley, 2015.

Rothman, William. *Hitchcock: The Murderous Gaze.* 2nd ed. Albany: SUNY Press, 2012.

Ryall, Tom. *Alfred Hitchcock and the British Cinema.* 2nd ed. London: Athlone, 1996.

Schatz, Thomas. *The Genius of the System: Hollywood Filmmaking in the Studio Era.* 2nd ed. Minneapolis: University of Minnesota Press, 2010.

Scheuer, Philip K. "Producer's Spurs Won by Woman: Member of Fair Sex Makes Good with First Film." *Los Angeles Times*, February 22, 1944. Harrison files, AMPAS.

Schiebe, Donna. "Screenwriting Last Entry for Women in Film Production." *Los Angeles Times*, April 27, 1967.

Schmenner, Will, and Corinne Granof, eds. *Casting a Shadow: Creating the Alfred Hitchcock Film.* Evanston, IL: Northwestern University Press, 2007.

Schwartz, Laura. *A Serious Endeavor: Gender, Education and Community at St. Hugh's, 1886–2011*. London: Profile Books, 2011.

Shnayerson, Michael. *Irwin Shaw: A Biography*. New York: G. P. Putnam's Sons, 1989.

Smith, Imogen Sarah. "A Light in the Dark: Ella Raines and Film Noir's Working Girls." *Noir City: A Publication of the Film Noir Foundation* (Fall 2015): 25–31.

Smyth, J. E. *Nobody's Girl Friday: The Women Who Ran Hollywood*. Oxford: Oxford University Press, 2018.

Snelson, Tim. *Phantom Ladies: Hollywood Horror and the Home Front*. New Brunswick, NJ: Rutgers University Press, 2014.

Spicer, Andrew. *Film Noir*. New York: Routledge, 2016.

——. *Historical Dictionary of Film Noir*. Lanham, MD: Scarecrow Press, 2010.

Spoto, Donald. *The Dark Side of Genius: The Life of Alfred Hitchcock*. New York: Ballantine Books, 2003.

Srebnick, Walter. "Working with Hitch: A Screenwriter's Forum with Evan Hunter, Arthur Laurents, and Joseph Stefano." In *The Hitchcock Annual Anthology: Selected Essays from Volumes 10–15*, edited by Sidney Gottlieb and Richard Allen, 15–39. London: Wallflower, 2009.

Stanley, Fred. "Hollywood Flash: Studios Scrap War Stories; The Horror Boys Convene." *New York Times*, April 16, 1944.

——. "Hollywood Shivers." *New York Times*, May 28, 1944.

Starr, Kevin. *The Dream Endures: California Enters the 1940s*. Oxford: Oxford University Press, 2002.

Swindell, Larry. *Screwball: The Life of Carole Lombard*. New York: William Morrow, 1975.

Taylor, John Russell. *Hitch: The Life and Times of Alfred Hitchcock*. New York: Bloomsbury Edition, 2016.

——. "Was Alfred Hitchcock a Mysogynist? He Was Adored by Actresses." *London Times*, September 6, 2008.

Telotte, J. P. *Voices in the Dark: The Narrative Patterns of Film Noir*. Chicago: University of Illinois Press, 1988.

Time. Cinema: The New Pictures. February 28, 1944.

Truffaut, François. *Hitchcock*. Rev. ed. New York: Simon & Schuster, 1985.

TV Guide. "Specialty: Murder, Alfred Hitchcock's Protégé Works at Crime Fifteen Hours a Day." March 8–14, 1958.

Universal Pictures. Press book for *Phantom Lady*. 1944. USC.

——. Press book for *Uncle Harry*. 1945. USC.

Walker, Joseph, ASC, and Juanita Walker. *The Light on Her Face*. Hollywood: ASC Press, 1984.

Walker, Michael. "Robert Siodmak." In *The Book of Film Noir*, edited by Ian Cameron, 110–151. London: Continuum, 1993.

Ware, John. "British Girl Becomes World's Top Ranking Film Producer." Coronado Productions, press release, ca. 1949.

Waterbury, Ruth. "How Clark Gable Is Conquering Loneliness." *Photoplay*, August 1942, 34.

West, Priscilla. "Reminiscences of Seven Decades." In *St. Hugh's: One Hundred Years of Women's Education in Oxford*, edited by Penny Griffin, 62–243. London: Macmillan, 1986.

Wilkonson, Lupton A. "He Makes the Movies Move." *Los Angeles Times*, January 5, 1941.

Woman's Hour. "Daphne du Maurier Walk, Jamaica Inn." BBC Radio, April 30, 2007. http://www.bbc.co.uk/radio4/womanshour/03/2007_18_mon.shtml.

———. "Money Comes Second." BBC Radio, September 7, 1949.

Wood, Linda. *British Films, 1927–1939*. London: BFI National Library, 2009.

Worland, Rick. "Before and After the Fact: Writing and Reading Hitchcock's *Suspicion*." *Cinema Journal* 41, no. 4 (2002): 3–26.

Yacowar, Maurice. *Hitchcock's British Films*. 2nd ed. Detroit, MI: Wayne State University Press, 2010.

Youngkin, Stephen D. *The Lost One: A Life of Peter Lorre*. Lexington: University Press of Kentucky, 2005.

Zolotow, Maurice. *Billy Wilder in Hollywood*. New York: Hal Leonard, 1977.

Original Interviews

Adamson, Kate (niece of Harrison). May 2013 and June 2017.

Allen, Jay Presson. July 2000.

Asher, Andrew (cousin of Harrison). June 2016.

Blyth, Ann. June 2016.

Buck, Joan Juliet (daughter of Joyce and Jules Buck). April 2019.

Chanock, Edith Tobias (daughter of Milton Tobias). May 2017.

Cockrell, Amanda (daughter of Marian and Francis Cockrell). July 2015.

Coppel, Chris (son of Alec and Myra Coppel, friends of Harrison). August 2015.

Gaynor, Patricia (Harrison and Ambler's personal secretary). August 2017.

Glaser, Allan (friend of Evelyn Keyes, executor of Keyes's estate). January 2019.

Henreid, Monika (daughter of Paul and Lisl Henreid). October 2015.

Kilgallen, Eleanor. August 2000.

Kohner, Susan. June 2018.

Lewi, Peter (son of Charlotte Armstrong, writer). September 2015.

Lloyd, Norman. August 2001, June 2015, and February 2017.

Lynley, Carol. June 2015.

Makkink, Jackie (Harrison's personal housekeeper, nurse). August and October 2015, May and August 2016, and August 2017.

Muller, Eddie. October 2015.

O'Connell, Patricia Hitchcock. June 2000.

Olds, Christina (daughter of Ella Raines). July 2017.

Rose, David (Guildford historian). July 2016.

Stefano, Joseph. November 1999.

Tone, Pascale "Pat" Franchot (son of Franchot Tone). June 2018.

Williams, Georgina (niece of housekeeper Nellie Williams). August and October 2016 and October 2018.

INDEX